1990 Supplement

CONSTITUTIONAL LAW

1990 Supplement

CONSTITUTIONAL LAW

Geoffrey R. Stone
Harry Kalven, Jr., Professor of Law and Dean
University of Chicago Law School

Louis M. Seidman
Professor of Law
Georgetown University Law Center

Cass R. Sunstein
Professor of Law
University of Chicago Law School

Mark V. Tushnet
Professor of Law
Georgetown University Law Center

Little, Brown and Company   *Boston   Toronto   London*

Library of Congress Catalog Card No. 85-81679

ISBN 0-316-81776-7

ICP

Published simultaneously in Canada
by Little, Brown & Company (Canada) Limited

PRINTED IN THE UNITED STATES OF AMERICA

Contents

Chapter Seven.   Freedom of Expression   197

Chapter Eight.   The Constitution and Religion   263

Table of Cases

Table of Cases

Table of Cases

Preface

We are grateful for the tireless research assistance from Linda Lauve, William Nolen, and Catherine O'Neil, and the careful, patient secretarial assistance provided by Mary Ann DeRosa, Brenda Butler, Brenda Greenfield, June Hardesty, Irene Kennedy, Marlene Vellinga, and other members of the University of Chicago secretarial staff and the Georgetown University Law Center Faculty Support Service.

G.R.S.
L.M.S.
C.R.S.
M.V.T.

August 1990

Acknowledgments

Excerpts from the following materials appear with the kind permission of the copyright holders:

D. Bell, And We Are Not Saved: The Elusive Quest for Racial Justice 48-49, 111-113. Copyright © 1987 by Basic Books, Inc. Reprinted by permission of Basic Books, Inc., Publishers.

Epstein, Unconstitutional Conditions, State Power, and the Limits of Consent, 102 Harv. L. Rev. 4, 83-85, 99-100 (1988). Copyright © 1988 by the Harvard Law Review Association.

H. Kalven, A Worthy Tradition: Freedom of Speech in America 158. Copyright © 1987 by Harper & Row, Publishers. Reprinted by permission.

C. MacKinnon, Feminism Unmodified: Discourses on Life and Law 3, 8-9. Copyright © 1987 by the President and Fellows of Harvard College. Reprinted by permission.

C. MacKinnon, Feminism Unmodified: Discourses on Life and Law 155, 155-156. Copyright © 1987 by the President and Fellows of Harvard College. Reprinted by permission. These portions of the book originally appeared as an article titled Not a Moral Issue, in 2 Yale L. & Poly. Rev. 321 (No. 2, Spring 1984). Copyright © 1984 by the Yale Law Journal Company and Fred B. Rothman & Company. Reprinted by permission.

W. Nelson, The Fourteenth Amendment: From Political Principle to Judicial Doctrine 8-10, 197-200. Copyright © 1988 by the President and Fellows of Harvard College. Reprinted by permission.

Post, Between Goverance and Management: The History and Theory of the Public Forum, 34 U.C.L.A. L. Rev. 1775-1777, 1782 (1987). Copyright © 1987 by the Regents of the University of California. Reprinted by permission.

Rapaczynski, Andrzej, From Sovereignty to Process: The Jurisprudence of Federalism after *Garcia*, 1985 Sup. Ct. Rev. 341. Copyright © 1985 by the University of Chicago Press. Reprinted by permission.

Rubenfeld, The Right of Privacy, 102 Harv. L. Rev. 737, 770, 782, 799-800 (1989). Copyright © 1989 by the Harvard Law Review Association.

Schneider, State Interest Analysis in Fourteenth Amendment "Privacy" Law: An Essay on the Constitutionalization of Social Issues, 51 L. & Contemp.

Prob. 79, 99, 102-103, 110-111 (1988). Copyright © 1988 by Duke University School of Law. Reprinted by permission.

1990 Supplement

CONSTITUTIONAL LAW

THE CONSTITUTION OF THE UNITED STATES

Page xlv. Art. II, sec. 4 should read:

"The President, Vice President and all civil Officers of the United States, shall be removed from Office on Impeachment for, and Conviction of, Treason, Bribery, or other high Crimes and Misdemeanors."

BIOGRAPHICAL NOTES ON SELECTED U.S. SUPREME COURT JUSTICES

Page lxiv. Before the biography of John Marshall, add the following:

ANTHONY M. KENNEDY (1936-   ):   President Reagan's effort to fill the seat vacated by the retirement of Justice Powell, who was widely viewed as a "swing vote" on a number of important issues, sparked an extraordinary controversy about the future direction of the Supreme Court. His first nominee, Robert Bork, was defeated on the Senate floor after a long and bitter debate that pitted "originalists" against those who would treat the Constitution as incorporating values not directly derived from the text. His second nominee, Douglas Ginsburg, was forced to withdraw from consideration after it was revealed that he had used marijuana. In the wake of these events, the Senate greeted with relief the nomination of Justice Kennedy, a relatively colorless and nonideological conservative. After graduating from Harvard Law School in 1961, Kennedy worked as a lawyer and lobbyist in California until his appointment to the Ninth Circuit by President Ford in 1975. While on the bench, he taught constitutional law at McGeorge School of Law and was perhaps best known for writing the lower court opinion striking down the legislative veto — a result subsequently affirmed by the Supreme Court in INS v. Chadha, 462 U.S. 919 (1983).

Page lxvii. Before the biography of Justice Stevens, add the following:

ANTONIN SCALIA (1936-   ):   The son of an Italian immigrant, Justice Scalia was the first Italian-American to be appointed to the Supreme Court. A former law professor and assistant attorney general, he earned a reputation as an intelligent, hardworking, and dedicated conservative while serving as a

1

judge on the United States Court of Appeals for the District of Columbia Circuit. Although he often clashed with some of his more liberal colleagues on that court, they uniformly praised his civility, reasonableness, and scholarship. Justice Scalia is known for his strong defense of the prerogatives of the executive branch, for his opposition to affirmative action, for his unwillingness to endorse the judicial creation of nontextual "privacy" rights, and for his narrow reading of the first amendment's free speech and press clauses.

Chapter One

The Role of the Supreme Court in the Constitutional Scheme

A. INTRODUCTION: SOME NOTES ON THE HISTORY AND THEORY OF THE CONSTITUTION

Page 17.   At the bottom of the page, add the following:

Consider the following defense of the modern relevance of the antifederalist position:

> [The] civic-republican tradition, currently resurgent in American constitutional-legal thought, offers historical validation for the ideal of freedom as self-government realized through politics, along with visionary resources for critical comprehension of the ideal and of specific institutional manifestations of it. If this positive-libertarian ideal is highly valued, then these observations may help explain the tradition's stubborn hold on a place in constitutional imagination — despite the historical defeat of its antifederalist defenders, despite its obvious impracticality in the national constitutional setting, and despite the unattractive or ominous features that the tradition also notoriously incorporates. Conversely, the tradition's persistence despite these adverse factors suggests that positive public freedom — active political self-government — is indeed an ideal more highly valued than actual constitutional practice might suggest.
>
> [As] a result, the courts, and especially the Supreme Court, seem to take on as one of their ascribed functions the modeling of active self-government that citizens find practically beyond reach. Unable as a nation to practice or own self-government, [we can] at least identify with the judiciary's as we idealistically construct it.

Michelman, Foreword: Traces of Self-Government, 100 Harv. L. Rev. 4, 74 (1986).

Consider the view that republican thought argues in favor of a deferential rather than aggressive judicial role. After all, it was the antifederalists who were least favorably disposed toward a powerful Supreme Court. On republican thought and current constitutional controversies, see Symposium, 97 Yale L.J. 1493 (1988).

See also Fallon, What is Republicanism, and Is It Worth Reviving?, 102 Harv. L. Rev. 1695 (1989); Kahn, Community in Contemporary Constitutional Theory, 99 Yale L.J. 1 (1989). Both Fallon and Kahn raise serious questions about the effort to revive republicanism in contemporary constitutional thought.

B. THE BASIC FRAMEWORK

Page 26. On line 30, the correct date for Stuart v. Laird is 1803.

Page 33. At line 6 from the top, after "public-spiritedness.", add the following:

See also Ackerman, Constitutional Politics/Constitutional Law, 99 Yale L.J. 433 (1989).

Page 33. Before the first full paragraph, add the following:

Does Ackerman's account romanticize "constitutional politics"? Consider Brest, Constitutional Citizenship, 34 Clev. St. L. Rev. 175, 187-188 (1986):

> Some of the Federalists, who urged ratification of the Constitution of 1787, and some of the Anti-Federalists, who opposed it, undoubtedly took the long view. The proponents and opponents were also concerned with immediate economic problems, and the solutions provided by the new Constitution — for example, a strong central government — were widely understood to serve the interests of some groups at the expense of others. . . .
>
> Considering issues from the moral point of view requires habits and attitudes that come from regular practice and that are not readily acquired on the spur of the moment. It is simply not plausible to expect citizens or officials to act out of self interest day to day, and adopt a very different perspective when the word "constitutional" is invoked.

See also Seidman, Public Principle and Private Choice: The Uneasy Case for a Boundary Maintenance Theory of Constitutional Law, 96 Yale L.J. 1006, 1021, 1050 (1987):

> Any theory about what constitutes the good life must recognize that people are both private and public regarding. We are all equal and entitled to equality of concern and respect, but we also need lovers, families, and friends for whom we care specially. . . .
>
> Some commentators have argued that the [constitutional] text [should] bind future generations because it was written during rare moments in our history when most of the country was politicized. In this view, the Constitution represents as pure an articulation of our public universalist values as we are likely ever to get. But precisely because the Constitution is a public document articulating public values, it would be undesirable to let the constitutional text alone mark the boundary between the public

and private spheres. Allowing a public document to determine the boundaries of private power would build into the system a bias in favor of public values.

Page 34.   At line 13 from the bottom, after "framers.", add the following:

For a vigorous defense of the view that courts should rely on the original meaning, see R. Bork, The Tempting of America (1989).

Page 37.   Before section 3 of the Note, add the following:

How do these various possible sources of constitutional decision fit together? Sometimes they will of course point in different directions, creating what might be called a "commensurability problem." Fallon, A Constructivist Coherence Theory of Constitutional Interpretation, 100 Harv. L. Rev. 1189 (1987). Professor Fallon's essay is a detailed exploration of the ways in which courts do and should resolve that problem in the face of inconsistency in the directions pointed to by various sources of constitutional argument.

Page 38.   After the block quotation, add the following:

See also Michelman, Foreword: Traces of Self-Government, 100 Harv. L. Rev. 4, 75 (1986):

> [For] citizens of the United States, national politics are not imaginably the arena of self-government in its positive, freedom-giving sense. As a constituted nation we are, it seems, necessarily committed to the sovereign separation of rulers from ruled. [Congress] is not us. The President is not us. ["We"] are not "in" those bodies. Their determinations are not our self-government. Judges overriding those determinations do not, therefore, necessarily subtract anything from our freedom, although the judges also, obviously are not us. Their actions may augment our freedom. As usual, it all depends. One thing it depends on, I believe, is the commitment of judges to the process of their own self-government.

Page 47.   Before section 3 of the Note, add the following:

Consider the views of Attorney General Edwin Meese in The Law of the Constitution, 61 Tul. L. Rev. 979 (1987):

> [There] is [a] necessary distinction between the Constitution and constitutional law. The two are not synonymous. . . .
> Obviously [a Supreme Court decision] does have binding quality: It binds the parties in a case and also the executive branch for whatever enforcement is necessary. But such a decision does not establish a "supreme Law of the Land" that is binding on all persons and parts of government, henceforth and forevermore. . . .
> The Supreme Court would face quite a dilemma if its own constitutional decisions really were "the supreme Law of the Land" binding on all persons and governmental

entities, including the Court itself, for then the Court would not be able to change its mind. It could not overrule itself in a constitutional case. . . .

To confuse the Constitution with judicial pronouncements allows no standard by which to criticize and to seek the overruling of [cases] such as *Dred Scott*, and Plessy v. Ferguson. To do otherwise, as Lincoln said, is to submit to government by judiciary. But such a state could never be consistent with the principles of our Constitution. Indeed, it would be utterly inconsistent with the very idea of the rule of law to which we, as a people, have always subscribed.

Attorney General Meese's comments generated a storm of protest. See, e.g., Taylor, Liberties Union Denounces Meese, N.Y. Times, Oct. 24, 1986, at A17, col. 1. Would acceptance of his views create "a grave threat to the rule of law" as Professor Tribe claimed, or cause the "system [to] break down" as Professor Gunther charged? Consider Tushnet, The Supreme Court, The Supreme Law of the Land, and Attorney-General Meese: A Comment, 61 Tul. L. Rev 1017 (1987):

"Anarchy" and "a threat to the rule of law" seem pretty strong words for people who, as academics, had to have known that Jefferson, Jackson, Lincoln, and Roosevelt had made statements at least similar to Meese's. . . .

The issues raised by Meese are troubling because, on analysis, they seem to imply that politics determines the line between politics and law. . . .

[Those] contemplating defiance of the Supreme Court, in the sense of insisting that they be made the targets of coercive judicial orders directed at them personally, must consider the implications of their proposed actions. Among those implications are the possibility of violent confrontations between the supporters of the Supreme Court and the supporters of defiance, the production of generalized instability about previously settled understandings, and the generation of litigation. And, of course, they must consider whether their defiance will accomplish anything. Whether defiance or acquiescence is acceptable is thus a question of political prudence. . . .

There may, therefore, be a sense in which Attorney General Meese's position does promote anarchy — not, as his critics suggested, in the immediate sense of urging "every person a law unto herself," but in the indirect sense of showing that law is another form of politics. But, of course, Attorney General Meese does not believe that either. For the point of his speech is to demonstrate that the Supreme Court's decisions [are] not properly regarded as "law" at all, but merely as expressions of the Justices' personal preferences. So, in the end, the problem is not so much that Meese is wrong or lawless; it is that he is hypocritical.

D. THE POWER OF REPRISAL: POLITICAL CONTROL OF THE SUPREME COURT

Page 67. On line 7, the correct citation is 97 Harv. L. Rev. 386 (1983).

Page 68.   Line 12 should read "No Supreme Court justice has been removed from office in the nation's history."

Page 68.   After the first full paragraph, add the following:

Consider in this regard the extraordinary public debate in 1987 over President Reagan's nomination of Judge Robert Bork. Judge Bork had been known as a distinguished lawyer, professor, and judge; he was also one of the most outspoken critics of what he saw as unjustified judicial activism on the part of the Supreme Court under Chief Justices Warren and Burger. An especially controversial article, Bork, Neutral Principles and Some First Amendment Problems, 47 Ind. L.J. 1 (1971), was taken by many readers as a broadside attack on the Supreme Court's decisions in such areas as privacy, voting rights, and sex discrimination. Judge Bork was one of the leading defenders of the view that the original intent of the framers ought to be of central importance to constitutional law, a view discussed in various places in the casebook. At least outside of certain areas, his belief in original intent was accompanied by a belief in judicial restraint.

That article — and other writings by Judge Bork — provided the focus for a heated and lengthy confirmation process in which the Senate Judiciary Committee heard testimony from Judge Bork himself and from numerous lawyers and law professors. There was intense lobbying on both sides; the lobbying efforts included national advertisements — in newspapers and journals as well as on television and radio — predicting the consequences of Judge Bork's confirmation. Some of the most controversial advertisements suggested that Judge Bork would seriously threaten many of the developments associated with the civil rights and women's movements. See generally The Bork Nomination, Essays and Reports, 9 Cardozo L. Rev. 1 (1987).

Judge Bork's nomination was defeated by the largest margin of any Supreme Court nominee in American history. What, if any, implications does the defeat have for constitutional interpretation? In the immediate aftermath of the confirmation process, the following views, among others, were expressed.

(1) Judge Bork's defeat should be understood as a kind of public referendum on his views of constitutional interpretation, and a public ratification of some of the methods of the Warren and Burger Courts. Ironically, those views — including belief in original intent and in judicial restraint, which are often defended as democratic — were rejected by the democratic process itself. In this sense, the rejection of Judge Bork was a kind of "constitutional moment," having significant consequences for future interpretation.

(2) Judge Bork's defeat was a tribute to the power of the status quo, not to any considered judgment by the American public about constitutional interpretation. In the end, the question was whether the conflicting direc-

tions marked out by the moderately activist, moderately conservative Court of the 1980s should be dramatically shifted. The American public expressed a negative judgment, largely because it did not want significant changes in existing practice — not because it had worked out any view about constitutional interpretation.

(3) Judge Bork's defeat was the result of a well-financed and at least partly dishonest public relations campaign and a particular, contingent array of forces, including a Judiciary Committee controlled by the Democratic Party and a somewhat weakened President Reagan. Well-organized interests were able to defeat the nomination, in large part because of the power wielded by the civil rights community over (ironically) southern Democrats. No broad lesson should be drawn from the result.

Does the experience with Judge Bork suggest that an aggressive senatorial role in the confirmation process is desirable? What does it suggest about the idea that the appointments process weakens the countermajoritarian difficulty? Issues of constitutional interpretation received considerable public attention, perhaps for the first time in at least a generation. Should other justices receive the same scrutiny from the public and the Senate? What are the dangers of an affirmative conclusion? For varying views on these and related questions, see Essays on the Supreme Court Appointment Process, 101 Harv. L. Rev. 1146 (1988). For Judge Bork's analysis of the confirmation process, and for a detailed statement of his approach to constitutional interpretation, see R. Bork, The Tempting of America (1989).

Page 75.   Before the Note, add the following:

For a careful elaboration of a position similar to that of Story, see Amar, A Neo-Federalist View of Article III: Separating the Two Tiers of Federal Jurisdiction, 65 B.U.L. Rev. 205 (1985).

E.   "CASE OR CONTROVERSY" REQUIREMENTS AND THE PASSIVE VIRTUES

Page 86.   At the bottom of the page, add the following:

For discussion of some of these considerations, see Meltzer, Deterring Constitutional Violations by Law Enforcement Officials: Plaintiffs and Defendants as Private Attorneys General, 88 Colum. L. Rev. 247 (1988).

Page 90.   Before subsection c of the Note, add the following:

In Bender v. Williamsport Area School District, 475 U.S. 534 (1986), the Court held in a 5 to 4 decision that an individual school board member, sued in his corporate capacity, lacked standing to appeal a judgment rendered against him when a majority of the board voted not to pursue an appeal. Plaintiffs, a group of high school students, were denied permission to meet on school premises for the purpose of reading passages from scripture and praying. They brought an action against the school board and individual school board members, alleging violation of their first amendment rights. After the district court granted their motion for summary judgment, the school board elected to comply with the judgment and not to seek an appeal. However, an individual board member filed a notice of appeal. The Court held that

> [as] a member of the School Board sued in his official capacity Mr. Youngman has no personal stake in the outcome of the litigation and therefore did not have standing to file the notice of appeal. [Generally] speaking, members of collegial bodies do not have standing to perfect an appeal the body itself has declined to take.

Page 93.   Before subsection d of the Note, add the following:

In Diamond v. Charles, 476 U.S. 54 (1986), the Court held that a pediatrician who had intervened below to defend a state's criminal statute regulating abortions lacked standing to appeal when the state itself failed to seek review of a decision enjoining enforcement of the statute. The Court pointed out that even if the abortion law were held constitutional, appellant "could not compel the State to enforce it against appellees because 'a private citizen lacks a judicially cognizable interest in the prosecution or nonprosecution of another.' [Linda R. S.]" Moreover, appellant was unable to assert injury in fact. Appellant claimed that as a pediatrician, he would benefit financially if there were more live births. The Court responded that "[the] possibilities that such fetuses would survive and then find their way as patients to [appellant] are speculative, and 'unadorned speculation will not suffice to invoke the federal judicial power.' [Simon.]" Nor could appellant assert the rights of unborn fetuses. "Only the State may invoke regulatory measures to protect that interest and only the State may invoke the power of the courts when those regulatory measures are subject to challenge." Finally, the Court held that an award of attorneys' fees against appellant failed to give him a direct stake in enforcement of the law.

> It is true that, were the Court to resolve the case on the merits against appellees, appellees would no longer be "prevailing parties" entitled to an award of fees. [But] the mere fact that continued adjudication would provide a remedy for an injury that is only a byproduct of the suit itself does not mean that the injury is cognizable under Art. III.

Compare Diamond with Maine v. Taylor, 477 U.S. 131 (1986). A federal statute makes it a federal criminal offense for a person to import any fish into a state in violation of the law of that state. Respondent, who operated a bait business in Maine, was prosecuted under the federal law for importing live baitfish into the state in violation of Maine law. He moved to dismiss the indictment on the ground that the Maine statute unconstitutionally burdened interstate commerce and, therefore, could not form the basis of the federal prosecution. The district judge allowed Maine to intervene to defend the constitutionality of its statute, and ruled that the statute was constitutional. On appeal, the court of appeals reversed. Although the United States, which had brought the initial prosecution, sought no further review, Maine appealed to the Supreme Court, and the Court held that the state had a sufficient stake in the outcome to give it standing to appeal.

> [If] the judgment of the Court of Appeals is left undisturbed, the State will be bound by the conclusive adjudication that its import ban is unconstitutional. And although private parties, and perhaps even separate sovereigns, have no legally cognizable interest in the prosecutorial decisions of the Federal government, cf., e.g., [Diamond; Linda R. S.] a State clearly has a legitimate interest in the continued enforceability of its own statutes.

Page 101.   After Baker v. Carr, add the following:

DAVIS v. BANDEMER, 478 U.S. 109 (1986):   This case concerned an equal protection challenge to "political gerrymandering" by the Indiana legislature. Although the legislative districts created by the Republican controlled legislature were substantially equal in population, the Democrats claimed that the district lines were deliberately drawn so as to understate Democratic voting strength. The trial court agreed and ordered preparation of a new plan. On appeal, a majority of the Supreme Court held that "political gerrymandering" was not a nonjusticiable political question. However, a plurality held that the trial court had erred in finding a substantive constitutional violation. (This aspect of the case is considered in greater detail at Supplement to Casebook page 786 infra.)

Justice White delivered the Court's opinion with respect to the political question issue: "Disposition of this question does not involve us in a matter more properly decided by a coequal branch of our Government. There is no risk of foreign or domestic disturbance, and in light of our cases since *Baker* we are not persuaded that there are no judicially discernible and manageable standards by which political gerrymander cases are to be decided.

"It is true that the type of claim that was presented in Baker v. Carr was subsequently resolved in this Court by the formulation of the 'one person, one vote' rule. [For a discussion of this rule, see pages 768-777 of the main text.] The mere fact, however, that we may not now similarly perceive a likely arithmetic presumption in the instant context does not compel a conclusion that the claims presented here are non-justiciable. The one person, one vote principle had not yet been developed when *Baker* was decided. At that time, the Court did not rely on the potential for such a rule in finding justiciability. Instead, [the] Court contemplated simply that legislative line-drawing in the districting context would be susceptible of adjudication under the applicable constitutional criteria. . . .

"[Justice O'Connor's dissent] would transform the narrow categories of 'political questions' that Baker v. Carr carefully defined into an ad hoc litmus test of this Court's reactions to the desirability of and need for judicial application of constitutional or statutory standards to a given type of claim. [She] concludes that because political gerrymandering may be a 'self-limiting enterprise' there is no need for judicial intervention. She also expresses concern that our decision today will lead to 'political instability and judicial malaise,' because nothing will prevent members of other identifiable groups from bringing similar claims. To begin with, Justice O'Connor's factual assumptions are by no means obviously correct: It is not clear that political gerrymandering *is* a self-limiting enterprise or that other groups will have any great incentive to bring gerrymandering claims, given the requirement of a showing of discriminatory intent. At a more fundamental level, however, Justice O'Connor's analysis is flawed because it focuses on the perceived need for judicial review and on the potential practical problems with allowing such review. Validation of the consideration of such amorphous and wide-ranging factors in assessing justiciability would alter substantially the analysis the Court enunciated in Baker v. Carr, and we decline Justice O'Connor's implicit invitation to rethink that approach."

Turning to the merits, Justice White (now writing for only a four-justice plurality of the Court) held that "a group's electoral power is not unconstitutionally diminished by the simple fact of an apportionment scheme that makes winning elections more difficult, and a failure of proportional representation alone does not constitute impermissible discrimination." In order to establish a constitutional violation, the party challenging a districting scheme must show that "the electoral system is arranged in a manner that will consistently degrade a voter's or a group of voters' influence on the political process as a whole." (See Supplement to Casebook page 786 infra for a fuller discussion.)

Justice O'Connor, joined by Chief Justice Burger and Justice Rehnquist, dissented from the Court's justiciability holding: "The step taken today is a momentous one, which if followed in the future can only lead to political instability and judicial malaise. If members of the majority political parties are protected by the Equal Protection Clause from dilution of their voting strength, then members of every identifiable group that possesses distinctive interests and tends to vote on the basis of those interests should be able to bring similar claims. Federal courts will have no alternative but to attempt to recreate the complex process of legislative apportionment in the context of adversary litigation in order to reconcile the competing claims of political, religious, ethnic, racial, occupational, and socioeconomic groups. [There] is

simply no clear stopping point to prevent the gradual evolution of a requirement of roughly proportional representation for every cohesive political
group.

"In my view, this enterprise is flawed from its inception. The Equal Protection Clause does not supply judicially manageable standards for resolving
purely political gerrymandering claims, and no group right to an equal share of
political power was ever intended by the Framers of the Fourteenth
Amendment. . . .

"[There] is good reason to think that political gerrymandering is a self-
limiting enterprise. In order to gerrymander, the legislative majority must
weaken some of its safe seats, thus exposing its own incumbents to greater risks
of defeat — risks they may refuse to accept past a certain point. [More]
generally, each major party presumably has ample weapons at its disposal to
conduct the partisan struggle that often leads to a partisan apportionment,
but also often leads to a bipartisan one. There is no proof before us that
political gerrymandering is an evil that cannot be checked or cured by the
people or by the parties themselves. . . .

"The standard the plurality proposes exemplifies the intractable difficulties
in deriving a judicially manageable standard from the Equal Protection Clause
for adjudicating political gerrymandering claims. [In] my view, this standard
will over time either prove unmanageable and arbitrary or else evolve towards
some loose form of proportionality. . . .

"Absent [a norm of proportionality] the inquiry the plurality proposes would
be so standardless as to make the adjudication of political gerrymandering
claims impossible. . . .

"Of course, in one sense a requirement of proportional representation,
whether loose or absolute, is judicially manageable. If this Court were to declare
that the Equal Protection Clause required proportional representation within
certain fixed tolerances, I have no doubt that district courts would be able to
apply this edict. The flaw in such a pronouncement, however, would be the use
of the Equal Protection Clause as the vehicle for making a fundamental policy
choice that is contrary to the intent of its Framers and to the traditions of this
republic. The political question doctrine as articulated in Baker v. Carr rightly
requires that we refrain from making such policy choices in order to evade what
would otherwise be a lack of judicially manageable standards."

Chief Justice Burger also wrote a short opinion arguing that the issue was
nonjusticiable.

Justice Powell, joined by Justice Stevens, wrote an opinion agreeing with
Justice White that this issue was justiciable, but arguing that the trial court had
applied the correct substantive standard and that its judgment should be
affirmed.

For criticism of *Bandemer*, see Schuck, The Thickest Thicket: Partisan Gerrymandering and Judicial Regulation of Politics, 87 Colum. L. Rev. 1325 (1987).

Page 108.   After the first paragraph in subsection d of the Note, add the following:

Consider Japan Whaling Assn. v. Baldridge, 478 U.S. 238 (1986). A federal statute requires the Secretary of Commerce to certify to the President whether a foreign country engaged in fishing operations is diminishing the effectiveness of quotas set by the International Whaling Commission (IWC). Once the certification is made, the President is required to impose economic sanctions against the offending nation. After Japan announced that it would not comply with IWC quotas, the United States and Japan entered into negotiations culminating in an executive agreement according to which Japan would cease commercial whaling by 1988 and the Secretary would not certify that Japan was in violation of the IWC quotas. This action was then filed by several conservation groups seeking to compel the Secretary to certify Japanese violations. In an opinion by Justice White, the Court rejected the contention that the political question doctrine barred adjudication of the dispute.

> The political question doctrine excludes from judicial review those controversies which revolve around policy choices and value determinations constitutionally committed for resolution to the halls of Congress or the confines of the Executive Branch. The judiciary is particularly ill-suited to make such decisions. . . .
>
> As *Baker* plainly held, however, the courts have the authority to construe treaties and executive agreements, and it goes without saying that interpreting congressional legislation is a recurring and accepted task for the federal courts. It is also evident that the challenge to the Secretary's decision not to certify Japan for harvesting whales in excess of IWC quotas presents a purely legal question of statutory interpretation.

The Court thereupon held that the Secretary's decision did not violate the statutory mandate.

F.   THE JURISDICTION OF THE SUPREME COURT

Page 111.   Eliminate the third paragraph of Note 1 and all of Note 2 on pages 112-113, and substitute the following:

The Supreme Court's mandatory (appeal) jurisdiction was almost entirely eliminated in 1988.

Chapter Two

The Powers of Congress

A. INTRODUCTION

Page 125. Before the paragraph beginning "A national government with plenary power might choose to exercise . . . ," add the following:

Compare Rapaczynski, From Sovereignty to Process: The Jurisprudence of Federalism after *Garcia*, 1985 Sup. Ct. Rev. 341, 400, 402-403, 407-408:

> [The] model of participatory government [views] political activity not as instrumental toward achieving a proportionate share in the distribution of available resources, to be used in a variety of private pursuits, but rather as a good in itself, something essentially implicated in the very concept of human freedom. [If] there is some genuine room for noninstrumental participation in American political life, it can realistically exist only on the local level. [The] existence of participatory politics on the state level [is] by no means a fiction. [The] most traditional American mechanism of participatory democracy — the town meeting — is very much alive in a large section of the country. [Further], throughout the country, there is significant citizen involvement in the local planning process, school boards, the budget process, and other governmental functions. [Finally], a special role of the most powerful tool of direct government on a larger scale — the referendum — must be mentioned. [One] of the basic purposes of federalism is to assure that, insofar as politics is per se an indispensable communal component of the good life, the nationalization of political decision making does not deprive the communities and individuals of an essential sphere of their self-realization.

Page 125. Before section 2 of the Note, add the following new subsection:

e. *Preventing tyranny*. Consider Rapaczynski, supra at 341, 385-386, 388-389:

> Many American liberals tend to look with skepticism on the states as the protectors of individual freedom and they point to a whole host of situations in which the states, much more than the federal government, have engaged in practices violative of individual rights. [But] if the liberal mistrust of the states' power is partially justified in this way, the more comprehensive neglect on the part of liberals of the importance

of the states for the prevention of governmental oppression is somewhat myopic. [While] the states are more easily captured by relatively undifferentiated majoritarian interests intent on suppressing small minorities, the federal government may be a more likely subject of capture by a set of special minoritarian interests, precisely because the majority interest of the national constituency is so large, diffuse, and enormously difficult to organize.

But the most influential protection that the states offer against tyranny is the protection against the special interest of the government itself. [Should] the federal government ever be captured by an authoritarian movement [the] resulting oppression would almost certainly be much more severe and durable than that of which any state would be capable. [It] is precisely because the states are governmental bodies that break the national authorities' monopoly on coercion that they constitute the most fundamental bastion against a successful conversion of the federal government into a vehicle of the worst kind of oppression.

Page 177.   Before United States v. Darby, add the following:

For a vigorous challenge to the post-New Deal expansion of the commerce power, see Epstein, The Proper Scope of the Commerce Power, 73 Va. L. Rev. 1387 (1987).

E.   THE PURPORTED DEMISE OF JUDICIALLY ENFORCED FEDERALISM LIMITS ON CONGRESSIONAL POWER

Page 187.   Before *Heart of Atlanta Motel,* add the following:

In Bowen v. American Hospital Assn., 476 U.S. 610 (1986), (the "Baby Doe" case), a plurality of the Court relied in part on federalism concerns when it found regulations adopted by the Department of Health and Human Services concerning health care for handicapped infants beyond the Department's authority under the Rehabilitation Act of 1973.

Section 504 of the Act prohibits discrimination against an "otherwise qualified handicapped individual" under any program receiving federal financial assistance. After a much publicized incident in which parents of a child with Down's syndrome refused to consent to lifesaving surgery for the child, the Department promulgated rules that required, inter alia, hospitals receiving federal assistance to post "informational notices" warning that withholding of nourishment and medically beneficial treatment from handicapped infants solely on the basis of their impairment violated federal law. The regulations also required state child protection agencies receiving federal funds to establish procedures ensuring utilization of their full authority pursuant to state law to prevent medical neglect of handicapped infants and requiring timely notification of the Department of every report of suspected unlawful medical neglect.

A plurality of the Court found that the Department had not shown that a regulation of this sort was needed. In the plurality opinion, Justice Stevens stated that

> The need for a proper evidentiary basis for agency action is especially acute in this case because Congress has failed to indicate, either in the statute or in the legislative history, that it envisioned federal superintendence of treatment decisions traditionally entrusted to state governance. [Congress] "[will] not be deemed to have significantly changed the federal-state balance," [*Bass*] — or to have authorized its delegates to do so — "unless otherwise the purpose of the Act would be defeated," Trade Commn. v. Bunte Bros., 312 U.S. 349 (1941). [The] administrative record does not contain the reasoning and evidence that is necessary to sustain federal intervention into a historically state-administered decisional process that appears — for lack of any evidence to the contrary — to be functioning in full compliance with §504.

The plurality was especially critical of those portions of the federal regulations directed against state child protection agencies. "State child protective services agencies are not field offices of the HHS bureaucracy, and they may not be conscripted against their will as the foot soldiers in a federal crusade."

Chief Justice Burger concurred in the judgment without opinion. Justice Rehnquist did not participate. Justices White, Brennan, and O'Connor dissented.

Page 208.   At the beginning of the Note, add the following:

Nine months after the Court's decision in *Garcia*, Congress enacted the Fair Labor Standards Amendments of 1985. Under the original Fair Labor Standards Act, private employers must pay overtime to employees who work more than a stated number of hours at a rate of 1½ times their regular pay. The amendments, responding to widespread practices in police and fire departments, allow public employers to substitute compensatory time-off for the overtime pay, again at the rate of 1½ hours compensatory time for each hour of overtime. Compensatory time-off is limited to 480 hours for public safety employees and employees in seasonal work, and 240 hours for other public employees; after that, public employers must pay for overtime. Does the adoption of the amendments demonstrate that *Garcia* was correctly decided? Does it show that the Court unnecessarily forced Congress to act so as to maintain the proper system of federal nonregulation of state employment practices? Note that the amendments do not restore the pre-*Garcia* status quo, because they define limits on the use of compensatory time-off.

Page 211.   After the first paragraph, add the following:

In Rockford Life Insurance Co. v. Illinois Dept. of Revenue, 482 U.S. 182 (1987), a unanimous Court held that the intergovernmental tax immunity doctrine did not preclude state taxation of "Ginnie Maes" — instruments issued by private financial institutions but guaranteed by the United States government.

F. OTHER POWERS OF CONGRESS: ARE THEY MORE (OR LESS) PLENARY THAN THE COMMERCE POWER?

Page 229. Before section 2 of the Note, add the following:

1A. *The modern view.* South Dakota v. Dole, 483 U.S. 203 (1987), upheld a federal statute that directed the Secretary of Transportation to withhold a portion of federal highway funds from states that do not prohibit the purchase of alcohol by people under the age of 21. Congress used this technique because of uncertainty about its power to impose a national minimum drinking age directly, in light of the twenty-first amendment. Although most of the opinion for the Court by Chief Justice Rehnquist discussed whether the twenty-first amendment was a limitation on Congress' power to spend, the opinion also contained some general observations about the scope of the conditional spending power:

> The spending power is of course not unlimited, but is instead subject to several general restrictions. [First,] the exercise of the spending power must be in pursuit of "the general welfare." [*Butler.*] In considering whether a particular expenditure is intended to serve general public purposes, courts should defer substantially to the judgment of Congress. Second, [if] Congress desires to condition the States' receipt of federal funds, it "must do so [unambiguously."] Third, our cases have suggested (without significant elaboration) that conditions on federal grants might be illegitimate if they are unrelated "to the federal interest in particular national projects or programs." Finally, [other] constitutional provisions may provide an independent bar to the conditional grant of federal funds.

The 21-year-old drinking age condition satisfied all of these requirements. It served the general welfare because different drinking ages in different states created incentives for young people "to combine their desire to drink with their ability to drive," and it was reasonably calculated to advance the general welfare. Further, "the condition imposed by Congress is directly related to one of the main purposes for which highway funds are expended — safe interstate travel." The Court noted that the cases it had decided in the past had not required that it "define the outer bounds of the 'germaneness' or 'relatedness' limitation on the imposition of conditions under the spending power," and that it need not do so here because "any such limitation on conditional federal spending [was] satisfied in this case in any event." It also concluded that the twenty-first amendment was not an "independent constitutional bar" on the spending power. The requirement that conditions on spending not violate such a bar "stands for the unexceptionable proposition that the power may not be used to induce the States to engage in activities that would themselves be unconstitutional. [A] grant of federal funds conditioned on [the] infliction of cruel and unusual punishment would be an illegitimate exercise of the Congress' broad spending power."

Finally, the Court discussed the question of coercion. It agreed with the suggestion in *Steward Machine Co.* that at some point "pressure turns into coercion." But here, because

> all South Dakota would lose if she adheres to her chosen course as to a suitable minimum drinking age is 5% of the funds otherwise obtainable under specified highway grant programs, the argument as to coercion is shown to be more rhetoric than fact. [Here] Congress has offered relatively mild encouragement to the States to enact higher minimum drinking ages than they would otherwise choose. [But] the enactment of such laws remains the prerogative of the States not merely in theory but in fact.

Justice O'Connor's dissenting opinion argued that the minimum drinking age "is not sufficiently related to interstate highway construction to justify" the condition placed on funds "appropriated for that purpose." If the condition was designed to deter drunken driving, it was "far too over- and under-inclusive," because "it stops teenagers from drinking even when they are not about to drive on interstate highways," and because

> teenagers pose only a small part of the drunken driving problem. [When] Congress appropriates money to build a highway, it is entitled to insist that the highway be a safe one. But it is not entitled to insist as a condition of the use of highway funds that the State impose or change regulations in other areas of the State's social and economic life because of an attenuated or tangential relationship to highway use or safety. [If] the rule were otherwise, the Congress could effectively regulate almost any area of a State's social, political, or economic life on the theory that use of the interstate transportation system is somehow enhanced.

She would have relied on an approach "hark[ing] back" to *Butler*, under which the test would be whether the condition is a regulation or a specification of "how the money should be spent." *Butler* was wrong only because of "its crabbed view of the extent of Congress' regulatory power under the Commerce Clause, not because it insisted that conditions on spending be non-regulatory."

Justice Brennan also dissented.

For a general discussion of the conditional spending power, see Rosenthal, Conditional Federal Spending and the Constitution, 39 Stan. L. Rev. 1103 (1987).

Page 243. At the end of section 3 of the Note, add the following:

Carter, The *Morgan* "Power" and the Forced Reconsideration of Constitutional Decisions, 53 U. Chi. L. Rev. 819, 824 (1986), argues that *Morgan* is "best understood as a tool that permits the Congress to use its power to enact ordinary legislation to engage the Court in a dialogue about our fundamental rights, thereby 'forcing' the Justices to take a fresh look at their own judgments." Compare this power with that of Congress to regulate (or restrict) the jurisdiction of the federal courts.

Chapter Three

Judicial Efforts to Protect the Expansion of the Market against Assertions of Local Power

A. THE FUNDAMENTAL FRAMEWORK

Page 250. **The third line from the bottom should refer to note 5 infra, rather than note 4.**

Page 251. **After subsection b of the Note, add the following:**

The Court relied on the directness test in Brown-Forman Distillers Corp. v. New York State Liquor Auth., 476 U.S. 573 (1986). New York required distillers to file a price schedule with the Authority each month. All sales during the following month had to be at the prices listed in the schedule. In addition, the schedule had to affirm that the prices in the schedule are no higher than the lowest price at which each item would be sold anywhere else in the United States during the covered month. The Court construed this affirmation as prohibiting distillers from lowering their prices in other states once the New York price had been filed. It said that this prohibition "regulates out-of-state transactions in violation of the Commerce Clause. [Forcing] a merchant to seek regulatory approval in one State before undertaking a transaction in another directly regulates interstate commerce." Justices Stevens, White, and Rehnquist dissented. For a follow-up to *Brown-Forman,* see Healy v. Beer Institute, Inc., 109 S. Ct. 249 (1989).

Page 257. **At the fourth line from the bottom, the sentence beginning "[In] the absence of affirmative consent" starts the quotation from Dowling cited on the following page.**

B. PROTECTION AGAINST DISCRIMINATION

Page 270. After subsection a of the Note, add the following:

Compare *City of Philadelphia* and *Hughes* with Maine v. Taylor, 477 U.S. 131 (1986), where the Court upheld the constitutionality of a Maine statute that prohibited the importation of live baitfish. Writing for eight justices, Justice Blackmun noted that the statute affirmatively discriminated against interstate transactions and, therefore, could be upheld only if it survived "the strictest scrutiny." Specifically, the burden was on the state to show that the statute served a legitimate local purpose and that the purpose could not be served as well by an available nondiscriminatory means. In this case, however, the Court held that, in light of the trial court's findings of fact, both branches of this test had been satisfied.

Evidence before the trial court indicated that Maine's population of wild fish might be placed at risk by parasites prevalent in out-of-state baitfish but not common in wild fish in Maine. Moreover, non-native species inadvertently included in shipments of live baitfish could disturb Maine's aquatic ecology to an unpredictable extent by competing with, or preying on, native species. Finally, there was no satisfactory way to inspect imported baitfish for parasites and commingled species. Based on this evidence, the trial court found that Maine clearly had a legitimate and substantial interest in excluding the baitfish because of the "substantial uncertainties" surrounding the consequences of their importation.

The Supreme Court held that these findings were sufficient to sustain the statute. Although it was not certain that importation of the baitfish would adversely affect the environment, "Maine has a legitimate interest in guarding against imperfectly understood environmental risks, despite the possibility that they may ultimately prove to be negligible." Moreover, the mere "abstract possibility" of developing an acceptable testing procedure did not constitute an available nondiscriminatory alternative. Nor was there convincing evidence that the statute was the product of a protectionist intent.

> Shielding in-state industries from out-of-state competition is almost never a legitimate local purpose, and state laws that amount to "simple economic protectionism" consequently have been subject to a "virtually per se rule of invalidity." [Philadelphia v. New Jersey.] But there is little reason in this case to believe that the legitimate justifications the State has put forward for its statute are merely a sham or a "post hoc rationalization." [*Hughes*.] . . .
>
> The fact that Maine allows importation of salmonids, for which standardized sampling and inspection procedures are available, hardly demonstrates that Maine has no legitimate interest in prohibiting the importation of baitfish, for which such procedures have not yet been devised. Nor is this demonstrated by the fact that other States may not have enacted similar bans, especially given the testimony that Maine's fisheries are unique and unusually fragile. Finally, it is of little relevance that fish can swim directly into Maine from New Hampshire. As the magistrate explained:

"The impediments to complete success . . . cannot be a grounds for preventing a state from using its best efforts to limit [an environmental] risk."

Justice Stevens wrote a dissenting opinion.

Page 290.   At the end of the Note, add the following:

Consider this summary of the economics of severance taxation on the coal industry:

> [With] respect to the coal industry, which [is] competitive, the existence of short-run supply elasticity suggests a market dominated by demand considerations with little forward shifting of state and local production taxes in the short run. Instead production taxes would be shifted backward to owners of capital or mineral rights and to labor and exported to the extent that such owners or workers are nonresidents. [This] conclusion must be modified to take account of institutional factors in the coal industry. Long-term coal contracts that pass the burden of production taxes on to utility purchasers as well as transportation costs that segment national markets and permit states to dominate subnational markets create an environment in which some forward shifting and exporting to out-of-state consumers is more likely. In the long run, due to the absence of market dominance, large domestic reserves of coal, renegotiability of contracts, and the availability of alternative energy sources, [the] burden of production taxes will be borne by mineral owners.

W. Hellerstein, State and Local Taxation of Natural Resources in the Federal System: Legal, Economic and Political Perspectives 125-126 (1986).

C.   FACIALLY NEUTRAL STATUTES WITH SIGNIFICANT EFFECTS ON INTERSTATE COMMERCE

Page 292.   Before the final paragraph, add the following:

For a useful historical analysis of the problem presented in H. P. Hood & Sons, see Comment, *Hood v. DuMond*: A Study of the Supreme Court and the Ideology of Capitalism, 134 U. Pa. L. Rev. 657 (1986).

Page 293.   After the first full paragraph, add the following:

Armco Inc. v. Hardesty, 467 U.S. 638 (1984), held unconstitutional West Virginia's gross receipts tax on wholesale sales because it exempted local manufacturers. The tax on wholesaling was .27 percent, and although local manufacturers were exempt from that tax, they did have to pay a tax of .88 percent on manufacturing and bore a higher tax burden in dollar terms. The Court held that the West Virginia tax system could not be justified as an integrated system in which some tax burdens were compensated for by exemptions from other taxes. It held that the Court would examine only taxes placed on "substantially equivalent" activities, and that manufacturing and wholesaling were not substantially equivalent activities.

In Tyler Pipe Industries, Inc. v. Washington State Department of Revenue, 483 U.S. 232 (1987), the Court relied on *Armco* to invalidate a similar system. *Tyler* distinguished Henneford v. Silas Mason in this way:

> We upheld the tax because, in the context of the overall tax structure, the burden it placed on goods purchased out-of-state was identical to that placed on an equivalent purchase within the State. This identical impact was no fortuity; it was guaranteed by the statutory exemption from the use tax for goods on which a sales tax had already been paid.

Consider the relation between the "substantially equivalent activities" test and the observation that the "identical impact was no fortuity."

Page 313.   At the end of Note 3, add the following:

Consider Justice Scalia's observation in his concurring opinion in CTS Corp. v. Dynamics Corp., 481 U.S. 69 (1987), where the Court rejected a commerce clause challenge to a state anti-takeover statute:

> I do not know what qualifies us to make [the] ultimate (and most ineffable) judgment as to whether, given the importance-level x, and effectiveness-level y, the worth of the statute is "outweighed" by impact-on-commerce z. One commentator has suggested that, at least much of the time, we do not in fact mean what we say when we declare that statutes which neither discriminate against commerce nor present a threat of multiple and inconsistent burdens might nonetheless be unconstitutional under a "balancing" test. [Regan, The Supreme Court and State Protectionism: Making Sense of the Dormant Commerce Clause, 84 Mich. L. Rev. 1091 (1986).] If he is not correct, he ought to be. As long as a State's [law does] not discriminate against out-of-state interests, it should survive this Court's scrutiny. [Beyond] that, it is for Congress to prescribe its invalidity.

Justice White's dissenting opinion, which was joined by Justices Blackmun and Stevens, objected that the statute "directly" regulated interstate commerce by limiting the ability of an out-of-state trader to sell shares to a different out-of-state purchaser.

Page 313.   After section 4 of the Note, add the following:

5. *State protectionism.* Regan, The Supreme Court and State Protectionism: Making Sense of the Dormant Commerce Clause, 84 Mich. L. Rev. 1091 (1986), deserves close attention. Regan argues, in detail, that

> [the] Court should prevent states from engaging in protectionism directed against other states. . . .

State protectionism is unacceptable because it is inconsistent with the very idea of political union, even a limited federal union. Protectionist legislation is the economic equivalent of war. It is hostile in its essence. . . .

[In addition], protectionist impositions cause resentment and invite protectionist retaliation. . . .

[Finally], protectionism is inefficient because it diverts business away from presumptively low-cost producers without any colorable justification in terms of a benefit that deserves approval from the point of view of the nation as a whole. [Id. at 1112-1114, 1118.]

Regan describes the compromise he finds in the Constitution "between unlimited state autonomy and perfect national unity":

[The] states may not single out foreigners for disadvantageous treatment just because of their foreignness. But, provided they do not single out foreigners, the states need not attend positively to the foreign effects of laws they adopt nor to the distribution between locals and foreigners of the benefits and burdens of those laws. "Singling out" foreigners does not necessarily involve explicitness. It does involve purpose. [Id. at 1165.]

In addition, he argues that the Court should also protect the national transportation network from state legislation that places excessive burdens on it, because in such cases "there is a national interest in the existence of an effective transportation network" linking the states. Id. at 1185. Is this approach consistent with the decided cases? Is it different from the economic-political analysis described above? What is the scope of the "transportation" exception? Consider whether *Exxon* should be treated as a transportation case in Regan's sense.

Page 320. At the end of the first full paragraph, insert the following:

See also English v. General Electric Co., 58 U.S.L.W. 4679 (June 4, 1990) (state action for intentional infliction of emotional distress arising out of retaliation for employee's reporting nuclear safety violations is not within field of nuclear safety and so is not preempted).

E. OTHER DOCTRINES PROTECTING THE NATIONAL MARKET

Page 327. Before section 2 of the Note, add the following:

Wisconsin Department of Industry, Labor & Human Relations v. Gould, 475 U.S. 282 (1986), held that the National Labor Relations Act (NLRA) preempted a Wisconsin statute that barred state agencies from making contracts with employers who had violated the NLRA three times within a five year period. The state agreed that the federal act would preempt any state effort to require private businesses to refrain from entering into contracts with such employers, and the Court agreed that "[nothing] in the NLRA [prevents] private purchasers from boycotting labor law violators." But the Court rejected the state's effort to invoke "market participant" ideas, because "for all practical purposes, [the state statute] is tantamount to regulation," and because "government occupies a unique position of power in our society, and its conduct [is] rightly subject to special restraints." The market participant doctrine "reflects the particular concerns underlying the Commerce Clause, not any general notion regarding the necessary extent of state power in areas where Congress has acted." According to the Court, the NLRA "treats state action differently from private action [because] in our system States simply are different from private parties and have a different role to play." Could not the same be said for purposes of commerce clause analysis about states as purchasers of goods?

Page 327. Before section 4 of the Note, add the following:

Regan, The Supreme Court and State Protectionism: Making Sense of the Dormant Commerce Clause, 84 Mich. L. Rev. 1091, 1194 (1986), defends the market-participant exception as applied to cases involving "state spending as opposed to mere regulation or the positive imposition of a tax" on the following grounds:

(1) "state spending programs are less coercive than regulatory programs or taxes with similar purposes;"

(2) such programs "seem less hostile to other states and less inconsistent with the conception of union than discriminatory regulation or taxation;"

(3) "many spending programs are positively beneficial from the point of view of the nation as a whole [but] many of these programs would not exist if the state could not channel the primary benefits to locals;"

(4) "the very fact that spending programs involve spending and are therefore relatively expensive as a way of securing local benefits [means that they are] less likely to proliferate than measures like tariffs;" and

(5) such measures "are less likely to produce resentment and retaliation."

Page 335. At the end of subsection 2 of the Note, add the following:

See also Supreme Court of Virginia v. Friedman, 487 U.S. 59 (1988), in which the Court, relying on *Piper*, invalidated a Virginia Supreme Court rule permitting resident, but not nonresident, attorneys who are members of the bar of another state to be admitted to the Virginia bar "on motion," that is, without taking the Virginia bar examination.

Page 337. After the last paragraph, add the following:

NOTE: CONCLUDING OBSERVATIONS

Consider Justice Scalia's assessment of the law in this area, as expressed in his opinion dissenting in relevant part in Tyler Pipe Industries, Inc. v. Washington State Department of Revenue, 483 U.S. 232 (1987), where the Court held unconstitutional some provisions of Washington's system of taxing goods in interstate commerce. Justice Scalia argued that

> to the extent that we have gone beyond guarding against rank discrimination against citizens of other States — which is regulated not by the Commerce Clause but by the Privileges and Immunities Clause — the Court for over a century has engaged in an enterprise that it has been unable to justify by textual support or even coherent nontextual theory, that it was almost certainly not intended to undertake, and that it has not undertaken very well.

He noted that "pre-emption of state legislation would automatically follow [if] the grant of power to Congress to regulate interstate commerce were exclusive," but added that

> the language of the Commerce Clause gives no indication of exclusivity. Nor can one assume generally that Congress' Article I powers are exclusive; many of them plainly coexist with concurrent authority in the States. Furthermore, there is no correlative denial of power over commerce to the States [as] there is [with] the power to coin money or make treaties. [The] exclusivity rationale is infinitely less attractive today than it was in 1847. Now that we know interstate commerce embraces such activities as growing wheat for home consumption [*Wickard*] and local loan sharking [*Perez*], it is more difficult to imagine what state activity would survive an exclusive Commerce Clause than to imagine what would be precluded.

Justice Scalia argued that the Court could not distinguish, as *Cooley* attempted to, among the subjects of the commerce power, because the Constitution treats commerce "as a unitary subject," or between preempting state laws "*intended* to regulate commerce (as opposed to those intended, for example, to promote health)," because the distinction was "metaphysical, [not] useful as a practical technique for marking out the powers of separate sovereigns." He called "least plausible" the theory that

> in enforcing the negative Commerce Clause the Court is not applying a constitutional command at all, but is merely interpreting the will of Congress, whose silence in certain fields of interstate commerce (but not in others) is to be taken as a prohibition of regulation. There is no conceivable reason why congressional inaction under the Commerce Clause should be deemed to have the same pre-emptive effect elsewhere accorded only to congressional action. There, as elsewhere, 'Congress' silence is just that — silence."

Consider whether the law in this area might be justified as articulating a series of canons of construction to be applied to whatever federal legislation there is that regulates the subject matter of the state laws at issue.

Chapter Four

The Distribution of National Powers

C. THE DISTRIBUTION OF NATIONAL POWERS IN AN ADMINISTRATIVE STATE

Page 369.   After the first paragraph, add the following:

In Skinner v. Mid-America Pipeline Co., 109 S. Ct. 1726 (1989), the Court held that the standard for determining the constitutionality of a delegation of authority to raise money by means of "user fees" was the same as the general standard for delegations.

Page 385.   Before "8. *Future directions.*" add the following:

See also Sunstein, Constitutionalism After The New Deal, 101 Harv. L. Rev. 421, 493-494 (1987):

> The last few years have seen a sharp rise of constitutional "formalism" in cases involving the separation of powers. Formalist decisions are premised on the beliefs that the text of the Constitution and the intent of its drafters are controlling and sometimes dispositive, that changed circumstances are irrelevant to constitutional outcomes, and that broader "policy" concerns should not play a role in legal decisions. . . . But the federal government and the executive branch in particular have changed so dramatically since the founding that "framers' intent" cannot be mechanically applied as if it settles the matter. . . . The modern presidency is so different from the entity contemplated by the framers that it is unrealistic simply to "apply" their choices to the present situation. At its inception, the American presidency was by modern standards weak, especially in domestic affairs. Its regulatory role was minimal.

In these circumstances, the article urges a "functional" approach examining "whether present practices undermine constitutional commitments that should be regarded as central." Id. at 495. Is an approach of that sort too open-ended to be helpful?

Page 394. Before section 5 of the Note, add the following:

In Young v. United States ex rel. Vuitton et Fils, 481 U.S. 787 (1987), the Supreme Court, in an opinion by Justice Brennan, upheld the inherent power of a federal court to appoint a private attorney to prosecute a criminal contempt growing out of alleged disobedience to the court's order. The Court held that contempt proceedings were "a part of the judicial function" and emphasized that they were "not intended to punish conduct proscribed as harmful by the general criminal laws." The Court also noted that a trial court "ordinarily should first request the appropriate prosecuting authority to prosecute contempt actions, and should appoint a private prosecutor only if that request is denied. Such a procedure ensures that the court will exercise its inherent power of self-protection only as a last resort."

In an opinion concurring in the judgment, Justice Scalia pointed out that no statute authorized the appointment of private counsel to prosecute contempts, and that the case therefore raised no issue regarding Congress's Article II power to vest appointment of inferior officers in courts of law.

Page 395. Before section D, add the following:

BOWSHER v. SYNAR
478 U.S. 714 (1986)

CHIEF JUSTICE BURGER delivered the opinion of the Court.

The question presented by these appeals is whether the assignment by Congress to the Comptroller General of the United States of certain functions under the Balanced Budget and Emergency Deficit Control Act of 1985 [the "Gramm-Rudman-Hollings Act"] violates the doctrine of separation of powers.

[The Comptroller General is the head of the General Accounting Office. His Office was created by the Budget and Accounting Act of 1921, which vested him with the duty, inter alia, of investigating all matters relating to the receipt and disbursement of public funds and of reporting to Congress and the President about these matters. Although the Comptroller General is nominated by the President from a list of three individuals recommended by the Speaker of the House of Representatives and the President pro tempore of the Senate, he is removable only at the initiative of Congress. He may be removed by impeachment, or by a Joint Resolution of Congress (subject to presidential veto) on the basis of permanent disability, inefficiency, neglect of duty, malfeasance, or commission of a felony or conduct involving moral turpitude.

The issue in this case concerned the Comptroller General's role in effectuating "automatic," across-the-board spending reductions mandated in certain circumstances by the Gramm-Rudman-Hollings Act. Passed during a period of mounting concern about the size of the federal budget deficit, this act establishes declining maximum deficit amounts for each fiscal year beginning in 1986, until the deficit is reduced to zero in fiscal year 1991. Each year the directors of the Office of Management and Budget (OMB) and the Congressional Budget Office (CBO) are required to estimate independently the amount of the federal budget deficit for the next fiscal year. If the deficit exceeds the target, the directors are required to calculate independently, on a program-by-program basis, the budget reductions necessary to meet the target and to report the results to the Comptroller General. The Comptroller General is thereupon directed to prepare a report to the President. Although he is obligated to have "due regard" for the estimates and reductions set forth in the joint report submitted to him by the directors of CBO and OMB, the act requires that he exercise independent judgment in evaluating those estimates. Upon receipt of the Comptroller General's report, the President is required to issue a "sequestration order" mandating the spending reductions specified by the Comptroller General, which after a specified period become final unless Congress legislates other spending reductions to obviate the need for the order.

This action was brought by Congressman Synar, who had voted against the act, and by the National Treasury Employees Union, which claimed that its members were injured because the automatic spending reduction provisions suspended certain cost-of-living benefit increases. A three-judge district court held that the act was unconstitutional on the ground that the Comptroller General exercised executive functions under the act — functions that could not constitutionally be exercised by an officer removable by Congress.]

That [the] system of division and separation of powers produces conflicts, confusion, and discordance at times is inherent, but it was deliberately so structured to assure full, vigorous and open debate on the great issues affecting the people and to provide avenues for the operation of checks on the exercise of governmental power.

The Constitution does not contemplate an active role for Congress in the supervision of officers charged with the execution of the laws it enacts. The President appoints "Officers of the United States" with the "Advice and Consent of the Senate. . . ." Article II, §2. Once the appointment has been made and confirmed, however, the Constitution explicitly provides for removal of Officers of the United States by Congress only upon impeachment by the House of Representatives and conviction by the Senate. An impeachment by the House and trial by the Senate can rest only on "Treason, Bribery or other high Crimes and Misdemeanors." Article II, §4. A direct congressional role in the removal of officers charged with the execution of the laws beyond this limited one is inconsistent with separation of powers. . . .

[In *Myers*, the Court addressed the constitutionality of a] statute providing that certain postmasters could be removed only "by and with the advice and consent of the Senate." The President removed one such postmaster without Senate approval, and a lawsuit ensued. Chief Justice Taft, writing for the Court, declared the statute unconstitutional on the ground that for Congress to "draw to itself, or to either branch of it, the power to remove or the right to participate in the exercise of that power . . . would be . . . to infringe the constitutional principle of the separation of governmental powers."

A decade later, in [*Humphrey's Executor*], relied upon heavily by appellants, a Federal Trade Commissioner who had been removed by the President sought back pay. *Humphrey's Executor* involved an issue not presented either in the *Myers* case or in this case — i.e., the power of Congress to limit the President's powers of removal of a Federal Trade Commissioner. [4] The relevant statute permitted removal "by the President," but only "for inefficiency, neglect of duty, or malfeasance in office." Justice Sutherland, speaking for the Court, upheld the statute, holding that "illimitable power of removal is not possessed by the President [with respect to Federal Trade Commissioners]." . . .

In light of these precedents, we conclude that Congress cannot reserve for itself the power of removal of an officer charged with the execution of the laws except by impeachment. To permit the execution of the laws to be vested in an officer answerable only to Congress would, in practical terms, reserve in Congress control over the execution of the laws. [The] structure of the Constitution does not permit Congress to execute the laws; it follows that Congress cannot grant to an officer under its control what it does not possess. . . .

To permit an officer controlled by Congress to execute the laws would be, in essence, to permit a congressional veto. Congress could simply remove, or threaten to remove, an officer for executing the laws in any fashion found to be unsatisfactory to Congress. This kind of congressional control over the execution of the laws, *Chadha* makes clear, is constitutionally impermissible. . . .

Appellants urge that the Comptroller General performs his duties independently and is not subservient to Congress. We agree with the District Court that this contention does not bear close scrutiny. . . .

The [Budget and Accounting Act of 1921] permits removal for "inefficiency," "neglect of duty," or "malfeasance." These terms are very broad and, as interpreted by Congress, could sustain removal of a Comptroller General for any number of actual or perceived transgressions of the legislative will. The Constitutional Convention chose to permit impeachment of executive officers only for "Treason, Bribery, or other high Crimes and Misdemeanors." It rejected language that would have permitted impeachment for "maladministra-

4. Appellants therefore are wide of the mark in arguing that an affirmance in this case requires casting doubt on the status of "independent" agencies because no issues involving such agencies are presented here. [This] case involves [a] statute that provides for direct Congressional involvement over the decision to remove the Comptroller General. Appellants have referred us to no independent agency whose members are removable by the Congress for certain causes short of impeachable offenses, as is the Comptroller General.

tion," with Madison arguing that "[s]o vague a term will be equivalent to a tenure during pleasure of the Senate.". . .

Justice White, however, assures us [in his dissenting opinion] that "[r]ealistic consideration" of the "practical result of the removal provision," reveals that the Comptroller General is unlikely to be removed by Congress. The separated powers of our government can not be permitted to turn on judicial assessment of whether an officer exercising executive power is on good terms with Congress. The Framers recognized that, in the long term, structural protections against abuse of power were critical to preserving liberty. In constitutional terms, the removal powers over the Comptroller General's office dictate that he will be subservient to Congress. . . .

It is clear that Congress has consistently viewed the Comptroller General as an officer of the Legislative Branch. The Reorganization Acts of 1945 and 1949, for example, both stated that the Comptroller General and the GAO are "a part of the legislative branch of the Government." Similarly, in the Accounting and Auditing Act of 1950, Congress required the Comptroller General to conduct audits "as an agent of the Congress."

Over the years, the Comptrollers General have also viewed themselves as part of the Legislative Branch. . . .

Against this background, we see no escape from the conclusion that, because Congress had retained removal authority over the Comptroller General, he may not be entrusted with executive powers. The remaining question is whether the Comptroller General has been assigned such powers in the [Gramm-Rudman-Hollings] Act. . . .

Appellants suggest that the duties assigned to the Comptroller General in the Act are essentially ministerial and mechanical so that their performance does not constitute "execution of the law" in a meaningful sense. On the contrary, we view these functions as plainly entailing execution of the law in constitutional terms. Interpreting a law enacted by Congress to implement the legislative mandate is the very essence of "execution" of the law. Under [the statute], the Comptroller General must exercise judgment concerning facts that affect the application of the Act. He must also interpret the provisions of the Act to determine precisely what budgetary calculations are required. Decisions of that kind are typically made by officers charged with executing a statute.

The executive nature of the Comptroller General's functions under the Act is revealed in §252(a)(3) which gives the Comptroller General the ultimate authority to determine the budget cuts to be made. Indeed, the Comptroller General commands the President himself to carry out, without the slightest variation (with exceptions not relevant to the constitutional issues presented), the directive of the Comptroller General as to the budget reductions. . . .

[As] *Chadha* makes clear, once Congress makes its choice in enacting legislation, its participation ends. Congress can thereafter control the execution of its enactment only indirectly — by passing new legislation. By placing the responsibility for execution of the Balanced Budget and Emergency Deficit Control Act in the hands of an officer who is subject to removal only by itself, Congress in effect has retained control over the execution of the Act and has intruded into the executive function. The Constitution does not permit such intrusion. . . .

Appellants urge that rather than striking down [the reporting provision] and invalidating the significant power Congress vested in the Comptroller General to meet a national fiscal emergency, we should take the lesser course of nullifying the statutory provisions of the 1921 Act that authorizes Congress to remove the Comptroller General. . . .

The language of the Balanced Budget and Emergency Deficit Control Act itself settles [this] issue. In §274(f), Congress has explicitly provided "fallback" provisions in the Act that take effect "[i]n the event . . . *any* of the reporting procedures described in section 251 are invalidated." [The "fallback" provisions state that, in the event any of the reporting procedures are invalidated, Congress shall consider a joint resolution (subject to presidential veto) embodying the reports of OMB and CBO. Upon its enactment, the joint resolution is then treated as the equivalent of the Comptroller General's report.] Assuming that appellants are correct in urging that this matter must be resolved on the basis of congressional intent, the intent appears to have been for §274(f) to be given effect in this situation. Indeed, striking the removal provisions would lead to a statute that Congress would probably have refused to adopt. As the District Court concluded,

> the grant of authority to the Comptroller General was a carefully considered protection against what the House conceived to be the pro-executive bias of the OMB. It is doubtful that the automatic deficit reduction process would have passed without such protection, and doubtful that the protection would have been considered present if the Comptroller General were not removable by Congress itself. . . .

Accordingly, rather than perform the type of creative and imaginative statutory surgery urged by appellants, our holding simply permits the fallback provisions to come into play.[10]

No one can doubt that Congress and the President are confronted with fiscal and economic problems of unprecedented magnitude, but "the fact that a given law or procedure is efficient, convenient, and useful in facilitating functions of government, standing alone, will not save it if it is contrary to the Constitution. Convenience and efficiency are not the primary objectives — or the hallmarks — of democratic government. . . ." *Chadha.* . . .

[The] judgment and order of the District Court are affirmed.

---

10. Because we conclude that the Comptroller General, as an officer removable by Congress, may not exercise the powers conferred upon him by the Act, we have no occasion for considering appellees' other challenges to the Act, including their argument that the assignment of powers to the Comptroller General in [the Act] violates the delegation doctrine.

Our judgment is stayed for a period not to exceed 60 days to permit Congress to implement the fallback provisions.

JUSTICE STEVENS, with whom JUSTICE MARSHALL joins, concurring in the judgment.

[I] agree with the Court that the "Gramm-Rudman-Hollings" Act contains a constitutional infirmity so severe that the flawed provision may not stand. I disagree with the Court, however, on the reasons why the Constitution prohibits the Comptroller General from exercising the powers assigned to him by [the] Act. It is not the dormant, carefully circumscribed congressional removal power that represents the primary constitutional evil. Nor do I agree with the conclusion of both the majority and the dissent that the analysis depends on a labeling of the functions assigned to the Comptroller General as "executive powers." Rather, I am convinced that the Comptroller General must be characterized as an agent of Congress because of his longstanding statutory responsibilities; that the powers assigned to him under the Gramm-Rudman-Hollings Act require him to make policy that will bind the Nation; and that, when Congress, or a component or an agent of Congress, seeks to make policy that will bind the Nation, it must follow the procedures mandated by Article I of the Constitution — through passage by both Houses and presentment to the President. . . .

Everyone agrees that the powers assigned to the Comptroller General by [the] Gramm-Rudman-Hollings Act are extremely important. They require him to exercise sophisticated economic judgment concerning anticipated trends in the Nation's economy, projected levels of unemployment, interest rates, and the special problems that may be confronted by the many components of a vast federal bureaucracy. His duties are anything but ministerial — he is not merely a clerk wearing a "green eye shade" as he undertakes these tasks. Rather, he is vested with the kind of responsibilities that Congress has elected to discharge itself under the fallback provision that will become effective if and when [the reporting provisions of the Act] are held invalid. Unless we make the naive assumption that the economic destiny of the Nation could be safely entrusted to a mindless bank of computers, the powers that this Act vests in the Comptroller General must be recognized as having transcendent importance.

The Court concludes that the Gramm-Rudman-Hollings Act impermissibly assigns the Comptroller General "executive powers." The dissent agrees that "the powers exercised by the Comptroller under the Act may be characterized as 'executive' in that they involve the interpretation and carrying out of the Act's mandate." This conclusion is not only far from obvious but also rests on the unstated and unsound premise that there is a definite line that distinguishes executive power from legislative power. . . .

The powers delegated to the Comptroller General by [the] Act before us today have a [chameleon-like] quality. The District Court persuasively explained why they may be appropriately characterized as executive powers. But, when that delegation is held invalid, the "fallback provision" provides that the report that would otherwise be issued by the Comptroller General shall be issued by Congress itself. In the event that the resolution is enacted, the congressional report will have the same legal consequences as if it had been issued by the Comptroller General. . . .

Under [the] analysis adopted by the majority today, it would therefore appear that the function at issue is "executive" if performed by the Comptroller General but "legislative" if performed by the Congress. In my view, however, the function may appropriately be labeled "legislative" even if performed by the Comptroller General or by an executive agency.

Despite the statement in Article I of the Constitution that "All legislative Powers herein granted shall be vested in a Congress of the United States," it is far from novel to acknowledge that independent agencies do indeed exercise legislative powers. . . .

Thus, I do not agree that the Comptroller General's responsibilities under the Gramm-Rudman-Hollings Act must be termed "executive powers," or even that our inquiry is much advanced by using that term. For, whatever the label given the functions to be performed by the Comptroller General under [the reporting provision] — or by the Congress under [the fallback provision] — the District Court had no difficulty in concluding that Congress could delegate the performance of those functions to another branch of the Government. If the delegation to a stranger is permissible, why may not Congress delegate the same responsibilities to one of its own agents? That is the central question before us today. . . .

The Gramm-Rudman-Hollings Act assigns to the Comptroller General the duty to make policy decisions that have the force of law. . . .

Article I of the Constitution specifies the procedures that Congress must follow when it makes policy that binds the Nation: its legislation must be approved by both Houses of Congress and presented to the President. . . .

> If Congress were free to delegate its policymaking authority to one of its components, or to one of its agents, it would be able to evade "the carefully crafted restraints spelled out in the Constitution." That danger — congressional action that evades constitutional restraints — is not present when Congress delegates lawmaking power to the executive or to an independent agency. . . . [*Buckley*].

In short, even though it is well settled that Congress may delegate legislative power to independent agencies or to the Executive, and thereby divest itself of a portion of its lawmaking power, when it elects to exercise such power itself, it may not authorize a lesser representative of the Legislative Branch to act on its behalf. It is for this reason that I believe [the reporting provisions] of the Act are unconstitutional. . . .

JUSTICE WHITE, dissenting.

The Court, acting in the name of separation of powers, takes upon itself to strike down the Gramm-Rudman-Hollings Act, one of the most novel and far-reaching legislative responses to a national crisis since the New Deal. The basis of the Court's action is a solitary provision of another statute that was passed over sixty years ago and has lain dormant since that time. I cannot concur in the Court's action. Like the Court, I will not purport to speak to the wisdom of the policies incorporated in the legislation the Court invalidates; that is a matter for the Congress and the Executive, *both* of which expressed their assent to the statute barely half a year ago. I will, however, address the wisdom of the Court's willingness to interpose its distressingly formalistic view of separation of powers as a bar to the attainment of governmental objectives through the means chosen by the Congress and the President in the legislative process established by the Constitution. . . .

[The] Court's decision rests on a feature of the legislative scheme that is of minimal practical significance and that presents no substantial threat to the basic scheme of separation of powers. In attaching dispositive significance to what should be regarded as a triviality, the Court neglects what has in the past been recognized as a fundamental principle governing consideration of disputes over separation of powers:

> The actual art of governing under our Constitution does not and cannot conform to judicial definitions of the power of any of its branches based on isolated clauses or even single Articles torn from context. While the Constitution diffuses power the better to secure liberty, it also contemplates that practice will integrate the dispersed powers into a workable government. [*Youngstown* (Jackson, J. concurring).] . . .

Before examining the merits of the Court's argument, I wish to emphasize what it is that the Court quite pointedly and correctly does *not* hold: namely, that "executive" powers of the sort granted the Comptroller by the Act may only be exercised by officers removable at will by the President. The Court's apparent unwillingness to accept this argument, [is] fully consistent with the Court's longstanding recognition that it is within the power of Congress under the "Necessary and Proper" Clause, Art. I, §8, to vest authority that falls within the Court's definition of executive power in officers who are not subject to removal at will by the President and are therefore not under the President's direct control. See, e.g., [*Humphrey's Executor; Wiener.*] . . .

The Court's recognition of the legitimacy of legislation vesting "executive" authority in officers independent of the President does not imply derogation of the President's own constitutional authority — indeed, duty — to "take Care that the Laws be faithfully executed," Art. II, §3, for any such duty is necessarily limited to a great extent by the content of the laws enacted by the Congress. [There] are undoubtedly executive functions that, regardless of the enactments of Congress, must be performed by officers subject to removal at will by the President. Whether a particular function falls within this class or within the far larger class that may be relegated to independent officers "will depend upon the character of the office." [*Humphrey's Executor*.]. . .

It is evident (and nothing in the Court's opinion is to the contrary) that the powers exercised by the Comptroller General under the Gramm-Rudman Act are not such that vesting them in an officer not subject to removal at will by the President would in itself improperly interfere with Presidential powers. Determining the level of spending by the Federal Government is not by nature a function central either to the exercise of the President's enumerated powers or to his general duty to ensure execution of the laws; rather, appropriating funds is a peculiarly legislative function.

[Delegating] the execution of this legislation — that is, the power to apply the Act's criteria and make the required calculations — to an officer independent of the President's will does not deprive the President of any power that he would otherwise have or that is essential to the performance of the duties of his office. Rather, the result of such a delegation, from the standpoint of the President, is no different from the result of more traditional forms of appropriation: under either system, the level of funds available to the Executive branch to carry out its duties is not within the President's discretionary control. [Given] that the exercise of policy choice by the officer executing the statute would be inimical to Congress' goal in enacting "automatic" budget-cutting measures, it is eminently reasonable and proper for Congress to vest the budget-cutting authority in an officer who is to the greatest degree possible nonpartisan and independent of the President and his political agenda and who therefore may be relied upon not to allow his calculations to be colored by political considerations. Such a delegation deprives the President of no authority that is rightfully his. . . .

[The] question remains whether, as the Court concludes, the fact that the officer to whom Congress has delegated the authority to implement the Act is removable by a joint resolution of Congress should require invalidation of the Act. . . .

I have no quarrel with the proposition that the powers exercised by the Comptroller under the Act may be characterized as "executive" in that they involve the interpretation and carrying out of the Act's mandate. I can also accept the general proposition that although Congress has considerable authority in designating the officers who are to execute legislation, the constitutional scheme of separated powers does prevent Congress from reserving an executive role for itself or for its "agents." [*Buckley* (White, J., concurring in part and dissenting in part).] I cannot accept, however, that the exercise of authority by an officer removable for cause by a joint resolution of Congress is analogous to the impermissible execution of the law by Congress itself, nor would I hold that the congressional role in the removal process renders the Comptroller an "agent" of the Congress, incapable of receiving "executive" power. . . .

Because the Comptroller is not an appointee of Congress but an officer of the United States appointed by the President with the advice and consent of the Senate, *Buckley* neither requires that he be characterized as an agent of the Congress nor in any other way calls into question his capacity to exercise "executive" authority.

As the majority points out, however, the Court's decision in [*Chadha*] recognizes additional limits on the ability of Congress to participate in or influence the execution of the laws. As interpreted in *Chadha*, the Constitution prevents Congress from interfering with the actions of officers of the United States through means short of legislation satisfying the demands of bicameral passage and presentment to the President for approval or disapproval. . . .

[The] Court baldly mischaracterizes the removal provision when it suggests that it allows Congress to remove the Comptroller for "executing the laws in any fashion found to be unsatisfactory"; in fact, Congress may remove the Comptroller only for one or more of five specified reasons, which "although not so narrow as to deny Congress any leeway, circumscribe Congress' power to some extent by providing a basis for judicial review of congressional removal." *Ameron, Inc. v. United States Army Corps of Engineers*, 787 F.2d 875, 895 (CA3 1986) (Becker, J., concurring in part). [More] to the point, the Court overlooks or deliberately ignores the decisive difference between the congressional removal provision and the legislative veto struck down in *Chadha*: under the Budget and Accounting Act, Congress may remove the Comptroller only through a joint resolution, which by definition must be passed by both Houses and signed by the President. In other words, a removal of the Comptroller under the statute *satisfies the requirements of bicameralism and presentment laid down in* Chadha. [7] . . .

That such action may represent a more or less successful attempt by Congress to "control" the actions of an officer of the United States surely does not in itself indicate that it is unconstitutional, for no one would dispute that Congress has the power to "control" administration through legislation imposing duties or

---

7. Because a joint resolution passed by both Houses of Congress and signed by the President (or repassed over the President's veto) is legislation having the same force as any other Act of Congress, it is somewhat mysterious why the Court focuses on the Budget and Accounting Act's authorization of removal of the Comptroller through such a resolution as an indicator that the Comptroller may not be vested with executive powers. After all, even without such prior statutory authorization, Congress could pass, and the President sign, a joint resolution purporting to remove the Comptroller, and the validity of such legislation would seem in no way dependent on previous legislation contemplating it. [A] joint resolution purporting to remove the Comptroller, or any other executive officer, might be constitutionally infirm, but Congress' advance assertion of the power to enact such legislation seems irrelevant to the question whether exercise of authority by an officer who might in the future be subject to such a possibly valid and possibly invalid resolution is permissible, since the provision contemplating a resolution of removal obviously cannot in any way add to Congress' power to enact such a resolution. . . . [Relocated footnote.]

substantive restraints on executive officers, through legislation increasing or decreasing the funds made available to such officers, or through legislation actually abolishing a particular office. . . .

That a joint resolution removing the Comptroller General would satisfy the requirements for legitimate legislative action laid down in *Chadha* does not fully answer the separation of powers argument, for it is apparent that even the results of the constitutional legislative process may be unconstitutional if those results are in fact destructive of the scheme of separation of powers. [Common] sense indicates that the existence of the removal provision poses no such threat to the principle of separation of powers.

The statute does not permit anyone to remove the Comptroller at will; removal is permitted only for specified cause, with the existence of cause to be determined by Congress following a hearing. Any removal under the statute would presumably be subject to post-termination judicial review to ensure that a hearing had in fact been held and that the finding of cause for removal was not arbitrary. These procedural and substantive limitations on the removal power militate strongly against the characterization of the Comptroller as a mere agent of Congress by virtue of the removal authority. [Removal] authority limited in such a manner is more properly viewed as motivating adherence to a substantive standard established by law than as inducing subservience to the particular institution that enforces that standard. That the agent enforcing the standard is Congress may be of some significance to the Comptroller, but Congress' substantively limited removal power will undoubtedly be less of a spur to subservience than Congress' unquestionable and unqualified power to enact legislation reducing the Comptroller's salary, cutting the funds available to his department, reducing his personnel, limiting or expanding his duties, or even abolishing his position altogether.

More importantly, the substantial role played by the President in the process of removal through joint resolution reduces to utter insignificance the possibility that the threat of removal will induce subservience to the Congress. [If] the Comptroller's conduct in office is not so unsatisfactory to the President as to convince the latter that removal is required under the statutory standard, Congress will have no independent power to coerce the Comptroller unless it can muster a two-thirds majority in both Houses — a feat of bipartisanship more difficult than that required to impeach and convict. The incremental *in terrorem* effect of the possibility of congressional removal in the face of a presidential veto is therefore exceedingly unlikely to have any discernible impact on the extent of congressional influence over the Comptroller.

The practical result of the removal provision is not to render the Comptroller unduly dependent upon or subservient to Congress, but to render him one of the most independent officers in the entire federal establishment. Those who have studied the office agree that the procedural and substantive limits on the power of Congress and the President to remove the Comptroller make dislodging him against his will practically impossible. . . .

The wisdom of vesting "executive" powers in an officer removable by joint resolution may indeed be debatable — as may be the wisdom of the entire scheme of permitting an unelected official to revise the budget enacted by Congress — but such matters are for the most part to be worked out between the Congress and the President through the legislative process, which affords each branch ample opportunity to defend its interests. The Act vesting budget-cutting authority in the Comptroller General represents Congress' judgment that the delegation of such authority to counteract ever-mounting deficits is "necessary and proper" to the exercise of the powers granted the Federal Government by the Constitution; and the President's approval of the statute signifies his unwillingness to reject the choice made by Congress. Under such circumstances, the role of this Court should be limited to determining whether the Act so alters the balance of authority among the branches of government as to pose a genuine threat to the basic division between the lawmaking power and the power to execute the law. Because I see no such threat, I cannot join the Court in striking down the Act.

I dissent.

JUSTICE BLACKMUN, dissenting.

The Court may be correct when it says that Congress cannot constitutionally exercise removal authority over an official vested with the budget-reduction powers that [the Gramm-Rudman-Hollings Act] gives to the Comptroller General. . . .

In my view, however, that important and difficult question need not be decided in this case, because no matter how it is resolved the plaintiffs, now appellees, are not entitled to the relief they have requested. Appellees have not sought invalidation of the 1921 provision that authorizes Congress to remove the Comptroller General by joint resolution; indeed, it is far from clear they would have standing to request such a judgment. The only relief sought in this case is nullification of the automatic budget-reduction provisions of the Deficit Control Act, and that relief should not be awarded even if the Court is correct that those provisions are constitutionally incompatible with Congress' authority to remove the Comptroller General by joint resolution. Any incompatibility, I feel, should be cured by refusing to allow congressional removal — if it ever is attempted — and not by striking down the central provisions of the Deficit Control Act. However wise or foolish it may be, that statute unquestionably ranks among the most important federal enactments of the past several decades. I cannot see the sense of invalidating legislation of this magnitude in order to preserve a cumbersome, 65-year-old removal power that has never been exercised and appears to have been all but forgotten until this litigation. . . .

I do not claim that the 1921 removal provision is a piece of statutory dead-wood utterly without contemporary significance. But it comes close. Rarely if ever invoked even for symbolic purposes, the removal provision certainly pales in importance beside the legislative scheme the Court strikes down today — an extraordinarily far-reaching response to a deficit problem of unprecedented proportions. Because I believe that the constitutional defect found by the Court cannot justify the remedy it has imposed, I respectfully dissent.

See Symposium: Bowsher v. Synar, 72 Cornell L. Rev. 421 (1987), especially Strauss, Formal and Functional Approaches to Separation of Powers Questions: A Foolish Inconsistency?, 72 Cornell L. Rev. 488 (1987).

MORRISON v. OLSON
487 U.S. 654 (1988)

CHIEF JUSTICE REHNQUIST delivered the opinion of the Court.

This case presents us with a challenge to the independent counsel provisions of the Ethics in Government Act of 1978. We hold today that these provisions of the Act do not violate the Appointments Clause of the Constitution, Art. II, §2, cl. 2, or the limitations of Article III, nor do they impermissibly interfere with the President's authority under Article II in violation of the constitutional principle of separation of powers.

I

Briefly stated, Title VI of the Ethics of Government Act allows for the appointment of an "independent counsel" to investigate and, if appropriate, prosecute certain high ranking government officials for violations of federal criminal laws. The Act requires the Attorney General, upon receipt of information that he determines is "sufficient to constitute grounds to investigate whether any person [covered by the Act] may have violated any Federal criminal law," to conduct a preliminary investigation of the matter. When the Attorney General has completed this investigation, or 90 days has elapsed, he is required to report to a special court (the Special Division) created by the Act "for the purpose of appointing independent counsels." If the Attorney General determines that "there are no reasonable grounds to believe that further investigation is warranted," then he must notify the Special Division of this result. In such a case, "the division of the court shall have no power to appoint an independent counsel." If, however, the Attorney General has determined that there are "reasonable grounds to believe that further investigation or prosecution is warranted," then he "shall apply to the division of the court for the appointment of an independent counsel." The Attorney General's application to the court "shall contain sufficient information to assist the [court] in selecting an independent counsel and in defining that independent counsel's prosecutorial jurisdiction." Upon receiving this application, the Special Division "shall appoint an appropriate independent counsel and shall define that independent counsel's prosecutorial jurisdiction."

With respect to all matters within the independent counsel's jurisdiction, the Act grants the counsel "full power and independent authority to exercise all investigative and prosecutorial functions and powers of the Department of Justice, the Attorney General, and any other officer or employee of the Department of Justice." The functions of the independent counsel include conducting grand jury proceedings and other investigations, participating in civil and criminal court proceedings and litigation, and appealing any decision in any case in which the counsel participates in an official capacity. . . . The Act also states that an independent counsel "shall, except where not possible, comply with the written or other established policies of the Department of Justice respecting enforcement of the criminal laws." In addition, whenever a matter has been referred to an independent counsel under the Act, the Attorney General and the Justice Department are required to suspend all investigations and proceedings regarding the matter. An independent counsel has "full authority to dismiss matters within [his] prosecutorial jurisdiction without conducting an investigation or at any subsequent time before prosecution, if to do so would be consistent" with Department of Justice policy.

Two statutory provisions govern the length of an independent counsel's tenure in office. The first defines the procedure for removing an independent counsel. Section 596(a)(1) provides:

> An independent counsel appointed under this chapter may be removed from office, other than by impeachment and conviction, only by the personal action of the Attorney General and only for good cause, physical disability, mental incapacity, or any other condition that substantially impairs the performance of such independent counsel's duties.

If an independent counsel is removed pursuant to this section, the Attorney General is required to submit a report to both the Special Division and the Judiciary Committees of the Senate and the House "specifying the facts found and the ultimate grounds for such removal." Under the current version of the Act, an independent counsel can obtain judicial review of the Attorney General's action by filing a civil action in the United States District Court for the District of Columbia. . . .

The other provision governing the tenure of the independent counsel defines the procedures for "terminating" the counsel's office. [T]he office of an independent counsel terminates when he notifies the Attorney General that he has completed or substantially completed any investigations or prosecutions undertaken pursuant to the Act. In addition, the Special Division, acting either on its own or on the suggestion of the Attorney General, may terminate the office of an independent counsel at any time if it finds that "the investigation of all matters within the prosecutorial jurisdiction of such independent counsel . . . have been completed or so substantially completed that it would be appropriate for the Department of Justice to complete such investigations and prosecutions."

Finally, the Act provides for Congressional oversight of the activities of independent counsels. An independent counsel may from time to time send Congress statements or reports on his activities. The "appropriate committees of the Congress" are given oversight jurisdiction in regard to the official conduct of an independent counsel, and the counsel is required by the Act to cooperate with Congress in the exercise of this jurisdiction. The counsel is required to inform the House of Representatives of "substantial and credible information which [the counsel] receives . . . that may constitute grounds for an impeachment." In addition, the Act gives certain Congressional Committee Members the power to "request in writing that the Attorney General apply for the appointment of an independent counsel." The Attorney General is required to respond to this request within a specified time but is not required to accede to the request.

The proceedings in this case provide an example of how the Act works in practice. In 1982, two subcommittees of the House of Representatives issued subpoenas directing the Environmental Protection Agency (EPA) to produce certain documents relating to the efforts of the EPA and the Land and Natural Resources Division of the Justice Department to enforce the "Superfund Law." At that time, appellee Olson was the Assistant Attorney General for the Office of Legal Counsel (OLC), appellee Schmults was Deputy Attorney General, and appellee Dinkins was the Assistant Attorney General for the Land and Natural Resources Division. Acting on the advice of the Justice Department, the President ordered the Administrator of EPA to invoke executive privilege to withhold certain of the documents on the ground that they contained "enforcement sensitive information." The Administrator obeyed this order and withheld the documents. In response, the House voted to hold the Administrator in contempt, after which the Administrator and the United States together filed a lawsuit against the House. The conflict abated in March 1983, when the Administration agreed to give the House committees limited access to the documents.

The following year, the House Judiciary Committee began an investigation into the Justice Department's role in the controversy over the EPA documents. During this investigation, appellee Olson testified before a House subcommittee on March 10, 1983. Both before and after that testimony, the Department complied with several Committee requests to produce certain documents. Other documents were at first withheld, although these documents were eventually disclosed by the Department after the Committee learned of their existence. In 1985, the majority members of the Judiciary Committee published a lengthy report on the Committee's investigation. The report not only criticized various officials in the Department of Justice for their role in the EPA executive privilege dispute, but it also suggested that appellee Olson had given false and misleading testimony to the subcommittee. . . . The Chairman of the Judiciary Committee forwarded a copy of the report to the Attorney General with a request . . . that he seek the appointment of an independent counsel to investigate the allegations against Olson, Schmults, and Dinkins.

The Attorney General directed the Public Integrity Section of the Criminal Division to conduct a preliminary investigation. . . . After consulting with other Department officials, however, the Attorney General chose to apply to the Special Division for the appointment of an independent counsel solely with respect to appellee Olson. . . .

On April 23, 1986, the Special Division appointed James C. McKay as independent counsel to investigate "whether the testimony of . . . Olson and his revision of such testimony on March 10, 1983, violated either 18 U.S.C. §1505 or §1001, or any other provision of federal law." . . . McKay later resigned as independent counsel, and on May 29, 1986, the Division appointed appellant Morrison as his replacement, with the same jurisdiction. . . .

A divided Court of Appeals [invalidated the Act]. We now reverse. . . .

III

The Appointments Clause of Article II reads as follows:

[The President] shall nominate, and by and with the Advice and Consent of the Senate, shall appoint Ambassadors, other public Ministers and Consuls, Judges of the supreme Court, and all other Officers of the United States, whose Appointments are not herein otherwise provided for, and which shall be established by Law: but the Congress may by Law vest the Appointment of such inferior Officers, as they think proper, in the President alone, in the Courts of Law, or in the Heads of Departments. U.S. Const., Art. II, §2, cl. 2. . . .

The line between "inferior" and "principal" officers is one that is far from clear, and the Framers provided little guidance into where it should be drawn. . . . We need not attempt here to decide exactly where the line falls between the two types of officers, because in our view appellant clearly falls on the "inferior officer" side of that line. Several factors lead to this conclusion.

First, appellant is subject to removal by a higher Executive Branch official. Although appellant may not be "subordinate" to the Attorney General (and the President) insofar as she possesses a degree of independent discretion to exercise the powers delegated to her under the Act, the fact that she can be removed by the Attorney General indicates that she is to some degree "inferior' in rank and authority. Second, appellant is empowered by the Act to perform only certain, limited duties. An independent counsel's role is restricted primarily to investigation and, if appropriate, prosecution for certain federal crimes. Admittedly, the Act delegates to appellant "full power and independent authority to exercise all investigative and prosecutorial functions and powers of the Department of Justice," but this grant of authority does not include any authority to formulate policy for the Government or the Executive Branch, nor does it give appellant any administrative duties outside of those necessary to operate her office. The Act specifically provides that in policy matters appellant is to comply to the extent possible with the policies of the Department.

Third, appellant's office is limited in jurisdiction. Not only is the Act itself restricted in applicability to certain federal officials suspected of certain serious federal crimes, but an independent counsel can only act within the scope of the jurisdiction that has been granted by the Special Division pursuant to a request by the Attorney General. Finally, appellant's office is limited in tenure. . . . [T]he office of independent counsel is "temporary" in the sense that an independent counsel is appointed essentially to accomplish a single task, and when that task is over the office is terminated, either by the counsel herself or by action of the Special Division. Unlike other prosecutors, appellant has no ongoing responsibilities that extend beyond the accomplishment of the mission that she was appointed for and authorized by the Special Division to undertake. In our view, these factors relating to the "ideas of tenure, duration . . . and duties" of the independent counsel are sufficient to establish that appellant is an "inferior" officer in the constitutional sense. . . .

This does not, however, end our inquiry under the Appointments Clause. Appellees argue that even if appellant is an "inferior" officer, the Clause does not empower Congress to place the power to appoint such an officer outside the Executive Branch. They contend that the Clause does not contemplate congressional authorization of "interbranch appointments," in which an officer of one branch is appointed by officers of another branch. The relevant language of the Appointments Clause is worth repeating. It reads: ". . . but the Congress may by Law vest the Appointment of such inferior Officers, as they think proper, in the President alone, in the courts of Law, or in the Heads of Departments." On its face, the language of this "excepting clause" admits of no limitation on interbranch appointments. Indeed, the inclusion of "as they think proper" seems clearly to give Congress significant discretion to determine whether it is "proper" to vest the appointment of, for example, executive officials in the "courts of Law." We recognized as much in one of our few decisions in this area, where we stated:

> It is no doubt usual and proper to vest the appointment of inferior officers in that department of the government, executive or judicial, or in that particular executive department to which the duties of such officers appertain. But there is no absolute requirement to this effect in the Constitution; and, if there were, it would be difficult in many cases to determine to which department an office properly belonged. . . .

But as the Constitution stands, the selection of the appointing power, as between the functionaries named, is a matter resting in the discretion of Congress. And, looking at the subject in a practical light, it is perhaps better that it should rest there, than that the country should be harassed by the endless controversies to which a more specific direction on this subject might have given rise. [Ex parte Siebold,] 100 U.S., at 397-398. . . .

We do not mean to say that Congress' power to provide for interbranch appointments of "inferior officers" is unlimited. In addition to separation of powers concerns, which would arise if such provisions for appointment had the potential to impair the constitutional functions assigned to one of the branches, *Siebold* itself suggested that Congress' decision to vest the appointment power in the courts would be improper if there was some "incongruity" between the functions normally performed by the courts and the performance of their duty to appoint. 100 U.S., at 398 ("the duty to appoint inferior officers, when required thereto by law, is a constitutional duty of the courts; and in the present case there is no such incongruity in the duty required as to excuse the courts from its performance, or to render their acts void"). In this case, however, we do not think it impermissible for Congress to vest the power to appoint independent counsels in a specially created federal court. We thus disagree with the Court of Appeals' conclusion that there is an inherent incongruity about a court having the power to appoint prosecutorial officers. [12] We have recognized that courts may appoint private attorneys to act as prosecutor for judicial contempt judgments. . . . Congress of course was concerned when it created the office of independent counsel with the conflicts of interest that could arise in situations when the Executive Branch is called upon to investigate its own high-ranking officers. If it were to remove the appointing authority from the Executive Branch, the most logical place to put it was in the Judicial Branch. In the light of the Act's provision making the judges of the Special Division ineligible to participate in any matters relating to an independent counsel they have appointed, we do not think that appointment of the independent counsels by the court runs afoul of the constitutional limitation on "incongruous" interbranch appointments.

IV

Appellees next contend that the powers vested in the Special Division by the Act conflict with Article III of the Constitution. We have long recognized that

12. Indeed, in light of judicial experience with prosecutors in criminal cases, it could be said that courts are especially well qualified to appoint prosecutors. This is not a case in which judges are given power to appoint an officer in an area in which they have no special knowledge or expertise, as in, for example, a statute authorizing the courts to appoint officials in the Department of Agriculture or the Federal Energy Regulatory Commission.

by the express provision of Article III, the judicial power of the United States is limited to "Cases" and "Controversies." As a general rule, we have broadly stated that "executive or administrative duties of a nonjudicial nature may not be imposed on judges holding office under Art. III of the Constitution." The purpose of this limitation is to help ensure the independence of the Judicial Branch and to prevent the judiciary from encroaching into areas reserved for the other branches. . . .

Leaving aside for the moment the Division's power to terminate an independent counsel, we do not think that Article III absolutely prevents Congress from vesting these other miscellaneous powers in the Special Division pursuant to the Act. . . . In this case, the miscellaneous powers . . . do not impermissibly trespass upon the authority of the Executive Branch. Some of these allegedly "supervisory" powers conferred on the court are passive: the Division merely "receives" reports from the counsel or the Attorney General, it is not entitled to act on them or to specifically approve or disapprove of their contents. Other provisions of the Act do require the court to exercise some judgment and discretion, but the powers granted by these provisions are themselves essentially ministerial. The Act simply does not give the Division the power to "supervise" the independent counsel in the exercise of her investigative or prosecutorial authority. . . .

We are more doubtful about the Special Divison's power to terminate the office of the independent counsel. . . . Nonetheless, we do not, as did the Court of Appeals, view this provision as a significant judicial encroachment upon executive power or upon the prosecutorial discretion of the independent counsel. . . .

The provision has not been tested in practice, and we do not mean to say that an adventurous special court could not reasonably construe the provision as did the Court of Appeals; but it is the duty of federal courts to construe a statute in order to save it from constitutional infirmities. . . . As we see it, "termination" may occur only when the duties of the counsel are truly "completed" or "so substantially completed" that there remains no need for any continuing action by the independent counsel. It is basically a device for removing from the public payroll an independent counsel who has served her purpose, but is unwilling to acknowledge the fact. So construed, the Special Division's power to terminate does not pose a sufficient threat of judicial intrusion into matters that are more properly within the Executive's authority to require that the Act be invalidated as inconsistent with Article III.

Nor do we believe, as appellees contend, that the Special Division's exercise of the various powers specifically granted to it under the Act poses any threat to the "impartial and independent federal adjudication of claims within the judicial power of the United States." We reach this conclusion for two reasons. First, the Act as it currently stands gives the Special Division itself no power to review any of the actions of the independent counsel or any of the actions of the Attorney General with regard to the counsel. . . . Second, the Act prevents members of the Special Division from participating in *"any* judicial proceeding concerning a matter which involves such independent counsel while such independent counsel is serving in that office or which involves the exercise of such independent counsel's official duties, regardless of whether such independent counsel is still serving in that office.". . .

V

We now turn to consider whether the Act is invalid under the constitutional principle of separation of powers. Two related issues must be addressed: The first is whether the provision of the Act restricting the Attorney General's power to remove the independent counsel to only those instances in which he can show "good cause," taken by itself, impermissibly interferes with the President's exercise of his constitutionally appointed functions. The second is whether, taken as a whole, the Act violates the separation of powers by reducing the President's ability to control the prosecutorial powers wielded by the independent counsel.

A

Two Terms ago we had occasion to consider whether it was consistent with the separation of powers for Congress to pass a statute that authorized a government official who is removable only by Congress to participate in what we found to be "executive powers." Bowsher v. Synar, 478 U.S. 714, 730 (1986). We held in *Bowsher* that "Congress cannot reserve for itself the power of removal of an officer charged with the execution of the laws except by impeachment." Id., at 726. A primary antecedent for this ruling was our 1925 decision in Myers v. United States, 272 U.S. 52 (1926). . . .

Unlike both *Bowsher* and *Myers*, this case does not involve an attempt by Congress itself to gain a role in the removal of executive officials other than its established powers of impeachment and conviction. The Act instead puts the removal power squarely in the hands of the Executive Branch; an independent counsel may be removed from office, "only by the personal action of the Attorney General, and only for good cause." There is no requirement of congressional approval of the Attorney General's removal decision, though the decision is subject to judicial review. In our view, the removal provisions of the Act make this case more analogous to Humphrey's Executor v. United States, 295 U.S. 602 (1935), and Weiner v. United States, 357 U.S. 349 (1958), than to *Myers* or *Bowsher*. . . .

Appellees contend that *Humphrey's Executor* and *Wiener* are distinguishable from this case because they did not involve officials who performed a "core executive function." They argue that our decision in *Humphrey's Executor* rests on a distinction between "purely executive" officials and officials who exercise "quasi-legislative" and "quasi-judicial" powers. . . .

We undoubtedly did rely on the terms "quasi-legislative" and "quasi-judicial" to distinguish the officials involved in *Humphrey's Executor* and *Wiener* from those in *Myers*, but our present considered view is that the determination of whether the Constitution allows Congress to impose a "good cause"-type restriction on the President's power to remove an official cannot be made to turn on whether or not that official is classified as "purely executive." The analysis contained in our removal cases is designed not to define rigid categories of those officials who may or may not be removed at will by the President, but to ensure that Congress does not interfere with the President's exercise of the "executive power" and his constitutionally appointed duty to "take care that the laws be faithfully executed" under Article II. . . . We do not mean to suggest that an analysis of the functions served by the officials at issue is irrelevant. But the real question is whether the removal restrictions are of such a nature that they impede the President's ability to perform his constitutional duty, and the functions of the officials in question must be analyzed in that light.

Considering for the moment the "good cause" removal provision in isolation from the other parts of the Act at issue in this case, we cannot say that the imposition of a "good cause" standard for removal by itself unduly trammels on executive authority. . . . Although the counsel exercises no small amount of discretion and judgment in deciding how to carry out her duties under the Act, we simply do not see how the President's need to control the exercise of that discretion is so central to the functioning of the Executive Branch as to require as a matter of constitutional law that the counsel be terminable at will by the President.

Nor do we think that the "good cause" removal provision at issue here impermissibly burdens the President's power to control or supervise the independent counsel, as an executive official, in the execution of her duties under the Act. This is not a case in which the power to remove an executive official has been completely stripped from the President, thus providing no means for the President to ensure the "faithful execution" of the laws. Rather, because the independent counsel may be terminated for "good cause," the Executive, through the Attorney General, retains ample authority to assure that the counsel is competently performing her statutory responsibilities in a manner that comports with the provisions of the Act. Although we need not decide in this case exactly what is encompassed with the term "good cause" under the Act, the legislative history of the removal provision also makes clear that the Attorney General may remove an independent counsel for "misconduct.". . . We do not think that this limitation as it presently stands sufficiently deprives the President of control over the independent counsel to interfere impermissibly with his constitutional obligation to ensure the faithful execution of the laws.

B

The final question to be addressed is whether the Act, taken as a whole, violates the principle of separation of powers by unduly interfering with the role of the Executive Branch. . . . [We] have never held that the Constitution requires that the three Branches of Government "operate with absolute independence.". . .

We observe first that this case does not involve an attempt by Congress to increase its own powers at the expense of the Executive Branch. Unlike some of our previous cases, most recently Bowsher v. Synar, this case simply does not pose a "dange[r] of congressional usurpation of Executive Branch functions," 478 U.S., at 727; see also INS v. Chadha, 462 U.S. 919, 958 (1983). . . .

Similarly, we do not think that the Act works any *judicial* usurpation of properly executive functions. . . .

Finally, we do not think that the Act "impermissibly undermine[s]" the powers of the Executive Branch, or "disrupts the proper balance between the coordinate branches [by] prevent[ing] the Executive Branch from accomplishing its constitutionally assigned functions." It is undeniable that the Act reduces the amount of control or supervision that the Attorney General and, through him, the President exercises over the investigation and prosecution of a certain class of alleged criminal activity. . . . Nonetheless, the Act does give the Attorney General several means of supervising or controlling the prosecutorial powers that may be wielded by an independent counsel. Most importantly, the Attorney General retains the power to remove the counsel for "good cause," a power that we have already concluded provides the Executive with substantial ability to ensure that the laws are "faithfully executed" by an independent counsel. No independent counsel may be appointed without a specific request by the Attorney General, and the Attorney General's decision not to request appointment if he finds "no reasonable grounds to believe that further investigation is warranted" is committed to his unreviewable discretion. The Act thus gives the Executive a degree of control over the power to initiate an investigation by the independent counsel. . . .

VI

In sum, we conclude today that it does not violate the Appointments Clause for Congress to vest the appointment of independent counsels in the Special Division; that the powers exercised by the Special Division under the Act do not violate Article III; and that the Act does not violate the separation of powers principle by impermissibly interfering with the functions of the Executive Branch. The decision of the Court of Appeals is therefore reversed.

Justice Kennedy took no part in the consideration or decision of this case.

JUSTICE SCALIA, dissenting. . . .

II

If to describe this case is not to decide it, the concept of a government of separate and coordinate powers no longer has meaning. The Court devotes most of its attention to such relatively technical details as the Appointments Clause and the removal power, addressing briefly and only at the end of its opinion the separation of powers. As my prologue suggests, I think that has it backwards. Our opinions are full of the recognition that it is the principle of separation of powers, and the inseparable corollary that each department's "defense must . . . be made commensurate to the danger of attack," Federalist No. 51, p.322 (J. Madison), which gives comprehensible content to the appointments clause, and determines the appropriate scope of the removal power. . . .

Art. II, §1, cl. 1 of the Constitution provides: "The executive Power shall be vested in a President of the United States." [T]his does not mean *some of* the executive power, but *all of* the executive power. It seems to me, therefore, that the decision of the Court of Appeals invalidating the present statute must be upheld on fundamental separation-of-powers principles if the following two questions are answered affirmatively: (1) Is the conduct of a criminal prosecution (and of an investigation to decide whether to prosecute) the exercise of purely executive power? (2) Does the statute deprive the President of the United States of exclusive control over the exercise of that power? Surprising to say, the Court appears to concede an affirmative answer to both questions, but seeks to avoid the inevitable conclusion that since the statute vests some purely executive power in a person who is not the President of the United States it is void.

The Court concedes that "[t]here is no real dispute that the functions performed by the independent counsel are 'executive'," though it qualifies that concession by adding "in the sense that they are 'law enforcement' functions that typically have been undertaken by officials within the Executive Branch." The qualifier adds nothing but atmosphere. In what *other* sense can one identify "the executive Power" that is supposed to be vested in the President (unless it includes everything the Executive Branch is given to do) *except* by reference to what has always and everywhere — if conducted by Government at all — been conducted never by the legislature, never by the courts, and always by the executive. There is no possible doubt that the independent counsel's functions fit this description. . . .

As for the second question, whether the statute before us deprives the President of exclusive control over that quintessentially executive activity. The Court does not, and could not possibly, assert that it does not. That is indeed the whole object of the statute. Instead, the Court points out that the President, through his Attorney General, has at least *some* control. That concession is alone enough to invalidate the statute, but I cannot refrain from pointing out that the Court greatly exaggerates the extent of that "some" presidential control. . . .

The utter incompatibility of the Court's approach with our constitutional traditions can be made more clear, perhaps, by applying it to the powers of the other two Branches. Is it conceivable that if Congress passed a statute depriving itself of less than full and entire control over some insignificant area of legislation, we would inquire whether the matter was "*so central* to the functioning of the Legislative Branch" as really to require complete control, or whether the statute gives Congress "*sufficient* control over the surrogate legislator to ensure that Congress is able to perform its constitutionally as-signed duties"? Of course we would have none of that. Once we determined that a purely legislative power was at issue we would require it to be exer-cised, wholly and entirely, by Congress. Or to bring the point closer to home, consider a statute giving to non-Article III judges just a tiny bit of purely judicial power in a relatively insignificant field, with substantial control, though not total control, in the courts — perhaps "clear error" review, which would be a fair judicial equivalent of the Attorney General's "for cause" removal power here. Is there any doubt that we would not pause to inquire whether the matter was "*so central* to the functioning of the Judicial Branch" as really to require complete control, or whether we retained "*sufficient* control over the matters to be decided that we are able to perform our constitutional-ly assigned duties"? We would say that our "constitutionally assigned duties" include *complete* control over all exercises of the judicial power — or, as the plurality opinion said in Northern Pipeline Construction Co. v. Marathon Pipe Line Co., 458 U.S. 50, 58-59 (1982), that "[t]he inexorable command of [Article III] is clear and definite: The judicial power of the United States must be exercised by courts having the attributes prescribed in Art. III." We should say here that the President's constitutionally assigned duties include *complete* control over investigation and prosecution of violations of the law, and that the inexorable command of Article II is clear and definite: the executive power must be vested in the President of the United States.

Is it unthinkable that the President should have such exclusive power, even when alleged crimes by him or his close associates are at issue? No more so than that Congress should have the exclusive power of legislation, even when what is at issue is its own exemption from the burdens of certain laws. No more so than that this Court should have the exclusive power to pronounce the final decision on justiciable cases and controversies, even those pertaining to the constitution-ality of a statute reducing the salaries of the Justices. A system of separate and coordinate powers necessarily involves an acceptance of exclusive power that can theoretically be abused. . . .

The Court has, nonetheless, replaced the clear constitutional prescription that the executive power belongs to the President with a "balancing test." What are the standards to determine how the balance is to be struck, that is, how much removal of presidential power is too much? Many countries of the world get along with an Executive that is much weaker than ours — in fact, entirely dependent upon the continued support of the legislature. Once we depart from the text of the Constitution, just where short of that do we stop? The most amazing feature of the Court's opinion is that it does not even purport to give an answer. It simply *announces*, with no analysis, that the ability to control the decision whether to investigate and prosecute the President's closest advisors, and indeed the President himself, is not "so central to the functioning of the Executive Branch" as to be constitutionally required to be within the President's control. . . .

Besides weakening the Presidency by reducing the zeal of his staff, it must also be obvious that the institution of the independent counsel enfeebles him more directly in his constant confrontations with Congress, by eroding his public support. Nothing is so politically effective as the ability to charge that one's opponent and his associates are not merely wrong-headed, naive, ineffective, but, in all probability, "crooks." And nothing so effectively gives an appearance of validity to such charges as a Justice Department investigation and, even better, prosecution. The present statute provides ample means for that sort of attack, assuring that massive and lengthy investigations will occur, not merely when the Justice Department in the application of its usual standards believes they are called for, but whenever it cannot be said that there are "no reasonable grounds to believe" they are called for. . . .

[T]he Court does not attempt to "decide exactly" what establishes the line between principal and "inferior" officers, but is confident that, whatever the line may be, appellant "clearly falls on the 'inferior officer' side" of it. . . .

Appellant is removable only for "good cause" or physical or mental incapacity. By contrast, most (if not all) *principal* officers in the Executive Branch may be removed by the President *at will*. I fail to see how the fact that appellant is more difficult to remove than most principal officers helps to establish that she is an inferior officer. And I do not see how it could possibly make any difference to her superior or inferior status that the President's limited power to remove her must be exercised through the Attorney General. If she were removable at will by the Attorney General, then she would be subordinate to him and thus properly designated as inferior; but the Court essentially admits that she is not subordinate. . . .

The second reason offered by the Court — that appellant performs only certain, limited duties — may be relevant to whether she is an inferior officer, but it mischaracterizes the extent of her powers. As the Court states: "Admittedly, the Act delegates to appellant [the] '*full power and independent authority to exercise all investigative and prosecutorial functions and powers of the Department of Justice.*' " *Ante*, at 13, quoting 28 U.S.C. §594(a) (emphasis added). . . .

The final set of reasons given by the Court for why the independent counsel clearly is an inferior officer emphasizes the limited nature of her jurisdiction and tenure. Taking the latter first, I find nothing unusually limited about the independent counsel's tenure. . . . I think it preferable to look to the text of the Constitution and the division of power that it establishes. These demonstrate, I think, that the independent counsel is not an inferior officer because she is not *subordinate* to any officer in the Executive Branch (indeed, not even to the President). Dictionaries in use at the time of the Constitutional Convention gave the word "inferiour" two meanings which it still bears today: (1) "[l]ower in place, . . . station, . . . rank of life, . . . value or excellency," and (2) "[s]ubordinate." S. Johnson, Dictionary of the English Language (6th ed. 1785). In a document dealing with the structure (the constitution) of a government, one would naturally expect the word to bear the latter meaning — indeed, in such a context it would be unpardonably careless to use the word *unless* a relationship of subordination was intended. . . .

The independent counsel is not even subordinate to the President. The Court essentially admits as much, noting that "appellant may not be 'subordinate' to the Attorney General (and the President) insofar as she possesses a degree of independent discretion to exercise the powers delegated to her under the Act." In fact, there is no doubt about it. As noted earlier, the Act specifically grants her the "*full* power and *independent* authority to exercise *all* investigative and prosecutorial functions of the Department of Justice," 28 U.S.C. §594(a), and makes her removable only for "good cause," a limitation specifically intended to ensure that she be *independent* of, not *subordinate* to, the President and the Attorney General. See H.R. Conf. Rep. No. 100-452, 37 (1987). . . .

IV . . .

There is of course no provision in the Constitution stating who may remove executive officers, except the provisions for removal by impeachment. Before the present decision it was established, however, (1) that the President's power to remove principal officers who exercise purely executive powers could not be restricted, see Myers v. United States, 272 U.S. 52, 127 (1926), and (2) that his power to remove inferior officers who exercise purely executive powers, and whose appointment Congress had removed from the usual procedure of presidential appointment with Senate consent, could be restricted, at least where the appointment had been made by an officer of the Executive Branch, see ibid.; United States v. Perkins, 116 U.S. 483, 485 (1886). . . .

Since our 1935 decision in Humphrey's Executor v. United States, 295 U.S. 602 — which was considered by many at the time the product of an activist, anti-New Deal court bent on reducing the power of President Franklin Roosevelt — it has been established that the line of permissible restriction upon removal of principal officers lies at the point at which the powers exercised by those officers are no longer purely executive. . . . What *Humphrey's Executor* (and presumably *Myers*) really means, we are now told, is not that there are any "rigid categories of those officials who may or may not be removed at will by the President," but simply that Congress cannot "interfere with the President's exercise of the 'executive power' and his constitutionally appointed duty to 'take care that the laws be faithfully executed.' ". . .

Humphrey's Executor at least had the decency formally to observe the constitutional principle that the President had to be the repository of *all* executive power, which, as *Myers* carefully explained, necessarily means that he must be able to discharge those who do not perform executive functions according to his liking. . . . By contrast, "our present considered view" is simply that *any* Executive officer's removal can be restricted, so long as the President remains "able to accomplish his constitutional role." There are now no lines. If the removal of a prosecutor, the virtual embodiment of the power to "take care that the laws be faithfully executed," can be restricted, what officer's removal cannot? This is an open invitation for Congress to experiment. What about a special Assistant Secretary of State, with responsibility for one very narrow area of foreign policy, who would not only have to be confirmed by the Senate but could also be removed only pursuant to certain carefully designed restrictions? Could this possibly render the President "[un]able to accomplish his constitutional role"? Or a special Assistant Secretary of Defense for Procurement? The possibilities are endless, and the Court does not understand what the separation of powers, what "[a]mbition . . . counteract[ing] ambition," Federalist No. 51, p.322 (Madison), is all about, if it does not expect Congress to try them. As far as I can discern from the Court's opinion, it is now open season upon the President's removal power for all executive officers, with not even the superficially principled restriction of *Humphrey's Executor* as cover. The Court essentially says to the President "Trust us. We will make sure that you are able to accomplish your constitutional role." I think the Constitution gives the President — and the people — more protection than that.

V

The purpose of the separation and equilibration of powers in general, and of the unitary Executive in particular, was not merely to assure effective government but to preserve individual freedom. Those who hold or have held offices covered by the Ethics in Government Act are entitled to that protection as much as the rest of us, and I conclude my discussion by considering the effect of the Act upon the fairness of the process they receive.

Only someone who has worked in the field of law enforcement can fully appreciate the vast power and the immense discretion that are placed in the hands of a prosecutor with respect to the objects of his investigation. . . .

Under our system of government, the primary check against prosecutorial abuse is a political one. The prosecutors who exercise this awesome discretion are selected and can be removed by a President, whom the people have trusted enough to elect. Moreover, when crimes are not investigated and prosecuted fairly, nonselectively, with a reasonable sense of proportion, the President pays the cost in political damage to his administration. . . .

That is the system of justice the rest of us are entitled to, but what of that select class consisting of present or former high-level executive-branch officials? If an allegation is made against them of any violation of any federal criminal law (except Class B or C misdemeanors or infractions) the Attorney General must give it his attention. That in itself is not objectionable. But if, after a 90-day investigation without the benefit of normal investigatory tools, the Attorney General is unable to say that there are "no reasonable grounds to believe" that further investigation is warranted, a process is set in motion that is *not* in the full control of persons "dependent on the people," and whose flaws cannot be blamed on the President. An independent counsel is selected, and the scope of her authority prescribed, by a panel of judges. What if they are politically partisan, as judges have been known to be, and select a prosecutor antagonistic to the administration, or even to the particular individual who has been selected for this special treatment? There is no remedy for that, not even a political one. . . . It is, in other words, an additional advantage of the unitary Executive that it can achieve a more uniform application of the law. Perhaps that is not always achieved, but the mechanism to achieve it is there. The mini-Executive that is the independent counsel, however, operating in an area where so little is law and so much is discretion, is intentionally cut off from the unifying influence of the Justice Department, and from the perspective that multiple responsibilities provide. What would normally be regarded as a technical violation (there are no rules defining such things), may in her small world assume the proportions of an indictable offense. . . .

By its short-sighted action today, I fear the Court has permanently encumbered the Republic with an institution that will do it great harm.

Worse than what it has done, however, is the manner in which it has done it. A government of laws means a government of rules. Today's decision on the basic issue of fragmentation of executive power is ungoverned by rule, and hence ungoverned by law. It extends into the very heart of our most significant constitutional function the "totality of the circumstances" mode of analysis that this Court has in recent years become fond of. Taking all things into account, we conclude that the power taken away from the President here is not really *too* much. The next time executive power is assigned to someone other than the President we may conclude, taking all things into account, that it *is* too much. That opinion, like this one, will not be confined by any rule. We will describe, as we have today (though I hope more accurately) the effects of the provision in question, and will authoritatively announce: "The President's need to control the exercise of the [subject officer's] discretion *is* so central to the functioning of the Executive Branch as to require complete control." This is not analysis; it is ad hoc judgment. And it fails to explain why it is not true that — as the text of the Constitution seems to require, as the Founders seemed to expect, and as our past cases have uniformly assumed — all purely executive power must be under the control of the President.

The ad hoc approach to constitutional adjudication has real attraction, even apart from its work-saving potential. It is guaranteed to produce a result, in every case, that will make a majority of the Court happy with the law. The law is, by definition, precisely what the majority thinks, taking all things into account, it *ought* to be. I prefer to rely upon the judgment of the wise men who constructed our system, and of the people who approved it, and of two centuries of history that have shown it to be sound. Like it or not, that judgment says, quite plainly, that "[t]he executive Power shall be vested in a President of the United States."

MISTRETTA v. UNITED STATES, 109 S. Ct. 647 (1989):   The United States Sentencing Commission has seven members appointed by the President, of whom three must be federal judges; the statute creating the Commission states that it is "an independent commission located in the judicial branch." The Commission was created in response to concern that sentences for similar offenses and of similar offenders in the federal system varied too substantially to promote the goals of sentencing. Its role is to create mandatory sentencing guidelines specifying rather narrow ranges of permissible sentences for different offenses, taking some account of the different circumstances under which different people commit crimes.

The Court, in an opinion by Justice Blackmun, rejected a variety of separation of powers challenges to the Commission. Relying on the "intelligible principle" test derived from prior nondelegation cases, the Court found that the Congress had given the Commission sufficiently detailed guidance as to the purposes its guidelines were to serve and the considerations the Commission was to take into account.

Addressing more general separation of powers concerns, the Court relied on Justice Jackson's opinion in *Youngstown* for "the pragmatic, flexible view of differentiated governmental power to which we are heir. [In] adopting this flexible understanding of separation of powers, we simply have recognized Madison's teaching that the greatest security against tyranny — the accumulation of excessive authority in a single branch — lies not in a hermetic division between the Branches, but in a carefully crafted system of checked and balanced power within each Branch. . . . It is this concern of encroachment and aggrandizement that has animated our separation-of-powers jurisprudence and aroused our vigilance against the 'hydraulic pressure inherent within each of the separate Branches to exceed the outer limits of its power.' [*Buckley*.]" "Close inspection" of the Commission's structure led the Court to conclude that, "although the unique composition and responsibilities of the Sentencing Commission give rise to serious concerns about a disruption of the appropriate balance

of governmental power among the coordinate branches, [fears] for the fundamental structural protections of the Constitution prove, at least in this case, to
be 'more smoke than fire.' "

The Court said that it has "recognized significant exceptions" to the general
rule that courts may not exercise executive and administrative duties of a
nonjudicial nature. "In keeping with Justice Jackson's *Youngstown* admonition
that the separation of powers contemplates the integration of dispersed powers
into a workable government, we have recognized the constitutionality of a
'twilight area' in which the activities of the separate Branches merge. . . . That
judicial rulemaking [falls] within this twilight area is no longer an issue for
dispute. . . . Consistent with the separation of powers, Congress may delegate
nonadjudicatory functions that do not trench upon the prerogatives of another
branch and that are appropriate to the central mission of the Judiciary." The
Sentencing Commission's location in the judicial branch "simply acknowledges
the role that the Judiciary always has played, and continues to play, in sentencing." Developing guidelines was similar to establishing rules of procedure for
the courts. "Just as the rules of procedure bind judges and courts in the proper
management of the cases before them, so the Guidelines bind judges and courts
in the exercise of their uncontested responsibility to pass sentence in criminal
cases," although "the degree of political judgment about crime and criminality
exercised by the Commission and the scope of the substantive effects of its work
does to some extent set its rulemaking powers apart from prior judicial
rulemaking."

Still, "the 'practical consequences' of locating the Commission within the
Judicial Branch pose no threat of undermining the integrity of the Judicial
Branch or of expanding the powers of the Judiciary beyond constitutional
bounds by uniting within the Branch the political or quasi-legislative power of
the Commission with the judicial power of the courts." The Commission was not
a court and was "fully accountable to Congress." Nor did the placement of the
Commission in the judicial branch increase that branch's authority, for "prior
to the passage of the Act, the Judicial Branch, as an aggregate, decided precisely
the questions assigned to the Commission: what sentence is appropriate to what
criminal conduct under what circumstances. [The] Sentencing Commission
does no more than this, albeit [through] the mechanism of sentencing guidelines, rather than entirely individualized sentencing determinations. [In] placing the Commission in the Judicial Branch, Congress cannot be said to have
[deprived] the Executive Branch of a power it once possessed. [And,] since
Congress did not unconstitutionally delegate its own authority, the Act does not
unconstitutionally diminish Congress' authority. . . . What Mistretta's argument comes down to, then, is [that the Judicial] Branch is inevitably weakened
by its participation in policymaking. [However,] despite the substantive nature
of its work, the Commission is not incongruous or inappropriate to the Branch.
[Although] the Guidelines are intended to have substantive effects on public

behavior, [they] do not bind or regulate the primary conduct of the public or vest in the Judicial Branch the legislative responsibility for establishing minimum and maximum penalties for every crime. They do no more than fetter the discretion of sentencing judges to do what they have done for generations. [Given] their limited reach, the special role of the Judicial Branch in the field of sentencing, and the fact that the Guidelines are promulgated by an independent agency and not a court, it follows that as a matter of 'practical consequences' the location of the Sentencing Commission within the Judicial Branch simply leaves with the Judiciary what long has belonged to it."

The Court found the requirement that the Commission have three federal judges on it "somewhat troublesome," but rejected the constitutional challenge to the composition of the Commission. "The text of the Constitution contains no prohibition against the service of active federal judges on independent commissions," and early historical practice allowed federal judges to undertake "extrajudicial duties." "The judges serve on the Sentencing Commission not pursuant to their status and authority as Article III judges, but solely because of their appointment by the President. [Such] power as these judges wield as Commissioners is not judicial power; it is administrative power. [The] Constitution [does] not forbid judges from wearing two hats; it merely forbids them from wearing both hats at the same time. . . . The ultimate inquiry remains whether a particular extrajudicial assignment undermines the integrity of the Judicial Branch." Because service by any particular judge on the Commission was voluntary, that service could not diminish the independence of the Judiciary. The Court was "somewhat more troubled by [the] argument that the Judiciary's entanglement in the political work of the Commission undermines public confidence in the disinterestedness of the Judicial Branch. While the problem of individual bias is usually cured through recusal, no such mechanism can overcome the appearance of institutional partiality that may arise from judiciary involvement in the making of policy. . . . Although it is a judgment that is not without difficulty, we conclude that the participation of federal judges on the Sentencing Commission does not threaten, either in fact or in appearance, the impartiality of the Judicial Branch" because the Commission "is devoted exclusively to the development of rules to rationalize a process that has been and will continue to be performed exclusively by the Judicial Branch. In our view, this is an essentially neutral endeavor and one in which judicial participation is peculiarly appropriate."

Finally, the Court concluded that the President's power to appoint judges to the Commission did not give him "influence over the Judicial Branch. [We] simply cannot imagine that federal judges will comport their actions to the wishes of the President for the purpose of receiving an appointment to the Sentencing Commission. The President's removal power over Commission members poses a similarly negligible threat to judicial independence. [Since] the President has no power to affect the tenure or compensation of Article III judges, even if the Act authorized him to remove judges from the Commission at will, he would have no power to coerce the judges in the exercise of their judicial duties," and any damage to reputation from a removal was undertaken voluntarily by judges who accepted appointments to the Commission.

Justice Scalia dissented. "[The] decisions made by the Commission are far from technical, but are heavily laden [with] value judgments and policy assessments." Justice Scalia sympathized with the nondelegation argument, but said that nondelegation "is not [readily] enforceable by the courts. Once it is conceded, as it must be, that no statute can be entirely precise, and that some judgments, even some judgments involving policy considerations, must be left to the officers executing the law and to the judges applying it, the debate over unconstitutional delegation becomes a debate not over a point of principle but over a question of degree. [Since] Congress is no less endowed with common sense than we are, and better equipped to inform itself of the 'necessities' of government; and since the factors bearing upon those necessities are both multifarious and (in the nonpartisan sense) highly political, [it] is small wonder that we have almost never felt qualified to second-guess Congress regarding the permissible degree of policy judgment that can be left to those executing or applying the law."

However, "[precisely] because the scope of delegation is largely uncontrollable by the courts, we must be particularly rigorous in preserving the Constitution's structural restrictions that deter excessive delegation. The major one [is] that the power to make law cannot be exercised by anyone other than Congress, except in conjunction with the lawful exercise of executive or judicial power. The whole theory of *lawful* congressional 'delegation' is [that] a certain degree of discretion, and thus of law-making, *inheres* in most executive or judicial action, and it is up to Congress, by the relative specificity or generality of its statutory commands to determine [how] small or how large that degree shall be." On this theory, "there is *no* acceptable delegation of legislative power," because whatever law-making occurs is ancillary to the exercise of executive or judicial power. Here, though, "the lawmaking function of the Sentencing Commission is completely divorced from any responsibility for the execution of the law or adjudication of private rights under the law." Thus, "the delegation of lawmaking authority to the Commission is [unsupported] by any legitimating theory to explain why it is not a delegation of legislative power. To disregard structural legitimacy is wrong in itself — but since structure has purpose, the disregard also has adverse practical consequences. In this case, [the] consequence is to facilitate and encourage judicially uncontrollable delegation. Until [Morrison v. Olsen,] it could have been said that Congress could delegate lawmaking authority only at the expense of increasing the power of either the President or the courts. Most often, as a practical matter, it would be the President, since the judicial process is unable to conduct the investigations and make the political assessments essential for most policymaking. Thus, the need for delegation would have to be important enough to induce Congress to aggrandize its primary competitor for political power, and the recipient of the policymaking authority, while not Congress itself, would at least be politically accountable. . . . [I] anticipate that Congress will find delegation of its lawmaking powers much more attractive in the future. If rulemaking can be entirely unrelated to the exercise of judicial or executive powers, I foresee all manner of 'expert' bodies, insulated from the political process, to which Congress will delegate various portions of its lawmaking responsibility. How tempting to create an expert Medical Commission [to] dispose of such thorny, 'no-win' political issues as the withholding of life-support systems in federally funded hospitals or the use of fetal tissue for research. This is an undemocratic precedent that we set — not because of the scope of the delegated power, but because its recipient is not one of the three Branches of Congress. The only governmental power the Commission possesses is the power to make law; and it is not the Congress."

"Today's decision follows the regrettable tendency of our recent separation-of-powers jurisprudence to treat the Constitution as though it were no more than a generalized prescription that the functions of the Branches should not be commingled too much — how much is too much to be determined, case-by-case, by this Court. The Constitution is not that. Rather, [it] is a prescribed structure, a framework, for the conduct of government. In designing that structure, the framers *themselves* considered how much commingling was, in the generality of things, acceptable, and set forth their conclusions in the document. That is the meaning of the statements concerning acceptable commingling made by Madison in defense of the proposed Constitutions, and now routinely used as an excuse for disregarding it." In Federalist 47, Madison's "point was that the commingling specifically provided for in the structure that he and his colleagues had designed [did] not violate a proper understanding of the separation of powers. He would be aghast, I think, to hear those words used as justification for ignoring that carefully designed structure so long as, in the changing view of the Supreme Court from time to time, 'too much commingling' does not occur. . . . I think the Court errs [not] so much because it mistakes the degree of commingling, but because it fails to recognize that this case is not about commingling, but about the creation of a new branch altogether, a sort of junior-varsity Congress. It may well be that in some circumstances such a branch would be desirable. [But] there are many desirable dispositions that do not accord with the constitutional structure we live under. And in the long run the improvisation of a constitutional structure on the basis of currently perceived utility will be disastrous."

NOTES

1. Does the decision in *Morrison* reflect the Court's rejection of the formalist approaches of *Bowsher* and *Chadha*? Consider the view that there are two lines of

cases here — one formalist, the other more functional in character — and that they are ultimately on a collision course. Also consider the view that it is possible to reconcile all of these cases in functional terms, since there was a genuine danger to central constitutional commitments in *Bowsher* and *Chadha*, but not in *Morrison*. Can this view be sustained in light of Justice Scalia's dissenting opinion?

2. After *Morrison*, it is quite difficult to describe in precise terms the nature of constitutional limitations on Congress' power (a) to vest the appointment of inferior officers (how defined?) outside of the executive branch, and (b) to immunize executive branch officials from presidential removal power. Suppose that Congress was disappointed with the performance of the Occupational Safety and Health Administration, or the Environmental Protection Agency, or even the Department of Justice. What steps might it take to protect officials in those entities from presidential control?

D. LEGISLATIVE AND EXECUTIVE IMMUNITIES: IMPEACHMENT

Page 398.   The correct date for United States v. Nixon is 1974.

Page 410.   At the end of section 3 of the Note, add the following:

For an interesting approach to interbranch negotiation of claims of executive privilege, see Shane, Legal Disagreement and Negotiation in a Government of Laws: The Case of Executive Privilege Claims against Congress, 71 Minn. L. Rev. 461 (1987).

E. FOREIGN AFFAIRS

Page 423.   After Note 3, add the following:

Consider Koh, Why the President (Almost) Always Wins in Foreign Affairs: Lessons of the Iran-Contra Affair, 97 Yale L.J. 1255, 1310-1311 (1988):

> Read together with [*Chadha*], *Dames & Moore* dramatically alters the application of *Youngstown*'s constitutional analysis in foreign affairs cases. For under [*Dames & Moore*], a court may construe congressional inaction or legislation in a related area as implicit approval for a challenged executive action. Yet under *Chadha*, Congress may definitively *disapprove* an executive act only by passing a joint resolution by a supermajority in both houses that is sufficient to override a subsequent presidential veto. These rulings create a one-way "ratchet effect" that effectively redraws the

categories described in Justice Jackson's *Youngstown* concurrence. For by treating all manner of ambiguous congressional action as "approval" [, a] court can manipulate almost any act out of the lower two Jackson categories, where it would be subject to challenge, into Jackson Category One, where the President's legal authority would be unassailable. Yet because *Chadha* demands an extraordinary display of political will to disapprove a presidential act, Congress could only rarely return those acts to Jackson Category Three. [These] decisions have the net effect of dramatically narrowing Jackson Category Three to those very few foreign affairs cases in which the President both lacks inherent constitutional powers and is foolish enough to act contrary to congressional intent clearly expressed on the face of a statute.

Chapter Five

Equality and the Constitution

A. RACE AND THE CONSTITUTION

Page 437. Before State v. Post, add the following:

In light of the provisions in the Constitution protecting slavery, should it have been ratified? Consider the views of Justice Thurgood Marshall:

I [do not] find the wisdom, foresight, and sense of justice exhibited by the framers particularly profound. To the contrary, the government they devised was defective from the start, requiring several amendments, a civil war, and momentous social transformation to attain the system of constitutional government, and its respect for the individual freedoms and human rights we hold as fundamental today. [Marshall, Remarks at the Annual Seminar of the San Francisco Patent and Trademark Law Assn. (May 6, 1987).]

Compare Levinson, Pledging Faith in the Civil Religion (Or, Would You Sign the Constitution?), Remarks at The Fourth Annual Bill of Rights Symposium, William and Mary Law School (Mar. 28, 1987):

[The] central problem with "disunionist" thinking [is] that it focuses more on the immorality of collaboration with slavery [than] on the question of how one most quickly can bring slavery to an end. We know that with ratification chattel slavery ended by 1865. Is there good reason to believe that it would have ended earlier had the Constitution not been ratified and balkanization followed? I suspect not. But the important point is surely this: Can one who believes that the ratification of the Constitution *did* enhance the prospects (and actuality) of chattel slavery sign the Constitution? What precisely is the value of the Constitution and of the concomitant nation that would justify even an extra week's slavery? What precisely is the omelet that justified breaking those particular eggs?

Page 439. At the end of section 2 of the Note, add the following:

According to Ernst, Legal Positivism, Abolitionist Litigation, and the New Jersey Slave Case of 1845, 4 Law & Hist. Rev. 337, 350-351 (1986), Stewart made four federal constitutional arguments against slavery: (1) that it deprived slaves of life, liberty, and property in violation of the due process clause of the fifth amendment; (2) that it deprived New Jersey of a "Republican form of Government" in violation of article IV; (3) that it stripped slaves of human rights that all constitutions are created to protect and thereby violated the preamble of the federal Constitution; and (4) that it violated the undertaking in the Treaty of Ghent, made binding on New Jersey by the supremacy clause, to end the traffic in slaves.

According to Ernst, Stewart

> maintained that the intent of the participants in the Federal Convention was irrelevant. [The] true adopters, whose intent *was* relevant, were the people of the individual states gathered in the ratifying conventions. If these "adopters ever thought of slavery, they did not think to name it, and must have supposed it near its end, and they did not wish to disgrace the nation by the admission that so foul and base a thing ever existed."

Page 467.   Before section 3 of the Note, add the following:

Consider the following argument, made by Geneva Crenshaw, the fictional heroine in D. Bell, And We Are Not Saved 111-113 (1987):

> We civil rights lawyers attacked segregation in the public schools because it was the weak link in the "separate but equal" chain. Our attack worked. But to equate integration with the effective education black children need — well, that was a mistake. . . .
>
> [I] don't agree that a better desegregation policy was beyond the reach of intelligent people whose minds were not clogged with integrationist dreams. [Suppose] the Court had issued the following orders:
>
> 1. Even though we encourage voluntary desegregation, we will not order racially integrated assignments of students or staff for ten years.
>
> 2. Even though "separate but equal" no longer meets the constitutional equal-protection standard, we will require immediate equalization of all facilities and resources.
>
> 3. Blacks must be represented on school boards and other policy-making bodies in proportions equal to those of black students in each school district.
>
> [Rather] than beat our heads against the wall seeking pupil-desegregation orders the courts were unwilling to enter or enforce, we could have organized parents and communities to ensure effective implementation for the equal-funding and equal-representation mandates.

Page 475.   After the third full paragraph, add the following:

Compare *Green* to Bazemore v. Friday, 478 U.S. 385 (1986). Prior to 1965, the North Carolina Agricultural Extension Service operated racially segregated 4-H and Homemaker Clubs. In response to the 1964 Civil Rights Act, the service discontinued its segregated club policy and opened any club to any otherwise eligible person regardless of race. Despite this change of policy, however, many clubs remained racially segregated and petitioners brought this action seeking to compel the Extension Service to take affirmative measures designed to integrate the clubs. The district court denied relief after finding that any racial imbalance was the result of a wholly voluntary choice by private individuals, and the Supreme Court affirmed. The Court, in an opinion by Justice White, distinguished *Green* as follows:

> While school children must go to school, there is no compulsion to join 4-H or Homemaker Clubs, and while School Boards customarily have the power to create school attendance areas and otherwise designate the school that particular students may attend, there is no statutory or regulatory authority to deny a young person the right to join any Club he or she wishes to join.

Is this distinction persuasive? Compare Justice Brennan's argument in a dissenting opinion joined by Justices Marshall, Blackmun, and Stevens:

> Prior to the early 1960's, the 4-H Clubs were organized in the public schools, which were at that time, of course, still segregated. Thus, those who wanted to join 4-H were, in effect, "assigned" to join the club in their segregated school. It is the racial segregation resulting from this practice that the State is under a duty to eradicate. As a result, this case is in fact indistinguishable from *Green*. . . .
>
> Nothing in our earlier cases suggests that the State's obligation to desegregate is confined only to those activities in which members of the public are compelled to participate. On the contrary, it is clear that the State's obligation to desegregate formerly segregated entities extends beyond those programs where participation is compulsory to voluntary public amenities such as parks and recreational facilities.

Page 490.   Before section 2 of the Note, add the following:

Are there any limits on the power of federal courts to order the expenditure of state resources to remedy segregated schools? Consider Missouri v. Jenkins, 110 S. Ct. 1651 (1990). After finding that the Kansas City, Missouri public schools were unconstitutionally segregated, a district judge ordered a sweeping remedy designed to create "magnet schools" that would attract white children into the district. In order to fund the program, the court ordered that the property tax levy within the school district be raised by almost 100 percent for the next fiscal year. On certiorari, the Supreme Court limited its review to the legitimacy of the judicially imposed tax increase and assumed, without deciding, that the underlying remedy was within the district court's powers. In a 5 to 4 decision, the Court, in an opinion by Justice White, held that the district judge had abused his discretion by ordering the tax increase. The Court went on to hold, however, that the District Judge could order a local government body to raise its own taxes even in excess of the limit set by state law.

> To hold otherwise would fail to take account of the obligations of local governments, under the Supremacy Clause, to fulfill the requirements that the Constitution imposes on them. However wide the discretion of local authorities in fashioning desegregation

remedies may be, "if a state-imposed limitation on a school authority's discretion operates to inhibit or obstruct the operation of a unitary school system or impede the disestablishing of a dual school system, it must fall; state policy must give way when it operates to hinder vindication of federal constitutional guarantees." [Quoting North Carolina State Bd. of Education v. Swann].

Justice Kennedy filed a dissenting opinion which Chief Justice Rehnquist and Justices O'Connor and Scalia joined:

Today's casual embrace of taxation imposed by the unelected, life-tenured federal judiciary disregards fundamental precepts for the democratic control of public institutions. . . .

Federal judges do not depend on the popular will for their office. They may not even share the burden of taxes they attempt to impose, for they may live outside the jurisdiction their orders affect. And federal judges have no fear that the competition for scarce public resources could result in a diminution of their salaries. It is not surprising that the imposition of taxes by an authority so insulated from public communication or control can lead to deep feelings of frustration, powerlessness, and anger on the part of taxpaying citizens.

Page 495.   Before Section B, add the following:

Consider the following summary, which Derrick Bell puts into the mouth of his fictional heroine, Geneva Crenshaw:

[Because] the Supreme Court is unable or unwilling to recognize and remedy the real losses resulting from long-held, race-based, subordinated status, the relief the Court has been willing to grant, while welcome, proves of less value than expected and exacts the exorbitant price of dividing the black community along economic lines. . . .

[There] seems little doubt that abandonment of overtly discriminatory policies has lowered racial barriers for some talented and skilled blacks seeking access to opportunity and advancement. Even their upward movement is, however, pointed to by much of the society as the final proof that racism is dead — a too hasty pronouncement which dilutes the achievement of those who have moved ahead and denies even society's sympathy to those less fortunate blacks whose opportunities and life fortunes are less promising today than they were twenty-five years ago.

D. Bell, And We Are Not Saved 48-49 (1987).

B.   EQUAL PROTECTION METHODOLOGY: RATIONAL BASIS REVIEW

Page 500.   At the end of Note 2, add the following:

For a helpful exposition of equal protection doctrine, see Simons, Overinclusion and Underinclusion: A New Model, 36 UCLA L. Rev. 447 (1989).

Page 500.   At the bottom of the page, add the following:

Compare Simons, Equality as a Comparative Right, 65 B.U.L. Rev. 387, 389 (1985):

> Westen's deconstruction of equality has power only because he artificially limits the conception of equality to "treating likes alike," that is, to the relationship of identity that a standard of measure entails. [A] different conception of equality, one more consistent with constitutional theory, [treats equality] as a *comparative* claim to receive a particular treatment just because another person or class receives it. The claim to that treatment is not absolute, but relative to whether others receive it. And the claim is satisfied by giving the comparatively situated classes the required equal treatment.

Page 509.   Before the Posner quotation, add the following:

Can deferential review be justified on the ground that more stringent scrutiny would discourage legislative reform? In Bowen v. Owens, 476 U.S. 1137 (1986), the Court defended deferential review of classifications contained in the Social Security laws as follows:

> Congress' adjustments of this complex system of entitlements necessarily create distinctions among categories of beneficiaries, a result that could be avoided only by making sweeping changes in the Act instead of incremental ones. A constitutional rule that would invalidate Congress' attempts to proceed cautiously in awarding increased benefits might deter Congress from making any increases at all.

Compare the views of Justice Marshall expressed in a dissenting opinion:

> [I] suspect that the Court is right to characterize the distinction drawn by [the act in question] as the product of Congress' decision to "take one step at a time." However under [equal protection principles] even legislative classifications that result from compromise must bear at least a rational relationship to a legitimate state purpose. Had Congress accommodated the House's reform goals with the Senate's more conservative outlook in this area by passing a law giving benefits to only those [born] on odd-numbered days of the calendar, we would surely have to strike the provision down as irrational.

Page 520.   Before the Note, add the following:

In recent cases, the Court has distinguished *Moreno* and upheld provisions of the Food Stamp Act against equal protection attack:

Castillo. Benefits under the federal food stamp program are determined by household. The statute treats all parents, children, and siblings who live together as a single household. However, more distant relatives and groups of unrelated persons living together are not a single "household" so long as they do not customarily buy food and prepare meals together. In Lyng v.

Castillo, 477 U.S. 635 (1986), appellees were closely related families who lived together but prepared meals separately. They were therefore treated as a single household and received smaller benefits than they would have if they had not been closely related and could have applied as more than one household. The district court held that this differential treatment violated the equal protection component of the due process clause, but the Supreme Court, in an opinion by Justice Stevens, reversed. The Court held that Congress had a rational basis for distinguishing between close and more distant relatives.

> Congress could reasonably determine that close relatives sharing a home — almost by definition — tend to purchase and prepare meals together while distant relatives and unrelated individuals might not be so inclined. In that event, even though close relatives are undoubtedly as honest as other food stamp recipients, the potential for mistaken or misstated claims of separate dining would be greater in the case of close relatives than would be true for those with weaker communal ties, simply because a greater percentage of the former category in fact prepare meals jointly than the comparable percentage in the latter category. [Congress] might [also] have reasoned that it would be somewhat easier for close relatives — again, almost by definition — to accommodate their living habits to a federal policy favoring common meal preparation than it would be for more distant relatives or unrelated persons to do so.

The Court distinguished *Moreno* as follows:

> Unlike the present statute, the [statute invalidated in *Moreno*] completely disqualified all households [containing an unrelated person]. Not only were all groups of unrelated persons ineligible for benefits, but even groups of related persons would lose their benefits if they admitted one nonrelative to their household.

Justice Marshall dissented:

> Despite the Court's attempts to distinguish this case from *Moreno*, the critical fact in both cases is that the statute drew a distinction that bears no necessary relation to the prevention of fraud. [In] the present case, the Government has provided no justification for the conclusion that related individuals living together are more likely to lie about their living arrangements than are unrelated individuals. Nor has it demonstrated that fraudulent conduct by related households is more difficult to detect than similar abuses by unrelated households.

See also Bowen v. Gilliard, 483 U.S. 587 (1987) (utilizing rational basis review to uphold an amendment to the Aid to Families with Dependent Children program that reduced benefit levels for covered families by the amount of child support received by the family from a noncustodial parent).

Consider the implications of the following case:

LYNG v. INTERNATIONAL UNION, UNITED AUTOMOBILE, AEROSPACE AND AGRICULTURAL IMPLEMENT WORKERS
485 U.S. 360 (1988)

JUSTICE WHITE delivered the opinion of the Court.

A 1981 amendment to the Food Stamp Act states that no household shall become eligible to participate in the food stamp program during the time that any member of the household is on strike or shall increase the allotment of food stamps that it was receiving already because the income of the striking member has decreased. We must decide whether this provision is valid under the First and the Fifth Amendments. . . .

In the Omnibus Budget Reconciliation Act of 1981, Pub. L. 97-35, 95 Stat. 357 (OBRA), Congress enacted a package of budget cuts throughout the Federal Government. Among the measures contained in OBRA were more than a dozen specific changes in the food stamp program. One of them was the amendment at issue in this case, which is set out in the margin. [2] The Committee Reports estimated that this measure alone would save a total of about $165 million in fiscal years 1982, 1983, and 1984. . . .

We deal first with the District Court's holding that §109 violates the associational and expressive rights of appellees under the First Amendment. These claimed constitutional infringements are also pressed as a basis for finding that appellees' rights of "fundamental importance" have been burdened, thus requiring this Court to examine appellees' equal protection claims under a heightened standard of review. Zablocki v. Redhail, 434 U.S. 374, 383 (1978). Since we conclude that the statute does not infringe either the associational or expressive rights of appellees, we must reject both parts of this analysis. . . .

The challenge to the statute based on the associational rights asserted by appellees is foreclosed by the reasoning this Court adopted in Lyng v. Castillo, 477 U.S. 635 (1986). There we considered a constitutional challenge to the definition of "household" in the Food Stamp Act, which treats parents, siblings, and children who live together, but not more distant relatives or unrelated persons who do so, as a single household for purposes of defining eligibility for

---

2. Notwithstanding any other provision of law, a household shall not participate in the food stamp program at any time that any member of the household, not exempt from the work registration requirements . . . is on strike as defined in section 142(2) of title 29, because of a labor dispute (other than a lockout) as defined in section 152(9) of title 29: *Provided,* That a household shall not lose its eligibility to participate in the food stamp program as a result of one of its members going on strike if the household was eligible for food stamps immediately prior to such strike, however, such household shall not receive an increased allotment as the result of a decrease in the income of the striking member or members of the household: *Provided further,* That such ineligibility shall not apply to any household that does not contain a member on strike, if any of its members refuses to accept employment at a plant or site because of a strike or lockout." OBRA §109, 95 Stat. 361, 7 U.S.C. §2015(d)(3).

food stamps. Although the challenge in that case was brought solely on equal protection grounds, and not under the First Amendment, the Court was obliged to decide whether the statutory classification should be reviewed under a stricter standard than mere rational-basis review because it " 'directly and substantially' interfere[s] with family living arrangements and thereby burden[s] a fundamental right." The Court held that it did not, explaining that the definition of "household" does not "order or prevent any group of persons from dining together. Indeed, in the overwhelming majority of cases it probably has no effect at all. It is exceedingly unlikely that close relatives would choose to live apart simply to increase their allotment of food stamps, for the costs of separate housing would almost certainly exceed the incremental value of the additional stamps."

The same rationale applies in this case. As was true of the provision at issue in *Castillo*, it is "exceedingly unlikely" that §109 will "prevent any group of persons from dining together." Even if isolated instances can be found in which a striking individual may have left the other members of the household in order to increase their allotment of food stamps, "in the overwhelming majority of cases [the statute] probably has no effect at all." The statute certainly does not "order" any individuals not to dine together; nor does it in any other way " 'directly and substantially' interfere with family living arrangements."

The statute also does not infringe the associational rights of appellee individuals and their unions. We have recognized that "one of the foundations of our society is the right of individuals to combine with other persons in pursuit of a common goal by lawful means," NAACP v. Claiborne Hardware Co., 458 U.S. 886, 933 (1982), and our recognition of this right encompasses the combination of individual workers together in order better to assert their lawful rights. See, e.g., Railroad Trainmen v. Virginia, 377 U.S. 1, 5-6 (1964). But in this case, the statute at issue does not " 'directly and substantially' interfere" with appellees' ability to associate for this purpose. *Lyng*, supra, at 638. It does not "order" appellees not to associate together for the purpose of conducting a strike, or for any other purpose, and it does not "prevent" them from associating together or burden their ability to do so in any significant manner. As we have just stated with respect to the effect of this statute on an individual's decision to remain in or to leave his or her household, it seems "exceedingly unlikely" that this statute will prevent individuals from continuing to associate together in unions to promote their lawful objectives. . . .

Any impact on associational rights in this case results from the Government's refusal to extend food stamp benefits to those on strike, who are now without their wage income. Denying such benefits makes it harder for strikers to maintain themselves and their families during the strike and exerts pressure on them to abandon their union. Strikers and their union would be much better off if food stamps were available, but the strikers' right of association does not require the Government to furnish funds to maximize the exercise of that right.

. . . The statute challenged in this case requires no exaction from any individual; it does not "coerce" belief; and it does not require appellees to participate in political activities or support political views with which they disagree. It merely declines to extend additional food stamp assistance to striking individuals merely because the decision to strike inevitably leads to a decline in their income. . . .

For the same reasons, we cannot agree that §109 abridges appellees' right to express themselves about union matters free of coercion by the Government. . . .

Because the statute challenged here has no substantial impact on any fundamental interest and does not "affect with particularity any protected class," we confine our consideration to whether the statutory classification "is rationally related to a legitimate governmental interest. . . ."

The Government submits that this statute serves three objectives. Most obvious, given its source in OBRA, is to cut federal expenditures. Second, the limited funds available were to be used when the need was likely to be greatest, an approach which Congress thought did not justify food stamps for strikers. Third was the concern that the food stamp program was being used to provide one-sided support for labor strikes; the Senate Report indicated that the amendment was intended to remove the basis for that perception and criticism. . . .

We have little trouble in concluding that §109 is rationally related to the legitimate governmental objective of avoiding undue favoritism to one side or the other in private labor disputes. The Senate Report declared: "Public policy demands an end to the food stamp subsidization of all strikers who become eligible for the program solely through the temporary loss of income during a strike. Union strike funds should be responsible for providing support and benefits to strikers during labor-management disputes." Ibid. It was no part of the purposes of the Food Stamp Act to establish a program that would serve as a weapon in labor disputes; the Act was passed to alleviate hunger and malnutrition and to strengthen the agricultural economy. 7 U.S.C. §2011. The Senate Report stated that "allowing strikers to be eligible for food stamps has damaged the program's public integrity" and thus endangers these other goals served by the program. Congress acted in response to these problems.

It would be difficult to deny that this statute works at least some discrimination against strikers and their households. For the duration of the strike, those households cannot increase their allotment of food stamps even though the loss of income occasioned by the strike may well be enough to qualify them for food stamps or to increase their allotment if the fact of the strike itself were ignored. Yet Congress was in a difficult position when it sought to address the problems it had identified. Because a striking individual faces an immediate and often total drop in income during a strike, a single controversy pitting an employer against its employees can lead to a large number of claims for food stamps for as long as the controversy endures. It is the disbursement of food stamps in response to such a controversy that constitutes the source of the concern, and of the dangers to the program, that Congress believed it was important to remedy. We are not free in this instance to reject Congress' views about "what constitutes wise economic or social policy."

It is true that in terms of the scope and extent of their ineligibility for food stamps, §109 is harder on strikers than on "voluntary quitters." But the concern about neutrality in labor disputes does not arise with respect to those who, for one reason or another, simply quit their jobs. As we have stated in a related context, even if the statute "provides only 'rough justice,' its treatment . . . is far from irrational." Congress need not draw a statutory classification to the satisfaction of the most sharp-eyed observers in order to meet the limitations that the Constitution imposes in this setting. And we are not authorized to ignore Congress' considered efforts to avoid favoritism in labor disputes, which are evidenced also by the two significant provisos contained in the statute. The first proviso preserves eligibility for the program of any household that was eligibile to receive stamps "immediately prior to such strike." 7 U.S.C. §2015(d)(3). The second proviso makes clear that the statutory ineligibility for food stamps does not apply "to any household that does not contain a member on strike, if any of its members refuses to accept employment at a plant or site because of a strike or lockout." In light of all this, the statute is rationally related to the stated objective of maintaining neutrality in private labor disputes.

In view of the foregoing, we need not determine whether either of the other two proffered justifications for §109 would alone suffice. But it is relevant to note that protecting the fiscal integrity of government programs, and of the Government as a whole, "is a legitimate concern of the State." This does not mean that Congress can pursue the objective of saving money by discriminating against individuals or groups. But our review of distinctions that Congress draws in order to make allocations from a finite pool of resources must be deferential, for the discretion about how best to spend money to improve the general welfare is lodged in Congress rather than the courts. "Fiscal considerations may compel certain difficult choices in order to improve the protection afforded to the entire benefited class." Harris v. McRae, 448 U.S., at 355 (STEVENS, J., dissenting). In OBRA Congress had already found it necessary to restrict eligibility in the food stamp program and to reduce the amount of deductions that were allowed to recipients. Rather than undertaking further budget cuts in these or other areas, and in order to avoid favoritism in labor disputes, Congress judged that it would do better to pass this statute along with its provisos. The Constitution does not permit us to disturb that judgment in this case.

Appellees contend and the District Court held that the legislative classification is irrational because of the "critical" fact that it "impermissibly strikes at the striker through his family." This, however, is nothing more than a description of how the food stamp program operates as a general matter, a fact that was acknowledged by the District Court. Whenever an individual takes any action that hampers his or her ability to meet the program's eligibility requirements, such as quitting a job or failing to comply with the work-registration requirements, the entire household suffers accordingly. We have never questioned the constitutionality of the entire Act on this basis, and we just recently upheld the validity of the Act's definition of "household" even though that definition embodies the basic fact that the Act determines benefits "on a 'household' rather than an individual basis." That aspect of the program does not violate the Constitution any more so today.

The decision of the District Court is therefore reversed.

JUSTICE KENNEDY took no part in the consideration or decision of this case.

JUSTICE MARSHALL, with whom JUSTICE BRENNAN and JUSTICE BLACK-MUN join, dissenting.

The Court today declares that it has "little trouble" in concluding that Congress's denial of food stamps to the households of striking workers is rationally related to a legitimate governmental objective. Ante, at 10. The ease with which the Court reaches this conclusion is reflected in the brevity of its Fifth Amendment analysis: the Court gives short shrift to appellees' Equal Protection challenge to the striker amendment even though this argument was the centerpiece of appellees' case in their briefs and at oral argument. I believe that the Court's dismissive approach has caused it to fail to register the full force of appellees' claim. After canvassing the many absurdities that afflict the striker amendment, I conclude that it fails to pass constitutional muster under even the most deferential scrutiny. I therefore would affirm the judgment below. . . .

The Secretary's argument that the striker amendment will save money proves far too much. According to the Secretary's reasoning, the exclusion of any unpopular group from a public benefit program would survive rational basis scrutiny, because exclusion always would result in a decrease in governmental expenditures. . . .

Perhaps recognizing this problem, the Secretary defends the singling out of strikers and their households as rationally related to the goal of channeling resources to those persons most " 'genuinely in need.' " As a threshold matter, however, households denied food stamps because of the presence of a striker are as "needy" in terms of financial resources as households that qualify for food stamps: the former are denied food stamps *despite* the fact that they meet the financial eligibility requirements of 7 U.S.C. §2014 (1982 ed. and Supp. IV), even after strike-fund payments are counted as household income. This point has particular poignancy for the infants and children of a striking worker. Their need for nourishment is in no logical way diminished by the striker's action. The denial to these children of what is often the only buffer between them and malnourishment and disease cannot be justified as a targeting of the most needy: they *are* the most needy. The record below bears witness to this point in a heartbreaking fashion.

The Secretary argues, however, that the striker amendment is related to need at least in the sense of willingness to work, if not in the strict sense of financial eligibility. Because the Food Stamp Act generally excludes persons unwilling to work — and their households — the Secretary argues that it is consistent to exclude strikers and their households as well, on the ground that strikers remain "unwilling to work," at least at the struck business, for the duration of the strike. In the Secretary's eyes, a striker is akin to an unemployed worker who day after day refuses to accept available work. One flaw in this argument is its false factual premise. It is simply not true, as the Secretary argues, that a striker always has a job that "remains available to him." Many strikes result in the complete cessation of a business's operations, so that the decision of an individual striker to return to work would be unavailing. Moreover, many of the businesses that continue to operate during a strike hire permanent replacements for the striking workers. In this situation as well, a striker no longer has the option of returning to work. In fact, the record in this case reveals that a number of appellees were denied food stamps even though they had been permanently replaced by their employers.

But even if it were true that strikers always can return to their jobs, the Secretary's "willingness to work" rationale falls apart in light of the glaring disparity between the treatment of strikers and the treatment of those who are unwilling to work for other reasons. People who voluntarily quit their jobs are not disqualified from receiving food stamps if, after notice and a hearing, they can demonstrate that they quit with "good cause." Moreover, even if the state agency determines that the quit was without good cause, the voluntary quitter is disqualified only for a period of 90 days, and the quitter's household is disqualified only if the quitter was the "head of household." In contrast, a striker is given no opportunity to demonstrate that the strike was for "good cause," even though strikers frequently allege that unfair labor practices by their employer precipitated the strike. In addition, strikers and their entire households, no matter how minimal the striker's contribution to the household's income may have been, are disqualified for the duration of the strike, even if the striker is permanently replaced or business operations temporarily cease. . . .

Unable to explain completely the striker amendment by the "willingness to work" rationale, the Secretary relies most heavily on yet a third rationale: the promotion of governmental neutrality in labor disputes. . . .

The "neutrality" argument on its merits is both deceptive and deeply flawed. Even on the most superficial level, the striker amendment does not treat the parties to a labor dispute evenhandedly; forepersons and other management employees who may become temporarily unemployed when a business ceases to operate during a strike remain eligible for food stamps. Management's burden during the course of the dispute is thus lessened by the receipt of public funds, whereas labor must struggle unaided. This disparity cannot be justified by the argument that the strike is labor's "fault," because strikes are often a direct response to illegal practices by management, such as failure to abide by the terms of a collective bargaining agreement or refusal to bargain in good faith.

On a deeper level, the "neutrality" argument reflects a profoundly inaccurate view of the relationship of the modern federal government to the various parties to a labor dispute. Both individuals and businesses are connected to the government by a complex web of supports and incentives. On the one hand, individuals may be eligible to receive a wide variety of health, education, and welfare-related benefits. On the other hand, businesses may be eligible to receive a myriad of tax subsidies through deductions, depreciation, and credits, or direct subsidies in the form of government loans through the Small Business Administration (SBA). Businesses also may receive lucrative government contracts and invoke the protections of the Bankruptcy Act against their creditors. None of these governmental subsidies to businesses is made contingent on the businesses' abstention from labor disputes, even if a labor dispute is the direct cause of the claim to a subsidy. . . . When viewed against the network of governmental support of both labor and management, the withdrawal of the single support of food stamps — a support critical to the continued life and health of an individual worker and his or her family — cannot be seen as a "neutral" act. Altering the backdrop of governmental support in this one-sided and devastating way amounts to a penalty on strikers, not neutrality . . . .

I agree with the Court that "[i]t was no part of the purposes of the Food Stamp Act to establish a program that would serve as a weapon in labor disputes." The striker amendment under consideration today, however, seems to have precisely that purpose — one admittedly irreconcilable with the legitimate goals of the food stamp program. No other purpose can adequately explain the especially harsh treatment reserved for strikers and their families by the 1981 enactment. Because I conclude that the striker amendment cannot survive even rational basis scrutiny, I would affirm the District Court's invalidation of the amendment. I dissent.

If Congress had frankly acknowledged that the amendment was designed to favor management over unions in labor disputes, would the amendment have been unconstitutional? Is there a constitutionally relevant difference between laws that disfavor strikers and those that disfavor "hippies"? Consider the view that *Lyng* depends on a common law baseline for deciding whether there is government "neutrality." How might that baseline be criticized in this context?

Epstein, Unconstitutional Conditions, State Power, and the Limits of Consent, 102 Harv. L. Rev. 4, 99-100 (1988), describes the general problem of identifying subsidies and penalties:

> The new constitutional order [comes] to us bereft of the old common law baselines, and without a new baseline to replace it. Given this legal void, it is quite impossible to say that a certain reform introduces either a subsidy or a penalty that needs to be constitutionally justified. Rather, it is just a change among the class of equally permissible permutations. Once all baselines are extinguished, [doctrine] has nothing on which to anchor itself, for there remains no dimension along which strategic behavior or the redistribution of wealth is forbidden. [Justice] Marshall tried to escape this problem by arguing that the mirage of government "neutrality" cannot possibly be used to uphold the statute. After all, employers themselves receive many benefits from the welfare state that are in no way conditioned upon their behavior in labor disputes. To hit union workers with an exclusion from this program fits poorly with the maintenance of government benefits on the other side. But the argument about "neutrality" fares no better [than] the argument about either penalty or subsidy. The complete response to Justice Marshall's point is that in the present constitutional world of labor relations, Congress could exclude employers from a wide variety of economic benefits [without] fear of overstepping constitutional limitations. [The] conscious, systematic elimination of all recognizable baselines makes the idea of "neutrality," powerful in a common law world, [as] empty as that of "penalty" or "subsidy." [The] absence of constitutional principle present no obstacle to the party that wants to sustain the statute. It is fatal only to the party, be it managment or labor, that wants to strike it down.

Page 521. After subsection b of the Note, add the following:

The Court returned to the problem of special benefits for in-state veterans in Attorney General of New York v. Soto-Lopez, 476 U.S. 898 (1986). New York law granted a civil service preference to current New York residents who served in the United States armed forces during time of war and were New York residents when they entered military service. Appellees, who were veterans and long-time residents of New York, were denied the preference because they were residents of Puerto Rico at the time they joined the military. The Court once again held that the discrimination against persons based on prior residency violated the equal protection clause. However, on this occasion, the plurality, in an opinion by Justice Brennan, did not utilize rational basis review. Instead, it held that the classification penalized persons who exercised the fundamental right of interstate migration and therefore had to satisfy strict scrutiny. (The Court's use of strict scrutiny for classifications penalizing the right to travel is discussed in the main text at pages 802-815 infra.) In separate concurrences, both Chief Justice Burger and Justice White argued that the Court should have utilized rational basis review to invalidate the statute. Justice Stevens and

Justice O'Connor, who was joined by Justices Stevens and Rehnquist, filed dissenting opinions.

C. EQUAL PROTECTION METHODOLOGY: HEIGHTENED SCRUTINY AND THE PROBLEM OF RACE

Page 535.   Before section 2 of the Note, add the following:

Compare Kaczorowski, Revolutionary Constitutionalism in the Era of the Civil War and Reconstruction, 61 N.Y.U. L. Rev. 863, 878-879 (1986):

> Racism notwithstanding, Republicans were morally committed to civil rights enforcement in 1866. They felt a general obligation to secure the rights of Americans because they believed that in return for an allegiance to government, citizens were entitled to the protection of the government. [Additionally], many Congressional Republicans felt a particular obligation to protect blacks because they [Republicans] were responsible for the changed status of the former slaves. They also felt obligated to blacks because of the latter's contribution to the Northern war effort during the Civil War.

Page 536.   Before section 3 of the Note, add the following:

Consider Strauss, The Myth of Colorblindness, 1986 Sup. Ct. Rev. 99, 119:

> To the extent these theories assert that racial generalizations are unacceptable because there is too great a danger that they will be factually inaccurate — for example, because they are based on inaccurate stereotypes — the theories miss the point of the prohibition against discrimination. If the prohibition against discrimination were based on the danger that racial generalizations tend to be overgeneralizations, states would be allowed to defend racial generalizations by showing that they are in fact accurate and are not overgeneralizations.
>
> [It] is quite clear, however, that this is not the way the prohibition against discrimination operates.

Page 539.   Before "5. *Group rights.*" add the following:

See Miller, The True Story of Carolene Products, 1987 Sup. Ct. Rev. 397, 428, concluding that the *Carolene Products* footnote

> is obviously misplaced. Public choice theory demonstrates that, in general, "discrete and insular minorities" are exactly the groups that are likely to obtain disproportionately large benefits from the political process. . . . The political theory underlying the *Carolene Products* footnote, now a half-century old, needs to be updated. The results of that process may call in question the Supreme Court's policy of blind deference to legislation favoring special industrial interests. Is it time to re-examine the wisdom of "see-no-evil, hear-no-evil" as the prevailing philosophy in economic regulation cases?

Page 540.   After the Fiss quotation, add the following:

Consider also Colker, Anti-subordination above All: Sex, Race, and Equal
Protection, 61 N.Y.U. L. Rev. 1003, 1005, 1007, 1012-1013 (1986):

> Under the anti-differentiation perspective, it is inappropriate to treat individuals
> differently on the basis of a particular normative view about [race]. . . .
> [In contrast, under] the anti-subordination perspective, it is inappropriate for
> certain groups in society to have subordinated status because of their lack of power in
> society as a whole. . . .
> [The] anti-subordination perspective is consistent with the history of the equal
> protection clause and reflects a living aspiration that will help us move towards a
> world of equality. Historically, the equal protection principle developed to remedy a
> history of subordination against [blacks]. Aspirationally, it reminds us that no group
> should remain subordinated in our [society].
> The anti-differentiation principle, in contrast, does a disservice to this history and
> fundamental aspiration by asserting that discrimination against whites is as problem-
> atic as discrimination against blacks. We have not decided, as a nation, that all
> distinctions are invidious. [We] only prohibit distinctions that we have good reason to
> believe are biased or irrational, and it is group-based experiences that primarily
> inform us as to which kinds of distinctions are biased or irrational, Thus, the anti-
> subordination principle [offers] a substantive explanation for why certain distinctions
> are subjected to closer scrutiny.

Page 541.   Before the Note, add the following:

Is special judicial scrutiny of racial classifications justified by the unconscious,
nonrational character of racial prejudice? Consider Lawrence, The Id, the Ego,
and Equal Protection: Reckoning with Unconscious Racism, 39 Stan. L. Rev.
317, 330, 349 (1987):

> Racism is irrational in the sense that we are not fully aware of the meanings we attach
> to race or why we have made race significant. It is also arguably dysfunctional to the
> extent that its irrationality prevents the optimal use of human resources. [But] unlike
> other forms of irrational and dysfunctional behavior, which we think of as deviant or
> abnormal, racism is "normal." It is a malady that we all share, because we have all
> been scarred by a common history. . . .
> [Unconscious] prejudice presents [a problem] in that it is not subject to self-
> correction within the political process. When racism operates at a conscious level,
> opposing forces can attempt to prevail upon the rationality and moral sensibility of
> racism's proponents. [But] when the discriminator is not aware of his prejudice and is
> convinced that he already walks in the path of righteousness, neither reason nor
> moral persuasion is likely to succeed. The process defect is all the more intractable,
> and judicial scrutiny becomes imperative.

Page 550. After the first paragraph, add the following:

By a 6 to 3 majority, the Court reaffirmed *Rose* in Vasquez v. Hillery, 474 U.S. 254 (1986). Consider the following criticism of the Court's position in Justice Powell's dissenting opinion:

> [The Court's] reasoning ignores established principles of equal protection jurisprudence. We have consistently declined to find a violation of the Equal Protection Clause absent a finding of intentional discrimination. There has been no showing in this case [that] the [grand] jury indicted respondent because of his race, or that the grand jury declined to indict white suspects in the face of similarly strong evidence. Nor is it sensible to assume that impermissible discrimination might have occurred simply because the grand jury had no black members. This Court has never suggested that the racial composition of a grand jury gives rise to the inference that indictments are racially motivated, any more than it has suggested that a suspect arrested by a policeman of a different race may challenge his subsequent conviction on that basis.

Page 551. Before the last paragraph, add the following:

This aspect of *Swain* was overruled in Batson v. Kentucky, 476 U.S. 79 (1986). In an opinion by Justice Powell, the Court held that

> [although] a prosecutor ordinarily is entitled to exercise permitted peremptory challenges "for any reason at all, as long as that reason is related to his view concerning the outcome" of the case to be tried, the Equal Protection Clause forbids the prosecutor to challenge potential jurors solely on account of their race or on the assumption that black jurors as a group will be unable impartially to consider the State's case against a black defendant.

The Court also outlined the procedure a trial judge should follow in evaluating a claim of discriminatory use of peremptory challenges.

> [The] defendant first must show that he is a member of a cognizable racial group and that the prosecutor has exercised peremptory challenges to remove from the venire members of the defendant's race. [The] defendant must [then] show that these facts and any other relevant circumstances raise an inference that the prosecutor used that practice to exclude the veniremen from the petit jury on account of their race. . . .
>
> In deciding whether the defendant has made the requisite showing, the trial court should consider all relevant circumstances. For example, a "pattern" of strikes against black jurors [might] give rise to an inference of discrimination. Similarly, the prosecutor's questions and statements during voir dire examination and in exercising his challenges may support or refute an inference of discriminatory purpose. These examples are merely illustrative. . . .
>
> Once the defendant makes a prima facie showing, the burden shifts to the State to come forward with a neutral explanation for challenging black jurors. Though this requirement imposes a limitation in some cases on the full peremptory character of

the historic challenge, we emphasize that the prosecutor's explanation need not rise to the level justifying exercise of a challenge for cause. But the prosecutor may not rebut the defendant's prima facie case of discrimination by stating merely that he challenged jurors of the defendant's race on the assumption — or his intuitive judgment — that they would be partial to the defendant because of their shared race.

Justices White (the author of *Swain*), Marshall, Stevens, and O'Connor wrote concurring opinions. In a dissenting opinion, Chief Justice Burger, joined by Justice Rehnquist, argued that

> peremptory challenges are often lodged, of necessity, for reasons "normally thought irrelevant to legal proceedings or official actions, namely, the race, religion, nationality, occupation or affiliation of people summoned for jury duty" [*Swain*]. Moreover, in making peremptory challenges, both the prosecutor and defense attorney necessarily act on only limited information or hunch. The process can not be indicted on the sole basis that such decisions are made on the basis of "assumption" or "intuitive judgment." As a result, unadulterated equal protection analysis is simply inapplicable to peremptory challenges exercised in any particular case.

Justice Rehnquist, joined by Chief Justice Burger, also wrote a dissenting opinion:

> [There] is simply nothing "unequal" about the State using its peremptory challenges to strike blacks from the jury in cases involving black defendants so long as such challenges are also used to exclude whites in cases involving white defendants, Hispanics in cases involving Hispanic defendants, Asians in cases involving Asian defendants, and so on. This case-specific use of peremptory challenges by the State does not single out blacks, or members of any other race for that matter, for discriminatory treatment. Such use of peremptories is at best based upon seat-of-the-pants instincts, which are undoubtedly crudely stereotypical and may in many cases be hopelessly mistaken. But as long as they are applied across the board to jurors of all races and nationalities, I do not see [how] their use violates the Equal Protection Clause.

Does *Batson* mean that the use of peremptory challenges to exclude black jurors would violate the equal protection rights of a white defendant? In Holland v. Illinois, — U.S. — (1990), the Court rejected a claim by a white defendant premised on the "fair cross-section" requirement of the sixth amendment jury trial guarantee. However, the Court did not reach the equal protection question, and five of the justices joined concurring and dissenting opinions intimating that a white defendant could object on equal protection grounds to the use of peremptory challenges to exclude blacks from the jury.

Does the Constitution obligate judges to disallow defense peremptory challenges based on race? Cf. Polk County v. Dodson, 454 U.S. 312 (1981) (state employed public defender does not act under color of state law when performing lawyer's traditional functions as counsel to defendant in criminal proceeding). If a defendant exercises peremptory challenges to eliminate black jurors, may the prosecutor constitutionally "even the score" by using peremptory challenges against whites?

Page 556. Before the Note, add the following:

McCLESKEY v. KEMP
481 U.S. 279 (1987)

JUSTICE POWELL delivered the opinion of the Court.

[McCleskey, a black, was convicted in a Georgia state court of murdering a white and sentenced to death. On habeas corpus, he alleged that the Georgia capital sentencing scheme was administered in a racially discriminatory manner in violation of the equal protection clause.

In support of this claim, he proffered a statistical study prepared by Professor David Baldus (the "Baldus study") that examined over 2,000 murder cases occurring in Georgia in the 1970s. The raw numbers collected by Baldus indicated that the death penalty was assessed in 22 percent of the cases involving black defendants and white victims; 8 percent of the cases involving white defendants and white victims; 1 percent of the cases involving black defendants and black victims; and 3 percent of the cases involving white defendants and black victims.

Baldus then subjected his data to statistical analysis that attempted to account for other variables that might have explained these differences on nonracial grounds. After taking into account a variety of nonracial variables, he concluded that defendants charged with killing whites were 4.3 times as likely to receive a death sentence as defendants charged with killing blacks. The study further indicated that black defendants who killed white victims had the greatest likelihood of receiving a death sentence.

The district court found the Baldus study flawed in several respects, held that it "[failed] to contribute anything of value" to McCleskey's claim, and dismissed the petition. The court of appeals affirmed. Although it assumed arguendo that the study was valid, the court held that the statistics were "insufficient to demonstrate discriminatory intent."]

Our analysis begins with the basic principle that a defendant who alleges an equal protection violation has the burden of proving "the existence of purposeful discrimination." [7] Thus, to prevail under the Equal Protection

---

7. [As] did the Court of Appeals, we assume the study is valid statistically without reviewing the factual findings of the District Court. Our assumption that the Baldus study is statistically valid does not include the assumption that the study shows that racial considerations actually enter into any sentencing decisions in Georgia. Even a sophisticated multiple regression analysis such as the Baldus study can only demonstrate a *risk* that the factor of race entered into some capital sentencing decisions and a necessarily lesser risk that race entered into any particular sentencing decision. [Relocated footnote.]

Clause, McCleskey must prove that the decisionmakers in *his* case acted with discriminatory purpose. He offers no evidence specific to his own case that would support an inference that racial considerations played a part in his sentence. . . .

The Court has accepted statistics as proof of intent to discriminate in certain limited contexts [such as jury discrimination cases and job discrimination cases brought under Title VII of the 1964 Civil Rights Act].

But the nature of the capital sentencing decision, and the relationship of the statistics to that decision, are fundamentally different from the corresponding elements in the venire-selection or Title VII cases. Most importantly, each particular decision to impose the death penalty is made by a petit jury selected from a properly constituted venire. Each jury is unique in its composition, and the Constitution requires that its decision rest on consideration of innumerable factors that vary according to the characteristics of the individual defendant and the facts of the particular capital offense. Thus, the application of an inference drawn from the general statistics to a specific decision in a trial and sentencing simply is not comparable to the application of an inference drawn from general statistics to a specific venire-selection or Title VII case. In those cases, the statistics relate to fewer entities, and fewer variables are relevant to the challenged decisions.

Another important difference [is] that, in the venire-selection and Title VII contexts, the decisionmaker has an opportunity to explain the statistical disparity. Here, the State has no practical opportunity to rebut the Baldus study. [The] policy considerations behind a prosecutor's traditionally "wide discretion" suggest the impropriety of our requiring prosecutors to defend their decisions to seek death penalties, "often years after they were made." [17] Moreover, absent far stronger proof, it is unnecessary to seek such a rebuttal, because a legitimate and unchallenged explanation for the decision is apparent from the record: McCleskey committed an act for which the United States Constitution and Georgia laws permit imposition of the death penalty.

Finally, McCleskey's statistical proffer must be viewed in the context of his challenge. McCleskey challenges decisions at the heart of the State's criminal justice system. [Because] discretion is essential to the criminal justice process, we would demand exceptionally clear proof before we would infer that the discretion has been abused. . . .

McCleskey also suggests that the Baldus study proves that the State as a whole has acted with a discriminatory purpose. He appears to argue that the State has violated the Equal Protection Clause by adopting the capital punishment statute and allowing it to remain in force despite its allegedly dis-

17. Requiring a prosecutor to rebut a study that analyzes the past conduct of scores of prosecutors is quite different from requiring a prosecutor to rebut a contemporaneous challenge to his own acts. See Batson v. Kentucky, 476 U. S. 79 (1986).

criminatory application. But " '[d]iscriminatory purpose' . . . implies more than intent as volition or intent as awareness of consequences. It implies that the decisionmaker, in this case a state legislature, selected or reaffirmed a particular course of action at least in part 'because of,' not merely 'in spite of,' its adverse effects upon an identifiable group." [*Feeney.*] For this claim to prevail, McCleskey would have to prove that the Georgia Legislature enacted or maintained the death penalty statute *because of* an anticipated racially discriminatory effect. [There is] no evidence [that] the Georgia Legislature enacted the capital punishment statute to further a racially discriminatory purpose.

Nor has McCleskey demonstrated that the legislature maintains the capital punishment statute because of the racially disproportionate impact suggested by the Baldus study. As legislatures necessarily have wide discretion in the choice of criminal laws and penalties, and as there were legitimate reasons for the Georgia Legislature to adopt and maintain capital punishment we will not infer a discriminatory purpose on the part of the State of Georgia. . . .

There is, of course, some risk of racial prejudice influencing a jury's decision in a criminal case. [The] question "is at what point that risk becomes constitutionally unacceptable," Turner v. Murray, 476 U. S. — , — , n. 8 (1986). McCleskey asks us to accept the likelihood allegedly shown by the Baldus study as the constitutional measure of an unacceptable risk of racial prejudice influencing capital sentencing decisions. This we decline to do.

Because of the risk that the factor of race may enter the criminal justice process, we have engaged in "unceasing efforts" to eradicate racial prejudice from our criminal justice system. Batson v. Kentucky, 476 U.S. — , — (1986). . . . Our efforts have been guided by our recognition that "the inestimable privilege of trial by jury . . . is a vital principle, underlying the whole administration of criminal justice," Ex parte Milligan, 4 Wall. 2, 123 (1866). . . .

[The] capital sentencing decision requires the individual jurors to focus their collective judgment on the unique characteristics of a particular criminal defendant. It is not surprising that such collective judgments often are difficult to explain. But the inherent lack of predictability of jury decisions does not justify their condemnation. On the contrary, it is the jury's function to make the difficult and uniquely human judgments that defy codification and that "buil[d] discretion, equity, and flexibility into a legal system." H. Kalven & H. Zeisel, The American Jury 498 (1966).

McCleskey's argument that the Constitution condemns the discretion allowed decisionmakers in the Georgia capital sentencing system is antithetical to the fundamental role of discretion in our criminal justice system. [Of] course, "the power to be lenient [also] is the power to discriminate," K. Davis, Discretionary Justice 170 (1973), but a capital-punishment system that did not allow for discretionary acts of leniency "would be totally alien to our notions of criminal justice." Gregg v. Georgia, 428 U.S. 153, 200, n. 50 (1976).

[Where] the discretion that is fundamental to our criminal process is involved, we decline to assume that what is unexplained is invidious. In light of the safeguards designed to minimize racial bias in the process, the fundamental value of jury trial in our criminal justice system, and the benefits that discretion provides to criminal defendants, we hold that the Baldus study does not demonstrate a constitutionally significant risk of racial bias affecting the Georgia capital-sentencing process.

Two additional concerns inform our decision in this case. First, McCleskey's claim, taken to its logical conclusion, throws into serious question the principles that underlie our entire criminal justice system. [If] we accepted McCleskey's claim that racial bias has impermissibly tainted the capital sentencing decision, we could soon be faced with similar claims as to other types of penalty. Moreover, the claim that his sentence rests on the irrelevant factor of race easily could be extended to apply to claims based on unexplained discrepancies that correlate to membership in other minority groups, and even to gender. [The] Constitution does not require that a State eliminate any demonstrable disparity that correlates with a potentially irrelevant factor in order to operate a criminal justice system that includes capital punishment. . . .

Second, McCleskey's arguments are best presented to the legislative bodies. It is not the responsibility — or indeed even the right — of this Court to determine the appropriate punishment for particular crimes. [Legislatures are] better qualified to weigh and "evaluate the results of statistical studies in terms of their own local conditions and with a flexibility of approach that is not available to the courts," [Gregg.] Capital punishment is now the law in more than two thirds of our States. It is the ultimate duty of courts to determine on a case-by-case basis whether these laws are applied consistently with the Constitution. Despite McCleskey's wide ranging arguments that basically challenge the validity of capital punishment in our multi-racial society, the only question before us is whether in his case the law of Georgia was properly applied. We agree with the District Court and the Court of Appeals . . . [that] this was carefully and correctly done in this case.

[Affirmed.]

JUSTICE BRENNAN, with whom JUSTICE MARSHALL, [JUSTICE BLACK-MUN, and JUSTICE STEVENS] join, dissenting. . . .

At some point in this case, Warren McCleskey doubtless asked his lawyer whether a jury was likely to sentence him to die. A candid reply to this question would have been disturbing. [The] story could be told in a variety of ways, but McCleskey could not fail to grasp its essential narrative line: there was a significant chance that race would play a prominent role in determing if he lived or died. . . .

The Baldus study indicates that, after taking into account some 230 nonracial factors that might legitimately influence a sentencer, the jury *more likely than not* would have spared McCleskey's life had his victim been black. . . .

Evaluation of McCleskey's evidence cannot rest solely on the numbers themselves. We must also ask whether the conclusion suggested by those numbers is consonant with our understanding of history and human experience. Georgia's legacy of a race-conscious criminal justice system, as well as this Court's own recognition of the persistent danger that racial attitudes may affect criminal proceedings, indicate that McCleskey's claim is not a fanciful product of mere statistical artifice.

For many years, Georgia operated openly and formally precisely the type of dual system the evidence shows is still effectively in place. The criminal law expressly differentiated between crimes committed by and against blacks and whites, distinctions whose lineage traced back to the time of slavery. . . .

This historical review of Georgia criminal law is not intended as a bill of indictment calling the State to account for past transgressions. Citation of past practices does not justify the automatic condemnation of current ones. But it would be unrealistic to ignore the influence of history in assessing the plausible implications of McCleskey's evidence. "[A]mericans share a historical experience that has resulted in individuals within the culture ubiquitously attaching a significance to race that is irrational and often outside their awareness." Lawrence, The Id, The Ego, and Equal Protection: Reckoning With Unconscious Racism, 39 Stan. L. Rev. 327 (1987). . . .

It is true that every nuance of decision cannot be statistically captured, nor can any individual judgment be plumbed with absolute certainty. Yet the fact that we must always act without the illumination of complete knowledge cannot induce paralysis when we confront what is literally an issue of life and death. Sentencing data, history, and experience all counsel that Georgia has provided insufficient assurance of the heightened rationality we have required in order to take a human life. . . .

The Court maintains that petitioner's claim "is antithetical to the fundamental role of discretion in our criminal justice system." . . .

Reliance on race in imposing capital punishment, however, is antithetical to the very rationale for granting sentencing discretion. Discretion is a means, not an end. . . .

Considering the race of a defendant or victim in deciding if the death penalty should be imposed is completely at odds with [the] concern that an individual be evaluated as a unique human being. Decisions influenced by race rest in part on a categorical assessment of the worth of human beings according to color, insensitive to whatever qualities the individuals in question may possess. . . .

The Court next states that its unwillingness to regard the petitioner's evidence as sufficient is based in part on the fear that recognition of McCleskey's claim would open the door to widespread challenges to all aspects of criminal sentencing. Taken on its face, such a statement seems to suggest a fear of too much justice. Yet surely the majority would acknowledge that if striking evidence indicated that other minority groups, or women, or even persons with blond hair, were disproportionately sentenced to death, such a state of affairs would be repugnant to deeply rooted conceptions of fairness. The prospect that there may be more widespread abuse than McCleskey documents may be dismaying, but it does not justify complete abdication of our judicial role. . . .

Finally, the Court justifies its rejection of McCleskey's claim by cautioning against usurpation of the legislatures' role in devising and monitoring criminal punishment. . . .

Those whom we would banish from society or from the human community itself often speak in too faint a voice to be heard above society's demand for punishment. It is the particular role of courts to hear these voices, for the Constitution declares that the majoritarian chorus may not alone dictate the conditions of social life. The Court thus fulfills, rather than disrupts, the scheme of separation of powers by closely scrutinizing the imposition of the death [penalty]. . . .

It is tempting to pretend that minorities on death row share a fate in no way connected to our own, that our treatment of them sounds no echoes beyond the chambers in which they die. Such an illusion is ultimately corrosive, for the reverberations of injustice are not so easily confined. "The destinies of the two races in this country are indissolubly linked together," [Plessy v. Ferguson (Harlan, J., dissenting)], and the way in which we choose those who will die reveals the depth of moral commitment among the living.

The Court's decision today will not change what attorneys in Georgia tell other Warren McCleskeys about their chances of execution. Nothing will soften the harsh message they must convey, nor alter the prospect that race undoubtedly will continue to be a topic of discussion. McCleskey's evidence will not have obtained judicial acceptance, but that will not affect what is said on death row. However many criticisms of today's decision may be rendered, these painful conversations will serve as the most eloquent dissents of all.

[A dissenting opinion by Justice Blackmun, joined by Justices Marshall and Stevens and, in part, by Justice Brennan, is omitted.]

JUSTICE STEVENS, with whom JUSTICE BLACKMUN joins, dissenting. . . .

The Court's decision appears to be based on a fear that the acceptance of McCleskey's claim would sound the death knell for capital punishment in Georgia. If society were indeed forced to choose between a racially discriminatory death penalty (one that provides heightened protection against murder "for whites only") and no death penalty at all, the choice mandated by the Constitution would be plain. But the Court's fear is unfounded. One of the lessons of the Baldus study is that there exist certain categories of extremely serious crimes for which prosecutors consistently seek, and juries consistently impose, the death penalty without regard to the race of the victim or the race of the offender. If Georgia were to narrow the class of death-eligible defendants to those categories, the danger of arbitrary and discriminatory imposition of the death penalty would be significantly decreased, if not eradicated. . . .

For critical discussion of *McCleskey*, see Kennedy, *McCleskey v. Kemp:* Rule, Capital Punishment, and the Supreme Court, 101 Harv. L. Rev. 1388 (1988), suggesting that one of the relevant rights in the case, unaddressed by the Court, was the right of black people to be protected against criminal violence on equal terms with white people. If the Court had focussed on this problem, how should it have written the opinion? See also Carter, When Victims Happen to be Black, 97 Yale L.J. 420 (1988), emphasizing judicial and societal devaluation of the interests of black victims of criminal violence.

On the basis of the arguments of Kennedy and Carter, can you construct a general argument to the effect that there is unconstitutionality in the differential risk of criminal violence faced by black people? Such an argument would have at least plausible foundations in the original understanding of the equal protection clause, which was designed in part to ensure that black people would be equally protected from private criminality. One might limit such an argument to the context of the death penalty; but its implications could be far broader. Consider the possibility that such an argument would call into question prosecutorial and sentencing decisions as well as the distribution of police protection. Could such an argument be made plausible in the context of sex discrimination?

Page 562.   Before the Note, add the following:

For a discussion of the appropriate role of purpose and effect in vote dilution cases involving political, as opposed to racial, gerrymandering, see Davis v. Bandemer, Supplement to Casebook page 786 infra.

Page 602.   Before the Note, add the following:

For a discussion of the Court's most recent efforts to resolve the benign discrimination problem, see Supplement to Casebook page 610 infra.

Page 604.   Before subsection c of the Note, add the following:

For an interesting discussion, see Sherry, Selective Judicial Activism in the Equal Protection Context: Democracy, Distrust, and Deconstruction, 73 Geo. L.J. 89, 114-118 (1984).

Page 606.   Before subsection f of the Note, add the following:

In Wygant v. Jackson Board of Education, 476 U.S. 267 (1986), a plurality of the Court held that a governmental entity could not constitutionally remedy prior employment discrimination through a program of race conscious layoffs. For a fuller discussion, see Supplement to Casebook page 610 infra.

In connection with the "innocent victim" argument, consider Sullivan, Sins of Discrimination: Last Term's Affirmative Action Cases, 100 Harv. L. Rev. 78, 80-81, 96 (1986):

> [The] Court has approved affirmative action only as precise penance for the specific sins of racism a government, union, or employer has committed in the past. Not surprisingly, this approach has invited claims [that] nonsinners — white workers "innocent" of their bosses' or union leadership's past discrimination — should not pay for "the sins of others of their own race," [*Fullilove*], nor should nonvictims benefit from their sacrifice. . . .
>
> But public and private employers often adopt affirmative action less to purge their past than to build their future. In so doing, they are not "engineering" racial balance as an end in itself but are promoting a variety of goals dependent on racial balance, from securing workplace peace to eliminating workplace caste. . . .
>
> If such aspirations for the future rather than past sin were the basis for affirmative action, would white claims of "innocence" count for less? They should, for it is easier to show that displacing "innocent" whites is narrowly tailored to goals that turn on integrating institutions now than it is to show that doing so is narrowly tailored to purging past sins of discrimination that the displaced whites did not themselves "commit."

Consider also Strauss, The Myth of Colorblindness, 1986 Sup. Ct. Rev. 99, 100, 105-106:

> The prohibition against discrimination established by *Brown* is not rooted in colorblindness at all. Instead, it is, like affirmative action, deeply race-conscious; like affirmative action, the prohibition against discrimination reflects a deliberate decision to treat blacks differently from other groups, even at the expense of innocent whites. It follows that affirmative action is not at odds with the principle of nondiscrimination established by *Brown* but is instead logically continuous with that principle. It also follows that the interesting question is not whether the Constitution permits affirmative action but why the Constitution does not require affirmative action.

Professor Strauss uses Palmore v. Sidoti to support this view:

> In *Palmore* Florida disadvantaged a black on the basis of a race-neutral "best interest of the child" criterion. In the ordinary university admissions process, Florida disadvantages (that is, rejects) many black applicants on the basis of race-neutral admissions criteria. What Florida did in *Palmore* was unconstitutional because it made decisive a black person's disability — Palmore's inability to provide a psychologically

healthy upbringing for the child — that was caused by racial prejudice in society as a whole. If blacks' deficiencies in undergraduate grades and standardized test scores are the causal product of racial prejudice in society as a whole, how does denying them admission differ from what Florida did in *Palmore*? Why isn't the application of a race-neutral admissions policy unconstitutional because, like the race-neutral "best interests of the child" criterion, it gives weight to disabilities that blacks genuinely have but that are the product of private prejudice.

Consider also the view that the attack on affirmative action — indeed the very term — depends on *Lochner*-like understandings that take the status quo as the baseline for distinguishing between action and inaction, or partisanship and neutrality. Does this view, or that of Professor Strauss, understate the socially corrosive effects of state action that takes race into account?

Page 610.   Before section D, add the following:

NOTE: FROM FULLILOVE TO CROSON: THE EMPLOYMENT CASES

1. *The pre-*Croson *compromise.* Between 1980, when the Court decided *Fullilove* and its 1989 decision in City of Richmond v. J. A. Croson Co., the Court decided a series of cases in which affirmative action measures were utilized to remedy employment discrimination. Throughout this period, the Court remained closely divided on the issues posed by these programs and continued to disagree concerning the appropriate goals and standard of review for them. Nevertheless, a few clear principles seemed to emerge. The Court appeared to steer a middle course between the extremes of completely outlawing affirmative action programs and granting them automatic approval.

On the one hand, the Court made plain that the voluntary use by government employers of race-conscious "goals" or "timetables" designed to remedy prior discrimination was not per se unconstitutional. It was also permissible for these race-conscious measures to provide for "class-wide" relief, and there was no requirement that they be limited to "making whole" the actual victims of prior discriminatory acts. Moreover, court-ordered affirmative action plans (directed at either public or private entities) to remedy violations of the Constitution or of the statutory mandate against employment discrimination were also not per se unconstitutional. (Whether such orders are within the power granted to federal courts under Title VII of the 1964 Civil Rights Act poses difficult issues of statutory construction that are touched upon only briefly in the materials that follow).

On the other hand, the Court repeatedly recognized that race-conscious remedies pose potentially serious constitutional problems and must therefore be carefully scrutinized. During this period, the Court failed to agree on a verbal formulation describing either the appropriate standard of review for such remedies or the characteristics a plan must have to survive review. The cases seemed to indicate, however, that the Court was unwilling to accept race-conscious measures as the norm. It was therefore important that affirmative action plans be bounded in some fashion. The Court made clear that it was unlikely to approve loosely drafted race-conscious measures not closely tied to remediation of prior violations. Moreover, the Court was sensitive to the claims of the "innocent victims" of race-conscious measures. The fact that there were such "victims" was not necessarily fatal to a race-conscious plan. But a plan was more likely to survive constitutional attack if its costs were broadly diffused and, in particular, if it did not interfere with the seniority-based expectations of present employees.

In reviewing the cases summarized below, consider whether they develop a coherent, analytically sound approach to the affirmative action problem. Should the holdings of these cases be applicable in contexts other than employment? Do they provide adequate guidance to lower courts and to governmental employers contemplating affirmative action plans? Are they sufficiently sensitive to the risks posed by a racial "spoils system"? To the plight of minorities held back by years of discrimination who, nonetheless, are unable to point to specific discriminatory conduct by a potential employer?

2. *The cases.* During this period, the Court decided three important affirmative action cases in the employment context.*

---

* Two other recent cases have upheld affirmative action plans against nonconstitutional attacks. Local No. 93, Intl. Assn. of Firefighters v. Cleveland, 478 U.S. 501 (1986), concerned a consent decree providing for race-conscious promotions in the Cleveland fire department. The decree terminated a suit brought against the city by a group of black and Hispanic firefighters. A local union, which had been permitted to intervene at the trial level, argued that the decree violated Title VII because it created a preference benefiting some minority workers who could not demonstrate that they had been personally victimized by prior acts of discrimination. In an opinion by Justice Brennan, the Court held that, whether or not such remedies could be legally imposed after trial, Title VII did not preclude the city from voluntarily entering a consent decree benefiting individuals who were not the actual victims of discrimination. Because the consent decree did not purport to resolve any of the constitutional issues posed by the affirmative action plan, and because the union had failed to raise these issues below, the Court did not address them.

In Johnson v. Transportation Agency, 480 U.S. 616 (1987), the Court upheld a voluntary affirmative action plan designed to increase the number of women working in traditionally male positions. Although not admitting any prior statutory or constitutional violation, the Santa Clara County Transit District Board of Supervisors found that women were significantly underrepresented in certain job categories, in part because women "had not traditionally been employed in these positions." Accordingly, it adopted an affirmative action plan that set aside no specific number of positions for women, but authorized consideration of gender as a factor when evaluating qualified candidates. When petitioner, a male employee, was passed over for promotion in favor of a woman, he brought suit claiming violation of Title VII.

The Court, in an opinion by Justice Brennan, held that the "manifest imbalance" in the number of women in the relevant job categories shielded the plan from Title VII attack even though the imbalance alone might not have been sufficient to make out a prima facie Title VII violation against the employer. The Court emphasized that gender was only one of numerous factors the

a. *Wygant.* Prior to 1954, the Jackson, Michigan, public schools employed no black teachers. In 1969, when minority representation had risen to only 3.9 percent, the NAACP filed a complaint with the Michigan Civil Rights Commission alleging employment discrimination. In settlement of the complaint, the commission issued an "order of adjustment" under which the Board of Education agreed to take "affirmative steps" to hire minority teachers.

As a result of these efforts, the percentage of minority teachers grew to 8.8 percent by 1971. In that year, however, faculty layoffs became necessary and seniority provisions in the collective bargaining agreement between the board and the teachers union resulted in the discharge of many of the newly hired black teachers. In 1972, with racial tensions in the schools rising, the board and union negotiated a new collective bargaining agreement. It provided, inter alia, that in the future, when the number of teachers was reduced through layoffs, teachers with the most seniority would be retained, except that at no time would the percentage of minorities to be laid off exceed the percentage of minorities employed at the time of the layoffs. As a result of this provision, some white teachers were laid off, despite the fact that they had more seniority than blacks who were retained. Laid-off white teachers brought this action alleging that the layoffs violated their rights under the equal protection clause.

The district court dismissed the action. It held that the preferential layoff provision need not be grounded on a finding of prior discrimination and was permissible as an attempt to correct societal discrimination by providing "role models" for minority school children. The court of appeals affirmed.

In Wygant v. Jackson Board of Education, 476 U.S. 267 (1986), a narrowly divided Court reversed and held the preferential layoff provision unconstitutional. Although five justices agreed that the provision violated the equal protection clause, the majority could not agree as to the reasons for its decision.

Justice Powell announced the Court's judgment. In portions of his opinion joined by Chief Justice Burger and Justices Rehnquist and O'Connor, he held that the goal of providing "minority role models" for black students in order to overcome societal discrimination was not sufficiently "compelling" to support the layoff provision.

> This Court never has held that societal discrimination alone is sufficient to justify a racial classification. Rather, the Court has insisted upon some showing of prior

---

agency considered in promotion decisions; that the plan set aside no positions for women; that it was designed to attain, rather than maintain an appropriate balance in the work force; and that it upset no "legitimate firmly rooted expectation" of the petitioner. No constitutional issues respecting the plan were raised below, and the Court therefore decided only the Title VII issues posed by it. Nonetheless, the Court's opinion was widely interpreted as setting out new guidelines for permissible affirmative action plans. How would (should) the Court have decided the constitutional issue posed by the plan? Consider whether *Johnson* marks the abandonment of the requirement that government-sponsored affirmative action plans be tied to the remediation of a past violation by the governmental unit adopting the plan.

discrimination by the governmental unit involved before allowing limited use of racial classifications in order to remedy such discrimination. . . .

The role model theory allows the Board to engage in discriminatory hiring and layoff practices long past the point required by any legitimate remedial purpose. . . .

Moreover, because the role model theory does not necessarily bear a relationship to the harm caused by prior discriminatory hiring practices, it actually could be used to escape the obligation to remedy such practices by justifying the small percentage of black teachers by reference to the small percentage of black students. . . .

No one doubts that there has been serious racial discrimination in this country. But as the basis for imposing discriminatory *legal* remedies that work against innocent people, societal discrimination is insufficient and over expansive. In the absence of particularized findings, a court could uphold remedies that are ageless in their reach into the past, and timeless in their ability to affect the future.

Having disposed of the district court's justification for the layoff provision, the plurality turned to the board's contention that the provision remedied prior specific acts of employment discrimination. With regard to this argument, the plurality noted that before adopting an affirmative action program, a public employer must have "convincing evidence that remedial action is warranted. That is, it must have sufficient evidence to justify the conclusion that there has been prior discrimination." It follows that when such a program is challenged in court, the trial judge

> must make a factual determination that the employer had a strong basis in evidence for its conclusion that remedial action was necessary. The ultimate burden remains with the employees to demonstrate the unconstitutionality of an affirmative action program. But unless such a determination is made, an appellate court reviewing a challenge to remedial action by nonminority employees cannot determine whether the race-based action is justified as a remedy for prior discrimination.

In this case, however, the plurality believed it unnecessary to decide whether the board should be afforded an opportunity to demonstrate past discrimination, since the layoff provision was not a legally appropriate means of achieving even the compelling purpose of remedying such discrimination. In a portion of his opinion joined only by Chief Justice Burger and Justice Rehnquist, Justice Powell argued that loss of an existing job imposed too severe a burden on nonminority employees to meet constitutional standards.

> While hiring goals impose a diffuse burden, often foreclosing only one of several opportunities, layoffs impose the entire burden of achieving racial equality on particular individuals, often resulting in serious disruption of their lives. That burden is too intrusive. We therefore hold that, as a means of accomplishing purposes that otherwise may be legitimate, the Board's layoff plan is not sufficiently narrowly tailored. Other, less intrusive means of accomplishing similar purposes — such as the adoption of hiring goals — are available.

In a short concurring opinion, Justice White agreed that

[whatever] the legitimacy of hiring goals or quotas may be, the discharge of white teachers to make room for blacks, none of whom has been shown to be a victim of any racial discrimination, is quite a different matter. I cannot believe that in order to integrate a work force, it would be permissible to discharge whites and hire blacks until the latter comprised a suitable percentage of the work force.

In a longer concurrence, Justice O'Connor noted her agreement with the plurality's rejection of the "societal discrimination" and "role model" theories. She emphasized, however, that she did not read the plurality as requiring, and would not herself require, an antecedent finding of prior discrimination before a public employer could adopt a voluntary affirmative action plan.

A violation of [constitutional] requirements does not arise with the making of a finding; it arises when the wrong is committed. Contemporaneous findings serve solely as a means by which it can be made absolutely certain that the governmental actor truly is attempting to remedy its own unlawful conduct when it adopts an affirmative action plan, rather than attempting to alleviate the wrongs suffered through general societal discrimination. . . .

The imposition of a requirement that public employers make findings that they have engaged in illegal discrimination before they engage in affirmative action programs would severely undermine public employers' incentive to meet voluntarily their civil rights obligations. . . .

[Moreover, imposing] a contemporaneous findings requirement would produce the anomalous result that what private employers may voluntarily do to correct apparent violations of Title VII, public employers are constitutionally forbidden to do to correct their statutory and constitutional transgressions.

Consequently, Justice O'Connor concluded, a remedial goal is sufficient to support an affirmative action plan, whether or not the employer has made particularized findings, unless the plaintiffs attacking the plan meet their burden of persuading the trial court that the employer's evidence did not support an inference of prior discrimination.

Like the rest of the plurality, Justice O'Connor thought it unnecessary to decide whether plaintiffs had met that burden in this case. But unlike the other plurality justices, she also would not have resolved the "troubling question" of whether layoffs were a constitutional means of remediation. Instead, she thought the provision was constitutionally deficient because

[the] hiring goal that the layoff provision was designed to safeguard was tied to the percentage of minority students in the school district, not to the percentage of qualified minority teachers within the relevant labor pool. [Because] the layoff provision here acts to maintain levels of minority hiring that have no relation to remedying employment discrimination, it cannot be adjudged "narrowly tailored" to effectuate its asserted remedial purpose.

In a dissenting opinion joined by Justices Brennan and Blackmun, Justice Marshall argued that the Court should leave undisturbed the voluntary, negotiated efforts to resolve disputes over minority hiring.

> I, too, believe that layoffs are unfair. But unfairness ought not be confused with constitutional injury. [The] plurality would nullify years of negotiation and compromise designed to solve serious educational problems in the public schools of Jackson, Michigan. Because I believe that a public employer, with the full agreement of its employees, should be permitted to preserve the benefits of a legitimate and constitutional affirmative-action hiring plan even while reducing its work force, I dissent.

In a separate dissenting opinion, Justice Stevens defended the "role model" justification for the provision.

> In the context of public education, it is quite obvious that a school board may reasonably conclude that an integrated faculty will be able to provide benefits to the student body that could not be provided by an all white, or nearly all white, faculty. For one of the most important lessons that the American public schools teach is that the diverse ethnic, cultural, and national backgrounds that have been brought together in our famous "melting pot" do not identify essential differences among the human beings that inhabit our land. It is one thing for a white child to be taught by a white teacher that color, like beauty, is only "skin deep"; it is far more convincing to experience that truth on a day to day basis during the routine, ongoing learning process.

b. *Sheet Metal Workers.* Local 28, Sheet Metal Workers Intl. Assn. v. EEOC, 478 U.S. 421 (1986), unlike *Wygant*, concerned affirmative action goals imposed by a court on an unwilling party. In 1975, a district court found that Local 28 of the Sheet Metal Workers Union had violated Title VII by discriminating against nonwhite workers in admission to the union. After finding that the union had flouted previous court mandates to desegregate, the court concluded that the imposition of a numerical "racial goal," tied to the percentage of nonwhites in the relevant workforce, was essential to remedy the Title VII violation. When the union failed to meet this goal, the trial court determined that its failure was due to continued efforts to impede the admission of nonwhites. It therefore held the union in contempt. In order to remedy the contempt, the court imposed a $150,000 fine to be placed in a fund designed to increase nonwhite membership in the apprenticeship program. The union thereupon sought review of the contempt citation, contending that the membership goal and the fund were unconstitutional and beyond the court's powers under Title VII because they extended race-conscious preferences to individuals who were not identified victims of the union's prior discrimination.

The Court rejected these arguments and affirmed the judgment below. Most of Justice Brennan's opinion announcing the judgment was devoted to demonstrating that the race-conscious remedies ordered by the trial judge were within his powers under Title VII. (Writing for four justices, the plurality concluded that although Title VII did not require employers to engage in affirmative action in order to avoid an initial violation of the law, once an egregious violation had been established, race-conscious measures were a permissible remedy.) At the conclusion of its opinion, however, the plurality turned to the constitutional issues posed by the membership goal and the fund. In a portion of his opinion joined by Justices Marshall, Blackmun, and Stevens, Justice Brennan made the following argument:

> We have consistently recognized that government bodies constitutionally may adopt racial classifications as a remedy for past discrimination. See [*Wygant; Fullilove; Bakke; Swann*]. We have not agreed, however, on the proper test to be applied in analyzing the constitutionality of race conscious remedial measures. We need not resolve this dispute here, since we conclude that the relief ordered in this case passes even the most rigorous test — it is narrowly tailored to further the Government's compelling interest in remedying past discrimination.
>
> In this case, there is no problem, as there was in *Wygant*, with a proper showing of prior discrimination that would justify the use of remedial racial classifications. [The] District Court's orders were properly tailored to accomplish [remediation. They] will have only a marginal impact on the interests of white workers. [Petitioners] concede that the District Court's orders did not disadvantage *existing* union members. While white applicants for union membership may be denied certain benefits available to their nonwhite counterparts, the court's orders do not stand as an absolute bar to the admission of such individuals.

In a concurring opinion, Justice Powell agreed that the finding below that the union had engaged in egregious Title VII violations provided a compelling governmental interest sufficient to justify a race-conscious remedy. He also agreed that the remedy was "narrowly tailored" to the goal of eradicating the union's prior discrimination. In support of this position, Justice Powell emphasized that on the facts before it, the trial court probably did not have available any other effective remedy. Moreover, the numerical goal was imposed for only a limited period, was directly related to the percentage of nonwhites in the workforce, and was flexible in its application. Justice Powell thought that this flexibility was especially significant because it

> [reflected] a recognition that neither the Constitution nor Title VII requires a particular racial balance in the workplace. Indeed, the Constitution forbids such a requirement if imposed for its own sake. [Thus], a court may not choose a remedy for the purpose of attaining a particular racial balance; rather, remedies properly are confined to the elimination of proven discrimination.

Finally, Justice Powell, like the plurality, thought it important that the trial court's order did not require the laying off of nonminority union members.

In separate opinions, Justices White, Rehnquist (in an opinion joined by Chief Justice Burger), and O'Connor all stated that they would reverse the lower court on statutory grounds. None of the opinions reached the union's constitutional claims.

c. *Paradise.* In 1972, a district court found that the Alabama Department of Public Safety had systematically excluded blacks from employment in violation of the equal protection clause. Almost twelve years later, and after extensive litigation and delay, the same court found that "the effects of [the Department's unconstitutional] policies and practices remain pervasive and conspicuous at all ranks above the entry level." After finding that the Department still lacked constitutionally adequate promotional procedures, and faced with the Department's immediate need to promote officers to the rank of corporal, the court ordered that "for a period of time" at least 50 percent of the promotions to this rank be awarded to black troopers if qualified black candidates were available. Moreover, in order to prevent further delay in the development of adequate promotion procedures for all ranks, the court imposed a 50 percent black promotional quota on all upper ranks so long as there were qualified black candidates, the rank was presently less than 25 percent black, and the Department had not developed and implemented a promotion plan without adverse impact on blacks for the relevant rank.

In United States v. Paradise, 480 U.S. 92 (1987), the Supreme Court affirmed the district court's order. In a plurality opinion joined by Justices Marshall, Blackmun, and Powell, Justice Brennan assumed, without deciding, that the remedial order had to survive strict scrutiny and held that it did so because it was "narrowly tailored" to serve a "compelling governmental purpose."

The plurality had no difficulty concluding that there was a compelling governmental interest in eradicating past and present discrimination by a state actor, as well as in enforcing prior judgments of federal courts. In determining whether the race conscious remedy was "narrowly tailored," the plurality looked to a number of factors, including the "necessity for the relief and efficacy of alternative remedies; the flexibility and duration of the relief, including the availability of waiver provisions; the relationship of the numerical goals to the relevant labor market; and the impact of relief on the rights of third parties."

Judged by these standards, the plurality argued, the district court's use of a one-for-one quota survived constitutional scrutiny. In light of the extensive record of delay, alternatives proposed by the Department, including a promise to develop fair promotion procedures in the future, would not have served the court's purposes. The requirement could be waived if no qualified black candidates were available. Moreover, the requirement was only temporary and endured "only until the Department comes up with a procedure that does not have a discriminatory impact on blacks — something the Department was enjoined to do in 1972 and expressly promised to do by 1980."

The plurality was also satisfied that the one-for-one requirement bore an adequate relationship to the percentage of nonwhites in the workforce, even though only 25 percent of the workforce was black.

> To achieve the goal of 25% black representation in the upper ranks, the court was not limited to ordering the promotion of only 25% blacks at any one time. Some promptness in the administration of relief was plainly justified in this case, and use of deadlines or end-dates had proven ineffective. In these circumstances, the use of a temporary requirement of 50% minority promotions, which [was] crafted and applied flexibly, was constitutionally permissible.

The plurality was also satisfied that the one-for-one requirement did not impose unacceptable burdens on innocent third parties.

> [The] temporary and extremely limited nature of the requirement substantially limits any potential burden on white applicants for promotion. [The] court [has not] imposed an "absolute bar" to white advancement [*Sheet Metal Workers*]. . . .
> The one-for-one requirement does not require the layoff and discharge of white employees and therefore does not impose burdens of the sort that concerned the plurality in *Wygant*. Because the one-for-one requirement is so limited in scope and duration, it only postpones the promotions of qualified whites.

Finally, the plurality emphasized that under the district court's order, black troopers had to be qualified in order to be promoted. "Qualified white candidates simply have to compete with qualified black candidates. To be sure, [black] applicants would receive some advantage. But this situation is only temporary, and is subject to amelioration by the action of the Department itself."

In a brief concurring opinion, Justice Powell emphasized that the Department "had engaged in persistent violation of constitutional rights and repeatedly failed to carry out court orders." In light of this record "[it] is reasonable to conclude that the District Court would have been 'powerless to provide an effective remedy' if it had lacked authority to establish a benchmark against which to measure progress in remedying the effects of the discrimination. [*Sheet Metal Workers*]."

Justice Stevens concurred in the judgment, but did not join the plurality opinion. He argued that it was crucial that the Department had previously been found to have violated the Constitution.

> A party who has been found guilty of repeated and persistent violations of the law bears the burden of demonstrating that the chancellor's efforts to fashion effective relief exceed the bounds of "reasonableness." The burden of proof in a case like this is precisely the opposite of that in cases such as [*Wygant* and *Fullilove*], which did not involve any proven violations of law. In such cases the governmental decisionmaker who would make race-conscious decisions must overcome a strong presumption against them. No such burden rests on a federal district judge who has found that the

governmental unit before him is guilty of racially discriminatory conduct that violates the Constitution.

Justice O'Connor, joined by Chief Justice Rehnquist and Justice Scalia, dissented. She agreed that the record demonstrated "pervasive, systematic, and obstinate discriminatory conduct" by the defendant and that the district court had the authority to fashion a remedy to end the "egregious history of discrimination." But the particular remedy adopted by the court was not sufficiently narrowly tailored.

> The one-for-one promotion quota used in this case far exceeded the percentage of blacks in the trooper force, and there is no evidence in the record that such an extreme quota was necessary to eradicate the effects of the Department's delay. The Court attempts to defend this one-for-one promotion quota as merely affecting the speed by which the Department attains the goal of 25% black representation in the upper ranks. Such a justification, however, necessarily eviscerates any notion of "narrowly tailored" because it has no stopping point; even a 100% quota could be defended on the ground that it merely "determined how quickly the Department progressed toward" some ultimate goal. . . .
>
> The District Court had available several alternatives that would have achieved full compliance with the [court orders] without trammeling on the rights of nonminority troopers. The court, for example, could have appointed a trustee to develop a promotion procedure that would satisfy the terms of the [orders]. [Alternatively], the District Court could have found the recalcitrant Department in contempt of court, and imposed stiff fines or other penalties for the contempt. Surely, some combination of penalties could have been designed that would have compelled compliance with the [orders].

Justice White also wrote a dissenting opinion.

3. *Some questions.* How much do *Wygant, Sheet Metal Workers,* and *Paradise* change the law of affirmative action? Does Justice Powell's "diversity" argument for affirmative action in *Bakke* survive the rejection of the "role model" argument in *Wygant*? Has the Court now rejected his *Bakke* contention that remediation is improper in the absence of a finding of prior discrimination by an appropriate governmental body? After *Wygant*, when a voluntary affirmative action plan is challenged, should the trial court determine the issue of prior discrimination de novo, or is it sufficient that the governmental entity adopting the program reasonably thought that there had been prior discrimination?

Was the *Sheet Metal Workers* Court properly attentive to the fact that the union was a private entity under no constitutional obligation to desegregate? Is there a "bootstrapping" problem when the government circumvents constitutional difficulties with race-conscious measures by first adopting a statute outlawing discrimination and then asserting a constitutionally compelling interest in enforcement of the statute?

A recurring theme in all recent cases is the impermissibility of using race-conscious measures to remedy discriminatory acts not committed by the governmental entity adopting the measures. Does this limitation make sense? Why does a state's decision to permit one of its governmental branches to remedy violations committed by another branch raise federal constitutional questions? Why can't a state entity undertake to remedy general "societal" discrimination?

4. *Unraveling of the compromise?* In 1987, Justice Powell retired. After his first nominee for the vacant seat failed to secure Senate confirmation and the second nominee withdrew, President Reagan nominated, and the Senate confirmed, Anthony Kennedy to replace Justice Powell. The appointment was widely viewed as creating a solid "conservative" majority on many constitutional issues. During Justice Kennedy's first term, the Court revisited the affirmative action problem — this time in the context of government contract "set asides." Consider how much of the pre-Croson approach survives its decision.

CITY OF RICHMOND v. J. A. CROSON CO.
— U.S. —, 109 S. Ct. 706 (1989)

JUSTICE O'CONNOR announced the judgment of the Court and delivered the opinion of the Court with respect to Parts I, III-B, and IV, an opinion with respect to Part II, in which THE CHIEF JUSTICE and JUSTICE WHITE join, and an opinion with respect to Parts III-A and V, in which THE CHIEF JUSTICE, JUSTICE WHITE and JUSTICE KENNEDY join.

I

[The city of Richmond adopted a set-aside program, modeled on the one upheld in *Fullilove* requiring prime contractors on city projects to subcontract at least 30% of the amount of the contract to Minority Business Enterprises (MBEs). Adopting the definition used by Congress in *Fullilove*, the Richmond City Council defined minority group members as "Blacks, Spanish-speaking, Orientals, Indians, Eskimos, or Aleuts." Regulations under the plan provided that no waivers would be granted except under exceptional circumstances, when "every feasible attempt has been made to comply, and it has been demonstrated that sufficient, relevant, qualified Minority Business Enterprises ... are unavailable or unwilling to participate in the contract."]

The Plan was adopted by the Richmond City Council after a public hearing. Seven members of the public spoke to the merits of the ordinance: five were in opposition, two in favor. Proponents of the set-aside provision relied on a study which indicated that, while the general population of

Richmond was 50% black, only .67% of the city's prime construction contracts had been awarded to minority businesses in the 5-year period from 1978 to 1983. It was also established that a variety of contractors' associations, whose representatives appeared in opposition to the ordinance, had virtually no minority businesses within their membership. The city's legal counsel indicated his view that the ordinance was constitutional under this Court's decision in Fullilove v. Klutznick. Councilperson Marsh, a proponent of the ordinance, made the following statement:

> There is some information, however, that I want to make sure that we put in the record. I have been practicing law in this community since 1961, and I am familiar with the practices in the construction industry in this area, in the State, and around the nation. And I can say without equivocation, that the general conduct of the construction industry in this area, and the State, and around the nation, is one in which race discrimination and exclusion on the basis of race is widespread.

There was no direct evidence of race discrimination on the part of the city in letting contracts or any evidence that the city's prime contractors had discriminated against minority-owned subcontractors. . . .

II

[Appellant] and its supporting *amici* rely heavily on *Fullilove* for the proposition that a city council, like Congress, need not make specific findings of discrimination to engage in race-conscious relief. Thus, appellant argues "[i]t would be a perversion of federalism to hold that the federal government has a compelling interest in remedying the effects of racial discrimination in its own public works program, but a city government does not."

What appellant ignores is that Congress, unlike any State or political subdivision, has a specific constitutional mandate to enforce the dictates of the Fourteenth Amendment. The power to "enforce" may at times also include the power to define situations which *Congress* determines threaten principles of equality and to adopt prophylactic rules to deal with those situations. See Katzenbach v. Morgan. The Civil War Amendments themselves worked a dramatic change in the balance between congressional and state power over matters of race. Speaking of the Thirteenth and Fourteenth Amendments in Ex parte Virginia, 100 U.S. 339, 345, (1880), the Court stated: "They were intended to be, what they really are, limitations of the powers of the States and enlargements of the power of Congress."

That Congress may identify and redress the effects of society-wide discrimination does not mean that, *a fortiori*, the States and their political subdivisions are free to decide that such remedies are appropriate. Section 1 of the Fourteenth Amendment is an explicit *constraint* on state power, and the States must undertake any remedial efforts in accordance with that provision. To hold otherwise would be to cede control over the content of the Equal Protection Clause to the 50 state legislatures and their myriad political subdivisions. The mere recitation of a benign or compensatory purpose for the use of a racial classification would essentially entitle the States to exercise the full power of Congress under §5 of the Fourteenth Amendment and insulate any racial classification from judicial scrutiny under §1. We believe that such a result would be contrary to the intentions of the Framers of the Fourteenth Amendment, who desired to place clear limits on the States' use of race as a criterion for legislative action, and to have the federal courts enforce those limitations.

We do not, as Justice Marshall's dissent suggests, find in §5 of the Fourteenth Amendment some form of federal pre-emption in matters of race. We simply note what should be apparent to all — §1 of the Fourteenth Amendment stemmed from a distrust of state legislative enactments based on race; §5 is, as the dissent notes, " 'a *positive* grant of legislative power' " to Congress. Thus, our treatment of an exercise of congressional power in *Fullilove* cannot be dispositive here. . . .

It would seem equally clear, however, that a state or local subdivision (if delegated the authority from the State) has the authority to eradicate the effects of private discrimination within its own legislative jurisdiction. This authority must, of course, be exercised within the constraints of §1 of the Fourteenth Amendment. Our decision in *Wygant* is not to the contrary. *Wygant* addressed the constitutionality of the use of racial quotas by local school authorities pursuant to an agreement reached with the local teachers' union. It was in the context of addressing the school board's power to adopt a race-based layoff program affecting its own work force that the *Wygant* plurality indicated that the Equal Protection Clause required "some showing of prior discrimination by the governmental unit involved." As a matter of state law, the city of Richmond has legislative authority over its procurement policies, and can use its spending powers to remedy private discrimination, if it identifies that discrimination with the particularity required by the Fourteenth Amendment. . . .

Thus, if the city could show that it had essentially become a "passive participant" in a system of racial exclusion practiced by elements of the local construction industry, we think it clear that the city could take affirmative steps to dismantle such a system. It is beyond dispute that any public entity, state or federal, has a compelling interest in assuring that public dollars, drawn from the tax contributions of all citizens, do not serve to finance the evil of private prejudice.

III

A

The Equal Protection Clause of the Fourteenth Amendment provides that "[N]o State shall . . . deny to *any person* within its jurisdiction the equal protection of the laws" (emphasis added). As this Court has noted in the past, the "rights created by the first section of the Fourteenth Amendment are, by its terms, guaranteed to the individual. The rights established are personal rights." Shelley v. Kraemer, 334 U.S. 1, 22 (1948). The Richmond Plan denies certain citizens the opportunity to compete for a fixed percentage of public contracts based solely upon their race. To whatever racial group these citizens belong, their "personal rights" to be treated with equal dignity and respect are implicated by a rigid rule erecting race as the sole criterion in an aspect of public decisionmaking.

Absent searching judicial inquiry into the justification for such race-based measures, there is simply no way of determining what classifications are "benign" or "remedial" and what classifications are in fact motivated by illegitimate notions of racial inferiority or simple racial politics. Indeed, the purpose of strict scrutiny is to "smoke out" illegitimate uses of race by assuring that the legislative body is pursuing a goal important enough to warrant use of a highly suspect tool. The test also ensures that the means chosen "fit" this compelling goal so closely that there is little or no possibility that the motive for the classification was illegitimate racial prejudice or stereotype.

Classifications based on race carry a danger of stigmatic harm. Unless they are strictly reserved for remedial settings, they may in fact promote notions of racial inferiority and lead to a politics of racial hostility. We thus reaffirm the view expressed by the plurality in *Wygant* that the standard of review under the Equal Protection Clause is not dependent on the race of those burdened or benefited by a particular classification.

Our continued adherence to the standard of review employed in *Wygant*, does not, as Justice Marshall's dissent suggests, indicate that we view "racial discrimination as largely a phenomenon of the past" or that "government bodies need no longer preoccupy themselves with rectifying racial injustice." As we indicate below, States and their local subdivisions have many legislative weapons at their disposal both to punish and prevent present discrimination and to remove arbitrary barriers to minority advancement. Rather, our interpretation of §1 stems from our agreement with the view expressed by Justice Powell in *Bakke*, that "[t]he guarantee of equal protection cannot mean one thing when applied to one individual and something else when applied to a person of another color." *Bakke*, 438 U.S., at 289-290.

Under the standard proposed by Justice Marshall's dissent, "[r]ace-conscious classifications designed to further remedial goals," are forthwith subject to a relaxed standard of review. How the dissent arrives at the legal conclusion that a racial classification is "designed to further remedial goals," without first engaging in an examination of the factual basis for its enactment and the nexus between its scope and that factual basis we are not told. However, once the "remedial" conclusion is reached, the dissent's standard is singularly deferential, and bears little resemblance to the close examination of legislative purpose we have engaged in when reviewing classifications based either on race or gender. The dissent's watered-down version of equal protection review effectively assures that race will always be relevant in American life, and that the "ultimate goal" of "eliminat[ing] entirely from governmental decisionmaking such irrelevant factors as a human being's race," *Wygant*, 476 U.S., at 320 (Stevens, J., dissenting), will never be achieved.

Even were we to accept a reading of the guarantee of equal protection under which the level of scrutiny varies according to the ability of different groups to defend their interests in the representative process, heightened scrutiny would still be appropriate in the circumstances of this case. One of the central arguments for applying a less exacting standard to "benign" racial classifications is that such measures essentially involve a choice made by dominant racial groups to disadvantage themselves. If one aspect of the judiciary's role under the Equal Protection Clause is to protect "discrete and insular minorities" from majoritarian prejudice or indifference, see United States v. Carolene Products Co., 304 U.S. 144, 153, n.4 (1938), some maintain that these concerns are not implicated when the "white majority" places burdens upon itself. See J. Ely, Democracy and Distrust 170 (1980).

In this case, blacks comprise approximately 50% of the population of the city of Richmond. Five of the nine seats on the City Council are held by blacks. The concern that a political majority will more easily act to the disadvantage of a minority based on unwarranted assumptions or incomplete facts would seem to militate for, not against, the application of heightened judicial scrutiny in this case. See Ely, The Constitutionality of Reverse Racial Discrimination, 41 U. Chi. L. Rev. 723, 739, n.58 (1974) ("Of course it works both ways: a law that favors Blacks over Whites would be suspect if it were enacted by a predominantly Black legislature"). . . .

B

We think it clear that the factual predicate offered in support of the Richmond Plan suffers from the same two defects identified as fatal in *Wygant*. The District Court found the city council's "findings sufficient to ensure that, in adopting the Plan, it was remedying the present effects of past discrimination in the *construction industry*." Like the "role model" theory employed in *Wygant*, a generalized assertion that there has been past discrimination in an entire industry provides no guidance for a legislative body to determine the precise scope of the injury it seeks to remedy. It "has no logical stopping point." *Wygant*, at 275, (plurality opinion). "Relief" for such an ill-defined wrong could extend until the percentage of public contracts awarded to MBEs in Richmond mirrored the percentage of minorities in the population as a whole.

Appellant argues that it is attempting to remedy various forms of past discrimination that are alleged to be responsible for the small number of minority businesses in the local contracting industry. Among these the city cites the exclusion of blacks from skilled construction trade unions and training programs. This past discrimination has prevented them "from following the traditional path from laborer to entrepreneur." The city also lists a host of nonracial factors which would seem to face a member of any racial group attempting to establish a new business enterprise, such as deficiencies in working capital, inability to meet bonding requirements, unfamiliarity with bidding procedures, and disability caused by an inadequate track record.

While there is no doubt that the sorry history of both private and public discrimination in this country has contributed to a lack of opportunities for black entrepreneurs, this observation, standing alone, cannot justify a rigid racial quota in the awarding of public contracts in Richmond, Virginia. Like the claim that discrimination in primary and secondary schooling justifies a rigid racial preference in medical school admissions, an amorphous claim that there has been past discrimination in a particular industry cannot justify the use of an unyielding racial quota.

It is sheer speculation how many minority firms there would be in Richmond absent past societal discrimination, just as it was sheer speculation how many minority medical students would have been admitted to the medical school at Davis absent past discrimination in educational opportunities. Defining these sorts of injuries as "identified discrimination" would give local governments license to create a patchwork of racial preferences based on statistical generalizations about any particular field of endeavor.

These defects are readily apparent in this case. The 30% quota cannot in any realistic sense be tied to any injury suffered by anyone. The District Court relied upon five predicate "facts" in reaching its conclusion that there was an adequate basis for the 30% quota: (1) the ordinance declares itself to be remedial; (2) several proponents of the measure stated their views that there had been past discrimination in the construction industry; (3) minority businesses received .67% of prime contracts from the city while minorities constituted 50% of the city's population; (4) there were very few minority contractors in local and state contractors' associations; and (5) in 1977, Congress made a determination that the effects of past discrimination had stifled minority participation in the construction industry nationally.

None of these "findings," singly or together, provide the city of Richmond with a "strong basis in evidence for its conclusion that remedial action was necessary." *Wygant*, 476 U.S., at 277 (plurality opinion). There is nothing approaching a prima facie case of a constitutional or statutory violation by *anyone* in the Richmond construction industry.

The District Court accorded great weight to the fact that the city council designated the Plan as "remedial." But the mere recitation of a "benign" or legitimate purpose for a racial classification, is entitled to little or no weight.

Racial classifications are suspect, and that means that simple legislative assurances of good intention cannot suffice.

The District Court also relied on the highly conclusionary statement of a proponent of the Plan that there was racial discrimination in the construction industry "in this area, and the State, and around the nation." It also noted that the city manager had related his view that racial discrimination still plagued the construction industry in his home city of Pittsburg. These statements are of little probative value in establishing identified discrimination in the Richmond construction industry. The fact-finding process of legislative bodies is generally entitled to a presumption of regularity and deferential review by the judiciary. See [Williamson v. Lee Optical]. But when a legislative body chooses to employ a suspect classification, it cannot rest upon a generalized assertion as to the classification's relevance to its goals. [A] governmental actor cannot render race a legitimate proxy for a particular condition merely by declaring that the condition exists. The history of racial classifications in this country suggests that blind judicial deference to legislative or executive pronouncements of necessity has no place in equal protection [analysis].

Reliance on the disparity between the number of prime contracts awarded to minority firms and the minority population of the city of Richmond is similarly misplaced. . . .

In this case, the city does not even know how many MBEs in the relevant market are qualified to undertake prime or subcontracting work in public construction projects. Nor does the city know what percentage of total city construction dollars minority firms now receive as subcontractors on prime contracts let by the city.

To a large extent, the set-aside of subcontracting dollars seems to rest on the unsupported assumption that white prime contractors simply will not hire minority firms. . . . Without any information on minority participation in subcontracting, it is quite simply impossible to evaluate overall minority representation in the city's construction expenditures.

The city and the District Court also relied on evidence that MBE membership in local contractors' associations was extremely low. Again, standing alone this evidence is not probative of any discrimination in the local construction industry. There are numerous explanations for this dearth of minority participation, including past societal discrimination in education and economic opportunities as well as both black and white career and entrepreneurial choices. Blacks may be disproportionately attracted to industries other than construction. . . .

For low minority membership in these associations to be relevant, the city would have to link it to the number of local MBEs eligible for membership. If the statistical disparity between eligible MBEs and MBE membership were great enough, an inference of discriminatory exclusion could arise. In such a case, the city would have a compelling interest in preventing its tax dollars from assisting these organizations in maintaining a racially segregated construction market.

Finally, the city and the District Court relied on Congress' finding in connection with the set-aside approved in *Fullilove* that there had been nationwide discrimination in the construction industry. The probative value of these findings for demonstrating the existence of discrimination in Richmond is extremely limited. By its inclusion of a waiver procedure in the national program addressed in *Fullilove*, Congress explicitly recognized that the scope of the problem would vary from market area to market area. . . .

Justice Marshall apparently views the requirement that Richmond identify the discrimination it seeks to remedy in its own jurisdiction as a mere administrative headache, an "onerous documentary obligatio[n]." We cannot agree. . . . The "evidence" relied upon by the dissent, the history of school desegregation in Richmond and numerous congressional reports, does little to define the scope of any injury to minority contractors in Richmond or the necessary remedy. The factors relied upon by the dissent could justify a preference of any size or duration.

Moreover, Justice Marshall's suggestion that findings of discrimination may be "shared" from jurisdiction to jurisdiction in the same manner as information concerning zoning and property values is unprecedented. Quoting Renton v. Playtime Theatres, Inc., 475 U.S. 41, 51-52 (1986). We have never approved the extrapolation of discrimination in one jurisdiction from the experience of another. . . .

To accept Richmond's claim that past societal discrimination alone can serve as the basis for rigid racial preferences would be to open the door to competing claims for "remedial relief" for every disadvantaged group. The dream of a Nation of equal citizens in a society where race is irrelevant to personal opportunity and achievement would be lost in a mosaic of shifting preferences based on inherently unmeasurable claims of past wrongs. . . . We think such a result would be contrary to both the letter and spirit of a constitutional provision whose central command is equality.

The foregoing analysis applies only to the inclusion of blacks within the Richmond set-aside program. There is *absolutely no evidence* of past discrimination against Spanish-speaking, Oriental, Indian, Eskimo, or Aleut persons in any aspect of the Richmond construction industry. The District Court took judicial notice of the fact that the vast majority of "minority" persons in Richmond were black. It may well be that Richmond has never had an Aleut or Eskimo citizen. The random inclusion of racial groups that, as a practical matter, may never have suffered from discrimination in the construction industry in Richmond, suggests that perhaps the city's purpose was not in fact to remedy past discrimination.

If a 30% set-aside was "narrowly tailored" to compensate black contractors for past discrimination, one may legitimately ask why they are forced to share this "remedial relief" with an Aleut citizen who moves to Richmond tomorrow? The gross overinclusiveness of Richmond's racial preference strongly impugns the city's claim of remedial motivation.

IV

As noted by the court below, it is almost impossible to assess whether the Richmond Plan is narrowly tailored to remedy prior discrimination since it is not linked to identified discrimination in any way. We limit ourselves to two observations in this regard.

First, there does not appear to have been any consideration of the use of race-neutral means to increase minority business participation in city contracting. Many of the barriers to minority participation in the construction industry relied upon by the city to justify a racial classification appear to be race neutral. If MBEs disproportionately lack capital or cannot meet bonding requirements, a race-neutral program of city financing for small firms would, *a fortiori*, lead to greater minority participation. . . .

Second, the 30% quota cannot be said to be narrowly tailored to any goal, except perhaps outright racial balancing. It rests upon the "completely unrealistic" assumption that minorities will choose a particular trade in lockstep proportion to their representation in the local population.

Since the city must already consider bids and waivers on a case-by-case basis, it is difficult to see the need for a rigid numerical quota. As noted above, the congressional scheme upheld in *Fullilove* allowed for a waiver of the set-aside provision where an MBE's higher price was not attributable to the effects of past discrimination. Based upon proper findings, such programs are less problematic from an equal protection standpoint because they treat all candidates individually, rather than making the color of an applicant's skin the sole relevant consideration. Unlike the program upheld in *Fullilove,* the Richmond Plan's waiver system focuses solely on the availability of MBEs; there is no inquiry into whether or not the particular MBE seeking a racial preference has suffered from the effects of past discrimination by the city or prime contractors.

Given the existence of an individualized procedure, the city's only interest in maintaining a quota system rather than investigating the need for remedial action in particular cases would seem to be simple administrative convenience. But the interest in avoiding the bureaucratic effort necessary to tailor remedial relief to those who truly have suffered the effects of prior discrimination cannot justify a rigid line drawn on the basis of a suspect classification. Under Richmond's scheme, a successful black, Hispanic, or Oriental entrepreneur from anywhere in the country enjoys an absolute preference over other citizens based solely on their race. We think it obvious that such a program is not narrowly tailored to remedy the effects of prior discrimination.

V

Nothing we say today precludes a state or local entity from taking action to rectify the effects of identified discrimination within its jurisdiction. If the city of Richmond had evidence before it that non-minority contractors were systematically excluding minority businesses from subcontracting opportunities it could take action to end the discriminatory exclusion. Where there is a significant statistical disparity between the number of qualified minority contractors willing and able to perform a particular service and the number of such contractors actually engaged by the locality or the locality's prime contractors, an inference of discriminatory exclusion could arise. Under such circumstances, the city could act to dismantle the closed business system by taking appropriate measures against those who discriminate on the basis of race or other illegitimate criteria. In the extreme case, some form of narrowly tailored racial preference might be necessary to break down patterns of deliberate exclusion.

Nor is local government powerless to deal with individual instances of racially motivated refusals to employ minority contractors. Where such discrimination occurs, a city would be justified in penalizing the discriminator and providing appropriate relief to the victim of such discrimination. Moreover, evidence of a pattern of individual discriminatory acts can, if supported by appropriate statistical proof, lend support to a local government's determination that broader remedial relief is justified.

Even in the absence of evidence of discrimination, the city has at its disposal a whole array of race-neutral devices to increase the accessibility of city contracting opportunities to small entrepreneurs of all races. . . . Business as usual should not mean business pursuant to the unthinking exclusion of certain members of our society from its rewards.

In the case at hand, the city has not ascertained how many minority enterprises are present in the local construction market nor the level of their participation in city construction projects. The city points to no evidence that qualified minority contractors have been passed over for city contracts or subcontracts, either as a group or in any individual case. . . .

Proper findings in this regard are necessary to define both the scope of the injury and the extent of the remedy necessary to cure its effects. Such findings also serve to assure all citizens that the deviation from the norm of equal treatment of all racial and ethnic groups is a temporary matter, a measure taken in the service of the goal of equality itself. . . . Because the city of Richmond has failed to identify the need for remedial action in the awarding of its public construction contracts, its treatment of its citizens on a racial basis violates the dictates of the Equal Protection Clause. Accordingly, the judgment of the Court of Appeals for the Fourth Circuit is

Affirmed.

JUSTICE STEVENS, concurring in part and concurring in the judgment.

. . . I write separately to emphasize three aspects of the case that are of special importance to me.

First, the city makes no claim that the public interest in the efficient performance of its construction contracts will be served by granting a preference to minority-business enterprises. This case is therefore completely unlike *Wygant*, in which I thought it quite obvious that the School Board had reasonably concluded that an integrated faculty could provide educational benefits to the entire student body that could not be provided by an all-white, or nearly all-white faculty. . . .

Second, this litigation involves an attempt by a legislative body, rather than a court, to fashion a remedy for a past wrong. Legislatures are primarily policy-making bodies that promulgate rules to govern future conduct. . . . It is the judicial system, rather than the legislative process, that is best equipped to identify past wrongdoers and to fashion remedies that will create the conditions that presumably would have existed had no wrong been committed. Thus, in cases involving the review of judicial remedies imposed against persons who have been proved guilty of violations of law, I would allow the courts in racial discrimination cases the same broad discretion that chancellors enjoy in other areas of the law.

Third, instead of engaging in a debate over the proper standard of review to apply in affirmative-action litigation, I believe it is more constructive to try to identify the characteristics of the advantaged and disadvantaged classes that may justify their disparate treatment. In this case that approach convinces me that, instead of carefully identifying the characteristics of the two classes of contractors that are respectively favored and disfavored by its ordinance, the Richmond City Council has merely engaged in the type of stereotypical analysis that is a hallmark of violations of the Equal Protection Clause.

The justification for the ordinance is the fact that in the past white contractors — and presumably other white citizens in Richmond — have discriminated against black contractors. The class of persons benefited by the ordinance is not, however, limited to victims of such discrimination — it encompasses persons who have never been in business in Richmond as well as minority contractors who may have been guilty of discriminating against members of other minority groups. Indeed, for all the record shows, all of the minority-business enterprises that have benefited from the ordinance may be firms that have prospered notwithstanding the discriminatory conduct that may have harmed other minority firms years ago. Ironically, minority firms that have survived in the competitive struggle, rather than those that have perished, are most likely to benefit from an ordinance of this kind.

The ordinance is equally vulnerable because of its failure to identify the characteristics of the disadvantaged class of white contractors that justify the disparate treatment. That class unquestionably includes some white contractors who are guilty of past discrimination against blacks, but it is only habit, rather than evidence or analysis, that makes it seem acceptable to assume that every white contractor covered by the ordinance shares in that guilt.[9]

[Justice Kennedy's opinion, concurring in part and concurring in the judgment, has been omitted.]

JUSTICE SCALIA, concurring in the judgment.

[I] do not agree [with] the Court's dicta suggesting that, despite the Fourteenth Amendment, state and local governments may in some circumstances discriminate on the basis of race in order (in a broad sense) "to ameliorate the effects of past discrimination." The benign purpose of compensating for social disadvantages, whether they have been acquired by reason of prior discrimination or otherwise, can no more be pursued by the illegitimate means of racial discrimination than can other assertedly benign purposes we have repeatedly rejected. The difficulty of overcoming the effects of past discrimination is as nothing compared with the difficulty of eradicating from our society the source of those effects, which is the tendency — fatal to a nation such as ours — to classify and judge men and women on the basis of their country of origin or the color of their skin. A solution to the first problem that aggravates the second is no solution at all. . . . At least where state or local action is at issue, only a social emergency rising to the level of imminent danger to life and limb — for example, a prison race riot, requiring temporary segregation of inmates — can justify an exception to the principle embodied in the Fourteenth Amendment that "[o]ur Constitution is color-blind, and neither knows nor tolerates classes among citizens," Plessy v. Ferguson, 163 U.S. 537, 559 (1896) (Harlan, J., dissenting). . . .

A sound distinction between federal and state (or local) action based on race rests not only upon the substance of the Civil War Amendments, but upon social reality and governmental theory. It is a simple fact that what Justice Stewart described in *Fullilove* as "the dispassionate objectivity [and] the flexibility that are needed to mold a race-conscious remedy around the single objective of eliminating the effects of past or present discrimination" — political qualities already to be doubted in a national legislature, *Fullilove,* at 527, (Stewart, J., with whom Rehnquist, J., joined, dissenting) — are substantially less likely to exist at the state or local level. The struggle for racial justice has historically been a struggle by the national society against oppression in the individual States. And the struggle retains that character in modern times. Not all of that

9. There is, of course, another possibility that should not be overlooked. The ordinance might be nothing more than a form of patronage. But racial patronage, like a racial gerrymander, is no more defensible than political patronage or a political gerrymander. A southern State with a long history of discrimination against Republicans in the awarding of public contracts could not rely on such past discrimination as a basis for granting a legislative preference to Republican contractors in the future. [Relocated Footnote.]

struggle has involved discrimination against blacks, and not all of it has been in the Old South. What the record shows, in other words, is that racial discrimination against any group finds a more ready expression at the state and local than at the federal level. To the children of the Founding Fathers, this should come as no surprise. An acute awareness of the heightened danger of oppression from political factions in small, rather than large, political units dates to the very beginning of our national history. As James Madison observed in support of the proposed Constitution's enhancement of national powers:

> The smaller the society, the fewer probably will be the distinct parties and interests composing it; the fewer the distinct parties and interests, the more frequently will a majority be found of the same party; and the smaller the number of individuals composing a majority, and the smaller the compass within which they are placed, the more easily will they concert and execute their plan of oppression. Extend the sphere and you take in a greater variety of parties and interests; you make it less probable that a majority of the whole will have a common motive to invade the rights of other citizens; or if such a common motive exists, it will be more difficult for all who feel it to discover their own strength and to act in unison with each other.

The Federalist No. 10, pp.82-84 (C. Rossiter ed. 1961).

The prophesy of these words came to fruition in Richmond in the enactment of a set-aside clearly and directly beneficial to the dominant political group, which happens also to be the dominant racial group. The same thing has no doubt happened before in other cities (though the racial basis of the preference has rarely been made textually explicit) — and blacks have often been on the receiving end of the injustice. Where injustice is the game, however, turn-about is not fair play.

In my view there is only one circumstance in which the States may act *by race* to "undo the effects of past discrimination": where that is necessary to eliminate their own maintenance of a system of unlawful racial classification. If, for example, a state agency has a discriminatory pay scale compensating black employees in all positions at 20% less than their nonblack counterparts, it may assuredly promulgate an order raising the salaries of "all black employees" by 20%. This distinction explains our school desegregation cases, in which we have made plain that States and localities sometimes have an obligation to adopt race-conscious remedies. . . .

I agree with the Court's dictum that a fundamental distinction must be drawn between the effects of "societal" discrimination and the effects of "identified" discrimination, and that the situation would be different if Richmond's plan were "tailored" to identify those particular bidders who "suffered from the effects of past discrimination by the city or prime contractors." In my view, however, the reason that would make a difference is not, as the Court states, that it would justify race-conscious action, but rather that it would enable race-neutral remediation. Nothing prevents Richmond from according a contracting preference to identified victims of discrimination. While most of the beneficiaries might be black, neither the beneficiaries nor those disadvantaged by the preference would be identified *on the basis of their race*. In other words, far from justifying racial classification, identification of actual victims of discrimination makes it less supportable than ever, because more obviously unneeded. . . .

It is plainly true that in our society blacks have suffered discrimination immeasurably greater than any directed at other racial groups. But those who believe that racial preferences can help to "even the score" display, and reinforce, a manner of thinking by race that was the source of the injustice and that will, if it endures within our society, be the source of more injustice still. The relevant proposition is not that it was blacks, or Jews, or Irish who were discriminated against, but that it was individual men and women, "created equal," who were discriminated against. And the relevant resolve is that that should never happen again. Racial preferences appear to "even the score" (in some small degree) only if one embraces the proposition that our society is appropriately viewed as divided into races, making it right that an injustice rendered in the past to a black man should be compensated for by discriminating against a white. Nothing is worth that embrace. Since blacks have been disproportionately disadvantaged by racial discrimination, any race-neutral remedial program aimed at the disadvantaged *as such* will have a disproportionately beneficial impact on blacks. Only such a program, and not one that operates on the basis of race, is in accord with the letter and the spirit of our Constitution.

Since I believe that the appellee here had a constitutional right to have its bid succeed or fail under a decisionmaking process uninfected with racial bias, I concur in the judgment of the Court.

JUSTICE MARSHALL, with whom JUSTICE BRENNAN and JUSTICE BLACKMUN join, dissenting.

It is a welcome symbol of racial progress when the former capital of the Confederacy acts forthrightly to confront the effects of racial discrimination in its midst. In my view, nothing in the Constitution can be construed to prevent Richmond, Virginia, from allocating a portion of its contracting dollars for businesses owned or controlled by members of minority groups. Indeed, Richmond's set-aside program is indistinguishable in all meaningful respects from — and in fact was patterned upon — the federal set-aside plan which this Court upheld in Fullilove v. Klutznick.

A majority of this Court holds today, however, that the Equal Protection Clause of the Fourteenth Amendment blocks Richmond's initiative. The essence of the majority's position is that Richmond has failed to catalogue adequate findings to prove that past discrimination has impeded minorities from joining or participating fully in Richmond's construction contracting industry. I find deep irony in second-guessing Richmond's judgment on this point. As much as any municipality in the United States, Richmond knows what racial discrimination is; a century of decisions by this and other federal courts has richly documented the city's disgraceful history of public and private racial discrimination. In any event, the Richmond City Council *has* supported its determination that minorities have been wrongly excluded from local construction contracting. Its proof includes statistics showing that minority-owned businesses have received virtually no city contracting dollars and rarely if ever belonged to area trade associations; testimony by municipal officials that discrimination has been widespread in the local construction industry; and the same exhaustive and widely publicized federal studies relied on in *Fullilove*, studies which showed that pervasive discrimination in the Nation's tight-knit construction industry had operated to exclude minorities from public contracting. These are precisely the types of statistical and testimonial evidence which, until today, this Court had credited in cases approving of race-conscious measures designed to remedy past discrimination.

More fundamentally, today's decision marks a deliberate and giant step backward in this Court's affirmative action jurisprudence. Cynical of one municipality's attempt to redress the effects of past racial discrimination in a particular industry, the majority launches a grapeshot attack on race-conscious remedies in general. The majority's unnecessary pronouncements will inevitably discourage or prevent governmental entities, particularly States and localities, from acting to rectify the scourge of past discrimination. This is the harsh reality of the majority's decision, but it is not the Constitution's command.

I

As an initial matter, the majority takes an exceedingly myopic view of the factual predicate on which the Richmond City Council relied when it passed the Minority Business Utilization Plan. The majority analyzes Richmond's initiative as if it were based solely upon the facts about local construction and contracting practices adduced during the City Council session at which the measure was enacted. In so doing, the majority down-plays the fact that the City Council had before it a rich trove of evidence that discrimination in the Nation's construction industry had seriously impaired the competitive position of businesses owned or controlled by members of minority groups. It is only against this backdrop of documented national discrimination, however, that the local evidence adduced by Richmond can be properly understood. The majority's refusal to recognize that Richmond has proven itself no exception to the dismaying pattern of national exclusion which Congress so painstakingly identified infects its entire analysis of this case. . . .

[As] of 1977, there was "abundant evidence" in the public domain "that minority businesses ha[d] been denied effective participation in public contracting opportunities by procurement practices that perpetuated the effects of prior discrimination." *Fullilove,* at 477-478. Significantly, this evidence demonstrated that discrimination had prevented existing or nascent minority-owned businesses from obtaining not only federal contracting assignments, but state and local ones as well.

The members of the Richmond City Council were well aware of these exhaustive congressional findings, a point the majority, tellingly, elides. The transcript of the session at which the Council enacted the local set-aside initiative contains numerous references to the 6-year-old congressional set-aside program, to the evidence of nationwide discrimination barriers described above, and to the *Fullilove* decision itself. . . .

II

A

1

[Richmond] has two powerful interests in setting aside a portion of public contracting funds for minority-owned enterprises. The first is the city's interest in eradicating the effects of past racial discrimination. It is far too late in the day to doubt that remedying such discrimination is a compelling, let alone an important, interest. . . .

Richmond has a second compelling interest in setting aside, where possible, a portion of its contracting dollars. That interest is the prospective one of preventing the city's own spending decisions from reinforcing and perpetuating the exclusionary effects of past discrimination.

The majority pays only lip service to this additional governmental interest. But our decisions have often emphasized the danger of the government tacitly adopting, encouraging, or furthering racial discrimination even by its own routine operations. . . .

The majority is wrong to trivialize the continuing impact of government acceptance or use of private institutions or structures once wrought by discrimination. When government channels all its contracting funds to a white-dominated community of established contractors whose racial homogeneity is the product of private discrimination, it does more than place its imprimatur on the practices which forged and which continue to define that community. It also provides a measurable boost to those economic entities that have thrived within it, while denying important economic benefits to those entities which, but for prior discrimination, might well be better qualified to receive valuable government contracts. . . .

2

The remaining question with respect to the "governmental interest" prong of equal protection analysis is whether Richmond has proffered satisfactory proof of past racial discrimination to support its twin interests in remediation and in governmental nonperpetuation. Although the Members of this Court have differed on the appropriate standard of review for race-conscious remedial measures, we have always regarded this factual inquiry as a practical one. Thus, the Court has eschewed rigid tests which require the provision of particular species of evidence, statistical or otherwise. At the same time we have required that government adduce evidence that, taken as a whole, is sufficient to support its claimed interest and to dispel the natural concern that it acted out of mere "paternalistic stereotyping, not on a careful consideration of modern social conditions." Fullilove v. Klutznick, 448 U.S., at 519 (Marshall, J., concurring in judgment). . . .

The varied body of evidence on which Richmond relied provides a "strong," "firm," and "unquestionably legitimate" basis upon which the City Council could determine that the effects of past racial discrimination warranted a remedial and prophylactic governmental response. [Richmond] acted against a backdrop of congressional and Executive Branch studies which demonstrated with such force the nationwide pervasiveness of prior discrimination that Congress presumed that " 'present economic inequities' " in construction contracting resulted from " 'past discriminatory systems.' " The city's local evidence confirmed that Richmond's construction industry did not deviate from this pernicious national pattern. The fact that just .67% of public construction expenditures over the previous five years had gone to minority-owned prime contractors, despite the city's racially mixed population, strongly suggests that construction contracting in the area was rife with "present economic inequities." To the extent this enormous disparity did not itself demonstrate that discrimination had occurred, the descriptive testimony of Richmond's elected and appointed leaders drew the necessary link between the pitifully small presence of minorities in construction contracting and past exclusionary practices. That *no one* who testified challenged this depiction of widespread racial discrimination in area construction contracting lent significant weight to these accounts. The fact that area trade associations had virtually no minority members dramatized the extent of present inequities and suggested the lasting power of past discriminatory systems. In sum, to suggest that the facts on which Richmond has relied do not provide a sound basis for its finding of past racial discrimination simply blinks credibility.

Richmond's reliance on localized, industry-specific findings is a far cry from the reliance on generalized "societal discrimination" which the majority decries as a basis for remedial action. But characterizing the plight of Richmond's minority contractors as mere "societal discrimination" is not the only respect in which the majority's critique shows an unwillingness to come to grips with why construction-contracting in Richmond is essentially a whites-only enterprise. The majority also takes the disingenuous approach of disaggregating Richmond's local evidence, attacking it piecemeal, and thereby concluding that no *single* piece of evidence adduced by the city, "standing alone," suffices to prove past discrimination. But items of evidence do not, of course, "stan[d] alone" or exist in alien juxtaposition; they necessarily work together, reinforcing or contradicting each other.

In any event, the majority's criticisms of individual items of Richmond's evidence rest on flimsy foundations. The majority states, for example, that reliance on the disparity between the share of city contracts awarded to minority firms (.67%) and the minority population of Richmond (approximately 50%) is "misplaced." It is true that, when the factual predicate needed to be proved is one of *present* discrimination, we have generally credited statistical contrasts between the racial composition of a work force and the general population as proving discrimination only where this contrast revealed "gross statistical disparities." But this principle does not impugn Richmond's statistical contrast, for two reasons. First, considering how minuscule the share of Richmond public construction contracting dollars received by minority-owned businesses is, it is hardly unreasonable to conclude that this case involves a "gross statistical disparit[y]." There are roughly equal numbers of minorities and nonminorities in Richmond — yet minority-owned businesses receive *one-seventy-fifth* the public contracting funds that other businesses receive.

Second, and more fundamentally, where the issue is not present discrimination but rather whether *past* discrimination has resulted in the *continuing exclusion* of minorities from an historically tight-knit industry, a contrast between population and work force is entirely appropriate to help gauge the degree of the exclusion. In Johnson v. Transportation Agency, Justice O'Connor specifically observed that, when it is alleged that discrimination has prevented blacks from "obtaining th[e] experience" needed to qualify for a position, the "relevant comparison" is not to the percentage of blacks in the pool of qualified candidates, but to "the total percentage of blacks in the labor force." 480 U.S., at 651. This contrast is especially illuminating in cases like this, where a main avenue of introduction into the work force — here, membership in the trade associations whose members presumably train apprentices and help them procure subcontracting assignments — is itself grossly dominated by nonminorities. The majority's assertion that the city "does not even know how many MBE's in the relevant market are qualified," is thus entirely beside the point. . . .

The majority's perfunctory dismissal of the testimony of Richmond's appointed and elected leaders is also deeply disturbing. . . .

Had the majority paused for a moment on the facts of the Richmond experience, it would have discovered that the city's leadership is deeply familiar with what racial discrimination is. The members of the Richmond City Council have spent long years witnessing multifarious acts of discrimination, including, but not limited to, the deliberate diminution of black residents' voting rights, resistance to school desegregation, and publicly sanctioned housing discrimination. Numerous decisions of federal courts chronicle this disgraceful recent history.

When the legislatures and leaders of cities with histories of pervasive discrimination testify that past discrimination has infected one of their industries, armchair cynicism like that exercised by the majority has no place. It may well be that "the autonomy of a state is an essential component of federalism," Garcia v. San Antonio Metropolitan Transit Authority, 469 U.S. 528, 588 (1985) (O'Connor, J., dissenting), and that "each State is sovereign within its own domain, governing its citizens and providing for their general welfare," FERC v. Mississippi, 456 U.S., at 777 (O'Connor, J., dissenting), but apparently this is not the case when federal judges, with nothing but their impressions to go on, choose to disbelieve the explanations of these local governments and officials. Disbelief is particularly inappropriate here in light of the fact that appellee Croson, which had the burden of proving unconstitutionality at trial, has *at no point* come forward with *any* direct evidence that the City Council's motives were anything other than sincere.

Finally, I vehemently disagree with the majority's dismissal of the congressional and Executive Branch findings noted in *Fullilove* as having "extremely limited" probative value in this case. The majority concedes that Congress established nothing less than a "presumption" that minority contracting firms have been disadvantaged by prior discrimination. The majority, inexplicably, would forbid Richmond to "share" in this information, and permit only Congress to take note of these ample findings. In thus requiring that Richmond's local evidence be severed from the context in which it was prepared, the majority would require cities seeking to eradicate the effects of past discrimination within their borders to reinvent the evidentiary wheel and engage in unnecessarily duplicative, costly, and time-consuming factfinding.

No principle of federalism or of federal power, however, forbids a state or local government from drawing upon a nationally relevant historical record prepared by the Federal Government. See Renton v. Playtime Theatres, Inc., 475 U.S. 41, 51-52 (1986). Of course, Richmond could have built an even more compendious record of past discrimination, one including additional stark statistics and additional individual accounts of past discrimination. But nothing in the Fourteenth Amendment imposes such onerous documentary obligations upon States and localities once the reality of past discrimination is apparent.

B

In my judgment, Richmond's set-aside plan also comports with the second prong of the equal protection inquiry, for it is substantially related to the interests it seeks to serve in remedying past discrimination and in ensuring that municipal contract procurement does not perpetuate that discrimination. The most striking aspect of the city's ordinance is the similarity it bears to the "appropriately limited" federal set-aside provision upheld in *Fullilove*.[10] Like the federal provision, Richmond's is limited to five years in duration, and was not renewed when it came up for reconsideration in 1988. Like the federal provision, Richmond's contains a waiver provision freeing from its subcontracting requirements those nonminority firms that demonstrate that they cannot comply with its provisions. Like the federal provision, Richmond's has a minimal impact on innocent third parties. While the measure affects 30% of *public* contracting dollars, that translates to only 3% of overall Richmond area contracting.

Finally, like the federal provision, Richmond's does not interfere with any vested right of a contractor to a particular contract; instead it operates entirely prospectively. Richmond's initiative affects only future economic arrangements and imposes only a diffuse burden on nonminority competitors — here, businesses owned or controlled by nonminorities which seek subcontracting work on public construction projects. . . .

[The] majority takes issue [with] two aspects of Richmond's tailoring: the city's refusal to explore the use of race-neutral measures to increase minority business participation in contracting, and the selection of a 30% set-aside figure. The majority's first criticism is flawed in two respects. First, the majority overlooks the fact that since 1975, Richmond has barred both discrimination by the city in awarding public contracts and discrimination by public contractors. The virtual absence of minority businesses from the city's contracting rolls, indicated by the fact that such businesses have received less than 1% of public contracting dollars, strongly suggests that this ban has not succeeded in redressing the impact of past discrimination or in preventing city contract procurement from reinforcing racial homogeneity. Second, the majority's suggestion that Richmond should have first undertaken such race-neutral measures as a program of city financing for small firms, ignores the fact that such measures, while theoretically appealing, have been discredited by Congress as ineffectual in eradicating the effects of past discrimination in this very industry. For this reason, this Court in *Fullilove* refused to fault Congress for not undertaking race-neutral measures as precursors to its race-conscious set-aside. The Equal Protection Clause does not require Richmond to retrace Congress' steps when Congress has found that those steps lead nowhere. Given the well-exposed limitations of race-neutral measures, it was thus appropriate for a municipality like Richmond to conclude that, in the words of Justice Blackmun, "[i]n order to get beyond racism, we

10. Although the majority sharply criticizes Richmond for using data which it did not itself develop, it is noteworthy that the federal set-aside program upheld in *Fullilove* was adopted as a floor amendment "without any congressional hearings or investigation whatsoever." L. Tribe, American Constitutional Law 345 (2d ed. 1988). The principal opinion in *Fullilove* justified the set-aside by relying heavily on the aforementioned studies by agencies like the Small Business Administration and on legislative reports prepared in connection with prior, failed legislation. [Relocated footnote.]

must first take account of race. There is no other way." University of California
Regents v. Bakke, 438 U.S., at 407 (1978) (separate opinion). [11]

As for Richmond's 30% target, the majority states that this figure "cannot be
said to be narrowly tailored to any goal, except perhaps outright racial balancing." The majority ignores two important facts. First, the set-aside measure
affects only 3% of overall city contracting; thus, any imprecision in tailoring has
far less impact than the majority suggests. But more important, the majority
ignores the fact that Richmond's 30% figure was patterned directly on the
Fullilove precedent. Congress' 10% figure fell "roughly halfway between the
present percentage of minority contractors and the percentage of minority
group members in the Nation." *Fullilove, supra,* 448 U.S., at 513-514 (Powell, J.,
concurring). The Richmond City Council's 30% figure similarly falls roughly
halfway between the present percentage of Richmond-based minority contractors (almost zero) and the percentage of minorities in Richmond (50%). In
faulting Richmond for not presenting a different explanation for its choice of a
set-aside figure, the majority honors *Fullilove* only in the breach.

III

I would ordinarily end my analysis at this point and conclude that Richmond's ordinance satisfies both the governmental interest and substantial relationship prongs of our Equal Protection Clause analysis. However, I am
compelled to add more, for the majority has gone beyond the facts of this case to
announce a set of principles which unnecessarily restrict the power of governmental entities to take race-conscious measures to redress the effects of prior
discrimination.

A

Today, for the first time, a majority of this Court has adopted strict scrutiny
as its standard of Equal Protection Clause review of race-conscious remedial
measures. This is an unwelcome development. A profound difference separates
governmental actions that themselves are racist, and governmental actions that
seek to remedy the effects of prior racism or to prevent neutral governmental
activity from perpetuating the effects of such racism.

---

11. The majority also faults Richmond's ordinance for including within its definition of "minority group members" not only black citizens, but also citizens who are "Spanish-speaking, Oriental,
Indian, Eskimo, or Aleut persons." This is, of course, precisely the same definition Congress adopted
in its set-aside legislation. Even accepting the majority's view that Richmond's ordinance is overbroad because it includes groups, such as Eskimos or Aleuts, about whom no evidence of local
discrimination has been proffered, it does not necessarily follow that the balance of Richmond's
ordinance should be invalidated.

Racial classifications "drawn on the presumption that one race is inferior to another or because they put the weight of government behind racial hatred and separatism" warrant the strictest judicial scrutiny because of the very irrelevance of these rationales. By contrast, racial classifications drawn for the purpose of remedying the effects of discrimination that itself was race-based have a highly pertinent basis: the tragic and indelible fact that discrimination against blacks and other racial minorities in this Nation has pervaded our Nation's history and continues to scar our society. . . .

In concluding that remedial classifications warrant no different standard of review under the Constitution than the most brute and repugnant forms of state-sponsored racism, a majority of this Court signals that it regards racial discrimination as largely a phenomenon of the past, and that government bodies need no longer preoccupy themselves with rectifying racial injustice. I, however, do not believe this Nation is anywhere close to eradicating racial discrimination or its vestiges. In constitutionalizing its wishful thinking, the majority today does a grave disservice not only to those victims of past and present racial discrimination in this Nation whom government has sought to assist, but also to this Court's long tradition of approaching issues of race with the utmost sensitivity.

B

I am also troubled by the majority's assertion that, even if it did not believe generally in strict scrutiny of race-based remedial measures, "the circumstances of this case" require this Court to look upon the Richmond City Council's measure with the strictest scrutiny. The sole such circumstance which the majority cites, however, is the fact that blacks in Richmond are a "dominant racial grou[p]" in the city. In support of this characterization of dominance, the majority observes that "blacks comprise approximately 50% of the population of the city of Richmond" and that "[f]ive of the nine seats on the City Council are held by blacks."

While I agree that the numerical and political supremacy of a given racial group is a factor bearing upon the level of scrutiny to be applied, this Court has never held that numerical inferiority, standing alone, makes a racial group "suspect" and thus entitled to strict scrutiny review. Rather, we have identified *other* "traditional indicia of suspectness": whether a group has been "saddled with such disabilities, or subjected to such a history of purposeful unequal treatment, or relegated to such a position of political powerlessness as to command extraordinary protection from the majoritarian political process." San Antonio Independent School District v. Rodriguez, 411 U.S. 1, 28 (1973).

It cannot seriously be suggested that nonminorities in Richmond have any "history of purposeful unequal treatment." Nor is there any indication that they have any of the disabilities that have characteristically afflicted those groups this Court has deemed suspect. Indeed, the numerical and political dominance of nonminorities within the State of Virginia and the Nation as a whole provide an enormous political check against the "simple racial politics" at the municipal level which the majority fears. If the majority really believes that groups like Richmond's non-minorities, which comprise approximately half the population but which are outnumbered even marginally in political fora, are deserving of suspect class status for these reasons alone, this Court's decisions denying suspect status to women, and to persons with below-average incomes, stand on extremely shaky ground.

In my view, the "circumstances of this case," underscore the importance of *not* subjecting to a strict scrutiny straitjacket the increasing number of cities which have recently come under minority leadership and are eager to rectify, or at least prevent the perpetuation of, past racial discrimination. In many cases, these cities will be the ones with the most in the way of prior discrimination to rectify. Richmond's leaders had just witnessed decades of publicly sanctioned racial discrimination in virtually all walks of life — discrimination amply documented in the decisions of the federal judiciary. This history of "purposefully unequal treatment" forced upon minorities, not imposed by them, should raise an inference that minorities in Richmond had much to remedy — and that the 1983 set-aside was undertaken with sincere remedial goals in mind, not "simple racial politics."

Richmond's own recent political history underscores the facile nature of the majority's assumption that elected officials' voting decisions are based on the color of their skins. In recent years, white and black councilmembers in Richmond have increasingly joined hands on controversial matters. When the Richmond City Council elected a black man Mayor in 1982, for example, his victory was won with the support of the City Council's four white members. The vote on the set-aside plan a year later also was not purely along racial lines. Of the four white councilmembers, one voted for the measure and another abstained. The majority's view that remedial measures undertaken by municipalities with black leadership must face a stiffer test of Equal Protection Clause scrutiny than remedial measures undertaken by municipalities with white leadership implies a lack of political maturity on the part of this Nation's elected minority officials that is totally unwarranted. Such insulting judgments have no place in constitutional jurisprudence.

C

Today's decision, finally, is particularly noteworthy for the daunting standard it imposes upon States and localities contemplating the use of race-conscious measures to eradicate the present effects of prior discrimination and prevent its perpetuation. The majority restricts the use of such measures to situations in which a State or locality can put forth "a prima facie case of a constitutional or statutory violation.". . .

[If] Congress tomorrow dramatically expanded Title VII of the Civil Rights Act of 1964 — or alternatively, if it repealed that legislation altogether — the meaning of equal protection would change precipitously along with it. Whatever the Framers of the Fourteenth Amendment had in mind in 1868, it certainly was not that the content of their Amendment would turn on the amendments to or the evolving interpretations of a federal statute passed nearly a century later.

To the degree that this parsimonious standard is grounded on a view that either §1 or §5 of the Fourteenth Amendment substantially disempowered States and localities from remedying past racial discrimination, the majority is seriously mistaken. With respect, first, to §5, our precedents have never suggested that this provision — or, for that matter, its companion federal-empowerment provisions in the Thirteenth and Fifteenth Amendments — was meant to pre-empt or limit state police power to undertake race-conscious remedial measures. . . .

As for §1, it is too late in the day to assert seriously that the Equal Protection Clause prohibits States — or for that matter, the Federal Government, to whom the equal protection guarantee has largely been applied — from enacting race-conscious remedies. Our cases in the areas of school desegregation, voting rights, and affirmative action have demonstrated time and again that race is constitutionally germane, precisely because race remains dismayingly relevant in American life.

In adopting its prima facie standard for States and localities, the majority closes its eyes to this constitutional history and social reality. So, too, does Justice Scalia. He would further limit consideration of race to those cases in which States find it "necessary to eliminate their own maintenance of a system of unlawful racial classification" — a "distinction" which, he states, "explains our school desegregation cases." But this Court's remedy-stage school desegregation decisions cannot so conveniently be cordoned off. These decisions (like those involving voting rights and affirmative action) stand for the same broad principles of equal protection which Richmond seeks to vindicate in this case: all persons have equal worth, and it is permissible, given a sufficient factual predicate and appropriate tailoring, for government to take account of race to eradicate the present effects of race-based subjugation denying that basic equality. Justice Scalia's artful distinction allows him to avoid having to repudiate "our school desegregation cases," but, like the arbitrary limitation on race-conscious relief adopted by the majority, his approach "would freeze the status quo that is the very target" of the remedial actions of States and localities.

The fact is that Congress' concern in passing the Reconstruction Amendments, and particularly their congressional authorization provisions, was that States would *not* adequately respond to racial violence or discrimination against newly freed slaves. To interpret any aspect of these Amendments as proscribing state remedial responses to these very problems turns the Amendments on their heads. . . .

[The] three Reconstruction Amendments undeniably "worked a dramatic change in the balance between congressional and state power:" they forbade state-sanctioned slavery, forbade the state-sanctioned denial of the right to vote, and (until the content of the Equal Protection Clause was substantially applied to the Federal Government through the Due Process Clause of the Fifth Amendment) uniquely forbade States from denying equal protection. The Amendments also specifically empowered the Federal Government to combat discrimination at a time when the breadth of federal power under the Constitution was less apparent than it is today. But nothing in the Amendments themselves, or in our long history of interpreting or applying those momentous charters, suggests that States, exercising their police power, are in any way constitutionally inhibited from working alongside the Federal Government in the fight against discrimination and its effects.

IV

The majority today sounds a full-scale retreat from the Court's longstanding solicitude to race-conscious remedial efforts "directed toward deliverance of the century-old promise of equality of economic opportunity." *Fullilove*, 448 U.S., at 463. The new and restrictive tests it applies scuttle one city's effort to surmount its discriminatory past, and imperil those of dozens more localities. I, however, profoundly disagree with the cramped vision of the Equal Protection Clause which the majority offers today and with its application of that vision to Richmond, Virginia's, laudable set-aside plan. The battle against pernicious racial discrimination or its effects is nowhere near won. I must dissent.

JUSTICE BLACKMUN, with whom JUSTICE BRENNAN joins, dissenting. . . .
I never thought that I would live to see the day when the city of Richmond, Virginia, the cradle of the Old Confederacy, sought on its own, within a narrow confine, to lessen the stark impact of persistent discrimination. But Richmond, to its great credit, acted. Yet this Court, the supposed bastion of equality, strikes down Richmond's efforts as though discrimination had never existed or was not demonstrated in this particular litigation. Justice Marshall convincingly discloses the fallacy and the shallowness of that approach. History is irrefutable, even though one might sympathize with those who — though possibly innocent in themselves — benefit from the wrongs of past decades.

So the Court today regresses. I am confident, however, that, given time, it one day again will do its best to fulfill the great promises of the Constitution's Preamble and of the guarantees embodied in the Bill of Rights — a fulfillment that would make this Nation very special.

METRO BROADCASTING, INC. v. FEDERAL COMMUNICA-
TIONS COMMISSION, – U.S. – (1990):   In this case, applicants for
broadcast licenses claimed that two FCC policies designed to favor minority
firms violated the equal protection component of the fifth amendment's due
process clause. Under one policy, the Commission considered minority ownership as a "plus" to be weighed with other factors in a comparative hearing
designed to determine which applicant should be awarded a license. The other
policy created an exception favoring minorities in cases where a licensee whose
qualifications to hold a license comes into question. Normally, such a licensee
may not transfer the license until the FCC has resolved the matter. However,
the FCC policy permitted such a licensee to assign the license to an FCC-
approved minority enterprise.

The Commission justified both policies on the ground that minorities were
inadequately represented in the broadcast media and that greater minority
representation would enhance the diversification of programming that was a
key object of the 1934 Federal Communications Act. While these cases were
pending, the FCC decided to reconsider its minority preference policies. The
reconsideration ended, however, when Congress enacted an appropriations
measure that prohibited the FCC from spending any appropriated funds to
examine or change its minority ownership policies.

In a 5-4 decision, the Court upheld the constitutionality of both policies.
Justice Brennan delivered the Court's opinion: "It is of overriding significance
in these cases that the FCC's minority ownership programs have been specifically approved – indeed, mandated – by Congress. . . .

"We hold that benign race-conscious measures mandated by Congress [12] –
even if those measures are not 'remedial' in the sense of being designed to
compensate victims of past governmental or society discrimination – are constitutionally permissible to the extent that they serve important governmental
objectives within the power of Congress and are substantially related to the
achievement of those objectives. . . .

"We hold that the FCC minority ownership policies pass muster under the
test we announce today. First, we find that they serve the important governmen-

---

12. "We fail to understand how Justice Kennedy can pretend that examples of 'benign' race-
conscious measures include South African apartheid, the 'separate-but-equal' law at issue in *Plessy v.
Ferguson*, and the internment of American citizens of Japanese ancestry upheld in *Korematsu v. United
States*. We are confident that an 'examination of the legislative scheme and its history,' [*Weinberger v.
Wisenfeld*] will separate benign measures from other types of racial classifications. Of course, 'the
mere recitation of a benign, compensatory purpose is not an automatic shield which protects against
any inquiry into the actual purposes underlying a statutory scheme.' [*Weinberger*] The concept of
benign race-conscious measures – even those with at least some non-remedial purposes – is as old
as the Fourteenth Amendment. For example, the Freedman's Bureau Acts authorized the provision
of land, education, medical care, and other assistance to Afro-Americans."

tal objective of broadcast diversity. Second, we conclude that they are substantially related to the achievement of that objective. . . .

"[The] interest in enhancing broadcast diversity is, at the very least, an important governmental objective and is therefore a sufficient basis for the Commission's minority ownership policies. Just as a 'diverse student body' contributing to a ' "robust exchange of ideas" ' is a 'constitutionally permissible goal' on which a race-conscious university admissions program may be predicated [*Bakke* (opinion of Powell, J.], the diversity of views and information on the airwaves serves important First Amendment values. Cf. [*Wygant* (Stevens, J., dissenting)]. . . .

"We also find that the minority ownership policies are substantially related to the achievement of the Government's interest.

"As revealed by the historical evolution of current federal policy, both Congress and the Commission have concluded that the minority ownership programs are critical means of promoting broadcast diversity. We must give great weight to their joint determination. . . .

"The judgment that there is a link between expanded minority ownership and broadcast diversity does not rest on impermissible stereotyping. [Rather], both Congress and the FCC maintain simply that expanded minority ownership of broadcast outlets will, in the aggregate, result in greater broadcast diversity. A broadcasting industry with representative minority participation will produce more variation and diversity than will one whose ownership is drawn from a single racially and ethnically homogeneous group. The predictive judgment about the overall result of minority entry into broadcasting is not a rigid assumption about how minority owners will behave in every case but rather is akin to Justice Powell's conclusion in *Bakke* that greater admission of minorities would contribute, on average, 'to the "robust exchange of ideas." ' . . .

"We find that the minority ownership policies are in other relevant respects substantially related to the goal of promoting broadcast diversity. [The] Commission adopted and Congress endorsed minority ownership preferences only after long study and painstaking consideration of all available alternatives. . . .

"The minority ownership policies are 'appropriately limited in extent and duration, and subject to reassessment and reevaluation by the Congress prior to any extension or reenactment.' [*Fullilove*]. . . .

"Congress and the Commission have adopted a policy of minority ownership not as an end in itself, but rather as a means of achieving greater programming diversity. Such a goal carries its own natural limit, for there will be no need for further minority preferences once sufficient diversity has been achieved. . . .

"In the context of broadcast licenses, the burden on nonminorities is slight. [Applicants] have no settled expectation that their applications will be granted without consideration of public interest factors such as minority ownership. Award of a preference [thus] contravenes 'no legitimate firmly rooted expectation[s]' of competing applicants."

Justice Stevens filed a concurring opinion.

Justice O'Connor filed a dissenting opinion that was joined by Chief Justice Rehnquist and Justices Scalia and Kennedy: "At the heart of the Constitution's guarantee of equal protection lies the simple command that the Government must treat citizens 'as *individuals*, not "as simply components of a racial, religious, sexual or national class." ' Arizona Governing Committee v. Norris, 463 U.S. 1073, 1083 (1983). Social scientists may debate how peoples' thoughts and behavior reflect their background, but the Constitution provides that the Government may not allocate benefits and burdens among individuals based on the assumption that race or enthicity determines how they act or think. To uphold the challenged programs, the Court departs from these fundamental principles and from our traditional requirement that racial classifications are permissible only if necessary and narrowly tailored to achieve a compelling interest. This departure marks a renewed toleration of racial classifications and a repudiation of our recent affirmation that the Constitution's equal protection guarantees extend equally to all citizens. . . .

"[The] congressional role in prolonging the FCC's policies [does not] justify any lower level of scrutiny. As with all instances of judicial review of federal legislation, the Court does not lightly set aside the considered judgment of a coordinate branch. Nonetheless, the respect due a coordinate branch yields neither less vigilance in defense of equal protection principles nor any corresponding diminution of the standard of review. . . .

"Congress has considerable latitude, presenting special concerns for judicial review, when it exercises its 'unique remedial powers . . . under §5 of the Fourteenth Amendment,' [*Croson*], but this case does not implicate those powers. Section 5 empowers Congress to act respecting the States, and of course this case concerns only the administration of federal programs by federal officials. . . .

"The FCC and Congress are clearly not acting for any remedial purpose, and the Court today expressly extends its standard to racial classifications that are not remedial in any sense. This case does not present [a] remedial effort or exercise of §5 powers. . . .

"Under the appropriate standard, strict scrutiny, only a compelling interest may support the Government's use of racial classifications. Modern equal protection doctrine has recognized only one such interest: remedying the effects of racial discrimination. The interest in increasing the diversity of broadcast viewpoints is clearly not a compelling interest. It is simply too amorphous, too insubstantial, and too unrelated to any legitimate basis for employing racial classifications. . . .

"Our traditional equal protection doctrine requires, in addition to a compelling state interest, that the Government's chosen means be necessary to accomplish and narrowly tailored to further the asserted interest. [The] FCC's policies [also fail] this requirement. . . .

"The FCC's choice to employ a racial criterion embodies the related notions that a particular and distinct viewpoint inheres in certain racial groups, and that a particular applicant, by virtue of race or ethnicity alone, is more valued than other applicants because 'likely to provide [that] distinct perspective.' [The] policies impermissibly value individuals because they presume that persons think in a manner associated with their race."

Justice Kennedy also filed a dissenting opinion, which Justice Scalia joined: "In abandoning strict scrutiny to endorse [the interest in broadcast diversity], the Court turns back the clock on the level of scrutiny applicable to federal race-conscious measures. Even strict scrutiny may not have sufficed to invalidate early race based laws of most doubtful validity, as we learned in [*Korematsu*]. But the relaxed standard of review embraced today would validate that case, and any number of future racial classifications the Government may find useful. . . .

"The Court insists that the programs under review are 'benign.' [A] fundamental error of the *Plessy* Court was its similar confidence in its ability to identify 'benign' discrimination. . . .

"Policies of racial separation and preference are almost always justified as benign, even when it is clear to any sensible observer that they are not. The following statement, for example, would fit well among those offered to uphold the Commission's racial preference policy: 'The policy is not based on any concept of superiority or inferiority, but merely on the fact that people differ, particularly in their group associations, loyalties, cultures, outlook, modes of life and standards of development.' See South Africa and the Rule of Law 37 (1968) (official publication of the South African Government). . . .

"Perhaps the Court can succeed in its assumed role of case-by-case arbiter of when it is desirable and benign for the Government to disfavor some citizens and favor others based on the color of their skin. Perhaps the tolerance and decency to which our people aspire will let the disfavored rise above hostility and the favored escape condescension. But history suggests much peril in this enterprise, and so the Constitution forbids us to undertake it. I regret that after a century of judicial opinions we interpret the Constitution to do no more than move us from 'separate but equal' to 'unequal but benign.' "

NOTE: THE FUTURE OF AFFIRMATIVE ACTION

1. *The impact of* Croson. Does *Croson* mark an important change in the law of affirmative action? Does it change the law of affirmative action in contexts other than "set asides"? In situations where a black majority is not favoring itself?

Arguably, the Richmond affirmative action plan was uniquely vulnerable to constitutional attack because of the perception (reality?) that set aside plans amount to no more than a racial spoils system and are singularly ineffective as a means of providing serious remediation for racial discrimination. But consider the proposition that historically, successive waves of ethnic groups have been integrated into American society by obtaining control of political offices in cities across the country and then directing municipal aid to members of their own groups. In light of this history, is there adequate justification for precluding blacks from following the same route to economic success when they have finally achieved some degree of political power? On this view, the efforts in the Progressive era to "professionalize" municipal administration achieved limited successes in the political process when various white ethnic groups controlled municipal politics, and achieved their greatest success through the judicial process when blacks eventually came to control or have substantial influence on municipal politics. Can this outcome be reconciled with the central purpose of the fourteenth amendment?

2. *Croson and the level of review.* On the doctrinal level, *Croson* marks the first time that a majority of the Court has been able to agree on a standard of review for affirmative action measures. Does it make a significant difference that such measures will now be subjected to "strict scrutiny" when adopted at the state level?

Consider the proposition that Justice O'Connor's enumeration of justifications that would satisfy the Constitution suggests that she is actually applying some form of nontraditional strict scrutiny, in that certain programs would survive even though their justifications were less than compelling in traditional terms. If that proposition is correct, does it mean that the Court has adopted a new form of strict scrutiny for all cases, or only for affirmative action cases? If the latter, why?

Note that with respect to the application of strict scrutiny, the plurality arguably expands the range of permissible affirmative action measures by endorsing the efforts of local government to remedy private discrimination occuring within its jurisdiction. It arguably contracts the permissible range of such measures by insisting on fairly rigorous proof of prior discrimination and by requiring that plans be very "narrowly tailored." Is the contraction more important than the expansion?

3. *The relation of congressional and state power.* In *Metro Broadcasting* the Court endorses "intermediate scrutiny" for "benign" measures adopted by Congress. Is this result consistent with *Croson*? Could Congress authorize the states to adopt set-aside programs like that in *J. A. Croson*? Recall the Court's assertion in Bolling v. Sharpe, page 464 of the main volume, that "[i]n view of our decision that the Constitution prohibits the States from maintaining racially segregated public schools, it would be unthinkable that the same Constitution would impose a lesser duty on the Federal Government." Is it still "unthinkable?"

Taken together, do *J. A. Croson* and *Metro Broadcasting* repudiate the "one-way ratchet" interpretation of §5 advanced by the Court in Katzenbach v. Morgan, page 233 of the main volume, by holding that Congress does have the power to "dilute" the equal protection guarantee as interpreted in *J. A. Croson?*

4. *Alternatives to set-asides.* After *J. A. Croson*, could a city adopt a regulation waiving bonding requirements for all minority business enterprises? For those that showed that their inability to obtain a bond (at competitive rates) resulted from their minority status? What if bonding companies refused bonds to newly established businesses, which are disproportionately minority owned?

Is Justice O'Connor's endorsement of race neutral alternatives to set-asides consistent with the proposition implicit in Washington v. Davis that even race neutral measures should be strictly scrutinized when they have a discriminatory purpose? Is there some reason why the Washington v. Davis doctrine should be inapplicable in the affirmative action context?

5. Croson *and originalism.* Most of the justices in the *Croson* majority are associated with originalist theories of judicial review. These theories hold that the Court should be deferential to judgments reached by the political branches, that it should respect the rights of states protected by the federalism principles embedded in the Constitution, and that it should not upset judgments reached in the political process except in circumstances where some clear provision of the constitutional text and the intent of its framers supports this result. Can *Croson* be reconciled with these tenets of originalism?

By its terms, the fourteenth amendment says nothing about heightened review for racial classifications contained in affirmative action measures. As noted above, see page 446 of the main volume, the original impetus for passage of the amendment was a desire to expand the scope of congressional power to enact the nineteenth century analogue of affirmative action measures. Congress wished to lay a firm constitutional grounding for Reconstruction statutes that had the specific purpose of benefiting and protecting the newly freed slaves. There is also a sense in which the amendment was designed to *restrict* judicial power. Members of the Reconstruction Congress feared that the Supreme Court would invalidate the 1866 Civil Rights Act and adopted the fourteenth amendment so as to avoid that result.

Does the plurality opinion deal satisfactorily with this history? Is it plausible that the Congress that wished to protect federal affirmative action measures from judicial attack also meant to authorize such attack when the very same measures were adopted by state and local governments? If *Croson* is inconsistent with an originalist approach to constitutional adjudication, what alternative approach explains (justifies) the result?

6. Metro *and judicial protection for minorities.* The justices in the *Metro* majority are often associated with the view that the judiciary has an important role to play in the protection of minorities from the political process. Is the Court's opinion in *Metro* consistent with this view? Notice that the Court might have reached the same result in a very different sort of opinion: It might have subjected the FCC policy to strict scrutiny and upheld it only after satisfying

itself that the policy in fact aided minority groups. Instead, the Court labeled the policy "benign" and then subjected it to a more relaxed standard of review, deferring to the congressional judgment regarding its merits.

What, precisely, makes the policy "benign"? The Court does not defend the diversification goal on remedial grounds and it treats diversity as a good that benefits the listening public as a whole rather than simply minorities. It also says that "the mere recitation of a benign, compensatory purpose is not an automatic shield which protects against any inquiry into the actual purpose underlying a statutory scheme." Does it follow that a federal statute would be subject to relaxed scrutiny even if it does not benefit minorities so long as its purpose is not to hurt them? Has the Court in effect extended the Washington v. Davis test to federally enacted race-based classifications? Does its opinion reflect the view that Congress is more likely to take adequate account of the welfare of minorities than the Court? If so, what has changed since *Korematsu*?

D. EQUAL PROTECTION METHODOLOGY: HEIGHTENED SCRUTINY AND THE PROBLEM OF GENDER

Page 634. After the second paragraph of section 2 of the Note, add the following:

Might the result in *Michael M.* be justified on the ground that many rape laws fail to deal adequately with acts of intercourse that do not involve overt force, yet are also not fully consensual? See, e.g., S. Estrich, Real Rape 29-41 (1987).

Consider Olsen, Statutory Rape: A Feminist Critique of Rights Analysis, 63 Tex. L. Rev. 387, 427-428 (1984):

> The opinions [in *Michael M.*] imply that there are two sharply distinct categories of sexual relations that together comprise all of sexuality. There is equal, consensual sexual intercourse on one hand, and bad, coercive sex imposed upon a female by a male aggressor on the other hand. But these two categories constitute a continuum of sexual relations; there is no bright line between them. Although most women do seek sexual contact with men, heterosexual behavior in our society is seldom fully voluntary. . . .
>
> The *Michael M.* opinions mystify the power relations involved in sexual intercourse by assuming that it is an equal activity. Most feminists would agree that sexual intercourse should be more equal. [But] it is not helpful to pretend that sexual intercourse is normally equal. This pretense is an unexamined assumption buried in the *Michael M.* opinions.

In a portion of his concurring opinion not reproduced in the main volume, Justice Blackmun notes that the complainant in *Michael M.* "appears not to have been an unwilling participant in at least the initial stages of the intimacies that took place," suggests that this fact made the case "an unattractive one to prosecute at all, and especially to prosecute as a felony," and concludes "reluctantly" that the facts "may fit the crime." However, the trial transcript, from which Justice Blackmun liberally quotes in a footnote, is open to a different interpretation:

> *The Witness:* [We were] laying there and we were kissing each other, and then he asked me if I wanted to walk him over to the park; so we walked over to the park and we sat down on the bench and then he started kissing me again and we were laying on the bench. And he told me to take my pants off.
>
> I said, "No" and I was trying to get up and he hit me back down on the bench and then I just said to myself, "Forget it," and I let him do what he wanted to do and he took my pants off and he was telling me to put my legs around him and stuff —
>
> *Q.* [You] said that he hit you?
> *A.* Yeah.
> *Q.* How did he hit you?
> *A.* He slugged me in the face.
> *The Court:* [Did] he hit you one time or did he hit you more than once?
> *The Witness:* He hit me about two or three times.

Page 639. At the end of section 5 of the Note, add the following:

Consider C. MacKinnon, Feminism Unmodified: Discourses on Life and Law 3, 8-9 (1987):

> [The] social relation between the sexes is organized so that men may dominate and women must submit and this relation is sexual — in fact, is sex. Men in particular, if not men alone, sexualize inequality, especially the inequality of the sexes. [To] treat gender as a difference (with or without a French accent) means to treat it as a bipolar distinction, each pole of which is defined in contrast to the other by opposed intrinsic attributes. Beloved of left and right alike, construing gender as a difference [obscures] and legitimizes the way gender is imposed by force. It hides that force behind a static description of gender as a biological or social or mythic or semantic partition, engraved or inscribed or inculcated by god, nature, society (agents unspecified), the unconscious, or the cosmos. The idea of gender difference helps keep the reality of male dominance in place. . . .
>
> Difference is the velvet glove on the iron fist of domination. This is as true when differences are affirmed as when they are denied, when their substance is applauded or when it is disparaged, when women are punished or [when] they are protected in their name. A sex inequality is not a difference gone wrong, a lesson the law of sex discrimination has yet to learn. One of the most deceptive antifeminisms in society, scholarship, politics, and law is the persistent treatment of gender as if it truly is a question of difference, rather than treating the gender difference as a construct of the difference gender makes.

Page 639. Before subsection 7, *"Beyond real differences."* add the following:

There is significant dissatisfaction with formal equality as a constitutional test in the area of gender. See the attack on formal equality in C. MacKinnon, Feminism Unmodified (1987). And consider Becker, Price Charming: Abstract Equality, Sup. Ct. Rev. 201, 247 (1988): "Formal equality . . . can effect only limited change. It cannot, for example, ensure that jobs are structured so that female workers and male workers are equally able to combine wage work and parenthood. Nor can it ensure that social security, unemployment compensation, and other safety nets are structured so as to provide for women's financial security as well as they provide for men's. Moreover, women, especially ordinary mothers and wives, have been harmed by the changes effected to date by the movement towards formal equality. Further movement in that direction could bring additional harm. Any other satisfactory and workable general standard to be applied by judges is as yet unimagined and likely to be so for the foreseeable future."

A different view is presented in Littleton, Reconstructing Sexual Equality, 75 Calif. L. Rev. 1279 (1987), urging a model of "equality as acceptance" that would make social or biological differences "costless." See also Minow, Foreword: Justice Engendered, 101 Harv. L. Rev. 4 (1987) (stressing that differences inhere in relationships).

How would constitutional doctrine have to be constructed to respond to these observations by M. Becker, Obscuring the Struggle: Sex Discrimination, Social Security, and Stone, Seidman, Sunstein & Tushnet's Constitutional Law, 89 Colum. L. Rev. 264, 283 (1989):

> [The] social security system fails to afford women as reliable an old-age security system as that afforded men. [Women] who lead ordinary lives are less likely to be well protected by the social security system than men who live ordinary lives because the system prefers those who have successfully fulfilled men's traditional breadwinner role over those who fulfilled women's traditional roles. Social security discriminates against women because it is designed so that women are at a much greater risk of poverty than are men. It exerts pressure on homemakers to depend economically on men in old age, despite the riskiness of such dependence.

To these observations by Z. Eisenstein, The Female Body and the Law 42-43 (1988):

> [Because] law is [structured] through the multiple oppositional layerings embedded in the dualism of man/woman, it is not able to move beyond the male referent as the standard for sex equality. [This] establishes men and women as opposites while privileging men. [The] legal notion of sex equality resulting from this stance is contradictory. It is progressive to the degree that it assumes men and women to be the same, and reactionary to the extent that its notion of what is "the same" derives from

the phallus. It is progressive to the degree that it recognizes sex difference(s) as potentially creative and productive, and reactionary to the extent that it differentiates women according to their gender.

Page 649.   Add the following as Note 1A:

1A. Goldfarb's *"significance."* Consider these observations by M. Becker, Obscuring the Struggle: Sex Discrimination, Social Security, and Stone, Seidman, Sunstein & Tushnet's Constitutional Law, 89 Colum. L. Rev. 264, 274-276 (1989):

> Relative to the changes necessary to achieve equality between the sexes, [*Goldfarb*] is trivial. [It] is trivial in another sense: it involves a challenge to the award of benefits to a man. [One] would expect the case to have had only the most limited effect on the status of women in the real world during their lives and marriages. True, after *Goldfarb,* a very few working women and retired women workers [could] sleep more soundly knowing that in the event of their deaths, their widowers would receive more money. But these women tend to be relatively powerful. [It] surely would be relevant to note that the Court developed its constitutional standard for sex equality in trivial cases. It seems likely that development in such a context might affect the effectiveness of a substantive standard.

Page 672.   Before section 4 of the Note, add the following new subsection:

d. Under California law, a child born to a married woman is presumed to be a child of the marriage, and the presumption can be overcome only in very limited circumstances. Victoria D. was born to Carole D. while she was married to Gerald D. However, blood tests demonstrated with near certainty that Victoria's biological father was Michael H. Michael filed an action to establish his paternity so that he could have visitation rights, and Victoria, through her guardian ad litem, joined in the action. The state court rejected the claim because of the statutory presumption. The Supreme Court, in an opinion by Justice Scalia, affirmed. The Court rejected

> [Victoria's] suggestion that her equal protection challenge must be assessed under a standard of strict scrutiny because, in denying her the right to maintain a filial relationship with Michael, the State is discriminating against her on the basis of her illegitimacy. Illegitimacy is a legal construct, not a natural traint. Under California law, Victoria is not illegitimate, and she is treated in the same manner as all other legitimate children: she is entitled to maintain a filial relationship with her legal parents. The Court held that the presumption easily survived rational relationship review because it served the state interest in preserving the integrity of a marital union.

E. EQUAL PROTECTION METHODOLOGY: OTHER CANDIDATES FOR HEIGHTENED SCRUTINY

Page 675.   Before section 5 of the Note, add the following new subsection:

e. Reed. In Reed v. Campbell, 476 U.S. 852 (1986), the Court summarized the "clear distinction" that had emerged from its nonmarital children cases as follows:

> [We] have unambiguously concluded that a State may not justify discriminatory treatment of illegitimates in order to express its disapproval of their parents' misconduct. We have, however, also recognized that there is a permissible basis for some "distinctions made in part on the basis of legitimacy" [Mathews v. Lucas]; specifically, we have upheld statutory provisions that have an evident and substantial relation to the State's interest in providing for the orderly and just distribution of a decedent's property at death. [This interest] may justify the imposition of special requirements upon an illegitimate child who asserts a right to inherit from her father, and, of course, it justifies the enforcement of generally applicable limitations on the time and the manner in which claims may be asserted.

Applying this test to the facts before it, the Court held that the state had no legitimate interest in the application of its total statutory ban on intestate inheritance by nonmarital children to estates that remained opened at the time *Trimble* was decided.

Page 687.   At the beginning of section 2 of the Note, add the following:

Are you persuaded by the *Cleburne* Court's argument that it should not extend quasi-suspect status to the mentally retarded because doing so would require it to provide similar treatment to a host of other groups? Consider the critique of "slippery slope" arguments such as this in Schauer, Slippery Slopes, 99 Harv. L. Rev. 361, 368-369 (1985):

> [A] slippery slope argument necessarily contains the *implicit concession* that the proposed resolution of the instant case is not itself troublesome. By focusing on the consequences for future cases, we implicitly concede that this instance is itself innocuous, or perhaps even desirable. . . .
> A slippery slope argument claims that permitting the instant case [will lead] to, or increase the likelihood of, the danger case. . . .
> But as thus isolated, the slippery slope argument seems weak. The drafter of the principle against which a slippery slope claim is made has usually taken pains to prevent the feared slide. Why, then, should a slippery slope claim have any persuasive force?

Page 688.   Before the first full paragraph, add the following:

In Lyng v. Castillo, 477 U.S. 635 (1986), the Court held that close relatives who live together are not a suspect or quasi-suspect class. Under the federal foodstamp program, unrelated and distantly related individuals living together can be considered separate "households" entitled to larger benefits if they do not eat or purchase food together. In contrast, siblings, parents, and children living together are treated as a single household even if they eat and purchase food separately. (For a more detailed description of the statutory scheme, see Supplement to Casebook page 520 supra.) A district court, applying heightened scrutiny, invalidated this distinction under the equal protection component of the fifth amendment due process clause, but the Supreme Court, in an opinion by Justice Stevens, reversed:

> Close relatives are not a "suspect" or "quasi-suspect" class. As a historical matter, they have not been subjected to discrimination; they do not exhibit obvious, immutable, or distinguishing characteristics that define them as a discrete group; and they are not a minority or politically powerless. In fact, quite the contrary is true.

Page 688.   After the Tribe quotation, add the following:

In Bowers v. Hardwick, 478 U.S. 186 (1986), the Court rejected a substantive due process attack on a Georgia sodomy statute brought by an adult male who had been criminally charged for a sexual act performed in his own bedroom with another adult male. (This aspect of *Bowers* is discussed at greater length at Supplement to Casebook page 897 infra.) On its face, the statute did not distinguish between heterosexual and homosexual sodomy, and the Court purported not to reach any equal protection questions raised by it. However, the Court also limited its holding to the question of homosexual sodomy posed by the facts before it and explicitly refused to decide whether the statute's application to heterosexuals would be constitutional. Does the Court's willingness to uphold the statute as applied to homosexuals while reserving the possibility that it might be unconstitutional as applied to heterosexuals implicitly resolve the equal protection question?

Consider the following argument advanced by Justice Blackmun writing for four justices in dissent:

> [Georgia's] exclusive stress before this Court on its interest in prosecuting homosexual activity despite the gender-neutral terms of the statute may raise serious questions of discriminatory enforcement, questions that cannot be disposed of before this Court on a motion to dismiss. See [*Yick Wo*]. The legislature having decided that the sex of the participants is irrelevant to the legality of the acts, I do not see why the State can defend [the statute] on the ground that individuals singled out for prosecution are of the same sex as their partners. Thus, under the circumstances of this case, a claim under the Equal Protection Clause may well be

available without having to reach the more controversial question whether homo-sexuals are a suspect class.

In Watkins v. United States Army, 837 F.2d 1428 (9th Cir. 1988), a divided court of appeals invoked the equal protection component of the due process clause in order to invalidate the dismissal from the Army of a serviceman having "homosexual tendencies." An Army regulation promulgated in 1981 required the discharge of all gays and lesbians regardless of merit. The court first con-cluded that Bowers v. Hardwick did not resolve the issue before it. According to the Court, the concerns in *Hardwick* "have little relevance to equal protection doctrine. . . . This principle of equal treatment, imposed against majoritarian rule, arises from the Constitution itself, not from judicial fiat." On the equal protection issue, the Court concluded that gays and lesbians were a suspect class entitled to strict scrutiny for disadvantageous classification, noting that "Lesbi-ans and gays have been the object of some of the deepest prejudice and hatred in American society. . . . Moreover, as the Army itself concluded, there is not a scintilla of evidence that Watkins' avowed homosexuality has either a degrad-ing effect upon unit performance, morale or discipline, or upon his own job performance."

On the problem of immutability, the court said that "Scientific research indicates that we have little control over our sexual orientation and that, once acquired, our sexual orientation is largely impervious to change. Scientific proof aside, it seems appropriate to ask whether heterosexuals feel capable of chang-ing their sexual orientation. Would heterosexuals living in a city that passed an ordinance banning those who engaged in or desired to engage in sex with persons of the opposite sex find it easy not only to abstain from heterosexual activity but also to shift the object of their sexual desires to persons of the same sex?"

The courts concluded that the Army regulation could not survive strict scrutiny, stating that the Army's attempted justifications "illegitimately cater to private biases" analogous to those that once justified racial segregation in the military.

Judge Reinhardt dissented. He suggested that "the Supreme Court egre-giously misinterpreted the Constitution in *Hardwick*. . . . I believe that history will view *Hardwick* much as it views Plessy v. Ferguson. . . ." Nonetheless, he argued that *Hardwick* controlled the problem in *Watkins*: "When conduct that plays a central role in defining a group may be prohibited by the state, it cannot be asserted with any legitimacy that the group is specifically protected by the Constitution."

Consider the suggestion in Sunstein, Sexual Orientation and the Constitution: A Note on the Relationship Between Due Process and Equal Protection, 55 U. Chicago L. Rev. 1161, 1163, that "the Due Process Clause has been interpreted largely (though not exclusively) to protect traditional practices against short-run departures [and] has therefore been associated with a [conception] of judicial review [that] sees the courts as safeguards against novel developments brought about by temporary majorities who are insufficiently sensitive to the claims of history," while "the Equal Protection Clause [has] been understood as an attempt to protect disadvantaged groups from discriminatory practices, however deeply engrained and longstanding. The Due Process Clause often looks backward; it is highly relevant to the Due Process issue whether an existing [convention] is violated by the practice under attack. [The] Equal Protection Clause looks forward, serving to invalidate practices that were widespread at the time of its ratification and that were expected to endure." How much weight can the "often" in this observation bear in distinguishing the two clauses?

For a discussion of whether and to what extent suspect categories should be expanded, see Scales-Trent, Black Women and the Constitution: Finding Our Place, Asserting Our Rights, 24 Harv. C.R.-C.L. L. Rev. 9 (1989).

Page 689.   At the end of section 3 of the Note, add the following:

Consider Minow, When Difference Has Its Home: Group Homes for the Mentally Retarded, Equal Protection and Legal Treatment of Difference, 22 Harv. C.R.-C.L. L. Rev. 111 (1987). Minow develops a "social relations" approach to the evaluation of discriminatory treatment of "deviant" groups such as the mentally retarded. This approach

> challenges the categories and differences used to define and describe people on a group basis. Such suspicion stems [from] a view that attribution itself hides the power of those who classify as well as those defined as different. A focus on social relations casts suspicion on the very claim to knowledge manifested by the labeling of any group as different, because that claim disguises the act of power by which the namers simultaneously assign names and deny their relationships with, and power over, the named.

Under such an approach "[attributions] of difference should be sustained only if they do not express or confirm the distribution of power in ways that harm the less powerful and benefit the more powerful." Id. at 128. Does such an approach take adequate account of the possibility that differences in power might themselves be a product of real differences that are not merely social constructs? Is it unduly optimistic about the ability of judges using the approach to transcend their own social position?

Chapter Six

Implied Fundamental Rights

A. INTRODUCTION

Page 693. After the quotation in section 3 of the Note, add the following:

For an extended elaboration of this view, see R. Bork, The Tempting of America (1989).

Compare Brest, Constitutional Citizenship, 34 Clev. St. L. Rev. 175, 181 n.16 (1986):

> What ever else may be said about [Bork's] positivist view of morality, it cannot provide a basis for *criticizing* judicial review. If all is preference, why should the preferences of a majority of legislators prevail over those of nine Supreme Court justices? [Some critics of judicial review hold that] majoritarian political processes are desirable because they respect the equality of citizens or because they tend to maximize aggregate preferences. But this is no less a moral theory than any other.

Page 693. At the end of subsection 4a of the Note, add the following:

See also Simon, The Authority of the Framers of the Constitution: Can Originalist Interpretation Be Justified?, 73 Cal. L. Rev. 1482 (1985).

An engaging presentation of the various difficulties in implementing an original intent approach to constitutional interpretation is Bittker, The Bicentennial of the Jurisprudence of Original Intent: The Recent Past, 77 Cal. L. Rev. 235 (1989).

Page 693. At the bottom of the page, add the following:

For a thoughtful counterargument, see Nelson, History and Neutrality in Constitutional Adjudication, 72 Va. L. Rev. 1237 (1986). For an analysis of the limits of historical inquiry, see Powell, Rules for Originalists, 73 Va. L. Rev. 659 (1987).

Page 694.   After the quotation from Grey in subsection 5a of the Note, add the following:

For a comprehensive historical discussion of the framers' intent, concluding that the "founding generation . . . expected the judiciary to keep legislatures from transgressing the natural rights of mankind, whether or not those rights found their way into the written Constitution," see Sherry, The Founders' Unwritten Constitution, 54 U. Chi. L. Rev. 1127, 1177 (1987).

Page 697.   After second Ely quotation, add the following:

Seidman, Ambivalence and Accountability, 61 S. Cal. L. Rev. 1571 (1988):

> [If] we could somehow ensure that judges in fact obeyed the tenets of [interpretivism] (and if we assume that text and intention are determinate) this obedience would indeed eliminate judicial discretion. But it does not follow that [interpretivism] would reconcile judicial decisionmaking with democracy. Of course, a current majority *might* favor [interpretivism]. But there is no guarantee that this would be so and, without a system of accountability, judges might easily adhere to [interpretivism] in the face of majority preferences for [noninterpretive] outcomes.

Page 697.   In subsection e of the Note, the correct citation for Tushnet, Darkness on the Edge of Town: The Contributions of John Hart Ely to Constitutional Theory is 89 Yale L.J. 1037.

Page 697.   In section 5 of the Note, before the citation to R. Berger, add the following:

Interpretation Symposium, 58 S. Cal. L. Rev. 1 (1985);

Page 697.   After the Bork quotation at the bottom of the page, add the following:

For an intriguing analysis of different schools of constitutional thought, with a suggestion that constitutional change should be sought through politics rather than through the courts, see West, Progressive and Conservative Constitutionalism, 88 Mich. L. Rev. 641 (1990).

f. *A mixed system of interpretivism and noninterpretivism.* Consider Clinton, Original Understanding, Legal Realism, and the Interpretation of "This Constitution," 72 Iowa L. Rev. 1177, 1278-1279 (1987):

> [B]oth originalist and nonoriginalist interpretive approaches are perfectly legitimate when properly employed. [The] framers of the [Constitution] intended to accomplish both flexible growth and evolution of the constitutional fabric, while maintaining sufficient constitutional stability to facilitate ordered change. Extraconstitutional interpretation facilitates evolution at a minimal cost to constitutional stability. On

the other hand, interpretations of the document that are fundamentally at odds with the historic meaning of those who drafted it — contraconstitutional interpretations — ultimately undermine societal faith in constitutional governance and judicial review, suggesting that in appropriate cases the demonstrated original understandings of the Constitution must be controlling. Only by applying a dynamic analysis that recognizes and accommodates the importance of each interpretive vision can the dual purposes of the Constitution [be] furthered, while reducing the level of dysfunctional political friction about the legitimacy of judicial enforcement of the Constitution.

Page 705. At the end of subsection 3a of the Note, add the following:

See also Kaczorowski, Revolutionary Constitutionalism in the Era of the Civil War and Reconstruction, 61 N.Y.U. L. Rev. 863 (1986).

D. SUBSTANTIVE DUE PROCESS: THE PROTECTION OF ECONOMIC INTERESTS

Page 735. Before section 3 of the Note, add the following:

For further discussion, see Baker, Property and Its Relation to Constitutionally Protected Liberty, 134 U. Pa. L. Rev. 741 (1986); Wright, Fundamental Property Rights, 21 Val. U. L. Rev. 75 (1986).

Page 739. At the end of section 6 of the Note, add the following:

For an articulation of the substantive view, see Sunstein, *Lochner's* Legacy, 87 Colum. L. Rev. 873, 874-875 (1987):

> The received wisdom is that *Lochner* was wrong because it involved "judicial activism." . . .
> [But it is possible] to understand *Lochner* from a different point of view. For the *Lochner* Court, neutrality, understood in a particular way, was a constitutional requirement. The key concepts here are threefold: governmental inaction, the existing distribution of wealth and entitlements, and the baseline set by the common law. Governmental intervention was constitutionally troublesome, whereas inaction was not; and both neutrality and inaction were defined as respect for the behavior of private actors pursuant to the common law, in light of the existing distribution of wealth and entitlements. . . .
> [If] *Lochner* is understood in these terms, its heirs are not Roe v. Wade and Miranda v. Arizona, but instead such decisions as Washington v. Davis, Buckley v. Valeo, Regents of California v. Bakke, and various cases immunizing those who are thought not to be "state actors" from constitutional constraints.

For a similar view, see Tribe, The Curvature of Constitutional Space: What Lawyers Can Learn from Modern Physics, 103 Harv. L. Rev. 1 (1989).

Page 739.   In the last line, after the word "see," add the following:

F. Strong, Substantive Due Process of Law: A Dichotomy of Sense and Nonsense (1986);

Page 746.   Before Williamson v. Lee Optical of Oklahoma, add the following:

For a detailed study of the problem in *Carolene Products*, see Miller, The True Story of Carolene Products, 1988 Sup. Ct. Rev. 397, 398-399, claiming that the

> statute upheld in the case was an utterly unprincipled example of special interest legislation. The purported "public interest" justifications so credulously reported by Justice Stone were patently bogus. . . . The consequence of the decision was to expropriate the property of a lawful and beneficial industry; to deprive working and poor people of a healthful, nutritious, and low-cost food; and to impair the health of the nation's children by encouraging the use as baby food of a sweetened condensed milk product that was 42 percent sugar.

Page 750.   At the bottom of the page, add the following:

For a critique of footnote 4, see Brilmayer, *Carolene*, Conflicts, and the Fate of the "Inside-Outsider," 134 U. Pa. L. Rev. 1291 (1986).

6. *The intent of the framers,* Lochner, *and* Carolene Products. Consider W. Nelson, The Fourteenth Amendment: From Political Principle to Judicial Doctrine 8-10, 197-200 (1988):

> [Those who wrote the Fourteenth Amendment] had a political agenda and a historical past that kept them from experiencing as clearly as we do the conflict between the protection of individual rights and the preservation of state legislative freedom. [Conflict] between these principles, though foreseeable, was not thought to be inevitable. [Indeed, the framers explained to their critics that no serious conflict was likely because] the amendment did not remove fundamental individual rights from the sphere of state control; [rather, it prohibited only] arbitrary and unreasonable lawmaking on the part of the States. [Although] this explanation remained at a vague level of rhetorical abstraction, [the framers left] the business of giving precise content to the Fourteenth Amendment [to] the Supreme Court. . . .
>
> Once the amendment had been adopted, the Supreme Court confronted the same two values, often in tension with one another. [Faithful] to the compromises that had taken place during the framing and ratification of the amendment, the late nineteenth-century Court [avoided] extreme positions and usually deferred to legislative judgments. Only when the Court found that legislative acts were plainly arbitrary would it declare them unconstitutional. [In *Lochner* and its progeny, however, the

Court read the Fourteenth Amendment as authorizing] the federal courts to immunize fundamental rights from all legislative regulation; it thereby transformed the Fourteenth Amendment from a bar to arbitrary and unequal state action into a charter identifying fundamental rights and immunizing them from all legislative regulation. [This view] ignored the original understanding of the framers that "[t]he preservation of the just powers of the states is quite as vital as the preservation of the powers of the general government," and thereby "enlarg[ed] the scope of the [Fourteenth] Amendment far beyond its original purpose." . . .

For reasons that the proponents of the Fourteenth Amendment had fully appreciated, [this] broad reading had to be rejected. But by the time it rejected the broad reading, the [Court] appears to have forgotten the line that the proponents of the Fourteenth Amendment and the late nineteenth-century judges had drawn in order to prevent the amendment from overwhelming the states. [For] whatever reason, the Court did not cut back on *Lochner* by distinguishing between reasonable and arbitrary state regulations, permitting the former and prohibiting the latter; instead, it distinguished in the *Carolene Products* case between economic and noneconomic rights, giving government plenary power to regulate the former and little power over the latter. A half century after *Carolene Products,* the nineteenth century's approach to limiting the reach of the Fourteenth Amendment had been largely forgotten.

E. "FUNDAMENTAL INTERESTS" AND THE EQUAL PROTECTION CLAUSE

Page 784. Before section 3 of the Note, add the following:

For a comprehensive discussion of the problem, see Symposium: Gerrymandering and the Courts, 22 UCLA L. Rev. 1 (1985).

Page 786. Before subsection c of the Note, add the following:

DAVIS v. BANDEMER
478 U.S. 109 (1986)

JUSTICE WHITE announced the judgment of the Court and delivered the opinion of the Court as to Part II and an opinion in which JUSTICE BRENNAN, JUSTICE MARSHALL, and JUSTICE BLACKMUN joined as to Parts I, III, and IV.

In this case, we review a judgment from a three-judge District Court, which sustained an equal protection challenge to Indiana's 1981 state apportionment on the basis that the law unconstitutionally diluted the votes of Indiana Democrats. Although we find such political gerrymandering to be justiciable, we conclude that the District Court applied an insufficiently demanding standard in finding unconstitutional vote dilution. Consequently, we reverse.

I

[The challenged apportionment plan, adopted by the Republican-controlled state legislature in 1981, provided for state Senate and House districts of substantially equal population. The Democrats nonetheless claimed that by using a mix of single and multimembered districts and gerrymandering district lines, the plan substantially understated Democratic voting strength. In elections held under the plan in 1982, the Democrats received 51.9 percent of the total House vote and 53.1 percent of the total Senate vote, yet won only 43 of 100 House seats and only 13 of 25 Senate seats.

According to facts contained in Justice Powell's dissenting opinion, the districting plan was written by a conference committee of the state legislature with the aid of a private computer firm. All members of the conference committee were Republicans, and the information fed into the computer primarily concerned the political complexion of the state's precincts. The redistricting process was conducted in secret, and the plan was not revealed until two days before the conclusion of the legislative session. On the last day of the session, it was adopted by party line votes in both houses.]

II

[In this section of his opinion, Justice White, writing for the Court, holds that the political question doctrine does not prevent the Court from reaching the merits. This portion of the opinion is discussed at Supplement to Casebook page 101 supra.]

III

[Parts III and IV of the opinion are joined only by Justices Brennan, Marshall, and Blackmun.]

[We agree] with the District Court that in order to succeed the [plaintiffs] were required to prove both intentional discrimination against an identifiable political group and an actual discriminatory effect on that group. Further, we are confident that if the law challenged here had discriminatory effects on Democrats, this record would support a finding that the discrimination was intentional. Thus, we decline to overturn the District Court's finding of discriminatory intent as clearly erroneous.

Indeed, quite aside from the anecdotal evidence, the shape of the House and Senate Districts, and the alleged disregard for political boundaries, we think it most likely that whenever a legislature redistricts, those responsible for the legislation will know the likely political composition of the new districts and will have a prediction as to whether a particular district is a safe one for a Democratic or Republican candidate or is a competitive district that either candidate might win. . . .

As long as redistricting is done by a legislature, it should not be very difficult to prove that the likely political consequences of the reapportionment were intended.

We do not accept, however, the District Court's legal and factual bases for concluding that the 1981 Act visited a sufficiently adverse effect on the appellees' constitutionally protected rights to make out a violation of the Equal Protection Clause. The District Court held that because any apportionment scheme that purposely prevents proportional representation is unconstitutional, Democratic voters need only show that their proportionate voting influence has been adversely affected. Our cases, however, clearly foreclose any claim that the Constitution requires proportional representation or that legislatures in reapportioning must draw district lines to come as near as possible to allocating seats to the contending parties in proportion to what their anticipated statewide vote will be.

The typical election for legislative seats in the United States is conducted in described geographical districts, with the candidate receiving the most votes in each district winning the seat allocated to that district. If all or most of the districts are competitive — defined by the District Court in this case as districts in which the anticipated split in the party vote is within the range of 45% to 55% — even a narrow statewide preference for either party would produce an overwhelming majority for the winning party in the state legislature. This consequence, however, is inherent in winner-take-all, district-based elections, and we cannot hold that such a reapportionment law would violate the Equal Protection Clause because the voters in the losing party do not have representation in the legislature in proportion to the statewide vote received by their party candidates. . . .

To draw district lines to maximize the representation of each major party would require creating as many safe seats for each party as the demographic and predicted political characteristics of the State would permit. This in turn would leave the minority in each safe district without a representative of its choice. We upheld this "political fairness" approach in Gaffney v. Cummings, despite its tendency to deny safe district minorities any realistic chance to elect their own representatives. But Gaffney in no way suggested that the Constitution requires the approach that Connecticut had adopted in that case. . . .

[The] mere fact that a particular apportionment scheme makes it more difficult for a particular group in a particular district to elect the representatives of its choice does not render that scheme constitutionally infirm. [The] power to influence the political process is not limited to winning elections. An individual or a group of individuals who votes for a losing candidate is usually deemed to be adequately represented by the winning candidate and to have as much opportunity to influence that candidate as other voters in the district. We cannot presume in such a situation, without actual proof to the contrary, that the candidate elected will entirely ignore the interests of those voters. This is true even in a safe district where the losing group loses election after election. Thus, a group's electoral power is not unconstitutionally diminished by the simple fact of an apportionment scheme that makes winning elections more difficult, and a failure of proportional representation alone does not constitute impermissible discrimination under the Equal Protection Clause.

As with individual districts, where unconstitutional vote dilution is alleged in the form of statewide political gerrymandering, the mere lack of proportional representation will not be sufficient to prove unconstitutional discrimination. [Unconstitutional] discrimination occurs only when the electoral system is arranged in a manner that will consistently degrade a voter's or a group of voters' influence on the political process as a whole. . . .

[An] equal protection violation may be found only where the electoral system substantially disadvantages certain voters in their opportunity to influence the political process effectively. In this context, such a finding of unconstitutionality must be supported by evidence of continued frustration of the will of a majority of the voters or effective denial to a minority of voters of a fair chance to influence the political process.

Based on these views, we would reject the District Court's apparent holding that *any* interference with an opportunity to elect a representative of one's choice would be sufficient to allege or make out an equal protection violation, unless justified by some acceptable state interest that the State would be required to demonstrate. In addition to being contrary to the above-described conception of an unconstitutional political gerrymander, such a low threshold for legal action would invite attack on all or almost all reapportionment statutes. [14] . . .

The District Court's findings do not satisfy this threshold condition to stating and proving a cause of action. . . .

Relying on a single election to prove unconstitutional discrimination is unsatisfactory. The District Court observed, and the parties do not disagree, that Indiana is a swing State. Voters sometimes prefer Democratic candidates, and sometimes Republican. The District Court did not find that because of the 1981 Act the Democrats could not in one of the next few elections secure a sufficient vote to take control of the assembly. Indeed, the District Court declined to hold that the 1982 election results were the predictable consequences of the 1981 Act and expressly refused to hold that those results were a reliable prediction of future ones. . . .

---

14. The requirement of a threshold showing is derived from the peculiar characteristics of these political gerrymandering claims. We do not contemplate that a similar requirement would apply to our Equal Protection cases outside of this particular context. [Relocated footnote.]

We recognize that our own view may be difficult of application. Determining when an electoral system has been "arranged in a manner that will consistently degrade a voter's or a group of voters' influence on the political process as a whole," is of necessity a difficult inquiry. Nevertheless, we believe that it recognizes the delicacy of intruding on this most political of legislative functions and is at the same time consistent with our prior cases regarding individual multi-member districts, which have formulated a parallel standard. [22]

IV

In sum, we hold that political gerrymandering cases are properly justiciable under the Equal Protection Clause. We also conclude, however, that a threshold showing of discriminatory vote dilution is required for a prima facie case of an equal protection violation. In this case, the findings made by the District Court of an adverse effect on the appellees do not surmount the threshold requirement. Consequently, the judgment of the District Court is reversed.

[Chief Justice Burger's opinion concurring in the judgment is omitted.

Justice O'Connor's opinion, joined by Chief Justice Burger and Justice Rehnquist, arguing that political gerrymandering poses a nonjusticiable political question, is discussed at Supplement to Casebook page 101 supra. In the course of arguing that there are no judicially manageable standards to resolve the controversy, she accused the plurality of moving toward a constitutionally mandated system of proportional representation for political parties:

> To be sure, the plurality has qualified its use of a *standard* of proportional representation in a variety of ways so as to avoid a *requirement* of proportional representation. The question is whether these qualifications are likely to be enduring in the face of the tremendous political pressures that courts will confront when called on to decide political gerrymandering claims. Because the most easily measured indicia of political power relate solely to winning and losing elections, there is a grave risk that the plurality's various attempts to qualify and condition the group right the Court has created will gradually pale in importance. What is likely to remain is a loose form of proportionality, under which *some* deviations from proportionality are permissible, but any significant, persistent deviations from proportionality are suspect.]

JUSTICE POWELL, with whom JUSTICE STEVENS joins, concurring in Part II, and dissenting.

---

22. We are puzzled by Justice Powell's conclusion that we contemplate a test under which only the "one person, one vote" requirement has any relevance. This opinion clearly does not adopt such a limited review.

This case presents the question whether a state legislature violates the Equal Protection Clause by adopting a redistricting plan designed solely to preserve the power of the dominant political party, when the plan follows the doctrine of "one person, one vote" but ignores all other neutral factors relevant to the fairness of redistricting.

In answering this question, the plurality expresses the view, with which I agree, that a partisan political gerrymander violates the Equal Protection Clause only on proof of "both intentional discrimination against an identifiable political group and an actual discriminatory effect on that group."

[The] plurality argues, however, that appellees failed to establish that their voting strength was diluted statewide despite uncontradicted proof that certain key districts were grotesquely gerrymandered to enhance the election prospects of Republican candidates. This argument appears to rest solely on the ground that the legislature accomplished its gerrymander consistent with "one person, one vote," in the sense that the legislature designed voting districts of approximately equal population and erected no direct barriers to Democratic voters' exercise of the franchise. Since the essence of a gerrymandering claim is that the members of a political party as a group have been denied their right to "fair and effective representation," [*Reynolds*], I believe that the claim cannot be tested solely by reference to "one person, one vote." Rather, a number of other relevant neutral factors must be considered. . . .

Gerrymandering is "the deliberate and arbitrary distortion of district boundaries and populations for partisan or personal political purposes." Kirkpatrick v. Preisler, 394 U.S. 526, 538 (1969) (Fortas, J., concurring). . . .

The term "gerrymandering," however, is also used loosely to describe the common practice of the party in power to choose the redistricting plan that gives it an advantage at the polls. An intent to discriminate in this sense may be present whenever redistricting occurs. . . .

Consequently, only a sensitive and searching inquiry can distinguish gerrymandering in the "loose" sense from gerrymandering that amounts to unconstitutional discrimination. Because it is difficult to develop and apply standards that will identify the unconstitutional gerrymander, courts may seek to avoid their responsibility to enforce the Equal Protection Clause by finding that a claim of gerrymandering is nonjusticiable. I agree with the plurality that such a course is mistaken, and that the allegations in this case raise a justiciable issue.

Moreover, I am convinced that appropriate judicial standards can and should be developed. Justice Fortas' definition of unconstitutional gerrymandering properly focuses on whether the boundaries of the voting districts have been distorted deliberately and arbitrarily to achieve illegitimate ends. [*Kirkpatrick*, at 538.] Under this definition, the merits of a gerrymandering claim must be determined by reference to the configurations of the districts, the observance of political subdivision lines, and other criteria that have independent relevance to the fairness of redistricting. . . .

The plurality [erroneously] characterizes the harm members of the losing party suffer as a group when they are deprived, through deliberate and arbitrary distortion of district boundaries, of the opportunity to elect representatives of their choosing. [7] It may be, as the plurality suggests, that representatives will not "entirely ignore the interests" of opposition voters. But it defies political reality to suppose that members of a losing party have as much political influence over state government as do members of the victorious party. Even the most conscientious state legislators do not disregard opportunities to reward persons or groups who were active supporters in their election campaigns. Similarly, no one doubts that partisan considerations play a major role in the passage of legislation and the appointment of state officers. Not surprisingly, therefore, the District Court expressly found that "[c]ontrol of the General Assembly is crucial" to members of the major political parties in Indiana. In light of those findings, I cannot accept the plurality's apparent conclusion that loss of this "crucial" position is constitutionally insignificant as long as the losers are not "entirely ignored" by the winners. . . .

The most important [factors in determining the constitutionality of redistricting plans] are the shapes of voting districts and adherence to established political subdivision boundaries. Other relevant considerations include the nature of the legislative procedures by which the apportionment law was adopted and legislative history reflecting contemporaneous legislative goals. To make out a case of unconstitutional partisan gerrymandering, the plaintiff should be required to offer proof concerning these factors, which bear directly on the fairness of a redistricting plan, as well as evidence concerning population disparities and statistics tending to show vote dilution. No one factor should be dispositive. [13]

In conclusion, I want to make clear the limits of the standard that I believe the Equal Protection Clause imposes on legislators engaged in redistricting. Traditionally, the determination of electoral districts within a State has been a matter left to the legislative branch of the state government. Apart from the doctrine of separa-

7. The plurality correctly concludes that a redistricting plan is not unconstitutional merely because the plan makes it more difficult for a group of voters to elect the candidate of its choice or merely because the plan does not provide proportional representation. [But] the plurality leaps from that conclusion to the assumption that "[a]n individual or group of individuals who votes for a losing candidate is usually deemed to be adequately represented by the winning candidate and to have as much opportunity to influence that candidate as other voters in the district." Thus, the plurality apparently believes that effects on election results are of little import, as long as the losers have some access to their representatives. Though effects on election results do not suffice to establish an unconstitutional gerrymander, they certainly are relevant to such a claim, and they may suffice to show that the claimants have been injured by the redistricting they challenge.

13. Groups may consistently fail to elect representatives under a perfectly neutral election scheme. Thus, a test that turns only on election results, as the plurality's standard apparently does, likely would identify an unconstitutional gerrymander where none existed. . . .

tion of powers and the federal system prescribed by the Constitution, federal judges are ill-equipped generally to review legislative decisions respecting redistricting. As the plurality opinion makes clear, however, our precedents hold that a colorable claim of discriminatory gerrymandering presents a justiciable controversy under the Equal Protection Clause. Federal courts in exercising their duty to adjudicate such claims should impose a heavy burden of proof on those who allege that a redistricting plan violates the Constitution. In light of Baker v. Carr, Reynolds v. Sims, and their progeny, including such comparatively recent decisions as Gaffney v. Cummings, this case presents a paradigm example of unconstitutional discrimination against the members of a political party that happened to be out of power. The well-grounded findings of the District Court to this effect have not been, and I believe cannot be, held clearly erroneous.

Accordingly, I would affirm the judgment of the District Court.[25]

Page 789. At the end of section 2 of the Note, add the following:

The Court relied on *Jenness* and *White* in Munro v. Socialist Workers Party, 479 U.S. 189 (1986), to uphold a state law that prevented minor party candidates from appearing on the general election ballot unless they received at least 1 percent of the votes cast in a "blanket primary" at which registered voters could vote for any candidate, irrespective of the candidate's political party affiliation.

Page 789. At the end of section 4 of the Note, add the following:

In Tashjian v. Republican Party, 479 U.S. 208 (1986), the Court distinguished *Storer* and invalidated a Connecticut statute requiring the voters in any party primary to be registered members of that party. The Republican party, which had adopted a party rule permitting independents to vote in its primary, challenged the provision. Writing for the Court, Justice Marshall distinguished *Storer* as follows:

The statute in *Storer* was designed to protect the parties and the party system against the disorganizing effect of independent candidacies launched by unsuccessful putative party nominees. This protection [was] undertaken to prevent the disruption of the political parties from without, and not, as in this case, to prevent the parties from taking internal steps affecting their own process for the selection of candidates. . . .

---

25. As is evident from the several opinions filed today, there is no "Court" for a standard that properly should be applied in determining whether a challenged redistricting plan is an unconstitutional partisan political gerrymander. The standard proposed by the plurality is explicitly rejected by two Justices, and three Justices also have expressed the view that the plurality's standard will "prove unmanageable and arbitrary." (O'Connor, J., joined by Burger, C.J., and Rehnquist, J., concurring in the judgment).

The Party's determination of the boundaries of its own association, and of the structure which best allows it to pursue its political goals, is protected by the Constitution.

Justice Stevens, joined by Justice Scalia, dissented. Justice Scalia also wrote a separate dissenting opinion, joined by Chief Justice Rehnquist and Justice O'Connor.

Page 791. At the end of section 6 of the Note, add the following:

For an argument in favor of a first amendment approach, see Calhoun, The First Amendment and Distributional Voting Rights Controversies, 52 Tenn. L. Rev. 549 (1985).

Page 810. Before section 2 of the Note, add the following:

In Attorney General of New York v. Soto-Lopez, 476 U.S. 898 (1986), the Court invalidated on "right to travel" grounds a New York statute granting an employment preference to resident veterans who resided in New York at the time that they entered military service. Although appellees were long-time New York residents, they were nonetheless denied the preference under the statute because they were not residents at the time they joined the military. Writing for a plurality of the Court, Justice Brennan explained that "the right to migrate protects residents of a State from being disadvantaged, or from being treated differently, simply because of the timing of their migration, from other similarly situated residents." In separate concurring opinions, Chief Justice Burger and Justice White argued that the statute should be invalidated under the rational basis test. Justices O'Connor, Stevens, and Rehnquist dissented.

Page 815. After the citation to Supreme Court of New Hampshire v. Piper in the final paragraph of subsection 5 of the Note, add the following:

Supreme Court of Virginia v. Friedman, 487 U.S. 59 (1988) (same);

Page 817. At the bottom of the page, add the following:

For the argument that the Constitution confers "rights of protection *from* rather than *by* the government," see Currie, Positive and Negative Constitutional Rights, 53 U. Chi. L. Rev. 864 (1986).

Page 831.   Before section 4 of the Note, add the following:

3A. *Territorial discrimination.* The school financing scheme upheld in *Rodriguez* treats individuals differently depending upon where they live in the state. How should the Court analyze such inequalities? Can a state constitutionally provide more money for the education of students who live in the northern part of the state? For discussion, see Neuman, Territorial Discrimination, Equal Protection, and Self-Determination, 135 U. Pa. L. Rev. 261 (1987).

Compare *Rodriguez* to Papasan v. Allain, 478 U.S. 265 (1986). While Mississippi was still a territory, Congress reserved certain plots of land within each township for support of public schools. However, Congress failed to reserve such lands in northern Mississippi, which was then held by the Chickasaw Indian Nation. In 1836, Congress sought to remedy this oversight by vesting certain lands in the state for the use of schools within the Chickasaw Cession, but the state (with the permission of Congress) sold these lands and invested the proceeds in railroads that were destroyed during the Civil War. The result is that today school districts in most of the state receive an average income of $75.34 per pupil from reserved lands located within their borders, while Chickasaw Cession schools receive annual appropriations, designed to compensate for the lost lands, of only 63 cents per pupil.

Petitioners filed this action claiming, inter alia, that the disparity in funding violated the equal protection clause. The court of appeals held that, in light of *Rodriguez*, the trial court correctly granted respondent's motion to dismiss, but the Supreme Court, in an opinion by Justice White, reversed. Because petitioners had not alleged any facts supporting the contention that they were denied a minimally adequate education, the Court found it unnecessary to determine whether such a denial would infringe upon a fundamental right and trigger strict scrutiny. Nonetheless, the Court ruled that the lower court had erred in holding that *Rodriguez* compelled dismissal of the suit:

> As we read their complaint, the petitioners do not challenge the overall organization of the Mississippi public school financing program. Instead, their challenge is restricted to one aspect of that program. . . .
> This case is [very] different from *Rodriguez*, where the differential financing available to school districts was traceable to school district funds available from local real estate taxation, not to a state decision to divide state resources unequally among school districts. The rationality of the disparity in *Rodriguez*, therefore, which rested on the fact that funding disparities based on differing local wealth were a necessary adjunct of allowing meaningful local control over school funding, does not settle the constitutionality of disparities alleged in this case.

The Court remanded the case so that the lower court could consider in the first instance whether, given state title to the lands, the equal protection clause permitted the state to distribute income from them unequally among school districts. Justice Powell, joined by Chief Justice Burger and Justice Rehnquist dissented. He pointed out that income from the lands accounted for only $1^1/_2$ percent of overall funding for the schools and argued that such de minimis variations in funding were insufficient to establish an equal protection clause violation.

F. "MODERN" SUBSTANTIVE DUE PROCESS: PRIVACY, PERSONHOOD, AND FAMILY

Page 840. Before subsection 3 of the Note, add the following:

2A. *The limits of* Plyler: Kadrmas. In Kadrmas v. Dickinson Public Schools, 487 U.S. 108 (1988), the Court, in a five-to-four decision, upheld a program whereby North Dakota permitted local school boards to assess a user fee for transporting students to and from public schools. Relying primarily on *Plyler*, appellants contended that the user fee, which could not exceed the estimated cost to the school district of providing the service, unconstitutionally deprived those who could not "afford to pay it of 'minimum access to education.'" The Court explained that it had not extended *Plyler* beyond its "unique circumstances." Moreover, *Plyler* did not govern this case, for the children in this case "had not been penalized by the government for illegal conduct by [their] parents," and the Court saw no "reason to suppose that this user fee will 'promot[e] the creation and perpetuation of a sub-class of illiterates.'" The Court emphasized that because the Constitution does not require the State to provide bus service at all, it surely does not require the State to provide free bus service to anyone.

Justice Marshall, joined by Justice Brennan, dissented:

> This case involves state action that places a special burden on poor families in their pursuit of education. [The] intent of the Fourteenth Amendment was to abolish class legislation. When state action has the predictable tendency to entrap the poor and create a permanent underclass, that intent is frustrated. Thus, to the extent that a law places discriminatory barriers between indigents and the basic tools and opportunities that might enable them to rise, exacting scrutiny should be applied.

Justice Stevens, joined by Justice Blackmun, also dissented.

Page 851. Before section 2 of the Note, add the following:

e. Nichol, Children of Distant Fathers: Sketching an Ethos of Constitutional Liberty, 1985 Wis. L. Rev. 1305, 1309, 1344:

> [There] is, among the unenumerated "rights" acknowledged by the ninth amendment, a liberty interest of broader scope than the isolated provisions of the Bill of Rights — [a] right of "self-governance." [This right, which embodies] the ability to

formulate, shape, and act upon the core aspects of one's sense of identity, character, and personality, [is] rooted in an American dedication to personal autonomy in moral decision-making. [We] allow people, so far as is possible, to choose the course of their lives because we know that, to be fully human, choice is demanded. We respect the choices of our fellow citizens so as to afford respect for their humanity. [The right] of self-governance [serves these] ends.

Page 852.   Add the following as Note 2(d):

d. Consider this exchange on the Ninth Amendment. Barber, The Ninth Amendment: Inkblot or Another Hard Nut to Crack?, 64 Chi.-Kent L. Rev. 67, 84-85 (1988):

[Friends] of the ninth amendment can argue [that] the nation should interpret the framers as having intended a continuing effort to bring our democracy and law as close to justice as we can, thus doing all we can to vindicate the claims that our democracy and our law have always made for themselves. [If] critics of the ninth amendment should stick by their basic position regarding the nation's alleged aspiration to simple justice, then they would have to say we cannot have a reason for preferring particular versions of other general norms, like democracy and the rest. They might then contend that we must settle for established beliefs about these things. And on our noting that the very debate among us indicates disagreements in crucial areas, [they] might believe we have no choice but to postulate answers and proceed from there. [But] it would take an enormous amount of political power and good fortune to transform a postulated answer into a political consensus.

McConnell, A Moral Realist Defense of Constitutional Democracy, 64 Chi.-Kent L. Rev. 89, 90-91 (1988):

[A] belief in natural rights [does not compel] a belief in *judicially-enforceable* unenumerated rights. [Barber's] fundamental fallacy is to confuse the willingness to recognize the authority of representative bodies with the belief that "in the principle the community can do no wrong." Proponents of constitutional democracy do not accede to the decisions of representative institutions because they are always right. We do so because the republican form of government seems more likely than the alternatives (including rule by judges) to reach right results over time in a wide range of cases. [Barber] directs his argument almost solely to the importance of natural rights, while giving little attention to the institutional question of how they can be identified and implemented. This is a peculiar and dangerous oversight. It is peculiar because the central questions addressed by our Constitution have to do with the allocation of power. It is dangerous because the power to identify and implement natural rights [is] an awesome power.

For a broad range of views on the Ninth Amendment, see the entire Symposium on Interpreting the Ninth Amendment, 64 Chicago-Kent L. Rev. 37 (1988).

Page 852.   At the end of the first paragraph of section 3 of the Note, add the following:

Consider D. Richards, Toleration and the Constitution 243-244 (1986):

[The] moral ground of the right to privacy justifies more [than informational privacy. There are] connections between privacy interests and the higher-order interests protected by the right to conscience itself. . . .

[The] scope of [the] private sphere includes those highly personal relationships and activities whose just moral independence requires special protection from a hostile public interest. [Intimate] relationships — which give play to love, devotion, friendship as organizing themes in self-conceptions of permanent value in living — are among the essential resources of moral independence. Protection from hostile interest thus nurtures these intimate personal resources, a wholeness of emotion, intellect, and self-image guided by the self-determining moral powers of a free person.

Page 864.   Before section 4, add the following:

For discussion of the abortion problem as one of sex discrimination, see L. Tribe, American Constitutional Law, 1350-1362 (2d ed. 1988); Ginsburg, Some Thoughts on Autonomy and Equality in Relation to Roe v. Wade, 63 N.C. L. Rev. 375 (1985).

Page 869.   After subsection c of the Note, add the following new section:

7A. *Reaffirmations of Roe.* On two occasions since 1973, the Court has strongly reaffirmed its holding in *Roe.* The first, City of Akron v. Akron Center for Reproductive Health, Inc., is discussed at page 874 infra of the main text. More recently, in Thornburgh v. American College of Obstetricians & Gynecologists, 476 U.S. 747 (1986), the Court, although narrowly divided, once again refused to retreat from *Roe.*

As litigated in the lower courts, *Thornburgh* did not involve a frontal assault on *Roe.* Instead, the case concerned the constitutionality of a series of ancillary state abortion regulations concerning matters such as informed consent, record keeping, and requirements for post-viability abortions. (These aspects of the decision are discussed at Supplement to Casebook page 886 infra.) However, when the case reached the Supreme Court, the Solicitor General of the United States filed an unusual amicus brief urging the Court to overrule *Roe.*

In an opinion written by Justice Blackmun, the Court made no direct reference to the brief. But the Court did acknowledge and respond to the public opposition sparked by *Roe:*

Constitutional rights do not always have easily ascertainable boundaries, and controversy over the meaning of our Nation's most majestic guarantees frequently has been turbulent. As judges, however, we are sworn to uphold the law even when its content gives rise to bitter dispute. See [Cooper v. Aaron]. We recognized at the very beginning of our opinion in *Roe* that abortion raises moral and spiritual questions over which honorable persons can disagree sincerely and profoundly. But those disagreements did not then and do not now relieve us of our duty to apply the Constitution faithfully.

Our cases long have recognized that the Constitution embodies a promise that a certain private sphere of individual liberty will be kept largely beyond the reach of government. That promise extends to women as well as to men. Few decisions are more personal and intimate, more properly private, or more basic to individual dignity and autonomy, than a woman's decision — with the guidance of her physician and within the limits specified in *Roe* — whether to end her pregnancy. A woman's right to make that choice freely is fundamental. Any other result, in our view, would protect inadequately a central part of the sphere of liberty that our law guarantees equally to all.

Although four justices dissented from the Court's opinion, only Justices White and Rehnquist, the sole dissenters in *Roe*, directly stated that they would overrule *Roe*'s core holding. Justice O'Connor, in an opinion joined by Justice Rehnquist, sharply attacked the Court for intervening prematurely in the litigation (the trial court had ruled only on plaintiff's motion for a preliminary injunction against the challenged statutes) and argued that the state regulations at issue were permissible. She stopped short, however, of urging that *Roe* be overruled. (Justice O'Connor's views are discussed at greater length at page 877 infra of the main text.) Chief Justice Burger wrote a separate dissent in *Thornburgh* noting that his concurrence in *Roe* was premised on the principle that the abortion right " 'is not unqualified and must be considered against important state interests in regulation.' " (Quoting from *Roe*.) Although in his view

> every member of the *Roe* Court [had] rejected the idea of abortion on demand, [the] Court's opinion today [plainly] undermines that important principle, and I regretfully conclude that some of the concerns of the dissenting Justices in *Roe*, as well as the concerns I expressed in my separate opinion, have now been realized.

He concluded by noting that "[the] soundness of our holdings must be tested by the decisions that purport to follow them. [If] today's holding really [means what it seems] to say, I agree we should reexamine *Roe*."

In a long, strongly worded dissent, Justice White, joined by Justice Rehnquist, argued that *Roe* was "fundamentally misguided since its inception" and ought to be overruled:

> The rule of stare decisis is essential if case-by-case judicial decisionmaking is to be reconciled with the principle of the rule of law. [But] decisions that find in the Constitution principles or values that cannot fairly be read into that document usurp the people's authority, for such decisions represent choices that the people have never made and that they cannot disavow through corrective legislation. For this reason, it is essential that this Court maintain the power to restore authority to its proper

possessors by correcting constitutional decisions that, on reconsideration, are found to be mistaken.

Justice White began his attack on *Roe*'s reasoning by acknowledging that

> this Court does not subscribe to the simplistic view that constitutional interpretation can possibly be limited to the "plain meaning" of the Constitution's text or to the subjective intention of the Framers. The Constitution is [a] document announcing fundamental principles in value-laden terms that leave ample scope for the exercise of normative judgment by those charged with interpreting and applying it.

He also conceded that a woman's ability to choose an abortion is a "liberty" subject to the "general protections" of the due process clause.

White took issue with the *Roe* Court, however, when it determined that the abortion right was a "fundamental" liberty interest triggering more than minimal judicial scrutiny when it was invaded. Although not denying that there were fundamental liberty interests nowhere mentioned in the constitutional text, he argued that when recognizing such nontextual interests, the Court "must [act] with more caution, lest it open itself to the accusation that, in the name of identifying constitutional principles to which the people have consented in framing their Constitution, the Court has done nothing more than impose its own controversial choices of value upon the people."

In White's view, prior decisions recognizing claims of personal autonomy in connection with family life, contraception, and capacity to procreate did not support denomination of the abortion right as fundamental:

> However one answers the metaphysical or theological question whether the fetus is a "human being" or the legal question whether it is a "person" as that term is used in the Constitution, one must at least recognize, first, that the fetus is an entity that bears in its cells all the genetic information that characterizes a member of the species homo sapiens, [and] second, that there is no nonarbitrary line separating a fetus from a child. [Given] that the continued existence and development — that is to say, the *life* — of such an entity are so directly at stake in the woman's decision whether or not to terminate her pregnancy, that decision must be recognized as sui generis, different in kind from the others that the Court has protected under the rubric of personal or family privacy and autonomy.

Nor could the abortion right be justified as "implicit in the concept of ordered liberty":

> [A] free, egalitarian, and democratic society does not presuppose any particular rule or set of rules with respect to abortion. [The] fact that many men and women of good will and high commitment to constitutional government place themselves on both sides of the abortion controversy strengthens my own conviction that the values animating the Constitution do not compel recognition of the abortion liberty as fundamental.

White also criticized the *Roe* Court's choice of "viability" as the point where the state's interest in regulating abortions becomes compelling:

> The governmental interests at issue is in protecting those who will be citizens if their lives are not ended in the womb. The substantiality of this interest is in no way dependent on the probability that the fetus may be capable of surviving outside the womb at any given point in its development, as the possibility of fetal survival is contingent on the state of medical practice and technology, factors that are in essence morally and constitutionally irrelevant. [Accordingly], the State's interest, if compelling after viability, is equally compelling before viability.

Justice White's opinion elicited a detailed rebuttal by Justice Stevens in a separate concurring opinion. Stevens found unconvincing White's effort to distinguish the Court's recognition of a fundamental liberty interest in the use of contraceptive devices:

> There may, of course, be a significant difference in the strength of the countervailing state interest, but I fail to see how a decision on child-bearing becomes *less* important the day after conception than the day before. Indeed, if one decision is more "fundamental" to the individual's freedom than the other, surely it is the post-conception decision that is more serious.

Stevens also rejected White's accusation that the Court was imposing its value preferences on the country:

> In a sense, the basic question is whether the "abortion decision" should be made by the individual or by the majority "in the unrestrained imposition of its own, extraconstitutional preferences." [Quoting from Justice White's opinion.] [Justice] White's characterization of the governmental interest as "protecting those who will be citizens if their lives are not ended in the womb," reveals that his opinion may be influenced as much by his own value preferences as by his view about the proper allocation of decisionmaking responsibilities between the individual and the State. For if federal judges must allow the State to make the abortion decision, presumably the State is free to decide that a woman may *never* abort, may *sometimes* abort, or, as in the People's Republic of China, must *always* abort if her family is already too large. In contrast, our cases represent a consistent view that the individual is primarily responsible for reproductive decisions, whether the State seeks to prohibit reproduction or to require it.

Stevens also defended the *Roe* Court's choice of "viability" as the point at which the state may assert a compelling interest in regulation:

> I should think it obvious that the state's interest in the protection of an embryo — even if that interest is defined as "protecting those who will be citizens" [quoting from Justice White's opinion] — increases progressively and dramatically as the organism's capacity to feel pain, to experience pleasure, to survive, and to react to its surroundings increases day by day. The development of a fetus — and pregnancy itself — are not static conditions, and the assertion that the government's interest is static simply ignores this reality.

Stevens concluded by noting that *Roe* left the majority

> free to preach the evils of birth control and abortion and to persuade others to make
> correct decisions while the individual faced with the reality of a difficult choice having
> serious and personal consequences of major importance to her own future — perhaps
> to the salvation of her own immortal soul — remains free to seek and to obtain
> sympathetic guidance from those who share her own value preferences.
>
> In the final analysis the holding in Roe v. Wade presumes that it is far better to
> permit some individuals to make incorrect decisions than to deny all individuals the
> right to make decisions that have a profound effect upon their destiny.

Page 874. At the end of section 3 of the Note, add the following:

Should *Maher* and *Harris* be analyzed as unconstitutional conditions cases? Under the unconstitutional conditions doctrine, it is sometimes said that government may not "penalize" people for exercising constitutional rights, or do indirectly what it cannot do directly. The unconstitutional conditions doctrine raises a number of puzzles, not least in the selection of the baseline from which to decide whether there has been an impermissible penalty or a permissible refusal to subsidize. See generally Sullivan, Unconstitutional Conditions, 102 Harv. L. Rev. 1413 (1989).

Sullivan argues that the "subsidy-penalty" distinction should be abandoned in favor of an inquiry into whether government has altered the "balance of power" between itself and rightholders; has skewed "the distribution of constitutional rights *among* rightholders because it necessarily discriminates facially between those who do and those who do not comply with the condition"; or has created "an undesirable caste hierarchy in the enjoyment of constitutional rights." Id. at 1490. Might inquiries of this sort introduce the same difficulties found in the subsidy-penalty inquiry? If these are the relevant inquiries, how do *Maher* and *Harris* come out?

Page 886. Before section 3, add the following:

In Thornburgh v. American College of Obstetricians and Gynecologists, 476 U.S. 747 (1986), the Court exhibited growing impatience with state efforts to regulate the abortion decision. The case concerned a Pennsylvania statute that, inter alia, required physicians to provide women seeking abortions with information allegedly designed to secure informed consent, required detailed record keeping concerning abortions, required use of the abortion technique that would provide the most protection for the life of the fetus in post-viability abortions unless the technique posed "significantly greater" medical risks to the pregnant mother, and required the presence of a second physician for post-viability abortions.

In a 5 to 4 decision, the Court, in an opinion by Justice Blackmun, held each of these provisions unconstitutional. The Court began its analysis by noting that

[in] the years since [*Roe*], States and municipalities have adopted a number of measures seemingly designed to prevent a woman, with the advice of her physician, from exercising her freedom of choice. [But "it] should go without saying that the vitality of these constitutional principles cannot be allowed to yield simply because of disagreement with them." [*Brown II.*] The States are not free, under the guise of protecting maternal health or potential life, to intimidate women into continuing pregnancies.

Turning to the specific provisions at issue, the Court first addressed the "informed consent" requirements. The statute required, inter alia, that the pregnant woman be informed of the possible detrimental physical and psychological effects, and all particular medical risks, of abortion as well as the medical risks of carrying the baby to term; that she be told that medical assistance benefits may be available for childbirth and that the father is liable to assist in the child's support; and that she be given the opportunity to read certain printed material. This material, in turn, described the anatomical characteristics of unborn children at two-week gestational increments, informed the woman of public and private agencies providing assistance with pregnancy and child rearing, and urged the woman to contact these agencies before deciding to have an abortion.

The Court found each of these informational requirements invalid:

> The printed materials [seem] to us to be nothing less than an out-right attempt to wedge the Commonwealth's message discouraging abortion into the privacy of the informed-consent dialogue between the woman and her physician. [Forcing] the physician or counselor to present the materials and the list to the woman makes him or her in effect an agent of the State in treating the woman and places his or her imprimatur upon both the materials and the list. All this is, or comes close to being, state medicine imposed upon the woman, not the professional medical guidance she seeks.

The other requirements were rejected because "[under] the guise of informed consent, the Act requires the dissemination of information that is not relevant to such consent." For example, the requirement that the woman be informed of medical risks "[compounds] the problem of medical attendance, [increases] the patient's anxiety, and [intrudes] upon the physician's exercise of proper professional judgment. This type of compelled information is the antithesis of informed consent."

The Court distinguished the reporting requirements from those upheld in *Danforth* on the ground that they went beyond health-related information to include the woman's method of payment, her personal history, and the bases for medical judgments. Moreover, unlike the Missouri records, which were to be kept solely for statistical purposes, the Pennsylvania records would be available for public copying.

The decision to terminate a pregnancy is an intensely private one that must be protected in a way that assures anonymity. [A] woman and her physician will necessarily be more reluctant to choose an abortion if there exists a possibility that her decision and her identity will become known publicly.

The Court found the standard of care requirements for post-viability abortions defective because, as interpreted by the Court, they required the attending physician to "trade off" maternal health for an increase in the chances of fetal survival.

Finally, the Court rejected the requirement that a second physician be present to aid the fetus in post-viability abortions because the provision, unlike that upheld in *Ashcroft*, contained no emergency exception for situations where the health of the mother would be endangered by waiting for the arrival of a second physician.

Chief Justice Burger, Justice White, with whom Justice Rehnquist joined, and Justice O'Connor, also joined by Justice Rehnquist, filed dissenting opinions.

In Webster v. Reproductive Health Services, 109 S. Ct. 3040 (1989), the Court upheld several provisions of a Missouri statute regulating abortions, and a plurality endorsed a reformulation of *Roe*'s trimester scheme. The Court found that a statement in the abortion statute's preamble that "the life of each human being begins at conception" was not in conflict with the statement in *Roe* that "a State may not adopt one theory of when life begins to justify its regulation of abortions," because *Roe* meant only that a state could not "justify" an abortion regulation "on the ground that it embodied the State's view about when life begins." The preamble simply "express[ed] . . . [a] value judgment" in the abstract.

Relying on *Harris v. McRae* and related cases, the Court also upheld a bar on state employees performing abortions and a ban on the use of public facilities for performing abortions, even when the patient paid for the abortion herself. "Missouri's refusal to allow public employees to perform abortions in public hospitals leaves a pregnant woman with the same choices as if the State had chosen not to operate any hospitals at all." The Court noted that "a different analysis might apply if a particular State had socialized medicine and all of its hospitals and physicians were publicly funded. This case also might be different if the State barred doctors who performed abortions in private facilities from the use of public facilities for any purpose." (Justice O'Connor's concurring opinion also stated that "there may be conceivable applications of the ban on the use of public facilities that would be unconstitutional," citing the suggestion by appellees that "the State could try to enforce the ban against private hospitals using public water and sewage lines," but found it unnecessary to decide whether these applications of the ban would be unconstitutional.)

The final provision at issue in *Webster,* as interpreted by the Court, required a physician, prior to performing an abortion "on a woman he has reason to believe is carrying an unborn child of twenty or more weeks gestational age," to perform tests which, in the physician's reasonable professional judgment, would be useful in determining the viability of the fetus. The plurality, in an opinion by Chief Justice Rehnquist, said that this statute, which regulated the performance of abortions in the second trimester in the interest not of maternal health but in the interest of protecting potential human life, conflicted with the trimester system articulated in *Roe* and applied in *Colautti,* Casebook p. 885. "It undoubtedly does superimpose state regulation on the medical determination of whether a particular fetus is viable." In addition, the plurality said that "to the extent that the viability tests increase the cost of what are in fact second-trimester abortions" — in cases where the tests show that the fetus was not viable — "their validity may also be questioned under *Akron.*" The plurality argued that *Roe's* trimester system should be abandoned.

> The rigid *Roe* framework is hardly consistent with the notion of a Constitution cast in general terms, as ours is, and usually speaking in general principles, as ours does. The key elements of the *Roe* framework [are] not found in the text of the Constitution or in any place else one would expect to find a constitutional principle. Since the bounds of the inquiry are essentially indeterminate, the result has been a web of legal rules that have become increasingly intricate, resembling a code of regulations rather than a body of constitutional doctrine. [Further,] we do not see why the State's interest in protecting potential human life should come into existence only at the point of viability, and that there should therefore be a rigid line allowing state regulation after viability but prohibiting it before viability. . . . The State here has chosen viability as the point at which its interest in potential human life must be safeguarded. [We] are satisfied that the requirement of these tests permissibly furthers the State's interest in protecting potential human life.

In response to the dissent's suggestion that an analysis that allowed states to protect potential human life at the point of viability necessarily implied that states could, if they chose, protect potential human life at the point of conception and therefore cast doubt on *Roe,* the plurality responded that it left *Roe* "undisturbed" because the Texas statute "criminalized the performance of *all* abortions, except when the mother's life was at stake." (Is this responsive to the dissent's objection?)

Justice O'Connor concurred in the result as to the testing provisions, arguing that they were permissible even within the *Roe* trimester framework. Relying on *Thornburgh,* she said that "regulations designed to protect the State's interest in potential life when viability is possible" were constitutional, and that inaccuracies in the determination of gestational life justified required viability testing at 20 weeks even though fetuses are viable no earlier than 23-24 weeks. Further, she said, "the costs of examinations and tests that could usefully and prudently be performed when a woman is 20-24 weeks pregnant to determine whether the fetus is viable would only marginally, if at all, increase the cost of an abortion."

Justice Scalia, believing that the analysis of the testing requirement in the opinions of the Chief Justice and Justice O'Connor, effectively overruled *Roe,* would have overruled *Roe* explicitly.

Justice Blackmun, joined by Justices Brennan and Marshall, dissented, saying the *Roe* "survive[d] but [was] not secure." He criticized the plurality's recasting of the relevant doctrine for failing to consider the dimensions of the individual right to privacy protected by the Constitution. "The trimester framework simply defines and limits that right to privacy in the abortion context to accommodate, not destroy, a State's legitimate interest in protecting the health of pregnant women and in preserving potential human life. Fashioning such accommodations between individual rights and the legitimate interests of government, establishing benchmarks and standards with which to evaluate the competing claims of individuals and government, lies at the very heart of constitutional adjudication." He also noted that "the 'critical elements' of countless constitutional doctrines nowhere appear in the Constitution's text." He would preserve "the viability standard" as "reflect[ing] the biological facts and truths of fetal development [that] a fetus [prior to viability] cannot survive separate from the woman and cannot reasonably and objectively be regarded as a subject of rights or interests distinct from, or paramount to, those of the pregnant woman." The plurality's standard, whether a regulation permissibly furthers the interest in protecting potential human life, was "circular and totally meaningless. Whether a challenged abortion regulation 'permissibly furthers' a legitimate state interest is the *question* that courts must answer in abortion cases, not the standard for courts to apply. [The standard] has no independent meaning and consists of nothing other than what a majority of this Court may believe at any given moment in any given case."

Justice Stevens also dissented; he would have invalidated not only the testing provision but also a portion of the preamble.

For discussion of *Webster,* see Colloquy, Webster v. Reproductive Health Services, 138 U. Pa. L. Rev. 83 (1989).

In Hodgson v. Minnesota, 100 S. Ct. — (1990) and Ohio v. Akron Center for Reproductive Health, 110 S. Ct. — (1990), the Court was confronted with two statutes regulating minors' access to abortion. In *Hodgson,* the Court invalidated a provision of a Minnesota statute that prohibited the performance of abortions on women under the age of 18 unless at least 48 hours had elapsed since the time when both parents were notified. In an opinion written by Justice Stevens and joined in principal part by Justices Brennan, Marshall, Blackmun, and O'Connor, the Court said that the two parent requirement was "not reasonably related to legitimate state interests."

The Court emphasized extensive testimony at trial to the effect that parents of minors seeking abortion were frequently divorced or separated, and that in these circumstances the two-parent notification requirement could have severe adverse effects on both the minor and the custodial parent. These adverse effects included the possibility of violence from fathers. The Court stessed that the trial court found that "many minors in Minnesota 'live in fear of violence by family members' and 'are, in fact, victims of rape, incest, neglect, and violence.' "

In a part of his opinion joined only by Justice O'Connor, Justice Stevens suggested that the state interests in the welfare of the pregnant minor and her parents, and in the family unit, could be served by single parent notification accompanied by the brief 48-hour delay. (Both the opinions in *Hodgson* and *Akron* reveal that a majority of the Court supports this position and would therefore uphold such a requirement. Justice Marshall, in a partial dissent joined by Justices Brennan and Blackmun, argued that such a provision would also be unconstitutional; he cited the increased health risks and costs of the delay.) The Court said that the two-parent notification requirement failed "to serve any state interest with respect to functioning families," and "disserves the state interest in protecting and assisting the minor with respect to dysfunctional families.

In a brief concurring opinion, Justice O'Connor reiterated her "undue burdens" test from *Akron,* and said that here there was no sufficient justification for two parent notification, especially in light of the fact that only half of the minors in Minnesota live with both biological parents. She argued that the statute's exception to notification for minors who are victims of neglect and abuse serves in practice as a means of contacting the parent, and therefore does not protect minors from neglectful or abusive parents at all.

Justice Kennedy, in an opinion joined by the Chief Justice and Justices White and Scalia, dissented on this point. He emphasized that "it was reasonable for the legislature to conclude that in most cases notice to both parents will work to the minor's benefit." The fact that in some cases there will be no such desirable results was not in his view fatal, because the statute contained exceptions sufficient "to ensure that the statutory notice requirement does not apply if it proves a serious threat to the minor's health or safety."

In *Hodgson,* a different majority of the Court upheld a part of the Minnesota statute to the effect that if the two parent requirement is found unconstitutional, the same notice requirement is effective *unless* the pregnant woman obtains a court order permitting the abortion to proceed. On this proposition, there was no opinion for the Court. The key vote came from Justice O'Connor, who said simply that "the interference with the internal operation of the family ... simply does not exist where the minor can avoid notifying one or both parents by use of the bypass procedure." On this point Justice Stevens dissented, saying that a "judicial bypass that is designed to handle exceptions from a reasonable general rule, ... is quite different from a requirement that a minor ... must apply to a court for permission to avoid the application of a rule that is not reasonably related to legitimate state goals. ... Where the parents are living together and have joint custody over the child, the State has no legitimate interests in the communication between father and mother about the child." And when there is a divorce, Justice Stevens argued, the question of notification is for the minor and the custodial parent rather than the state.

In his partial dissent, Justice Marshall argued that a judge cannot be given an absolute veto over a minor's decision to terminate a pregnancy. In his view, "many women will carry the fetus to term rather than notify a parent. Other women may decide to inform a parent but then confront parental pressure or abuse so severe as to obstruct the abortion. For these women, the judge's refusal to authorize an abortion effectively constitutes an absolute veto." He also emphasized the findings of the trial court, which showed "significant burdens on minors," including delays of a week or more, long distant transport to obtain a hearing, significant absences from home and school, and "trauma" for young women.

In a brief separate opinion, Justice Scalia dissented "from this enterprise of devising an Abortion Code, and from the illusion that we have authority to do so."

In *Akron,* the Court upheld an Ohio statute that, with certain exceptions, prohibited any person from performing an abortion on an unmarried, unemancipated minor without giving notice to one of her parents or receiving a court order of approval. Twenty-four hours after notice, an abortion would be permitted. No notice would be required, moreover, if the minor and another relative filed an affidavit stating that the minor fears physical, sexual, or severe emotional abuse from the parent. The notice provisions could also be bypassed entirely if the minor could file a complaint showing that notice is not in her best interests, or that she has sufficient maturity and information to make an intelligent decision without notice, or that one of her parents has engaged in a pattern of physical, sexual, or emotional abuse.

In an opinion by Justice Kennedy, the Court said that it did not have to decide whether notice statutes must provide bypass procedures at all. In this case, the procedures were adequate. They allowed the minor to prove maturity and information; they contained a general "best interests" exception; they guaranteed anonymity to the minor; and they ensured that the procedure would be conducted with expedition (here, within 22 days as a "worst case," and in all likelihood significantly less time).

Justice Blackmun, joined by Justices Brennan and Marshall, dissented. He emphasized that in practice, the Ohio system created an "obstacle course," involving an "unfamiliar and mystifying court system on an intensely intimate matter." In his view, the bypass procedure was, in practical reality, a way of discouraging abortions rather than ensuring maturity or protecting against abusive, neglectful, or violent parents. The complex pleading system, in his view, amounted to a "barricade" designed to confuse young women and to increase anxiety. Justice Blackmun also argued that the potential for a three week delay revealed an insufficiently expeditious procedure. He emphasized that the complexity of the procedure would have particularly severe effects "on sexually or physically abused minors."

Page 890.   Before section 5 of the Note, add the following new section:

4A. Compare *Moore* with Lyng v. Castillo, 477 U.S. 635 (1986). In *Lyng*, the Court, in an opinion by Justice Stevens, upheld a provision of the federal foodstamp act that treated parents, children, and siblings living together as a single household whether or not they purchased food and prepared meals together. In contrast, unrelated individuals who lived together could establish separate "households," and thereby qualify for enhanced benefits so long as they did not buy and prepare food together. The Court rejected the argument that the classification should be subjected to heightened scrutiny because it interfered with family living arrangements, thereby burdening a fundamental right:

> The "household" definition does not order or prevent any group of persons from dining together. Indeed, in the overwhelming majority of cases it probably has no effect at all. It is exceedingly unlikely that close relatives would choose to live apart simply to increase their allotment of food stamps, for the cost of separate housing would almost certainly exceed the incremental value of the additional stamps.

Justice Marshall dissented:

> The food stamp benefits at issue are necessary for the affected families' very survival, and the Federal Government denies that benefit to families who do not, by preparing their meals together, structure themselves in a manner that the Government believes will minimize unnecessary expenditures. [The] Government has thus chosen to intrude into the family dining room — a place where I would have thought the right to privacy exists in its strongest form. What possible interest can the Government have in preventing members of a family from dining as they choose? It is simply none of the Government's business.

Consider also Bowen v. Gilliard, 483 U.S. 587 (1987). An amendment to the Aid to Families with Dependent Children program required recipient families to include within the family unit all children living within the household, including children receiving child support payments from noncustodial parents. The family's benefit level was then reduced by the amount of these payments. The Court, in an opinion by Justice Stevens, rejected appellee's argument that these requirements should be subject to heightened scrutiny because they interfered with family living arrangements.

> That some families may decide to modify their living arrangements in order to avoid the effect of the amendment, does not transform the amendment into an act whose design and direct effect is to "intrud[e] on choices concerning family living arrangements." [*Moore.*]

Justice Brennan, joined by Justice Marshall, dissented:

The Government has told a child who lives with a mother receiving public assistance that it cannot both live with its mother and be supported by its father. The child must either leave the care and custody of the mother, or forgo the support of the father and become a Government client. The child is put to this choice not because it seeks Government benefits for itself, but because of a fact over which it has no control: the need of *other* household members for public assistance.

Justice Blackmun also filed a short dissent.

Page 893.   Before Stanley v. Illinois, add the following:

5. In Turner v. Safley, 482 U.S. 78 (1987), a unanimous Court relied upon *Zablocki* to invalidate a prison regulation that permitted inmates to marry only when the superintendent found compelling reasons to grant permission. In practice, such reasons were found only in cases of pregnancy or the birth of a nonmarital child. The Court, in an opinion by Justice O'Connor, held that "the right to marry, like many other rights, is subject to substantial restrictions as a result of incarceration. Many important attributes of marriage remain, however, after taking into account the limitations imposed by prison life." Although "legitimate security concerns" might require "reasonable restrictions" on the exercise of the right to marry and might "justify requiring the approval of the superintendent," this regulation represented "an exaggerated response to [security] objectives" and was therefore invalid.

6. One of the central issues in these cases is the identification, on the appropriate level of abstraction, of the traditional liberty protected by the Due Process Clause: If the tradition is defined too narrowly, the legislation at issue simply will illustrate the tradition, thereby depriving the appeal to tradition of any power to check legislative action. If the tradition is defined too broadly, judges will be able to appeal to it to invalidate whatever legislation they choose to characterize as inconsistent with tradition. This problem was the subject of an exchange between Justices Scalia and Brennan in Michael H. v. Gerald D., 109 S. Ct. 2333 (1989). A California statute provided that a child born to a married woman living with her husband is conclusively presumed to be a child of the marriage; this presumption has consequences for the visitation rights of the genetic father of such a child. A majority of the Court held that this statute did not violate the Constitution. A plurality opinion by Justice Scalia said that for the genetic father to have a liberty interest in establishing his paternity, that interest had to be both "fundamental" and "an interest traditionally protected by our society." To the plurality, the relevant tradition involved "the historic respect — indeed, sanctity would not be too strong a term — traditionally accorded to the relationships that develop within the unitary family." Because Michael H. was not part of such a unitary family, he had no interest of the necessary sort.

In a long footnote, Justice Scalia defended his reliance on "historical traditions specifically relating to the rights of an adulterous natural father, rather than [as Justice Brennan urged] inquiring more generally 'whether parenthood is an interest that historically has received our attention and protection.' " He asked,

> Why should the relevant category not be even more general — perhaps "family relationships"; or "personal relationships"; or even "emotional attachments in general"? Though [Justice Brennan] has no basis for the level of generality [he] would select, we do: We refer to the most specific level at which a relevant tradition protecting, or denying protection to, the asserted right can be identified. If [there] were no societal tradition, either way, regarding the rights of the natural father or a child adulterously conceived, we would have to consult and if possible reason from, the traditions regarding natural fathers in general. But there is such a more specific tradition, and it unqualifiedly denies protection to such a parent. . . . Because [general] traditions provide such imprecise guidance, they permit judges to dictate rather than discern the society's views. [Although] assuredly having the virtue (if it be that) of leaving judges free to decide as they think best when the unanticipated occurs, a rule of law that binds neither by text nor by any particular, identifiable tradition, is no rule of law at all.

(Although Justices O'Connor and Kennedy joined most of the plurality opinion, they specifically declined to join this footnote.)

Justice Brennan responded:

> If we had looked to tradition with such specificity in past cases, many a decision would have reached a different result. [*Eisenstadt, Griswold, Stanley.*] [The] plurality's interpretative method [ignores] the good reasons for limiting the role of "tradition" in interpreting the Constitution's deliberately capacious language. [By] suggesting that our sole function is to "*discern* the society's views," the plurality acts as if the only purpose of the Due Process Clause is to confirm the importance of interests already protected by a majority of the States. [In] construing the Fourteenth Amendment to offer shelter only to those interests specifically protected by historical practice, [the] plurality ignores the kind of society in which our Constitution exists. We are not an assimilative, homogeneous society, but a facilitative, pluralistic one, in which we must be willing to abide someone else's unfamiliar or even repellant practice because the same tolerant impulse protects our own idiosyncracies. Even if we can agree [that] "family" and "parenthood" are part of the good life, it is absurd to assume that we can agree on the content of those terms and destructive to pretend that we do. In a community such as ours, "liberty" must include the freedom not to conform. The plurality today squashes this freedom by requiring specific approval from history before protecting anything in the name of liberty.

To Justice Brennan, the case merely involved the protection of "the interest of a parent and child in their relationship with each other."

Justice Stevens, who contributed the fifth vote to support the constitutionality of the California statute, agreed that Michael H. had a liberty interest but argued that the California statutes recognized that interest to the extent required by the Due Process Clause.

Page 896.   Before section 2 of the Note, add the following:

1A. *Freedom of cultural association.* Is there a constitutional right of cultural association? Can the state constitutionally require an organization dedicated to maintaining Irish traditions and celebrating Irish heritage to admit Italians or Blacks? For a discussion of this issue, see Marshall, Discrimination and the Right of Association, 81 Nw. U.L. Rev. 68 (1986); Karst, Paths to Belonging: The Constitution and Cultural Identity, 64 N.C. L. Rev. 303 (1986).

Page 897.   After the word "argument" in line 16, add the following:

BOWERS v. HARDWICK
478 U.S. 186 (1986)

JUSTICE WHITE delivered the opinion of the Court.

[Respondent, an adult male, was criminally charged for violating Georgia's sodomy statute by committing a sexual act with another adult male in his own bedroom. The statute defined sodomy as committing or submitting to "any sexual act involving the sex organs of one person and the mouth or anus of another." After the prosecutor elected not to present the case to the grand jury, respondent brought this suit in federal court challenging the constitutionality of the statute. The district court upheld the statute, but the court of appeals reversed.]

We agree with the State that the Court of Appeals erred, and hence reverse its judgment. . . .

We first register our disagreement with the Court of Appeals and with respondent that the Court's prior cases have construed the Constitution to confer a right of privacy that extends to homosexual sodomy[2] and for all intents and purposes have decided this case. . . .

[We] think it evident that none of the rights announced in [such cases as *Pierce, Skinner, Griswold,* and *Roe*] bears any resemblance to the claimed constitutional right of homosexuals to engage in acts of sodomy that is asserted in this

2. The only claim properly before the Court [is] Hardwick's challenge to the Georgia statute as applied to consensual homosexual sodomy. We express no opinion on the constitutionality of the Georgia Statute as applied to other acts of sodomy. [Relocated footnote.]

case. No connection between family, marriage, or procreation on the one hand and homosexual activity on the other has been demonstrated, either by the Court of Appeals or by respondent. Moreover, any claim that these cases nevertheless stand for the proposition that any kind of private sexual conduct between consenting adults is constitutionally insulated from state proscription is unsupportable. . . .

Precedent aside, however, respondent would have us announce, as the Court of Appeals did, a fundamental right to engage in homosexual sodomy. This we are quite unwilling to do. . . .

Striving to assure itself and the public that announcing rights not readily identifiable in the Constitution's text involves much more than the imposition of the Justices' own choice of values on the States and the Federal Government, the Court has sought to identify the nature of the rights qualifying for heightened judicial protection. In [Palko] it was said that this category includes those fundamental liberties that are "implicit in the concept of ordered liberty," such that "neither liberty nor justice would exist if [they] were sacrificed." A different description of fundamental liberties appeared in [Moore] (opinion of Powell, J.), where they are characterized as those liberties that are "deeply rooted in this Nation's history and tradition." See also [Griswold].

It is obvious to us that neither of these formulations would extend a fundamental right to homosexuals to engage in acts of consensual sodomy. Proscriptions against that conduct have ancient roots. Sodomy was a criminal offense at common law and was forbidden by the laws of the original thirteen states when they ratified the Bill of Rights. In 1868, when the Fourteenth Amendment was ratified, all but 5 of the 37 States of the Union had criminal sodomy laws. In fact, until 1961, all 50 States outlawed sodomy, and today, 24 States and the District of Columbia continue to provide criminal penalties for sodomy performed in private and between consenting adults. Against this background, to claim that a right to engage in such conduct is "deeply rooted in this Nation's history and tradition" or "implicit in the concept of ordered liberty" is, at best, facetious.

Nor are we inclined to take a more expansive view of our authority to discover new fundamental rights imbedded in the Due Process Clause. The Court is most vulnerable and comes nearest to illegitimacy when it deals with judge-made constitutional law having little or no cognizable roots in the language or design of the Constitution. That this is so was painfully demonstrated by the face-off between the Executive and the Court in the 1930's, which resulted in the repudiation on much of the substantive gloss that the Court had placed on the Due Process Clause of the Fifth and Fourteenth Amendments. There should be, therefore, great resistance to expand the substantive reach of those Clauses, particularly if it requires redefining the category of rights deemed to be fundamental. Otherwise, the Judiciary necessarily takes to itself further authority to govern the country without express constitutional authority. The claimed right pressed on us today falls far short of overcoming this resistance.

Respondent, however, asserts that the result should be different where the homosexual conducts occurs in the privacy of the home. He relies on Stanley v. Georgia [page 1123 infra of the main text], where the Court held that the First Amendment prevents conviction for possessing and reading obscene material in the privacy of his home. . . .

Stanley did protect conduct that would not have been protected outside the home, and it partially prevented the enforcement of state obscenity laws; but the decision was firmly grounded in the First Amendment. The right pressed upon us here has no similar support in the text of the Constitution, and it does not qualify for recognition under the prevailing principles for construing the Fourteenth Amendment. Its limits are also difficult to discern. Plainly enough, otherwise illegal conduct is not always immunized whenever it occurs in the home. Victimless crimes, such as the possession and use of illegal drugs do not escape the law where they are committed at home. *Stanley* itself recognized that its holdings offered no protection for the possession in the home of drugs, firearms, or stolen goods. And if respondent's submission is limited to the voluntary sexual conduct between consenting adults, it would be difficult, except by fiat, to limit the claimed right to homosexual conduct while leaving exposed to prosecution adultery, incest, and other sexual crimes even though they are committed in the home. We are unwilling to start down that road.

Even if the conduct at issue here is not a fundamental right, respondent asserts that there must be a rational basis for the law and that there is none in this case other than the presumed belief of a majority of the electorate in Georgia that homosexual sodomy is immoral and unacceptable. This is said to be an inadequate rationale to support the law. The law, however, is constantly based on notions of morality, and if all laws representing essentially moral choices are to be invalidated under the Due Process Clause, the courts will be very busy indeed. Even respondent makes no such claim, but insists that majority sentiments about the morality of homosexuality should be declared inadequate. We do not agree, and are unpersuaded that the sodomy laws of some 25 States should be invalidated on this basis.[8]

Accordingly, the judgment of the Court of Appeals is reversed.

CHIEF JUSTICE BURGER, concurring.

I join the Court's opinion, but I write separately to underscore my view that in constitutional terms there is no such thing as a fundamental right to commit homosexual sodomy.

---

8. Respondent does not defend the judgment below based on the Ninth Amendment, the Equal Protecton Clause or the Eighth Amendment.

As the Court notes, the proscriptions against sodomy have very "Ancient roots." Decisions of individuals relating to homosexual conduct have been subject to state intervention throughout the history of Western Civilization. Condemnation of those practices is firmly rooted in Judeo-Christian moral and ethical standards. [Blackstone] described "the infamous crime against nature" as an offense of "deeper malignity" than rape, an heinous act "the very mention of which is a disgrace to human nature," and "a crime not fit to be named."

[To] hold that the act of homosexual sodomy is somehow protected as a fundamental right would be to cast aside millennia of moral teaching.

This is essentially not a question of personal "preferences" but rather of the legislative authority of the State. I find nothing in the Constitution depriving a State of the power to enact the statute challenged here.

JUSTICE POWELL, concurring.

[I] agree with the Court that there is no fundamental right — i.e., no substantive right under the Due Process Clause — such as that claimed by respondent, and found to exist by the Court of Appeals. This is not to suggest, however, that respondent may not be protected by the [cruel and unusual punishment clause of the] Eighth Amendment of the Constitution. The Georgia statute at issue in this case, authorizes a court to imprison a person for up to 20 years for a single private, consensual act of sodomy. In my view, a prison sentence for such conduct — certainly a sentence of long duration — would create a serious Eighth Amendment issue. . . .

Justice Blackmun, with whom Justice Brennan, Justice Marshall, and Justice Stevens join, dissenting.

This case is no more about "a fundamental right to engage in homosexual sodomy," as the Court purports to declare, than Stanley v. Georgia, 394 U.S. 557 (1969), was about a fundamental right to watch obscene movies, or Katz v. United States, 389 U.S. 347 (1967), was about a fundamental right to place interstate bets from a telephone booth. Rather, this case is about "the most comprehensive of rights and the right most valued by civilized men," namely, "the right to be let alone." Olmstead v. United States, 277 U.S. 438, 478 (1928) (Brandeis, J., dissenting).

The statute at issue denies individuals the right to decide for themselves whether to engage in particular forms of private, consensual sexual activity. The Court concludes that [the statute] is valid essentially because "the laws of . . . many States . . . still make such conduct illegal and have done so for a very long time." But the fact that the moral judgments expressed by statutes like [this one] may be "natural and familiar . . . ought not to conclude our judgment upon the question whether statutes embodying them conflict with the Constitution of the United States." [*Roe*, quoting *Lochner* (Holmes, J., dissenting).]

The Court concludes today that none of our prior cases dealing with various decisions that individuals are entitled to make free of governmental interference "bears any resemblance to the claimed constitutional right of homosexuals to engage in acts of sodomy that is asserted in this case." While it is true that these cases may be characterized by their connection to protection of the family, see Roberts v. United States Jaycees, the Court's conclusion that they extend no further than this boundary ignores the warning in [*Moore*] against "clos[ing] our eyes to the basic reasons why certain rights associated with the family have been accorded shelter under the Fourteenth Amendment's Due Process Clause." We protect those rights not because they contribute, in some direct and material way, to the general public welfare, but because they form so central a part of an individual's life. . . .

Only the most willful blindness could obscure the fact that sexual intimacy is "a sensitive, key relationship of human existence, central to family life, community welfare, and the development of human personality," Paris Adult Theatre I v. Slayton, 413 U.S. 49, 63 (1973).

[The] fact that individuals define themselves in a significant way through their intimate sexual relationships with others suggests, in a Nation as diverse as ours, that there may be many "right" ways of conducting those relationships, and that much of the richness of a relationship will come from the freedom an individual has to *choose* the form and nature of these intensely personal bonds. . . .

The Court claims that its decision today merely refuses to recognize a fundamental right to engage in homosexual sodomy; what the Court really has refused to recognize is the fundamental interest all individuals have in controlling the nature of their intimate associations with others.

The behavior for which Hardwick faces prosecution occurred in his own home, a place to which the Fourth Amendment attaches special significance. . . .

The Court's interpretation of the pivotal case of Stanley v. Georgia is entirely unconvincing. *Stanley* held that Georgia's undoubted power to punish the public distribution of constitutionally unprotected, obscene material did not permit the State to punish the private possession of such material. According to the majority here, *Stanley* relied entirely on the First Amendment, and thus, it is claimed, sheds no light on cases not involving printed materials. But that is not what *Stanley* said. Rather, the *Stanley* Court anchored its holding in the Fourth Amendment's special protection for the individual in his home. . . .

The Court's failure to comprehend the magnitude of the liberty interests at stake in this case leads it to slight the question whether petitioner, on behalf of the State, has justified Georgia's infringement on these interests. I believe that neither of the two general justifications for [the statute] that petitioner has advanced warrants dismissing respondent's challenge for failure to state a claim.

First, petitioner asserts that the acts made criminal by the statute may have serious adverse consequences for "the general public health and welfare," such as spreading communicable diseases or fostering other criminal activity. Inasmuch as this case was dismissed by the District Court on the pleadings, it is not surprising that the record before us is barren of any evidence to support petitioner's claim. In light of the state of the record, I see no justification for the Court's attempt to equate the private, consensual sexual activity at issue here with the "possession in the home of drugs, firearms, or stolen goods," to which *Stanley* refused to extend its protection. . . .

The core of petitioner's defense of [the statute], however, is that respondent and others who engage in the conduct prohibited by [it] interfere with Georgia's exercise of the " 'right of the Nation and of the States to maintain a decent society,' " Paris Adult Theater I v. Slaton, 413 U.S., at 59-60, quoting Jacobellis v. Ohio, 378 U.S. 184, 199 (1964) (Warren, C. J., dissenting). . . .

The assertion that "traditional Judeo-Christian values proscribe" the conduct involved cannot provide an adequate justification for [the statute]. That certain, but by no means all, religious groups condemn the behavior at issue gives the State no license to impose their judgments on the entire citizenry. The legitimacy of secular legislation depends instead on whether the State can advance some justification for its law beyond its conformity to religious doctrine. . . .

Certainly, some private behavior can affect the fabric of society as a whole. [Statutes] banning public sexual activity are entirely consistent with protecting the individual's liberty interest in decisions concerning sexual relations: the same recognition that those decisions are intensely private which justifies protecting them from governmental interference can justify protecting individuals from unwilling exposure to the sexual activities of others. But the mere fact that intimate behavior may be punished when it takes place in public cannot dictate how States can regulate intimate behavior that occurs in intimate places. . . .

I can only hope that [the] Court soon will reconsider its analysis and conclude that depriving individuals of the right to choose for themselves how to conduct their intimate relationships poses a far greater threat to the values most deeply rooted in our Nation's history than tolerance of nonconformity could ever do. Because I think the Court today betrays those values, I dissent.

JUSTICE STEVENS, with whom JUSTICE BRENNAN and JUSTICE MARSHALL join, dissenting.

Like the statute that is challenged in this case, the rationale of the Court's opinion applies equally to the prohibited conduct regardless of whether the parties who engage in it are married or unmarried, or are of the same or different sexes. Sodomy was condemned as an odious and sinful type of behavior during the formative period of the common law. That condemnation was equally damning for heterosexual and homosexual sodomy. Moreover, it provided no special exemption for married couples. . . .

Because the Georgia statute expresses the traditional view that sodomy is an immoral kind of conduct regardless of the identity of the persons who engage in it, I believe that a proper analysis of its constitutionality requires consideration of two questions: First, may a State totally prohibit the described conduct by means of a neutral law applying without exception to all persons subject to its jurisdiction? If not, may the State save the statute by announcing that it will only enforce the law against homosexuals? . . .

[Individual] decisions by married persons, concerning the intimacies of their physical relationship, even when not intended to produce offspring, are a form of "liberty" protected by the Due Process Clause of the Fourteenth Amendment. [*Griswold.*] Moreover, this protection extends to intimate choices by unmarried as well as married persons. [*Carey; Eisenstadt.*] . . .

Society has every right to encourage its individual members to follow particular traditions in expressing affection for one another and in gratifying their personal desires. It, of course, may prohibit an individual from imposing his will on another to satisfy his own selfish interests. It also may prevent an individual from interfering with, or violating, a legally sanctioned and protected relationship, such as marriage. And it may explain the relative advantages and disadvantages of different forms of intimate expression. But when individual married couples are isolated from observation by others, the way in which they voluntarily choose to conduct their intimate relations is a matter for them — not the State — to decide. The essential "liberty" that animated the development of the law in cases like *Griswold, Eisenstadt,* and *Carey* surely embraces the right to engage in nonreproductive, sexual conduct that others may consider offensive or immoral.

Paradoxical as it may seem, our prior cases thus establish that a State may not prohibit sodomy within "the sacred precincts of marital bedrooms," *Griswold,* or indeed, between unmarried heterosexual adults. *Eisenstadt.* . . .

If the Georgia statute cannot be enforced as it is written — if the conduct it seeks to prohibit is a protected form of liberty for the vast majority of Georgia's citizens — the State must assume the burden of justifying a selective application of its law. Either the persons to whom Georgia seeks to apply its statute do not have the same interest in "liberty" that others have, or there must be a reason why the State may be permitted to apply a generally applicable law to certain persons that it does not apply to others.

The first possibility is plainly unacceptable. Although the meaning of the principle that "all men are created equal" is not always clear, it surely must mean that every free citizen has the same interest in "liberty" that the members of the majority share. From the standpoint of the individual, the homosexual and the heterosexual have the same interest in deciding how he will live his own life, and, more narrowly, how he will conduct himself in his personal and voluntary associations with his companions. State intrusion into the private conduct of either is equally burdensome.

The second possibility is similarly unacceptable. A policy of selective application must be supported by a neutral and legitimate interest — something more substantial than a habitual dislike for, or ignorance about, the disfavored group. Neither the State nor the Court has identified any such interest in this case. The Court has posited as a justification for the Georgia statute "the presumed belief of a majority of the electorate in Georgia that homosexual sodomy is immoral and unacceptable." But the Georgia electorate has expressed no such belief — instead, its representatives enacted a law that presumably reflects the belief that *all sodomy* is immoral and unacceptable. Unless the Court is prepared to conclude that such a law is constitutional, it may not rely on the work product of the Georgia Legislature to support its holding. For the Georgia statute does not single out homosexuals as a separate class meriting special disfavored treatment. . . .

Both the Georgia statute and the Georgia prosecutor thus completely fail to provide the Court with any support for the conclusion that homosexual sodomy, *simpliciter*, is considered unacceptable conduct in that State, and that the burden of justifying a selective application of the generally applicable law has been met. . . .

I respectfully dissent.

NOTE: THE SECOND DEATH OF SUBSTANTIVE DUE PROCESS?

Does *Bowers* signal the end of the modern substantive due process era? Consider Conkle, The Second Death of Substantive Due Process, 62 Ind. L.J. 215, 232-233, 235, 242 (1987):

> Under [*Eisenstadt* and *Roe*], an individual, whether married or single, has the right [to] practice birth control through the use of contraceptives [or] abortion. As a result, *Eisenstadt* and *Roe* necessarily protect [the] right of heterosexuals to engage in nonprocreative sexual relations, even outside the traditional setting of marriage. [It] is difficult to imagine how the individual interest presented in *Bowers* was less important than the interest protected in [the] earlier decisions. [Moreover,] the countervailing governmental interests asserted in *Bowers* were far less substantial than the interests asserted in *Roe*. [*Roe*] and *Bowers* are [thus] inconsistent and irreconcilable. [Viewed in this light, *Bowers*] represents the death of substantive due process as a principled doctrine of law.

Consider the argument in Schneider, State-Interest Analysis in Fourteenth Amendment "Privacy" Law: An Essay on the Constitutionalization of Social Issues, 51 L. & Contemp. Prob. 79, 99, 102–103, 110-111 (1988):

> Statutes of the kind challenged in privacy cases may often be understood as attempting to influence behavior indirectly, by reinforcing in people attitudes that encourage restraint in family and sexual settings. They may seek to induce [ascetic] attitudes

towards family and sexual life [by a] "socializing strategy." . . . It may be reasonable to say that, when deciding whether to impinge on a fundamental privacy right, a legislature may not be judicially prevented from consulting a theory like a theory of human nature at least where the theory has been substantially relied on in the past and where it has substantial intellectual antecedents. . . . The view of human nature on which these statutes seem to rely [is] the pessimistic view [that] believes man is easily led to harm himself and other people by his own self-interestedness. [It] contrives to channel [the] pleasures [of the senses] into the service of good, as when it summons sexual passion to exalt love in marriage. Insofar as [they] cannot be channelled into good, [it] hopes to curb those propensities by social conditioning which seeks to internalize self-restraint. [Despite] the many forces that impel the United States as a whole toward dissensus, there are probably still states and even regions in which traditional social norms are widely accepted. [If] social dissensus [is] not inevitable, and if a particular state has something like social consensus, [that] state's legislature ought to be constitutionally able to make the socialization policy one of its interests. [Recognizing] the socializing strategy [would] ease social compromise, [which] is desirable where substantial numbers [of] reasonable citizens differ on legitimate grounds as to matters about which they feel deeply and as to which losing (especially losing in a way which emphasizes the illegitimacy of their opinions) will deprive them of a sense – or worse, the reality – of participation in the polity.

How does this argument apply to *Roe* and *Bowers*?

Consider Rubenfeld, The Right of Privacy, 102 Harv. L. Rev. 737, 770, 782, 799-800 (1989):

[Personhood as the basis for privacy] cannot exclude "intolerant" identities without abandoning its value-neutrality as between identities, and abandoning such value-neutrality undermines personhood's normative foundations. [It must] deliver a conception of personal identity that could explain which decisions, being central to identity, deserve constitutional protection and which decisions [do] not. [Personhood] finally comes to rest its case on the fundamental importance of sexuality: a person's sexual life [is] simply more definitive of and more deeply rooted in who that person is than his neighbors' conduct can ever be.

[But personhood] betrays privacy's [political] aspirations. By conceiving of the conduct that it purports to protect as "essential to the individual's identity" personhood reintroduces into privacy analysis the very premise of the invidious uses of state power it seeks to overcome. [For example,] personhood must defend the right to abortion on the ground that abortion is essential to the woman's self-definition. But underlying the idea that a women is *defining her identity* by determining not to have a child is the very premise of those institutionalized sexual roles through which the subordination of women has for so long been maintained. Only if it were "natural" for a woman to want to bear children [would] it make sense to insist that the decision not to have a child at one given moment was centrally definitive of a woman's identity. [Rather,] women should be able to abort their pregnancies so that they may *avoid being forced into an identity*, not because they are defining their identities through the decision itself.

[Laws] against homosexual sex have an effect that most laws do not. They forcibly channel certain individuals [into] a network of social institutions and relations that will occupy their lives to a substantial degree. [The] prohibition against homosexual sex channels individuals' sexual desires into *reproductive* outlets. Although the prohibition does not, like the law against abortions, produce as an imminent consequence compulsory child-bearing, it nonetheless forcibly directs individuals into the pathways of reproductive sexuality.

Consider the extent to which the force of this argument depends on its implicit definition of coercion, and consider once again the relation between *Roe* v. *Wade* and *Bowers*, and *Lochner*: Can it be said that *Lochner*'s mistake was to assume that decisions made within the general structure of property relations established by the government were *not* the result of government decisions, that *Roe* rests on the contrary assumption that decisions — whether they be to bear a child or to have an abortion — made within the general structure of social relations supported by the government *are* the result of government decisions, and that *Bowers* is inconsistent with *Roe* because it rejects that assumption?

Page 900.   After line 4, add a new section:

4. *The Right to Die*

CRUZAN v. DIRECTOR, MISSOURI DEPT. OF HEALTH
110 S. Ct. — (1990)

CHIEF JUSTICE REHNQUIST delivered the opinion of the Court.

On the night of January 11, 1983, Nancy Cruzan lost control of her car as she traveled down Elm Road in Jasper County, Missouri. The vehicle overturned, and Cruzan was discovered lying face down in a ditch without detectable respiratory or cardiac function. Paramedics were able to restore her breathing and heartbeat at the accident site, and she was transported to a hospital in an unconscious state. . . . She remained in a coma for approximately three weeks and then progressed to an unconscious state in which she was able to orally ingest some nutrition. In order to ease feeding and further the recovery, surgeons implanted a gastrostomy feeding and hydration tube in Cruzan with the consent of her then husband. Subsequent rehabilitative efforts proved unavailing. She now lies in a Missouri state hospital in what is commonly referred to as a persistent vegetative state: generally, a condition in which a person exhibits motor reflexes but evinces no indications of significant cognitive function. The State of Missouri is bearing the cost of her care.

After it had become apparent that Nancy Cruzan had virtually no chance of regaining her mental faculties her parents asked hospital employees to terminate the artificial nutrition and hydration procedures. All agree that such a removal would cause her death. The employees refused to honor the request without court approval. . . .

We granted certiorari to consider the question of whether Cruzan has a right under the United States Constitution which would require the hospital to withdraw life-sustaining treatment from her under these circumstances.

At common law, even the touching of one person by another without consent and without legal justification was a battery.

The logical corollary of the doctrine of informed consent is that the patient generally possesses the right not to consent, that is, to refuse treatment. Until about 15 years ago and the seminal decision in *In re Quinlan*, 70 N. J. 10, 355 A.2d 647, *cert. denied sub nom., Garger v. New Jersey,* 429 U.S. 922 (1976), the number of right-to-refuse-treatment decisions were relatively few. Most of the earlier cases involved patients who refused medical treatment forbidden by their religious beliefs, thus implicating First Amendment rights as well as common law rights of self-determination. More recently, however, with the advance of medical technology capable of sustaining life well past the point where natural forces would have brought certain death in earlier times, cases involving the right to refuse life-sustaining treatment have burgeoned. . . .

[The] common-law doctrine of informed consent is viewed as generally encompassing the right of a competent individual to refuse medical treatment.

. . . In this Court, the question is simply and starkly whether the United States Constitution prohibits Missouri from choosing the rule of decision which it did. This is the first case in which we have been squarely presented with the issue of whether the United States Constitution grants what is in common parlance referred to as a "right to die." We follow the judicious counsel of our decision in *Twin City Bank v. Nebeker*, 167 U.S. 196, 202 (1897), where we said that in deciding "a question of such magnitude and importance . . . it is the [better] part of wisdom not to attempt, by any general statement, to cover every possible phase of the subject."

The Fourteenth Amendment provides that no State shall "deprive any person of life, liberty, or property, without due process of law." The principle that a competent person has a constitutionally protected liberty interest in refusing unwanted medical treatment may be inferred from our prior decisions. In *Jacobson v. Massachusetts*, 197 U.S. 11, 24-30 (1905), for instance, the Court balanced an individual's liberty interest in declining an unwanted smallpox vaccine against the State's interest in preventing disease. . . .

Just this Term, in the course of holding that a State's procedures for administering antipsychotic medication to prisoners were sufficient to satisfy due process concerns, we recognized that prisoners possess "a significant liberty interest in avoiding the unwanted administration of antipsychotic drugs under the Due Process Clause of the Fourteenth Amendment." *Washington* v. *Harper*, – U.S. – , – (1990). . . .

But determining that a person has a "liberty interest", under the Due Process Clause does not end the inquiry; [7] "whether respondent's constitutional rights have been violated must be determined by balancing his liberty interests against the relevant state interests." *Youngberg* v. *Romeo,* 457 U.S. 307, 321 (1982). . . .

Petitioners insist that under the general holdings of our cases, the forced administration of life-sustaining medical treatment, and even of artificially-delivered food and water essential to life, would implicate a competent person's liberty interest. Although we think the logic of the cases discussed above would embrace such a liberty interest, the dramatic consequences involved in refusal of such treatment would inform the inquiry as to whether the deprivation of that interest is constitutionally permissible. But for purposes of this case, we assume that the United States Constitution would grant a competent person a constitutionally protected right to refuse lifesaving hydration and nutrition.

Petitioners go on to assert that an incompetent person should possess the same right in this respect as is possessed by a competent person. . . .

The difficulty with petitioners' claim is that in a sense it begs the question: an incompetent person is not able to make an informed and voluntary choice to exercise a hypothetical right to refuse treatment or any other right. Such a "right" must be exercised for her, if at all, by some sort of surrogate. Here, Missouri has in effect recognized that under certain circumstances a surrogate may act for the patient in electing to have hydration and nutrition withdrawn in such a way as to cause death, but it has established a procedural safeguard to assure that the action of the surrogate conforms as best it may to the wishes expressed by the patient while competent. Missouri requires that evidence of the incompetent's wishes as to the withdrawal of treatment be proved by clear and convincing evidence. The question, then, is whether the United States Constitution forbids the establishment of this procedural requirement by the State. We hold that it does not.

Whether or not Missouri's clear and convincing evidence requirement comports with the United States Constitution depends in part on what interests the State may properly seek to protect in this situation. Missouri relies on its interest in the protection and preservation of human life, and there can be no gainsaying this interest. As a general matter, the States — indeed, all civilized nations — demonstrate their commitment to life by treating homicide as serious crime. Moreover, the majority of States in this country have laws imposing criminal penalties on one who assists another to commit suicide. We do not think a State is required to remain neutral in the face of an informed and voluntary decision by a physically-able adult to starve to death.

7. Although many state courts have held that a right to refuse treatment is encompassed by a generalized constitutional right of privacy, we have never so held. We believe this issue is more properly analyzed in terms of a Fourteenth Amendment liberty interest. See *Bowers* v. *Hardwick*, 478 U.S. 186, 194-195 (1986).

But in the context presented here, a State has more particular interests at stake. The choice between life and death is a deeply personal decision of obvious and overwhelming finality. We believe Missouri may legitimately seek to safeguard the personal element of this choice through the imposition of heightened evidentiary requirements. It cannot be disputed that the Due Process Clause protects an interest in life as well as an interest in refusing life-sustaining medical treatment. Not all incompetent patients will have loved ones available to serve as surrogate decisionmakers. And even where family members are present, "[t]here will, of course, be some unfortunate situations in which family members will not act to protect a patient." *In re Jobes*, 108 N.J. 394, 419, 529 A.2d 434, 477 (1987). A State is entitled to guard against potential abuses in such situations. Similarly, a State is entitled to consider that a judicial proceeding to make a determination regarding an incompetent's wishes may very well not be an adversarial one, with the added guarantee of accurate factfinding that the adversary process brings with it. See *Ohio* v. *Akron Center for Reproductive Health*, — U.S. — , — (1990) (slip op., at 10-11). Finally, we think a State may properly decline to make judgments about the "quality" of life that a particular individual may enjoy, and simply assert an unqualified interest in the preservation of human life to be weighed against the constitutionally protected interests of the individual.

In our view, Missouri has permissibly sought to advance these interests through the adoption of a "clear and convincing" standard of proof to govern such proceedings. . . .

We think it self-evident that the interests at stake in the instant proceedings are more substantial, both on an individual and societal level, than those involved in a run-of-the-mine civil dispute. But not only does the standard of proof reflect the importance of a particular adjudication, it also serves as "a societal judgment about how the risk of error should be distributed between the litigants." The more stringent the burden of proof a party must bear, the more that party bears the risk of an erroneous decision. We believe that Missouri may permissibly place an increased risk of an erroneous decision on those seeking to terminate an incompetent individual's life-sustaining treatment.

In sum, we conclude that a State may apply a clear and convincing evidence standard in proceedings where a guardian seeks to discontinue nutrition and hydration of a person diagnosed to be in a persistent vegetative state.

The Supreme Court of Missouri held that in this case the testimony adduced at trial did not amount to clear and convincing proof of the patient's desire to have hydration and nutrition withdrawn. In so doing, it reversed a decision of the Missouri trial court which had found that the evidence "suggest[ed]" Nancy Cruzan would not have desired to continue such measures, App. to Pet. for Cert. A98, but which had not adopted the standard of "clear and convincing evidence" enunciated by the Supreme Court. The testimony adduced at trial consisted primarily of Nancy Cruzan's statements made to a housemate about a year before her accident that she would not want to live should she face life as a "vegetable," and other observations to the same effect. The observations did not deal in terms with withdrawal of medical treatment or of hydration and nutrition. We cannot say that the Supreme Court of Missouri committed constitutional error in reaching the conclusion that it did.

Petitioners alternatively contend that Missouri must accept the "substituted judgment" of close family members even in the absence of substantial proof that their views reflect the views of the patient. They rely primarily upon our decisions in *Michael H.* v. *Gerald D.*, 491 U.S. — (1989), and *Parham* v. *J. R.*, 442 U.S. 584 (1979). But we do not think these cases support their claim. In *Michael H.*, we *upheld* the constitutionality of California's favored treatment of traditional family relationships; such a holding may not be turned around into a constitutional requirement that a State *must* recognize the primacy of those relationships in a situation like this. And in *Parham*, where the patient was a minor, we also *upheld* the constitutionality of a state scheme in which parents made certain decisions for mentally ill minors. Here again petitioners would seek to turn a decision which allowed a State to rely on family decisionmaking into a constitutional requirement that the State recognize such decisionmaking. But constitutional law does not work that way.

No doubt is engendered by anything in this record but that Nancy Cruzan's mother and father are loving and caring parents. If the State were required by the United States Constitution to repose a right of "substituted judgment" with anyone, the Cruzans would surely qualify. But we do not think the Due Process Clause requires the State to repose judgment on these matters with anyone but the patient herself. Close family members may have a strong feeling — a feeling not at all ignoble or unworthy, but not entirely disinterested, either — that they do not wish to witness the continuation of the life of a loved one which they regard as hopeless, meaningless, and even degrading. But there is no automatic assurance that the view of close family members will necessarily be the same as the patient's would have been had she been confronted with the prospect of her situation while competent. All of the reasons previously discussed for allowing Missouri to require clear and convincing evidence of the patient's wishes lead us to conclude that the State may choose to defer only to those wishes, rather than confide the decision to close family members. [12]

12. We are not faced in this case with the question of whether a State might be required to defer to the decision of a surrogate if competent and probative evidence established that the patient herself had expressed a desire that the decision to terminate life-sustaining treatment be made for her by that individual.

Petitioners also adumbrate in their brief a claim based on the Equal Protection Clause of the Fourteenth Amendment to the effect that Missouri has impermissibly treated incompetent patients differently from competent ones, citing the statement in *Cleburne* v. *Cleburne Living Center, Inc.*, 473 U.S. 432, 439 (1985), that the clause is "essentially a direction that all persons similarly situated should be treated alike." The differences between the choice made *by* a competent person to refuse

The judgment of the Supreme Court of Missouri is *affirmed.*

JUSTICE O'CONNOR, concurring.

I agree that a protected liberty interest in refusing unwanted medical treatment may be inferred from our prior decisions, and that the refusal of artificially delivered food and water is encompassed within that liberty interest. I write separately to clarify why I believe this to be so.

As the Court notes, the liberty interest in refusing medical treatment flows from decisions involving the State's invasions into the body. Because our notions of liberty are inextricably entwined with our idea of physical freedom and self-determination, the Court has often deemed state incursions into the body repugnant to the interests protected by the Due Process Clause. . . .

The State's imposition of medical treatment on an unwilling competent adult necessarily involves some form of restraint and intrusion. A seriously ill or dying patient whose wishes are not honored may feel a captive of the machinery required for life-sustaining measures or other medical interventions. Such forced treatment may burden that individual's liberty interests as much as any state coercion. . . .

The State's artificial provision of nutrition and hydration implicates identical concerns. Artificial feeding cannot readily be distinguished from other forms of medical treatment. . . .

I also write separately to emphasize that the Court does not today decide the issue whether a State must also give effect to the decisions of a surrogate decisionmaker. In my view, such a duty may well be constitutionally required to protect the patient's liberty interest in refusing medical treatment. Few individuals provide explicit oral or written instructions regarding their intent to refuse medical treatment should they become incompetent. . . .

Today's decision, holding only that the Constitution permits a State to require clear and convincing evidence of Nancy Cruzan's desire to have artificial hydration and nutrition withdrawn, does not preclude a future determination that the Constitution requires the States to implement the decisions of a patient's duly appointed surrogate. Nor does it prevent States from developing other approaches for protecting an incompetent individual's liberty interest in refusing medical treatment. . . .

JUSTICE SCALIA, concurring.

The various opinions in this case portray quite clearly the difficult, indeed agonizing, questions that are presented by the constantly increasing power of science to keep the human body alive for longer than any reasonable person

---

medical treatment, and the choice made *for* an incompetent person by someone else to refuse medical treatment, are so obviously different that the State is warranted in establishing rigorous procedures for the latter class of cases which do not apply to the former class.

would want to inhabit it. The States have begun to grapple with these problems through legislation. I am concerned, from the tenor of today's opinions, that we are poised to confuse that enterprise as successfully as we have confused the enterprise of legislating concerning abortion — requiring it to be conducted against a background of federal constitutional imperatives that are unknown because they are being newly crafted from Term to Term. That would be a great misfortune.

While I agree with the Court's analysis today, and therefore join in its opinion, I would have preferred that we announce, clearly and promptly, that the federal courts have no business in this field; that American law has always accorded the State the power to prevent, by force if necessary, suicide — including suicide by refusing to take appropriate measures necessary to preserve one's life; that the point at which life becomes "worthless," and the point at which the means necessary to preserve it become "extraordinary" or "inappropriate," are neither set forth in the Constitution nor known to the nine Justices of this Court any better than they are known to nine people picked at random from the Kansas City telephone directory; and hence, that even when it *is* demonstrated by clear and convincing evidence that a patient no longer wishes certain measures to be taken to preserve her life, it is up to the citizens of Missouri to decide, through their elected representatives, whether that wish will be honored. It is quite impossible (because the Constitution says nothing about the matter) that those citizens will decide upon a line less lawful than the one we would choose; and it is unlikely (because we know no more about "life-and-death" than they do) that they will decide upon a line less reasonable.

The text of the Due Process Clause does not protect individuals against deprivations of liberty *simpliciter*. It protects them against deprivations of liberty "without due process of law." To determine that such a deprivation would not occur if Nancy Cruzan were forced to take nourishment against her will, it is unnecessary to reopen the historically recurrent debate over whether "due process" includes substantive restrictions.

. . . It is at least true that no "substantive due process" claim can be maintained unless the claimant demonstrates that the State has deprived him of a right historically and traditionally protected against State interference. *Michael H.* v. *Gerald D.*, 491 U.S. — , — (1989) (plurality opinion); *Bowers*, v. *Hardwick*, 478 U.S. 186, 192 (1986); *Moore, supra*, at 502-503 (plurality opinion). That cannot possibly be established here.

At common law in England, a suicide — defined as one who "deliberately puts an end to his own existence, or commits any unlawful malicious act, the consequence of which is his own death," 4 W. Blackstone, Commentaries *189 — was criminally liable. . . . And most States that did not explicitly prohibit assisted suicide in 1868 recognized, when the issue arose in the 50 years following the Fourteenth Amendment's ratification, that assisted and (in some cases) attempted suicide were unlawful. Thus, "there is no significant support for the claim that a right to suicide is so rooted in our tradition that it may be deemed 'fundamental' or 'implicit in the concept of ordered liberty.' "

Petitioners rely on three distinctions to separate Nancy Cruzan's case from ordinary suicide: (1) that she is permanently incapacited and in pain; (2) that she would bring on her death not by an affirmative act but by merely declining treatment that provides nourishment; and (3) that preventing her from effectuating her presumed wish to die requires violation of her bodily integrity. None of these suffices.

The dissents of Justices Brennan and Stevens make a plausible case for our intervention here only by embracing — the latter explicitly and the former by implication — a political principle that the States are free to adopt, but that is demonstrably not imposed by the Constitution.

What I have said above is not meant to suggest that I would think it desirable, if we were sure that Nancy Cruzan wanted to die, to keep her alive by the means at issue here. I assert only that the Constitution has nothing to say about the subject. To raise up a constitutional right here we would have to create out of nothing (for it exists neither in text nor tradition) some constitutional principle whereby, although the State may insist that an individual come in out of the cold and eat food, it may not insist that he take medicine; and although it may pump his stomach empty of poison he has ingested, it may not fill his stomach with food he has failed to ingest. Are there, then, no reasonable and human limits that ought not to be exceeded in requiring an individual to preserve his own life? There obviously are, but they are not set forth in the Due Process Clause. What assures us that those limits will not be exceeded is the same constitutional guarantee that is the source of most of our protection — what protects us, for example, from being assessed a tax of 100% of our income above the subsistence level, from being forbidden to drive cars, or from being required to send our children to school for 10 hours a day, none of which horribles is categorically prohibited by the Constitution. Our salvation is the Equal Protection Clause, which requires the democratic majority to accept for themselves and their loved ones what they impose on you and me. This Court need not, and has no authority to, inject itself into every field of human activity where irrationality and oppression may theoretically occur, and if it tries to do so it will destroy itself.

JUSTICE BRENNAN, with whom JUSTICE MARSHALL and JUSTICE BLACKMUN join, dissenting. . . .

The starting point for our legal analysis must be whether a competent person has a constitutional right to avoid unwanted medical care. Earlier this Term, this Court held that the Due Process Clause of the Fourteenth Amendment confers a significant liberty interest in avoiding unwanted medical treatment. *Washington* v. *Harper*, 494 U.S. — , — (1990). Today, the Court concedes that our prior decisions "support the recognition of a general liberty interest in refusing medical treatment." See *ante,* at 14. The Court, however, avoids discussing either the measure of that liberty interest or its application by assuming, for purposes of this case only, that a competent person has a constitutionally protected liberty interest in being free of unwanted artificial nutrition and hydration. . . .

But if a competent person has a liberty interest to be free of unwanted medical treatment, as both the majority and JUSTICE O'CONNOR concede, it must be fundamental. "We are dealing here with [a decision] which involves one of the basic civil rights of man." *Skinner* v. *Oklahoma ex rel. Williamson,* 316 U.S. 535, 541 (1942) (invalidating a statute authorizing sterilization of certain felons). Whatever other liberties protected by the Due Process Clause are fundamental, "those liberties that are 'deeply rooted in this Nation's history and tradition' " are among them. . . .

The right to be free from unwanted medical attention is a right to evaluate the potential benefit of treatment and its possible consequences according to one's own values and to make a personal decision whether to subject oneself to the intrusion. For a patient like Nancy Cruzan, the sole benefit of medical treatment is being kept metabolically alive. Neither artificial nutrition nor any other form of medical treatment available today can cure or in any way ameliorate her condition. Irreversibly vegetative patients are devoid of thought, emotion and sensation; they are permanently and completely unconscious.

Although the right to be free of unwanted medical intervention, like other constitutionally protected interests, may not be absolute, no State interest could outweigh the rights of an individual in Nancy Cruzan's position. Whatever a State's possible interests in mandating life-support treatment under other circumstances, there is no good to be obtained here by Missouri's insistence that Nancy Cruzan remain on life-support systems if it is indeed her wish not to do so. Missouri does not claim, nor could it, that society as a whole will be benefited by Nancy's receiving medical treatment. No third party's situation will be improved and no harm to others will be averted.

The only state interest asserted here is a general interest in the preservation of life. But the State has no legitimate general interest in someone's life, completely abstracted from the interest of the person living that life, that could outweigh the person's choice to avoid medical treatment. . . .

This is not to say that the State has no legitimate interests to assert here. As the majority recognizes, Missouri has a *parens patriae* interest in providing Nancy Cruzan, now incompetent, with as accurate as possible a determination of how she would exercise her rights under these circumstances. Second, if and when it is determined that Nancy Cruzan would want to continue treatment, the State may legitimately assert an interest in providing that treatment. But until Nancy's wishes have been determined, the only state interest that may be asserted is an interest in safe-guarding the accuracy of that determination.

Accuracy, therefore, must be our touchstone. Missouri may constitutionally impose only those procedural requirements that serve to enhance the accuracy of a determination of Nancy Cruzan's wishes or are at least consistent with an accurate determination. The Missouri "safeguard" that the Court upholds today does not meet that standard. The determination needed in this context is whether the incompetent person would choose to live in a persistent vegetative state on life-support or to avoid this medical treatment. Missouri's rule of decision imposes a markedly asymmetrical evidentiary burden. Only evidence of specific statements of treatment choice made by the patient when competent is admissible to support a finding that the patient, now in a persistent vegetative state, would wish to avoid further medical treatment. Moreover, this evidence must be clear and convincing. No proof is required to support a finding that the incompetent person would wish to continue treatment. . . .

Even more than its heightened evidentiary standard, the Missouri court's categorical exclusion of relevant evidence dispenses with any semblence of accurate factfinding. The court adverted to no evidence supporting its decision, but held that no clear and convincing, inherently reliable evidence had been presented to show that Nancy would want to avoid further treatment. In doing so, the court failed to consider statements Nancy had made to family members and a close friend. The court also failed to consider testimony from Nancy's mother and sister that they were certain that Nancy would want to discontinue to artificial nutrition and hydration, even after the court found that Nancy's family was loving and without malignant motive. . . .

Too few people execute living wills or equivalently formal directives for such an evidentiary rule to ensure adequately that the wishes of incompetent persons will be honored. While it might be a wise social policy to encourage people to furnish such instructions, no general conclusion about a patient's choice can be drawn from the absence of formalities. The probability of becoming irreversibly vegetative is so low that many people may not feel an urgency to marshal formal evidence of their preferences. Some may not wish to dwell on their own physical deterioration and mortality. Even someone with a resolute determination to avoid life-support under circumstances such as Nancy's would still need to know that such things as living wills exist and how to execute one. Often legal help would be necessary, especially given the majority's apparent willingness to permit States to insist that a person's wishes are not truly known unless the particular medical treatment is specified. . . .

To be constitutionally permissible, Missouri's intrusion upon these fundamental liberties must, at a minimum, bear a reasonable relationship to a legitimate state end. See, e.g., *Meyer* v. *Nebraska*, 262 U.S., at 400; *Dee* v. *Bolton*, 410 U.S. 179, 194-195, 199 (1973). Missouri asserts that its policy is related to a state interest in the protection of life. In my view, however, it is an effort to define life, rather than to protect it, that is the heart of Missouri's policy. Missouri insists, without regard to Nancy Cruzan's own interests, upon equating her life with the biological persistence of her bodily functions. Nancy Cruzan, it must be remembered, is not now simply incompetent. She is in a persistent vegetative state, and has been so for seven years. The trial court found, and no party contested, that Nancy has no possibility of recovery and no consciousness.

It seems to me that the Court errs insofar as it characterizes this case as involving "judgments about the 'quality' of life that a particular individual may enjoy." Nancy Cruzan is obviously "*alive*" in a physiological sense. But for patients like Nancy Cruzan, who have no consciousness and no chance of recovery, there is a serious question as to whether the mere persistence of their bodies is "*life*" as that word is commonly understood, or as it is used in both the Constitution and the Declaration of Independence. The State's unflagging determination to perpetuate Nancy Cruzan's physical existence is comprehensible only as an effort to define life's meaning, not as an attempt to preserve its sanctity. . . .

In short, there is no reasonable ground for believing that Nancy Beth Cruzan has any *personal* interest in the perpetuation of what the State has decided is her life. As I have already suggested, it would be possible to hypothesize such an interest on the basis of theological or philosophical conjecture. But even to posit such a basis for the State's action is to condemn it. It is not within the province of secular government to circumscribe the liberties of the people by regulations designed wholly for the purpose of establishing a sectarian definition of life.

My disagreement with the Court is thus unrelated to its endorsement of the clear and convincing standard of proof for cases of this kind. Indeed, I agree that the controlling facts must be established with unmistakable clarity. The critical question, however, is not how to prove the controlling facts but rather what proven facts should be controlling. In my view, the constitutional answer is clear: the best interests of the individual, especially when buttressed by the interests of all related third parties, must prevail over any general state policy that simply ignores those interests. Indeed, the only apparent *secular* basis for the State's interest in life is the policy's persuasive impact upon people other than Nancy and her family. . . .

Only because Missouri has arrogated to itself the power to define life, and only because the Court permits this usurpation, are Nancy Cruzan's life and liberty put into disquieting conflict. If Nancy Cruzan's life were defined by reference to her own interests, so that her life expired when her biological existence ceased serving *any* of her own interests, then her constitutionally protected interest in freedom from unwanted treatment would not come into conflict with her constitutionally protected interest in life. Conversely, if there were any evidence that Nancy Cruzan herself defined life to encompass every form of biological persistence by a human being, so that the continuation of treatment would serve Nancy's own liberty, then once again there would be no conflict between life and liberty. The opposition of life and liberty in this case are thus not the result of Nancy Cruzan's tragic accident, but are instead the artificial consequence of Missouri's effort, and this Court's willingness, to abstract Nancy Cruzan's life from Nancy Cruzan's person. . . .

The Cruzan family's continuing concern provides a concrete reminder that Nancy Cruzan's interests did not disappear with her vitality or her consciousness. However commendable may be the State's interest in human life, it cannot pursue that interest by appropriating Nancy Cruzan's life as a symbol for its own purposes. Lives do not exist in abstraction from persons, and to pretend otherwise is not to honor but to desecrate the State's responsibility for protecting life. A State that seeks to demonstrate its commitment to life may do so by aiding those who are actively struggling for life and health. In this endeavor, unfortunately, no State can lack for opportunities: there can be no need to make an example of tragic cases like that of Nancy Cruzan.

I respectfully dissent.

NOTE: THE RIGHT TO DIE

1. To what extent does *Cruzan* recognize a right to die? Note that the Court recognizes a "liberty interest," but it does not say whether that interest is fundamental or not, and it does not explain whether and when the state has sufficient reasons to intrude on that interest. For this reason the decision appears exceedingly narrow.

2. One might ask about the relationship between the right to die (said by the Court to represent liberty rather than privacy) and the previous privacy cases. After Bowers v. Hardwick, it seemed that a tradition of recognition would be a necessary condition for constitutional protection. Moreover, the *Hardwick* Court appeared to characterize the relevant tradition narrowly rather than broadly. (See also Michael H. v. Gerald D., in which Justice Scalia, speaking for a plurality, made precisely this point.) One might doubt whether there is a tradition of recognition of a right to die in cases like Cruzan's; indeed, one might doubt whether there has been sufficient time to build up any such tradition. Does the tone of the opinions in *Cruzan* suggest a greater willingness to characterize a tradition broadly than is suggested by the other recent cases? How does one explain the differences (if there differences) between *Hardwick* and *Cruzan*?

3. Evaluate the following argument: The state has no legitimate interest in interfering with the parents' decision in cases like *Cruzan*. The only possible interests are religious in nature or are patently absurd. The compulsion to keep Cruzan alive in her then-current state is therefore without the secular justification necessary to survive rationality review.

4. Compare with *Cruzan* the decision in Washington v. Harper, 110 S. Ct. — (1990). There the Court held that a mentally ill prisoner had "a significant liberty interest in avoiding the unwanted administration of antipsychotic drugs." At the same time, the Court said that this interest could be countered by

the state's "interests in prison safety and security . . . even when the constitutional right claimed to have been infringed is fundamental, and the State under other circumstances would have been required to satisfy a more rigorous standard of review." Strongly emphasizing the prison setting, the Court upheld the application of these drugs, for purposes of treatment only and by a licensed psychiatrist, "to inmates who are mentally ill and who, as a result of their illness, are gravely disabled or represent a significant danger to themselves or others." Justice Stevens, joined by Justices Brennan and Marshall, dissented.

G. PROCEDURAL DUE PROCESS

Page 910.   After subsection b of the Note, add the following:

Consider in this connection Regents of the University of Michigan v. Ewing, 474 U.S. 214 (1985). Respondent, who was dismissed from the University of Michigan medical school after failing a written examination, alleged that the university acted arbitrarily in not permitting him to retake the examination. He claimed that he had a property interest in continued enrollment and that his dismissal violated his substantive due process rights. In an opinion written by Justice Stevens, a unanimous Court rejected the claim. The Court assumed, arguendo, that respondent had a constitutionally protected property interest in continued enrollment free from arbitrary state action, but held that even if he had such an interest, the record disclosed no such action. In a concurring opinion, Justice Powell argued that "not every [property] right is entitled to the protection of substantive due process. While a property interest is derived from state law rather than the Constitution [*Roth*], substantive due process rights are created only by the Constitution."

Page 912.   Before section 3 of the Note, add the following:

In Board of Pardons v. Allen, 482 U.S. 369 (1987), the Court, in an opinion by Justice Brennan, held that Montana's parole statute established a sufficient expectancy of release to create a liberty interest. Although acknowledging the subjective nature of the parole board's decision and the broad discretion vested in it, the Court held that the mandatory language of the parole statute created an expectancy of release. Justice O'Connor, joined by Chief Justice Rehnquist and Justice Scalia, dissented.

Page 919.   Before section 2 of the Note, add the following:

Justice Stevens renewed his call for a bright line rule in a dissenting opinion in Brock v. Roadway Express, Inc., 481 U.S. 252 (1987):

The Court's willingness to sacrifice due process to the Government's obscure suggestion of necessity reveals the serious flaws in its due process analysis. It is wrong to
approach the due process analysis in each case by asking anew what procedures seem
worthwhile and not too costly. Unless a case falls within a recognized exception, we
should adhere to the strongest presumption that the Government may not take away
life, liberty, or property before making a meaningful hearing available.

Page 920. Before section 3 of the Note, add the following:

In Brock v. Roadway Express, Inc., 481 U.S. 252 (1987), the Court considered the converse of the problem posed by *Arnett* and *Loudermill* — i.e., the kind
of process that is due before an employer can be forced to reinstate a discharged
worker. A federal statute protects employees in the transportation industry from
discharge in retaliation for refusing to operate a motor vehicle that does not
comply with state and federal safety regulations. The statute provides that if the
Secretary of Labor finds reasonable cause to believe that an employee has been
discharged in violation of the act, he can issue an order reinstating the employee. An employer is entitled to a full evidentiary hearing only after the
reinstatement.

In an opinion written by Justice Marshall, a plurality of the Court held that
the Constitution did not require an evidentiary hearing and an opportunity to
cross examine witnesses before the government ordered temporary reinstatement. Although acknowledging the employer's substantial interest in controlling the makeup of its workforce, the plurality emphasized the government's
countervailing interest in promoting highway safety and the employee's interest
in retaining his job.

> So long as the prereinstatement procedures establish a reliable "initial check against
> mistaken decisions," [*Loudermill*], and complete and expeditious review is available,
> [they] fairly [balance] the competing interests of the Government, the employer, and
> the [employee].

The plurality went on to hold, however, that the procedures would only
satisfy this reliability standard if the employer received notice of the employee's
allegations, notice of the substance of the relevant supporting evidence, an
opportunity to submit a written response, and an opportunity to meet with the
investigator and present statements from rebuttal witnesses.

In separate opinions, Justices Brennan and Stevens each argued that the due
process clause required a full evidentiary hearing prior to a reinstatement order.
Justice White, in an opinion joined by Chief Justice Rehnquist and Justice
Scalia, argued that due process did not require that the employer be provided
with information on which the reinstatement order is based, including names of
witnesses, prior to reinstatement.

Page 921.   After the second full paragraph, add the following:

In Daniels v. Williams, 474 U.S. 327 (1986), the Court overruled *Parratt* insofar as that case had suggested that a negligently inflicted loss could amount to a deprivation of due process in the absence of a state tort remedy. Petitioner, an inmate in a city jail, claimed that he was deprived of a liberty interest when he slipped on a pillow negligently left on the stairs by a state official. He attempted to distinguish *Ingraham* and *Parratt* on the ground that the state sovereign immunity doctrine deprived him of an adequate state remedy. In an opinion by Justice Rehnquist, the Court "[concluded] that the Due Process Clause is simply not implicated by a *negligent* act of an official causing unintended loss of or injury to life, liberty or property."

Although all nine justices joined the result in *Daniels*, a second case, also involving negligence by a state official and decided on the same day, evoked more controversy. In Davidson v. Cannon, 474 U.S. 344 (1986), the Court rejected the due process claim of a state prisoner who alleged that he was seriously injured when prison officials negligently failed to protect him from another inmate. Justice Rehnquist again wrote the Court's opinion: "[Where] a government official is merely negligent in causing the injury, no procedure for compensation is constitutionally required. [The] guarantee of due process has never been understood to mean that the State must guarantee due care on the part of its officials."

Justice Stevens wrote an opinion concurring in the results in both *Daniels* and *Davidson*, but solely on the ground that in neither case were state remedies for the deprivations constitutionally inadequate.

In a short opinion dissenting in *Davidson*, Justice Brennan agreed that "merely negligent conduct by a state official, even though causing personal injury, does not constitute a deprivation of liberty under the Due Process Clause." He argued, however, that "official conduct which causes personal injury due to recklessness or deliberate indifference, does deprive the victim of liberty within the meaning of the Fourteenth Amendment."

In a longer dissenting opinion, Justice Blackmun, joined by Justice Marshall, also attempted to distinguish *Daniels*:

> It is one thing to hold that a commonplace slip and fall, or the loss of a $23.50 hobby kit, see [*Parratt*] does not rise to the dignified level of a constitutional violation. It is a somewhat different thing to say that negligence that permits anticipated inmate violence resulting in injury, or perhaps leads to the execution of the wrong prisoner, does not implicate the Constitution's guarantee of due process. When the State incarcerated Daniels, it left intact his own faculties for avoiding a slip and a fall. But the State prevented Davidson from defending himself, and therefore assumed some responsibility to protect him from the dangers to which he was exposed.

Compare *Daniels* and *Davidson* to the Court's treatment under the equal protection clause of classifications not enacted for a discriminatory purpose that disproportionately impact on disadvantaged groups. See pages 543-565 supra of the main text. Might Washington v. Davis, page 543 supra, be treated as a case involving "mere" negligent injury? In *Davidson*, the Court notes that

> Far from abusing governmental power, or employing it as an instrument of oppression, respondent [mistakenly] believed that the situation was not particularly serious. [The] guarantee of due process has never been understood to mean that the State must guarantee due care on the part of its officials. [Petitioner's] claim, based on respondents' negligence, is quite different from one involving injuries caused by an unjustified attack by prison guards themselves, or by another prisoner where officials simply stood by and permitted the attack to proceed.

Is there good reason in either the due process or equal protection context to distinguish between affirmative acts by government officials bringing about an injury and failures to act that produce the same injury?

Chapter Seven

Freedom of Expression

A. INTRODUCTION

Page 929. Before section 4 of the Note, add the following:

See also Mayton, From a Legacy of Suppression to the "Metaphor of the Fourth Estate," 39 Stan. L. Rev. 139 (1986).

Page 929. At the end of section 4 of the Note, add the following:

For discussion of the limitation of the text of the first amendment to "Congress," see Denbeaux, The First Word of the First Amendment, 80 Nw. U.L. Rev. 1156 (1986).

Page 933. Before subsection 2 of the Note, add the following:

e. Greenawalt, Free Speech Justifications, 89 Colum. L. Rev. 119, 135-136 (1989):

> The critical question is not how well truth will advance absolutely in conditions of freedom, but how well it will advance in conditions of freedom as compared with some alternative set of conditions. Suppose one were highly pessimistic about the capacity of people to ascertain important kinds of truths, but believed that governments that suppress ideas almost always manage to promote [falsehoods]. One might then support freedom of speech as less damaging to truth than an alternative social practice. One's overall judgment on this subject must depend on a delicate judgment about people's responses to claimed truth, about the effects of inequality of private power over what is communicated, and about the soundness of government determinations about valid ideas.

Page 935. At the end of subsection 3a of the Note, add the following:

Professor Richards has elaborated on this theory of the first amendment in D. Richards, Toleration and the Constitution 168-169 (1986):

The right to conscience rests [on] equal respect for persons, interpreted by reference to the highest-order twin moral powers of rationality and reasonableness: rationality in a person's self-conception of a life well lived, reasonableness in regulating such self-conceptions by an acknowledgment of the just claims of others. . . .

[This] ethical independence [is] imperiled [by nonneutral] state judgments about the worth of communications that usurp a person's control over the range of communications of facts and values central to the self-determination of rational and reasonable powers. In the same way that state imposition of judgments about the worth of religious beliefs chooses one such conception among others equally reasonable, comparable state judgments of the value of communications illegitimately prejudge the nature and weight of the communications relevant to the exercise of these powers.

Page 937.   At the end of section 4 of the Note, add the following new subsection:

c. *The tolerant society.* Consider L. Bollinger, The Tolerant Society: Freedom of Speech and Extremist Speech in America 9-10, 107 (1986):

[While] free speech theory has traditionally focused on the value of the protected activity (speech), [the theory offered here] seeks a justification by looking at the disvalue of the [frequently intolerant] response to that activity. [The] rationality and wisdom of choosing the course of tolerance can be derived from a neglected insight — namely, that the problematic feelings evoked [by] speech activity are precisely the same kinds of feelings evoked by a myriad of interactions in the society, not the least of which are the reactions we take toward nonspeech behavior. [The free speech principle] involves a special act of carving out one area of social interaction for extraordinary self-restraint, the purpose of which is to develop and demonstrate a social capacity to control feelings evoked by a host of social encounters. [The free speech principle is thus] concerned with nothing less than helping to shape the intellectual character of the society.

Compare Strauss, Why Be Tolerant?, 53 U. Chi. L. Rev. 1485, 1491 (1986) ("One might ask why [we should be required] to tolerate offensive *expression* [rather than] other offensive things, like loud noises or foul odors.")

Page 938.   At the end of section 5 of the Note that begins on the preceding page, add the following:

For the view that first amendment theory should be directed away from the "affirmative" promotion of certain core "values," and directed instead at the "negative" prevention of certain core evils (most centrally "self-interested" regulation of speech by government officials), see Cass, The Perils of Positive Thinking: Constitutional Interpretation and Negative First Amendment Theory, 34 U.C.L.A. L. Rev. 1305 (1987). For a critique of efforts to construct a "grand theory" of first amendment jurisprudence out of certain core "values," and a call for greater reliance on "practical reason," see Farber & Frickey, Practical Reason and the First Amendment, 34 U.C.L.A. L. Rev. 1615 (1987).

Page 952.   Before section 1 of the Note, add the following:

1. *Historical context.* For a lively telling of the full story of the *Abrams* case, see R. Polenberg, Fighting Faiths (1987).

B. CONTENT-BASED RESTRICTIONS: DANGEROUS IDEAS AND INFORMATION

Page 960.   Before the citation to Rogat & O'Fallon in section 4 of the Note, add the following:

Consider Stone, Reflections of the First Amendment: The Evolution of the American Jurisprudence of Free Expression, 131 J. Am. Phil. Soc. 251, 253 (1987):

> [The central principle of first amendment jurisprudence is that] the Government may *never* restrict the expression of particular ideas because it fears that citizens may adopt those ideas in the political process. As Alexander Meiklejohn explained, this principle is rooted "in the very foundations of the self-governing process," for when individuals "govern themselves it is they — and no one else — who must pass judgment upon unwisdom, unfairness and danger." Under this view, "no suggestion of policy" may be denied a hearing "because someone in control thinks it unwise."
>
> Now, there is an anomaly in this principle. As Meiklejohn explained, this principle lies deep within the "foundations of the self-governing process." But if the essential goal is to preserve self-governance, why can't citizens, acting in their capacity as self-governors, decide that certain policies are simply out-of-bounds and thus prohibit further debate on such issues? Under this view, it is not the Government, as some independent entity, that is closing off debate, but citizens themselves, and they are doing so through the very self-governing process that the First Amendment is designed to promote.
>
> The answer, I think, is that the First Amendment, which was itself adopted through the self-governing process, places out of bounds any law that attempts to freeze public debate at a particular moment in time. Under this view, a majority at any moment has the power to decide an issue of policy for itself, but it has no power irrevocably to decide that issue for future citizens by preventing them from continuing to debate the issue. This is [what] Justice Holmes described as the great First Amendment "experiment."

Page 960.   At the end of the first paragraph of Whitney v. California, add the following (inside the bracket):

For an excellent account of Ms. Whitney's life and of the trial and appellate proceedings in the case, see Blasi, The First Amendment and the Ideal of Civic

Courage: The Brandeis Opinion in *Whitney v. California*, 29 Wm. & Mary L. Rev. 653 (1988).

Page 965.   At the end of the first paragraph of section 1 of the Note, add the following:

Consider Blasi, The First Amendment and the Ideal of Civic Courage: The Brandeis Opinion in *Whitney v. California*, 29 Wm. & Mary L. Rev. 653, 679-680, 689-691 (1988):

> Brandeis valued a strong doctrine of free speech largely for its contribution to the character of the political community, particularly the character of those who possess the power to regulate. [To] Brandeis, the measure of courage in the civic realm is the capacity to experience or anticipate change — even rapid and fundamental change — without losing perspective or confidence. [The] courageous attitude, Brandeis asserts, is that of receptivity to new arrangements and new ways of thinking. Progress, the value literally at the root of the progressive philosophy, depends on receptivity to change. [All] of us need to be emancipated from "the bondage of irrational fears" as we encounter unsettling proposals for political change. The essence of civic courage is a healthy mentality regarding change.

Page 965.   Before section 2 of the Note, add the following:

1A. *The limits of judicial dissent.* Consider H. Kalven, A Worthy Tradition: Freedom of Speech in America 158 (1988):

> Although *Whitney* marks the sixth consecutive decision in which the majority has either ignored the clear and present danger test or found it inapplicable, Justice Brandeis [continues to assert that it "has been settled" that clear and present danger is the test for restrictions of speech]. The stamina and tactics of these classic dissents are remarkable. In professional lawyering terms, the performance of Justices Holmes and Brandeis is outrageous. They keep insisting that they are adhering to the Court's true rule adopted in *Schenck* [even though they] have been told [repeatedly] by the majority that clear and present danger is not now and never was the general [test]. Yet we are all deeply in their debt for their outrageous behavior. They have kept alive a counter-tension in the tradition, and their towering prestige has invested the slogan with almost mesmerizing force. Like twin Moses come down from Mount Sinai bearing the true Commandment, they see little need to argue that the formula is rightly derived from the First Amendment, merely that it is.

Page 978.   Before section 4 of the Note, add the following:

3A. *An expanded* Dennis *Formula.* Building upon the free speech formula that the plurality adopted in *Dennis*, Richard Posner has proposed that government may regulate speech "if but only if $B < PL$, where B is the cost of the regulation, $[P]$ is the probability that the speech sought to be suppressed will do harm, and L is the magnitude (social cost) of the harm." Posner has explained that B

consists of both "the social loss from suppressing valuable information" and the "legal-error costs incurred in trying to distinguish the information that society desires to suppress from valuable information," and that L must be discounted to present value:

> As between two catastrophes, one of which will occur tomorrow and the other in forty years, most of us think the former prospect the more costly. But this point was rejected [in *Dennis*]. This was a critical step in [the Court's] analysis; it allowed [the Court] to figure the costs of violent revolution as if it were to occur tomorrow, and not in twenty, fifty, or one hundred [years]. This failure to discount is questionable. [If] the question were whether to devote a given amount of resources to preventing a violent revolution in one hundred years, or an equivalent disaster in ten, the common-sense answer would be the latter; and that implies a positive social discount rate. [But] even if the social discount rate is set equal to the private discount rate (say as measured by the interest rate on long-term securities) remote harms, if large enough, will sometimes merit immediate corrective measures.

Posner, Free Speech in an Economic Perspective, 20 Suffolk U.L. Rev. 1, 8, 34-35 (1986).

Page 978.   Add the following new subsection 4-a to the Note and change the existing subsections to b, c, and d:

aa. Kahn, The Court, the Community and the Judicial Balance: The Jurisprudence of Justice Powell, 97 Yale L.J. 1, 3-4 (1987):

> To invoke a balance is to recognize that legitimate, judicially cognizable interests are in tension and that not all can be completely satisfied. [Within] the broad category of "balancing" are three distinguishable models, which I term "representative," "administrative," and "zero-sum" balancing. The representative and zero-sum balances refer to two different perspectives on the problem of resolving conflicts among competing claims. Representative balancing seeks to accommodate each claim; it does not completely reject any claim. Zero-sum balancing [makes] an exclusive choice rather than an accommodation. Instead of a "balanced" outcome, zero-sum balancing determines which claim is weightier and elevates that claim over others. The distinctive quality of the administrative balance is its quantitative character. It presents a quantitative assessment and comparison of competing claims [and] can be used to achieve either a representative or a zero-sum balance.

Page 979.   Before section 5 of the Note, add the following:

d. Aleinikoff, Constitutional Law in the Age of Balancing, 96 Yale L.J. 943, 952, 962-963 (1987):

> [Balancing] appeared as an explicit method of constitutional interpretation in the mid-twentieth century. [Ways] of thinking about constitutional law and constitution-

al reasoning [had] changed and that change was reflected in the new form of opinion writing.

[But] balancing presented constitutional jurisprudence with a difficult problem. As a methodology for bringing pragmatic instrumentalism to constitutional doctrine, it seemed to be precisely the activist, policy-oriented approach to constitutional law about which the public and the academy had been complaining for a quarter of a century. [The] defense of formalism ("we just find the law") was obviously no longer available: Balancers lived in a post-Realist age, and they were painfully aware that judging entailed choice, not deduction. How, then, could choices be made without reintroducing the bane of constitutional law — the judge's personal preference?

The answer lay in externalizing the balancing process. Judges ought to search for the relevant interests in society at large and give them the weight that history, tradition, and current society attributed to them. The social science-like methodology of balancing instructed the judge to look for values "out there." Balancing could be seen as primarily descriptive. Just as a physicist could measure atomic weights without inquiring into values, so the balancer could discover that free speech outweighed governmental interest in public order without expressing a personal view on the result. . . .

The balancers' belief in an external resolution of constitutional cases was important because they were fighting on two fronts. Not only did they need an alternative to Lochnerism; they also needed a response to Legal Realism which, in its most extreme moments, spoke in nihilistic tones. Although balancing was, in part, an outgrowth of the Realist critique of formalism, it was also a response to Realism. It attempted to overcome the problems of indeterminacy and subjectivity that some Realists had preached were inevitable. Balancing was a progressive, up-beat, "can-do" judicial attitude. It was certainly likely to appeal to judges who could not forget the lessons of Realism, but still had to decide constitutional cases.

Page 979. After the first paragraph of section 5 of the Note, add the following:

Consider H. Kalven, A Worthy Tradition: Freedom of Speech in America, 208 (1988):

The most curious aspect of Justice Frankfurter's performance is his handling of the *Gitlow* distinction. He has argued that speech cases are just like other instances of judicial review, that balancing of interests is called for, and that the primary responsibility for balancing rests with the legislature. [Thus], the Sanford opinion in *Gitlow* would seem to embody his argument. [Yet] he does not rest his case on *Gitlow*. The reason, I suspect, is that he cannot desert his hero: Holmes thought it absurd to convict Gitlow [and] Frankfurter perforce must think so too. [It] is not easy to see how Frankfurter can reject the legislative judgment as applied in *Gitlow* without introducing a criterion of danger in the particular circumstances. Thus, his nod to Holmes seems to impeach the whole rationale of his opinion.

Page 980. After the citation to the Van Alstyne article, add the following:

Zacharias, Flowcharting the First Amendment, 72 Cornell L. Rev. 936 (1987).

Page 980. Before section 7 of the Note, add the following:

For a critique of definitional balancing, see Aleinikoff, Constitutional Law in the Age of Balancing, 96 Yale L.J. 943, 979-981 (1987).

Page 990. At the end of section 4 of the Note, add the following:

For critical analyses of the "pathological perspective," see Redish, The Role of Pathology in First Amendment Theory: A Skeptical Examination, 38 Case W. Res. L. Rev. 618 (1988); Christie, Why the First Amendment Should Not Be Interpreted from the Pathological Perspective, 1986 Duke L.J. 683.

Page 1014. Before section 4 of the Note, add the following:

e. In City of Houston v. Hill, 482 U.S. 451 (1987), the Court, in an opinion by Justice Brennan, invalidated a Houston ordinance that made it unlawful for any person "in any manner [to] oppose, molest, abuse or interrupt any police-man in the execution of his duty." The ordinance, in the Court's view, was "much more sweeping" than that invalidated in *Lewis*. "It is not limited to fighting words nor even to obscene or opprobrious language, but prohibits speech that 'in any manner . . . interrupt[s]' an officer. The Constitution does not allow such speech to be made a crime."

Compare the views of Justice Powell in an opinion concurring in part and dissenting in part.

[*Lewis*] is clearly distinguishable. [On] its face, the [*Lewis*] ordinance criminalizes only the use of language. [By] contrast, [this] ordinance could be applied to activity that involves no element of speech or communication. . . .

I do agree that the ordinance can be applied to speech in some cases. [But] I question the implication of the Court's opinion that the First Amendment generally protects verbal "challenge[s] directed at police officers." [For example], a person observing an officer pursuing a person suspected of a felony could run beside him in a public street shouting at the officer. . . .

Despite these reservations, however, Justice Powell agreed that the "ambiguous terms" of the ordinance conferred too much discretion on the police to arrest persons for violations.

Page 1017.   Before *Landmark Communications*, add the following:

Consider DuVal, The Occasions of Secrecy, 47 U. Pitt. L. Rev. 579, 585-586 (1986):

> In the case of government secrets, [it] is precisely the truth of the communications that makes them dangerous. [The] whole point of such restrictions is to prevent ignorance from being dispelled.
>
> [Restraints] of this character pose a difficult challenge to any first amendment theory that takes the quest for truth seriously. If a major goal of the first amendment is to facilitate the discovery and dissemination of knowledge, it is paradoxical to suggest that communications may be suppressed because they lead to the acquisition or dissemination of knowledge.

Page 1019.   After section 3 of the Note, add the following:

4. In Butterworth v. Smith, 110 S. Ct. 1376 (1990), the Court invalidated a Florida statute that prohibited grand jury witnesses from ever publicly disclosing their own testimony. The Court explained that it must "balance [the witness'] First Amendment rights against Florida's interests in preserving the confidentiality of its grand jury proceedings." Noting that "neither the drafters of the Federal Rules of Criminal Procedure, nor the drafters of the similar rules in the majority of the States, found it necessary to impose [such] an obligation of secrecy on grand jury witnesses," the Court concluded that the State's "substantial interest" in protecting the reputations of persons " 'who are accused but exonerated by the grand jury' " was insufficient to "warrant a permanent ban on the disclosure by a witness of his own testimony once a grand jury has been discharged."

Page 1019.   Before *Nebraska Press Association*, add the following:

In recent years, exit polls have increasingly been used to predict election results while voters are still in the process of voting. Concluding that "early projections of election results have an adverse impact on the electoral process," Congress adopted a resolution that urged the networks to refrain voluntarily from projecting results of an election before all polls for the office closed. See H.R. Con. Res. 321, 98th Cong., 2d Sess. (1984). Consider the constitutionality of a law prohibiting the publication or broadcasting of such results. Would a law prohibiting any person from conducting an exit poll be constitutional? See DuVal, The Occasions of Secrecy, 47 U. Pitt. L. Rev. 579, 661-662 (1986).

Page 1032.   Before section 7 of the Note, add the following:

Consider Sunstein, Government Control of Information, 74 Calif. L. Rev. 889, 901-902, 904 (1986):

> [Bickel's] equilibrium theory is vulnerable because it does not address three critical matters: the actual incentives of the press and the government; the respective power of the countervailing forces; and what the proper baseline for evaluating outcomes should be.
>
> [The] equilibrium theory [is] impressionistic and relies on premises that are both unsupported and unlikely. The sharp distinction between rights of access and rights of publication thus rests on unstable foundations.

Page 1033.   Before the Note, add the following:

For analysis of the constitutional status of technical data, see Sunstein, Government Control of Information, 74 Calif. L. Rev. 889, 905-912 (1986).

C.   OVERBREADTH, VAGUENESS, AND PRIOR RESTRAINT

Page 1041.   At the end of the first paragraph of section 3 of the Note, add the following:

Consider Osborne v. Ohio, 110 S. Ct. 1691 (1990), in which the Court upheld a child pornography statute, as construed by the state supreme court on appeal in the same case. Although the statute, as written, was clearly unconstitutionally overbroad, the Court held that it was saved from invalidation by the state supreme court's narrowing construction and that the statute, as construed, could " 'be applied to conduct occurring prior to the construction, provided such application affords fair warning to the defendant.' " In *Osborne,* the Court concluded that the statute afforded "fair warning" because the defendant "would not [have been] surprised to learn that his possession of [the] photographs at issue [constituted] a crime." Nonetheless, the Court held that the defendant's conviction violated due process because the jury had not been instructed in accord with the state supreme court's subsequent narrowing construction of the law. Compare Massachusetts v. Oakes, 109 S. Ct. 2633 (1990) (an overbroad statute that is "narrowed" by legislative amendment rather than by judicial construction cannot constitutionally be applied to acts that occurred prior to the amendment).

Page 1043.   Before section 6 of the Note, add the following:

In Board of Airport Commissioners v. Jews for Jesus, 482 U.S. 569 (1987), a unanimous Court, in an opinion by Justice O'Connor, invalidated as substantially overbroad a rule banning all "First Amendment activities" within the

Central Terminal Area of the Los Angeles International Airport. Respondents, who were prevented from distributing religious literature on a pedestrian walkway in the airport, brought an action challenging the rule. Without deciding whether their conduct was constitutionally protected, the Court held that the rule was facially void.

> The [rule] does not merely reach the activity of [respondents]; it prohibits even talking and reading, or the wearing of campaign buttons or symbolic clothing. Under such a sweeping ban, virtually every individual who enters [the airport] may be found to violate the [rule] by engaging in some "First Amendment activit[y]." We think it obvious that such a ban cannot be [justified].

Because there was no apparent saving construction of the rule, it was "difficult to imagine that [it] could be limited by anything less than a series of adjudications, and the chilling effect of the [rule] on protected speech in the meantime would make such a case-by-case adjudication intolerable."

In City of Houston v. Hill, 482 U.S. 451 (1987), decided on the same day as *Board of Airport Commissioners,* the Court again utilized the substantial overbreadth technique. A Houston ordinance made it unlawful for any person to "oppose, molest, abuse or interrupt any policeman in the execution of his duty." Appellee, who had been arrested repeatedly under the ordinance, brought suit seeking to enjoin its enforcement on the ground that it was unconstitutionally overbroad under the first amendment. The Court, in an opinion by Justice Brennan, rejected the City's contention that the ordinance should be upheld because it banned "core criminal conduct" not protected by the first amendment.

> The freedom of individuals verbally to oppose or challenge police action without thereby risking arrest is one of the principal characteristics by which we distinguish a free nation from a police state. . . .
>
> [The ordinance] is not narrowly tailored to prohibit only disorderly conduct or fighting [words]. Although we appreciate the difficulties of drafting precise laws, we have repeatedly invalidated laws that provide the police with unfettered discretion to arrest individuals for words or conduct that annoy or offend them.

Page 1048.   At the end of the first paragraph of subsection 1 of the Note, add the following:

In City of Lakewood v. Plain Dealer Pub. Co., 486 U.S. 750 (1988), the Court applied the *Lovell* principle to invalidate an ordinance that gave a mayor standardless discretion to grant or deny permits to place newsracks on public property. The Court explained that the evils of standardless licensing "can be effectively alleviated only through a facial challenge":

> First, the mere existence of the licensor's unfettered discretion, coupled with the power of prior restraint, intimidates parties into censoring their own speech, even if the discretion and power are never actually abused. [Self-censorship] is immune to an

"as applied" challenge, for it derives from the individual's own actions, not an abuse of government power. [Only] standards limiting the licensor's discretion will eliminate this danger by adding an element of certain to fatal self-censorship. And only a facial challenge can effectively test the statute for these standards.

Second, the absence of express standards makes it difficult to distinguish, "as applied," between a licensor's legitimate denial of a permit and its illegitimate abuse of censorial power. Standards provide the guideposts that check the licensor and allow courts quickly and easily to determine whether the licensor is discriminating against disfavored speech. Without these guideposts, post hoc rationalizations by the licensing official and the use of shifting or illegitimate criteria are far too easy, making it difficult for courts to determine in any particular case whether the licensor is permitting favorable, and suppressing unfavorable, expression.

Page 1048.   At the end of subsection 1 of the Note, add the following:

1A. *Standardless licensing of expressive acts that are not themselves protected by the first amendment.* In dissent in City of Lakewood v. Plain Dealer Pub. Co., 486 U.S. 750 (1988), Justice White maintained that the *Lovell* principle was not applicable to the standardless newsrack ordinance because in all past decisions in which the principle had been invoked the challenged law had authorized standardless licensing of expressive activity that was itself protected by the first amendment, such as speaking in public parks or distributing leaflets. Justice White argued that this was not the case in *City of Lakewood* because there is no first amendment right to place newsracks on public property. In such circumstances, Justice White concluded, "as applied" review was sufficient. Otherwise, every program of standardless licensing would be invalid under the *Lovell* principle, even if the activity regulated had nothing to do with free expression. For example, even a licensing scheme for placing soft-drink machines on public property could be applied in a manner that discriminated against those taking a politically unfavorable position. If that risk was itself sufficient to invoke *Lovell*, all standardless licensing violates the first amendment.

In response, the Court maintained that Justice White's approach too severely limited the scope of the *Lovell* principle. Thus, the Court held that the *Lovell* principle applies whenever a standardless licensing scheme has "a close enough nexus to expression, or to conduct commonly associated with expression, to pose a real and substantial threat of [the] censorship risks" associated with this form of prior restraint. Applying that standard, the Court held that the *City of Lakewood* ordinance was subject to facial rather than "as applied" review because it required newspapers to "apply annually for newsrack licenses" and was "directed narrowly and specifically at expression or conduct commonly associated with expression: the circulation of newspapers."

Page 1051.   Before section 6 of the Note, add the following:

In FW/PBS, Inc. v. City of Dallas, 110 S. Ct. 596 (1990), the Court divided sharply on the applicability of *Freedman* to a comprehensive licensing scheme for "sexually oriented businesses," such as adult bookstores, adult movie theaters, and escort agencies. Justices Brennan, Marshall, and Blackmun concluded that *Freedman* was applicable; Chief Justice Rehnquist and Justice White concluded that *Freedman* was inapplicable because, unlike the licensing scheme at issue in *Freedman,* this scheme was not "aimed directly at speech," but covered all sexually oriented businesses, "including those not involved in expressive activity such as escort agencies"; and Justices Stevens, O'Connor, and Scalia, in an opinion by Justice O'Connor, concluded that *Freedman* was applicable, but only in part. Justice O'Connor reasoned that *Freedman* was applicable because the challenged scheme "largely targets businesses purveying sexually explicit speech [that is] protected by the First Amendment," but that it was not wholly applicable because the licensing authority focused on such matters as health and building code inspections, rather than on "direct censorship of particular expressive material," and because in this situation, where the applicant's entire business is at stake, there is a greater incentive "to pursue a license denial through court" than where "only one film was censored." Justice O'Connor therefore concluded that licensing decisions in this context must be made within a reasonable period, that there must be an opportunity for prompt judicial review of adverse decisions, but that the censor need not "go to court to bear the burden [of] justifying the denial."

Page 1054.   At the beginning of section 1 of the Note, add the following:

The first amendment states that "*Congress* shall make no law [abridging] the freedom of speech." In light of the express reference to Congress, how can it be said to restrict *judicially* imposed prior restraints? For discussion of this issue, see Denbeaux, The First Word of the First Amendment, 80 Nw. U.L. Rev. 1156 (1986).

Page 1058.   At the end of section 6 of the Note, add the following:

Consider also Scordato, Distinction Without a Difference: A Reappraisal of the Doctrine of Prior Restraint, 68 N.C.L. Rev. 1, 34 (1989), suggesting that the "definition of prior restraint [should] be changed to include only those government actions that result in the [actual] *physical* interception and suppression of speech prior to its public expression."

D. CONTENT-BASED RESTRICTIONS: "LOW" VALUE SPEECH

Page 1065.   At the end of section 2 of the Note, add the following:

Is balancing appropriate in the libel context, not because libel involves false statements of fact, but because libel laws are "ideologically neutral"? Consider L. Tribe, American Constitutional Law 878 (2d ed. 1988):

> Where the law is closely confined to the narrow purpose of compensating private individuals for injury to their reputational interests, the law is aimed at something other than content, at least in the sense that the objective is unrelated to whether government approves or disapproves the content of the message. Defamation law in this sense is ideologically neutral, and therefore is appropriately remitted to a "balancing" test.

Page 1065.   Before section 4 of the Note, add the following:

For a critique of definitional balancing, see Aleinikoff, Constitutional Law in the Age of Balancing, 96 Yale L.J. 943, 979-981 (1987).

Page 1066.   At the end of subsection 4c of the Note, add the following:

For analysis of the constituent elements of reputation — honor, property, and dignity — and how consideration of these elements can clarify first amendment analysis, see Post, The Social Foundations of Defamation Law: Reputation and the Constitution, 74 Calif. L. Rev. 691 (1986).

Page 1066.   At the end of subsection 4d of the Note, add the following:

For a similar suggestion, see Leval, The No-Money, No-Fault Libel Suit: Keeping *Sullivan* in Its Proper Place, 101 Harv. L. Rev. 1287 (1988) (proposing that an action for a declaration of falsity, requiring no showing of fault and authorizing no award of damages, is consistent with *New York Times.*)

Page 1066.   Before section 5 of the Note, add the following:

e. Bezanson, Libel Law and the Realities of Litigation: Setting the Record Straight, 71 Iowa L. Rev. 226, 229-230 (1985):

The requirement that fault be found [has] become more than a preliminary inquiry in the adjudication of the tort. Instead, it has pervasively transformed the entire process of adjudicating libel disputes, requiring intrusion into the subjective aspects of the reporting and editorial processes, committing vast judicial resources in advance of trial, and permeating the factfinding process throughout litigation. An astounding eighty-three percent of media libel cases involve a formal judicial proceeding on the merits of the libel claim *before* trial [and] an equally astonishing sixty percent of these cases involve at least one level of pretrial appeal. Questions of constitutional privilege are raised in virtually every case and are determinative in eighty-eight percent of the cases.

As a practical matter, the truth or falsity of the challenged statement is no longer pertinent to the libel action. [The] tort, in short, has been transformed from a tort of libel to a tort for abuse of constitutional privilege, regardless of truth or falsity and irrespective of reputational harm.

f. Epstein, Was *New York Times v. Sullivan* Wrong?, 53 U. Chi. L. Rev. 782, 797, 804 (1986):

The general tendency in defamation cases has always been for a powerful rule of strict liability. [This] rests upon commendable moral instincts. [Defamation] is made to third persons about the plaintiff, so that prima facie the plaintiff is in no way responsible for the commission of the wrong and typically could do very little, if anything, to protect himself. . . .

In strict liability the probability of recovery is relatively large and the damages can be kept relatively small. With actual malice the probability of recovery is relatively small and damages are relatively large. It takes little mathematical sophistication to realize that if success is more likely with strict liability, and damages are more generous with actual malice, it becomes uncertain whether the total liabilities [are] greater under the strict liability rule or the actual malice rule. [Epstein concludes that, once one takes into account "litigation costs" and "reputational effects," the common law rule of strict liability is preferable to the actual malice rule of New York Times v. Sullivan.]

Page 1067.   Before section 6 of the Note, add the following:

d. LeBel, Reforming the Tort of Defamation: An Accommodation of the Competing Interests Within the Current Constitutional Framework, 66 Neb. L. Rev. 249, 293 (1987):

If one is to take seriously the image of the marketplace of ideas, one is entitled to be extremely skeptical about the claims of the judiciary to be competent to act as some sort of Consumer Product Safety Commission for that marketplace. This skepticism is particularly well placed when it is a branch of that same government that is putting itself into a definitive position to label as false a statement about government.

The only truly adequate protection for criticism of government is an absolute privilege to say whatever one wishes about government without being called to account in any governmental forum.

Page 1077.   Before section 5 of the Note, add the following new section:

4A. *Burden of proof.* In two recent cases, the Court has extended the constitutional protection afforded to media defendants by further elaborating on the burden of proof that a libel plaintiff must satisfy.

In Philadelphia Newspapers, Inc. v. Hepps, 475 U.S. 767 (1986), the Court held that when a newspaper publishes speech of public concern, a private-figure plaintiff must bear the burden of proving that the statements at issue are false. In an opinion by Justice O'Connor, the Court held that

> placement by state law of the burden of proving truth upon media defendants who publish speech of public concern deters such speech because of the fear that liability will unjustifiably result. Because such a "chilling" effect would be antithetical to the First Amendment's protection of true speech on matters of public concern, we believe that a private-figure plaintiff must bear the burden of showing that the speech at issue is false before recovering damages for defamation from a media defendant.

In a dissenting opinion joined by Chief Justice Burger and Justices White and Rehnquist, Justice Stevens pointed out that the issue at stake

> will make a difference in only one category of cases — those in which a private individual can prove that he was libeled by a defendant who was at least negligent. For unless such a plaintiff can overcome the burden imposed by [*Gertz*], he cannot recover regardless of how the burden of proof on the issue or truth of falsity is allocated.

With respect to this category of cases, Stevens rejected the view that

> a private individual [must] bear the risk that a defamatory statement — uttered either with a mind toward assassinating his good name or with careless indifference to that possibility — cannot be proven false. By attaching no weight to the state's interest in protecting the private individual's good name, the Court has reached a pernicious result.

In Anderson v. Liberty Lobby, Inc., 477 U.S. 242 (1986), the Court addressed the burden that a public figure must meet in a libel action in order to overcome the defendant's motion for summary judgment. *Gertz* and *New York Times* required a public figure libel plaintiff to establish actual malice with "convincing clarity" in order to prevail at trial. In *Anderson* the Court, in an opinion by Justice White, held that a trial judge ruling on a defendant's motion for summary judgment filed pursuant to Rule 56 of the Federal Rules of Civil Procedure, must utilize the "convincing clarity" standard when determining whether there was a genuine issue of fact concerning actual malice. If the trial judge concludes that a reasonable jury could not find "clear and convincing" evidence of malice, then the summary judgment motion should be granted. Moreover, the plaintiff who produces no evidence of his own to establish malice cannot defeat the motion merely by asserting that the jury might disbelieve the defendant's denial of malice. Justice Brennan and Justice Rehnquist, joined by Chief Justice Burger, dissented.

For an overview of a range of procedural issues that affect defamation litigation, see Matheson, Procedure in Public Defamation Cases: The Impact of the First Amendment, 66 Tex. L. Rev. 215 (1987).

4B. *Opinions v. facts.* In Milkovich v. Lorain Journal Co., 110 S. Ct. — (1990), the Court, in an opinion by Chief Justice Rehnquist, held that the first amendment does not require "the creation of an artificial dichotomy between 'opinion' and fact." The Court explained that such a "dichotomy" is unnecessary because *Hepps* already "stands for the proposition that a statement on matters of public concern must be provable as false before there can be liability [where] a media defendant is involved."

> If a speaker says, "In my opinion [Jones] is a liar," he implies a knowledge of facts which lead to the conclusion that Jones told an untruth. [Simply] couching such statements in terms of opinion does not dispel these implications; and [such a] statement [can] cause as much damage to reputation as the statement, "Jones is a liar." "[It] would be destructive of the law of libel if a writer could escape liability for accusations of [defamatory conduct] simply by using, explicitly or implicitly, the words 'I think.'"
>
> [On the other hand], unlike the statement, "In my opinion [Jones] is a liar," the statement, "In my opinion [Jones] shows his abysmal ignorance by accepting the teachings of Marx and Lenin," would not be actionable [under existing law, for] *Hepps* ensures that a statement of opinion relating to matters of public concern which does not contain a provably false factual connotation will receive full constitutional protection.

Although agreeing with the Court's overall analysis, Justice Brennan, joined by Justice Marshall, disagreed with the Court's application of this analysis to the specific facts of the case. The libel action in *Milkovich* arose out of a newspaper column in which the columnist, after stating several specific facts, concluded that Milkovich had lied in court. The Court held that this assertion could be the basis for a libel action because it contained "a provably false factual connotation," whereas the dissenters maintained that, in the circumstances of the case, the assertion should be understood as constitutionally protected "conjecture." See also Greenbelt Cooperative Publishing Assn., Inc. v. Bresler, 398 U.S. 6 (1970) (a libel plaintiff cannot constitutionally recover for use of the phrase "blackmail" where it would reasonably be understood as hyperbole); Letter Carriers v. Austin, 418 U.S. 264 (1974) (a libel plaintiff cannot constitutionally recover for use of the phrase "traitor" where it would reasonably be understood as a metaphor).

Page 1081.   At the bottom of the page, add the following:

1a. Intentional Infliction of Emotional Distress

In Hustler Magazine v. Falwell, 485 U.S. 46 (1988), the Court held that the first amendment barred an action by the nationally known minister Jerry Falwell against Hustler magazine for a "parody" of an advertisement. The relevant item contained the name and picture of Reverend Falwell and provided an "interview" in which Falwell said that his "first time" was during a drunken incestuous rendezvous with his mother in an outhouse. In the Court's words, the parody suggested that Falwell "is a hypocrite who preaches only when he is drunk." Small print at the bottom of the page noted "ad parody — not to be taken seriously."

Falwell brought suit for libel, invasion of privacy, and intentional infliction of emotional distress; the jury found for Falwell on the last claim. The Supreme Court held that a public figure may not "recover damages for emotional harm caused by the publication of an ad parody offensive to him, and doubtless gross and repugnant in the eyes of most." In a unanimous opinion, the Court said:

> Were we to hold otherwise, there can be little doubt that political cartoonists and satirists would be subjected to damages awards without any showing that their work falsely defamed its subject. Webster's defines a caricature as "the deliberately distorted picturing or imitating of a person, literary style, etc. by exaggerating features or mannerisms for satirical effect." Webster's New Unabridged Twentieth Century Dictionary of the English Language 275 (2d ed. 1979). The appeal of the political cartoon or caricature is often based on exploration of unfortunate physical traits or politically embarrassing events — an exploration often calculated to injure the feelings of the subject of the portrayal. The art of the cartoonist is often not reasoned or evenhanded, but slashing and one-sided. . . .
>
> Respondent contends, however, that the caricature in question here was so "outrageous" as to distinguish it from more traditional political cartoons. There is no doubt that the caricature of respondent and his mother published in Hustler is at best a distant cousin of the political cartoons described above, and a rather poor relation at that. If it were possible by laying down a principled standard to separate the one from the other, public discourse would probably suffer little or no harm. But we doubt that there is any such standard, and we are quite sure that the pejorative description "outrageous" does not supply one. "Outrageousness" in the area of political and social discourse has an inherent subjectiveness about it which would allow a jury to impose liability on the basis of the jurors' tastes or views, or perhaps on the basis of their dislike of a particular expression. . . .
>
> We conclude that public figures and public officials may not recover for the tort of intentional infliction of emotional distress by reason of publications such as the one here at issue without showing in addition that the publication contains a false statement of fact which was made with "actual malice," i.e., with knowledge that the statement was false or with reckless disregard as to whether or not it was true.

Consider Post, "The Constitutional Concept of Public Discourse: Outrageous Opinion, Democratic Deliberation and *Hustler Magazine v. Falwell*, 103 Harv. L. Rev. 601, 624-625, 631-632 (1990):

[The] Court stated that "in the area of political and social discourse" the distinction between outrageous and non-outrageous [opinion] "has an inherent subjectiveness about it." [This] reasoning seems deeply misplaced in the context of a tort that appeals to *inter*subjective, rather than to private, standards of judgment. [To] claim that speech is outrageous is to assert much more than that it is personally unpleasant or disagreeable; it is to claim that [it is] inconsistent with common canons of decency. Such a claim may be controversial, but it need be neither arbitrary nor subjective. . . .

[Thus, the] "outrageousness" standard [can] have meaning [within] the commonly accepted norms of a particular community. But the constitutional concept of public discourse forbids the state from enforcing such a standard [because] to do so would privilege [one community over others]. Outrageous speech calls community identity into question [and thus] has unique power to focus attention, dislocate old assumptions, and shock its audience into the recognition of unfamiliar forms of life. [On] this account, an "outrageousness" standard is unacceptable not because it [is subjective, but] because it would enable a single community to use the authority of the state to confine speech within its own notions of propriety. [We might say] that the concept of public discourse requires the state to remain neutral in the "marketplace of communities."

Page 1086. After subsection c of the Note, add the following:

d. Consider Matsuda, Public Response to Racist Speech: Considering the Victim's Story, 87 Mich. L. Rev. 2320, 2332, 2336-2337, 2357, 2359 (1989):

The claim that a legal response to racist speech is required stems from a recognition of the structural reality of racism in America. Racism, as used here, comprises the ideology of racial supremacy and the mechanisms for keeping selected victim groups in subordinated positions. [Victims of] hate propaganda have experienced [fear, nightmares], post-traumatic stress disorder, hypertension, psychosis, and suicide. [In] order to avoid receiving hate messages, victims [of such speech] have had to quit jobs, forgo education, leave their homes, avoid certain public places, curtail their own exercise of free speech rights, and otherwise modify their behavior. . . .

Racist speech is best treated as a *sui generis* category, presenting an idea so historically untenable, so dangerous, and so tied to perpetuation of violence and degradation [that] it is properly treated as outside the realm of protected discourse. [The] identifying characteristics [of] racist hate [speech are]: 1. The message is of racial inferiority; 2. The message is directed against a historically oppressed group; and 3. The message is persecutorial, hateful, and degrading. . . .

How can one argue for censorship of racist hate messages without encouraging a revival of McCarthyism? There is an important difference that comes from human experience, our only source of collective knowledge. [The] doctrines of racial supremacy and racial hatred [are] uniformly rejected. [We] have fought wars and spilled blood to establish [this principle]. The universality of this principle, in a world bereft of agreement on many things, is a mark of collective human progress.

See also Delgado, Words That Wound: A Tort Action for Racial Insults, Epithets and Name-Calling, 1982 Harv. Civ. Rts.-Civ. Lib. L. Rev. 133.

Page 1091. At the end of section 4 of the Note, add the following:

In The Florida Star v. B.J.F., 109 S. Ct. 2603 (1989), the Court held that it violated the Constitution to impose civil liability for publishing the name of a rape victim, where the publisher had obtained the name from a police report that had been inadvertently disclosed to the public. Justice White, joined by Chief Justice Rehnquist and Justice O'Connor, dissented, distinguishing *Cox* as involving judicial proceedings.

Page 1100. At the end of subsection d of the Note, add the following:

For a defense of the Court's overall commercial speech jurisprudence from a "collective choice" perspective, see Cass, Commercial Speech, Constitutionalism, Collective Choice, 56 U. Cinn. L. Rev. 1317 (1988).

Page 1104. At the conclusion of section 1 of the Note, add the following:

Consider Posadas de Puerto Rico Assocs. v. Tourism Company of Puerto Rico, 478 U.S. 328 (1986). A Puerto Rican statute legalizing certain forms of casino gambling also prohibited advertising of such facilities directed to residents of Puerto Rico. In the course of upholding the statute, the Court, in an opinion by Justice Rehnquist, made the following argument:

> [The] greater power to completely ban casino gambling necessarily includes the lesser power to ban advertising of casino gambling. . . .
>   It would surely be a Pyrrhic victory for casino owners [to] gain recognition of a First Amendment right to advertise their casinos [only] to thereby force the legislature into banning casino gambling [altogether]. It would just as surely be a strange constitutional doctrine which would concede to the legislature the authority to totally ban a product or activity, but deny to the legislature the authority to forbid the stimulation of demand for the product or activity through [advertising].

In a dissenting opinion joined by Justices Marshall and Blackmun, Justice Brennan responded as follows:

> I do not agree that a ban on casino advertising is "less intrusive" than an outright prohibition of such activity. A majority of States have chosen not to legalize casino gambling, and we have never suggested that this might be unconstitutional. However, having decided to legalize casino gambling, Puerto Rico's decision to ban truthful speech concerning entirely lawful activity raises serious First Amendment problems. Thus, the "constitutional doctrine" which bans Puerto Rico from banning

advertisements concerning lawful casino gambling is not so strange a restraint — it is called the First Amendment.

Page 1105.   At the end of section 4 of the Note, add the following:

See Peel v. Attorney Registration and Disciplinary Commission of Illinois, 110 S. Ct. — (1990), in which the Court, in invalidating a disciplinary rule prohibiting lawyers from holding themselves out as "certified" or as "specialists" in particular fields, rejected the argument that such descriptions are "inherently misleading."

Page 1107.   Before Central Hudson, add the following:

See also Shapero v. Kentucky Bar Association, 486 U.S. 466 (1988), in which the Court invalidated a rule categorically prohibiting lawyers from soliciting business for pecuniary gain by mailing truthful and nondeceptive letters to potential clients known to face specific legal problems, and distinguished *Ohralik* on the ground that mail solicitation poses much less risk of "overreaching or undue influence" than in-person solicitation.

Page 1111.   After *Metromedia, Inc.,* add the following:

POSADAS DE PUERTO RICO ASSOCS. v. TOURISM COMPANY OF PUERTO RICO, 478 U.S. 328 (1986):   A Puerto Rican statute legalized certain forms of casino gambling but prohibited casinos from advertising their facilities to the public of Puerto Rico. The Puerto Rico Superior Court found that the statute had been administered in an arbitrary and confusing fashion and, in order to avoid declaring it unconstitutional, construed it to ban only advertisements directed at Puerto Ricans and listed the kinds of advertisements that the court considered permissible under the act. The Supreme Court accepted this construction as binding upon it and upheld the constitutionality of the act as so construed.

Justice Rehnquist delivered the Court's opinion: "The particular kind of commercial speech at issue here [concerns] a lawful activity and is not misleading or [fraudulent]. We must therefore proceed to the three remaining steps of the *Central Hudson* analysis in order to determine whether Puerto Rico's advertising restrictions run afoul of the First Amendment. The first of these three steps involves an assessment of the strength of the government's interest in restricting the speech. The interest at stake in this case [is] the reduction of demand for casino gambling by the residents of Puerto Rico. [We] have no difficulty in concluding that the Puerto Rico Legislature's interest in the health, safety, and welfare of its citizens constitutes a 'substantial' governmental interest. . . .

"Step three asks the question whether the challenged restrictions on commercial speech 'directly advance' the government's asserted interest. [The] Puerto Rico Legislature obviously believed, when it enacted the advertising restrictions at issue here, that advertising of casino gambling aimed at the residents of Puerto Rico would serve to increase the demand for the product advertised. We think the legislature's belief is a reasonable one, and the fact that appellant has chosen to litigate this case all the way to this Court indicates that appellant shares the legislature's view. . . .

"We also think it clear beyond peradventure that the challenged statute and regulations satisfy the fourth and last step of the *Central Hudson* analysis, namely, whether the restrictions on commercial speech are no more extensive than necessary to serve the government's interest. The narrowing constructions of the advertising restrictions announced by the Superior Court ensure that the restrictions will not affect advertising of casino gambling aimed at tourists, but will apply only to such advertising when aimed at the residents of Puerto Rico. Appellant contends, however, that the First Amendment requires the Puerto Rico Legislature to reduce demand for casino gambling among the residents of Puerto Rico not by suppressing commercial speech that might *encourage* such gambling, but by promulgating additional speech designed to *discourage* it. We reject this contention. We think it is up to the legislature to decide whether or not such a 'counterspeech' policy would be as effective in reducing the demand for casino gambling as a restriction on advertising. . . .

"Appellant [argues] that, having chosen to legalize casino gambling for residents of Puerto Rico, the First Amendment prohibits the legislature from using restrictions on advertising to accomplish its goal of reducing demand for such gambling. We disagree. In our view, appellant has the argument backwards. [It] is precisely *because* the government could have enacted a wholesale prohibition of the underlying conduct that it is permissible for the government to take the less intrusive step of allowing the conduct, but reducing the demand through restrictions on advertising."

Justice Brennan, joined by Justices Marshall and Blackmun, dissented: "I do not believe that Puerto Rico constitutionally may suppress truthful commercial speech in order to discourage its residents from engaging in lawful activity. . . .

"While tipping its hat to [the *Central Hudson*] standards, the Court does little more than defer to what it perceives to be the determination by Puerto Rico's legislature that a ban on casino advertising aimed at residents is reasonable. . . .

"[In] light of the legislature's determination that serious harm will *not* result if residents are permitted [to] gamble, I do not see how Puerto Rico's interest in discouraging its residents from engaging in casino gambling can be characterized as 'substantial,' even if the legislature had actually asserted such an interest which, of course, it has not."

Justice Stevens, in an opinion joined by Justices Marshall and Blackmun, also dissented: "Whether a State may ban all advertising of an activity that it permits but could prohibit — such as gambling, prostitution, or the consumption of marijuana or liquor — is an elegant question of constitutional law. It is not, however, appropriate to address that question in this case because Puerto Rico's rather bizarre restraints on speech are so plainly forbidden by the First Amendment. . . .

"The regulation [poses] what might be viewed as a reverse Privileges and Immunities problem: Puerto Rico's residents are singled out for disfavored treatment in comparison to all other Americans. But nothing so fancy is required to recognize the obvious First Amendment problem in this kind of audience discrimination. I cannot imagine that this Court would uphold an Illinois regulation that forbade advertising 'addressed' to Illinois residents while allowing the same advertiser to communicate his message to visitors and commuters; we should be no more willing to uphold a Puerto Rico regulation that forbids advertising 'addressed' to Puerto Rico residents."

Consider Kurland, Posadas de Puerto Rico v. Tourism Company: " 'Twas Strange, 'Twas Passing Strange; 'Twas Pitiful, 'Twas Wondrous Pitiful," 1986 Sup. Ct. Rev. 1, 2, 6:

> The Posadas opinion makes a reader think [of] Lewis Carroll's Alice in Wonderland and Franz Kafka's The Castle, as words take on new meanings and bureaucracy triumphs over the rule of law. If however, the Supreme Court is to afford guidance for future decisions, lower courts and future litigants are entitled to more cogent or at least more lucid reasoning than was afforded here. As it stands, one is relegated to the faith that Justice Field once expressed when he wrote in dissent: "I have an abiding faith that this, like other errors, will, in the end 'die among the worshippers.' "
>
> [When] Oliver Wendell Holmes told us that: "The life of law has not been logic; it has been experience," he was not suggesting the abandonment of reason.

In Board of Trustees of SUNY v. Fox, 109 S. Ct. 3028 (1989), the Court held that the fourth element of *Central Hudson,* that the regulation be no more extensive than necessary, does not require that the regulation be the least restrictive measure that could effectively protect the government's interest.

> [The] government goal [must] be substantial, and the cost [carefully] calculated. Moreover, [the State] bears the burden of justifying its restrictions. By declining to impose [a] least-restrictive-means requirement, we take account of the difficulty of establishing with precision the point at which restrictions become more extensive than their objective requires, and provide the legislative and executive branches needed leeway in a field (commercial speech) "traditionally subject to governmental regulation" [Ohralik.]

Page 1117.   At the end of section 1 of the Note, add the following:

For a more thorough explication of the values of aesthetic expression, see Nahmod, Artistic Expression and Aesthetic Theory: The Beautiful, The Sublime and The First Amendment, 1987 Wis. L. Rev. 221.

Page 1118.   At the end of subsection 2b of the Note, add the following:

For a critique of Schauer's view, see Gey, The Apologetics of Suppression: The Regulation of Pornography as Act and Idea, 86 Mich. L. Rev. 1564 (1988).

Page 1119.   At the end of subsection 3a of the Note, add the following:

For further discussion of the "causation" issue, see Schauer, Causation Theory and the Causes of Sexual Violence, 1987 Am. Bar Found. Res. J. 737.

Sixteen years after publication of the Commission on Obscenity and Pornography Report, a new government commission — The Attorney General's Commission on Pornography — determined that at least certain forms of obscenity could cause violent antisocial conduct. After reviewing available social science evidence, the Attorney General's Commission concluded that there was a causal relationship between exposure to sexually violent material and aggressive behavior toward women. With respect to nonviolent, but "degrading" sexually explicit material, the commission found the evidence "more tentative," but nonetheless concluded that "substantial exposure to material of this type will increase acceptance of the proposition that women like to be forced into sexual practices." Although finding less evidence linking this material to sexual aggression, the commission reasoned that "[over] a large enough sample a population that believes that many women like to be raped [will] commit more acts of sexual violence [than] would a population holding these beliefs to a lesser extent." Moreover, the commission found that "substantial exposure to materials of this type bears some causal relationship to the incidence of various non-violent forms of discrimination against or subordination of women in our society." With regard to nonviolent, "nondegrading" material, the commission concluded that there was no currently available evidence supporting a causal relationship between exposure to it and acts of sexual violence.

The commission's report stirred immediate controversy and some of the social scientists whose work the commission relied upon insisted that their studies did not support the conclusions the commission drew from them.

Page 1124. At the end of section 5 of the Note, add the following:

See also Osborne v. Ohio, 110 S. Ct. 1691 (1990) (holding *Stanley* inapplicable to the possession of child pornography).

Page 1135. At the end of section 5 of the Note, add the following:

e. In Pope v. Illinois, 481 U.S. 497 (1987), the Court held that it was error to utilize community standards to decide whether a work lacked serious literary, artistic, political, or scientific value. In a prosecution for sale of obscene materials, the trial judge instructed the jury that it should decide the "value" question by determining how the work would be viewed by ordinary adults in the state. In an opinion by Justice White, the Court held that this instruction violated the first amendment:

> Just as the ideas a work represents need not obtain majority approval to merit protection, neither, insofar as the First Amendment is concerned, does the value of the work vary from community to community based on the degree of local acceptance it has won. The proper inquiry is not whether an ordinary member of any given community would find serious [value] in allegedly obscene material, but whether a reasonable person would find such value in the [material].

Justice Scalia wrote a separate concurring opinion:

> [It] is quite impossible to come to an objective assessment of (at least) literary or artistic value, there being many accomplished people who have found literature in Dada, and art in the replication of a soup can. Since ratiocination has little to do with esthetics, the fabled "reasonable man" is of little help in the inquiry, and would have to be replaced with, perhaps, the "man of tolerably good taste" — a description that betrays the lack of an ascertainable standard. [I] think we would be better advised to adopt as a legal maxim what has long been the wisdom of mankind: *De gustibus non est disputandum.* Just as there is no use arguing about taste, there is no use litigating about it. . . .
>
> All of today's opinions, I suggest, display the need for reexamination of *Miller.*

In a dissenting opinion joined by Justice Marshall, Justice Stevens also attacked the "reasonable person" standard.

> The problem with [the Court's] formulation is that it assumes that all reasonable persons would resolve the value inquiry in the same way. In fact, there are many cases in which *some* reasonable people would find that [the materials] have serious [value], while *other* reasonable people would conclude that they have no such value. . . .
>
> In my judgment, communicative material of this sort is entitled to the protection of the First Amendment if *some reasonable persons* could consider it as having serious [value].

Justice Stevens went on to note an "even more basic reason" for reversal:

Under ordinary circumstances, ignorance of the law is no excuse for committing a crime. But that principle presupposes a penal statute that adequately puts citizens on notice of what is illegal. The Constitution cannot tolerate schemes that criminalize categories of speech that the Court has conceded to be so vague and uncertain that they cannot "be defined legislatively." [Smith v. United States.] . . .

Concern with the vagueness inherent in criminal obscenity statutes is not the only constitutional objection to [such laws]. [*Stanley*] was grounded upon a recognition that "[o]ur whole constitutional heritage rebels at the thought of giving government the power to control men's minds." . . .

The Court has adopted a restrictive reading of *Stanley*, opining that it has no implications to the criminalization of the sale or distribution of obscenity. But such a crabbed approach offends the overarching First Amendment principles discussed in *Stanley*, almost as much as it insults the citizenry by declaring its right to read and possess material which it may not legally obtain.

Justice Blackmun filed a separate opinion concurring in part and dissenting in part, and Justice Brennan filed a separate dissenting opinion.

Page 1137.   At the end of subsection b of the Note, add the following:

See also C. MacKinnon, Feminism Unmodified: Discourses on Life and Law 155 (1987):

The theory of the First Amendment under which most pornography is protected from governmental restriction proceeds from liberal assumptions that do not apply to the situation of women. First Amendment theory, like virtually all liberal legal theory, presumes the validity of the distinction between public and [private]. On this basis, courts distinguish between obscenity in public (which can be regulated) [and] the private possession of obscenity in the home. The problem is that not only the public but also the private *is* a "sphere of social power" of sexism. On paper and in life pornography is thrust upon unwilling women in their homes. The distinction between public and private does not cut the same for women as for men. It is men's right to inflict pornography upon women in private that is protected.

Page 1138.   At the conclusion of subsection e of the Note, add the following:

See also C. MacKinnon, Feminism Unmodified: Discourses on Life and Law 155-156 (1987):

Laissez faire might be an adequate theory of the social preconditions for knowledge in a nonhierarchical society. But in a society of gender inequality, the speech of the powerful impresses its view upon the world, concealing the truth of powerlessness under that despairing acquiescence that provides the appearance of consent and makes protest inaudible as well as rare. Pornography can invent women because it has the power to make its vision into reality, which then passes, objectively, for truth. So while the First Amendment supports pornography, believing that consensus and progress are facilitated by allowing all views, however divergent and unorthodox, it fails to notice that pornography [is] not at all divergent or unorthodox. [While] defenders of pornography argue that allowing all speech, including pornography, frees the mind to fulfill itself, pornography freely enslaves women's minds and bodies inseparably, normalizing the terror that enforces silence from women's point of view.

But consider West, The Feminist-Conservative Anti-Pornography Alliance and the 1986 Attorney General's Commission on Pornography Report, 1987 Am. Bar Found. Res. J. 681, 686, 691-692:

A woman-centered conception of pornography [has] two dimensions: for many women (perhaps most), pornography is primarily victimizing, threatening and oppressive, [but] for others [it] is on occasion liberating and transformative. [Indeed, some pornography assaults] a source of oppression: the marital, familial, productive, and reproductive values that the conservative wrongly identifies as necessary to the creation of a virtuous life and a virtuous society. [According] to women who enjoy pornography, the validation of pleasure, desire, and sexuality found in some pornography is [a] healthy attack on a stifling and oppressive societal denial of female sexuality. [It can be] something to celebrate, rather than something to condemn.

Page 1139.   Before *Ferber,* add the following:

For the Supreme Court's summary affirmance of *Hudnut,* see 475 U.S. 1001 (1986).

g. The conclusion that antipornography legislation is impermissible because it is viewpoint discrimination has been challenged. Consider Sunstein, Pornography and the First Amendment, 1986 Duke L.J. 589, 612 (1986):

The initial response to a claim that antipornography legislation is viewpoint-based should be straightforward. The legislation aimed at pornography [is] directed at harm rather than at viewpoint. Its purpose [is] to prevent sexual violence and discrimination, not to suppress expression of a point of view. Only pornography — not sexist material in general or material that reinforces notions of female subordination — is regulated. Because of its focus on harm, antipornography legislation [does] not pose the dangers associated with viewpoint-based restrictions.

Consider also Posner, Free Speech in an Economic Perspective, 20 Suffolk U.L. Rev. 1, 38 (1986):

[The] harms which a law is validly concerned with preventing may be a function of a particular viewpoint. The Indianapolis ordinance would apparently have fared better in the courts if it had punished sexually explicit material which showed men being degraded by women as well as material that showed women being degraded by men. But as no one supposes that any form of pornography results in crimes by women against men, to prohibit pornography in which women are shown inflicting pain on men would [be unconstitutionally overbroad because it would prohibit essentially harmless speech].

For the opposing view, consider L. Tribe, American Constitutional Law 925-926 (2d ed. 1988):

It is an inadequate response to argue [that pornography] ordinances take aim at harms, not at expression. *All* viewpoint-based regulations are targeted at some supposed harm, whether it be linked to an unsettling ideology like Communism [or] to socially shunned practices like adultery. [It] is beyond dispute that government may choose to outlaw the incitement of various acts independently deemed crimes — including murder, rape, or, indeed, the violent overthrow of government. Likewise, government may surely outlaw the direct incitement of sexual violence against women. [It] is, however, altogether different, and far more constitutionally tenuous, for government to outlaw [the] incitement of violence against women *only* when such incitement is caused by words or pictures that express a particular point of view: that women are meant for domination. The analogue would be a ban on anti-capitalist speeches that incite robbery, leaving other equally effective incitements to robbery unprohibited.

Page 1141. After *Ferber,* add the following:

In Massachusetts v. Oakes, 109 S. Ct. 2633 (1989), the Court avoided deciding whether a Massachusetts statute that prohibited posing children under eighteen "in a state of nudity" was unconstitutionally overbroad; the statute had been amended to require that the action be done with lascivious intent.

Similarly, in Osborne v. Ohio, 110 S. Ct. 1691 (1990), the Court upheld a child pornography statute directed at material "that shows a minor . . . in a state of nudity." Although emphasizing that "depictions of nudity, without more, constitute protected expression," the Court upheld the statute because the state supreme court had construed it as limited to nudity that "constitutes a lewd exhibition or involves a graphic focus on the genitals."

Page 1141. Before the Note, add the following:

In Osborne v. Ohio, 110 S. Ct. 1691 (1990), the Court held that Stanley v. Georgia does not extend to the private possession of child pornography. The Court, in an opinion by Justice White, explained:

[T]he interests underlying child pornography prohibitions far exceed the interests justifying [the] law at issue in *Stanley.* [In] *Stanley,* Georgia primarily sought to proscribe the private possession of obscenity because it was concerned that obscenity will poison the mind of its viewers. [The] difference here is obvious: the State does not rely on a paternalistic interest in regulating [the defendant's] mind. Rather, [the law is designed] to protect the victims of child pornography; it hopes to destroy a national market for the exploitative use of children.

Justices Brennan, Marshall, and Stevens dissented.

Page 1144.   After line 10, add the following:

In New York v. P.J. Video, Inc., 475 U.S. 868 (1986), the Court held that a warrant authorizing the seizure of materials presumptively protected by the first amendment need not be evaluated under an enhanced probable cause requirement. The Court further held that a magistrate may issue a warrant based on an affidavit describing the material in question without personally viewing it. Justice Marshall, joined by Justices Brennan and Stevens, dissented.

Fort Wayne Books, Inc. v. Indiana, – U.S. – , 109 S. Ct. 916 (1989), held that although it was constitutional to use the enhanced penalty system of racketeering statutes in obscenity prosecutions, the wholesale seizure of the books and films at an adult bookstore required a judicial determination that the articles seized were obscene.

Page 1167.   Before the Note, add the following:

CITY OF RENTON v. PLAYTIME THEATRES
475 U.S. 41 (1986)

JUSTICE REHNQUIST delivered the opinion of the Court.

[The City of Renton, Washington, adopted an ordinance prohibiting adult motion picture theaters from locating within 1,000 feet of any residential zone, single- or multiple-family dwelling, church, park or school. The ordinance defined "adult motion picture theatre" as "[an] enclosed building used for presenting motion picture films, video cassettes, cable television, or any other such visual media, distinguished or [characterized] by an emphasis on matter depicting, describing or relating to 'specified sexual activities' or 'specified anatomical areas' [for] observation by patrons therein." Appellees, who owned two theaters in downtown Renton, brought this action in federal district court seeking to enjoin enforcement of the ordinance on first amendment grounds. While the action was pending, the City Council amended the ordinance by, inter alia, adding a provision explaining that its intention was "to promote the City of Renton's great interest in protecting and preserving the quality of its neighborhoods, commercial districts, and the quality of urban life through effective land use planning." The district court granted the city's motion for summary judgment, but the court of appeals reversed.]

In our view, the resolution of this case is largely dictated by our decision in Young v. American Mini Theatres, Inc. [The] Renton ordinance, like the one in *American Mini Theatres*, does not ban adult theaters altogether, but merely provides that such theaters may not be located within 1,000 feet of any residential zone, single- or multiple-family dwelling, church, park, or school. The ordinance is therefore properly analyzed as a form of time, place, and manner regulation. . . .

This Court has long held that regulations enacted for the purpose of restraining speech on the basis of its content presumptively violate the First Amendment. On the other hand, so-called "content-neutral" time, place, and manner regulations are acceptable so long as they are designed to serve a substantial governmental interest and do not unreasonably limit alternative avenues of communication.

At first glance, the Renton ordinance, like the ordinance in *American Mini Theatres*, does not appear to fit neatly into either the "content-based" or the "content-neutral" category. To be sure, the ordinance treats theaters that specialize in adult films differently from other kinds of theaters. Nevertheless, as the District Court concluded, the Renton ordinance is aimed not at the *content* of the films shown at "adult motion picture theatres," but rather at the *secondary effects* of such theaters on the surrounding community. The District Court found that the City Council's "*predominate* concerns" were with the secondary effects of adult theaters, and not with the content of adult films themselves. But the Court of Appeals [held] that this was not enough to sustain the ordinance. According to the Court of Appeals, if "*a motivating factor*" in enacting the ordinance was to restrict respondents' exercise of First Amendment rights the ordinance would be invalid, apparently no matter how small a part this motivating factor may have played in the City Council's decision. This view of the law was rejected in United States v. O'Brien, [see page 1202 supra of the main text]:

> It is a familiar principle of constitutional law that this Court will not strike down an otherwise constitutional statute on the basis of an alleged illicit legislative motive. . . .
>
> What motivates one legislator to make a speech about a statute is not necessarily what motivates scores of others to enact it, and the stakes are sufficiently high for us to eschew guesswork.

The District Court's finding as to "predominate" intent, left undisturbed by the Court of Appeals, is more than adequate to establish that the city's pursuit of its zoning interests here was unrelated to the suppression of free expression. . . .

In short, the Renton ordinance is completely consistent with our definition of "content-neutral" speech regulations as those that "are *justified* without reference to the content of the regulated speech." [Virginia Pharmacy Board v. Virginia Citizens Consumer Council, Inc.] The ordinance does not contravene the fundamental principle that underlies our concern about "content-based" speech regulations: that "government may not grant the use of a forum to people whose views it finds acceptable, but deny use to those wishing to express less favored or more controversial views. [Police Dept. of Chicago v. Mosley, see page 1244 of the main text.]

The appropriate inquiry in this case, then, is whether the Renton ordinance is designed to serve a substantial governmental interest and allows for reasonable alternative avenues of communication. It is clear that the ordinance meets such a standard. As a majority of this Court recognized in *American Mini Theatres*, a city's "interest in attempting to preserve the quality of urban life is one that must be accorded high respect". . . .

The Court of Appeals ruled, however, that because the Renton ordinance was enacted without the benefit of studies specifically relating to "the particular problems or needs of Renton," the city's justifications for the ordinance were "conclusory and speculative." We think the Court of Appeals imposed on the city an unnecessarily rigid burden of proof. The record in this case reveals that Renton relied heavily on the experience of, and studies produced by, the city of Seattle. . . .

We also find no constitutional defect in the method chosen by Renton to further its substantial interests. Cities may regulate adult theaters by dispersing them, as in Detroit, or by effectively concentrating them, as in Renton. [Moreover,] the Renton ordinance is "narrowly tailored" to affect only that category of theaters shown to produce the unwanted secondary effects, thus avoiding the flaw that proved fatal to the regulations in [*Schad*] and [*Erznoznik*].

Respondents contend that the Renton ordinance is "underinclusive," in that it fails to regulate other kinds of adult businesses that are likely to produce secondary effects similar to those produced by adult theaters. [That] Renton chose first to address the potential problems created by one particular kind of adult business in no way suggests that the city has "singled out" adult theaters for discriminatory treatment. We simply have no basis on this record for assuming that Renton will not, in the future, amend its ordinance to include other kinds of adult businesses that have been shown to produce the same kinds of secondary effects as adult theaters.

Finally, turning to the question whether the Renton ordinance allows for reasonable alternative avenues of communication, we note that the ordinance leaves some 520 acres, or more than five percent of the entire land area of Renton, open to use as adult theater sites. . . .

[Playtime Theatres] argue, however, that some of the land in question is already occupied by existing businesses, that "practically none" of the undeveloped land is currently for sale or lease, and that in general there are no "commercially viable" adult theater sites within the 520 acres left open by the Renton ordinance. . . .

[But] although we have cautioned against the enactment of zoning regulations that have "the effect of suppressing, or greatly restricting access to, lawful speech," [*American Mini Theatres*] we have never suggested that the First Amendment compels the Government to ensure that adult theaters, or any other kinds of speech-related businesses for that matter, will be able to obtain sites at bargain prices. In our view, the First Amendment requires only that Renton refrain from effectively denying respondents a reasonable opportunity to open and operate an adult theater within the city, and the ordinance before us easily meets this requirement. . . .

In sum, we find that the Renton ordinance represents a valid governmental response to the "admittedly serious problems" created by adult theaters. Renton has not used "the power to zone as a pretext for suppressing expression," but rather has sought to make some areas available for adult theaters and their patrons, while at the same time preserving the quality of life in the community at large by preventing those theaters from locating in other areas. This, after all, is the essence of zoning. [The] judgment of the Court of Appeals is therefore reversed.

JUSTICE BLACKMUN concurs in the result.

JUSTICE BRENNAN joined by JUSTICE MARSHALL, dissenting.

Renton's zoning ordinance selectively imposes limitations on the location of a movie theater based exclusively on the content of the films shown there. The constitutionality of the ordinance is therefore not correctly analyzed under standards applied to content-neutral time, place, and manner restrictions. [The] fact that adult movie theaters may cause harmful "secondary" land use effects [does] not mean [that] such regulations are content-neutral. Because the ordinance imposes special restrictions on certain kinds of speech on the basis of *content*, I cannot simply accept, as the Court does, Renton's claim that the ordinance was not designed to suppress the content of adult movies. . . .

[In any event] the ordinance is invalid because it does not provide for reasonable alternative avenues of communication. The District Court found that the ordinance left 520 acres in Renton available for adult theater sites, an area comprising about five percent of the city. However, the Court of Appeals found that because much of this land was already occupied, "[l]imiting adult theater uses to these areas is a substantial restriction on speech." Many "available" sites are also largely unsuited for use by movie theaters. Again, these facts serve to distinguish this case from *American Mini Theatres*, where there was no indication that the Detroit zoning ordinance seriously limited the locations available for adult businesses. . . .

The Court [argues] that the First Amendment does not compel "the government to ensure that adult theatres, or any other kinds of speech-related businesses for that matter, will be able to obtain sites at bargain prices." However, [Playtime Theatres] do not ask Renton to guarantee low-price sites for their businesses, but seek only a reasonable opportunity to operate adult theaters in the city. By denying them this opportunity, Renton can effectively ban a form of protected speech from its borders. The ordinance "greatly restrict[s] access to, lawful speech," [*American Mini Theatres* (plurality opinion)], and is plainly unconstitutional.

Page 1167. At the end of section 1 of the Note, add the following:

In Sable Communications, Inc. v. Federal Communications Commission, 109 S. Ct. 2829 (1989), the Court unanimously held unconstitutional a federal statute prohibiting the interstate transmission of indecent (but not obscene) commercial telephone messages ("dial-a-porn" services). The Court distinguished the "emphatically narrow holding" of *Pacifica,* which did not involve a total ban on broadcasting indecent material, and involved the unique intrusiveness of broadcasting, unlike telephone communications, which require the listener to take "affirmative steps" to receive the message. "Placing a telephone call is not the same as turning on a radio and being taken by surprise by an indecent message." The government's interest in protecting children could be served by various technical means other than a total ban on the transmission of indecent messages; although some limited numbers of children might be able to defeat these devices, the prohibition "has the invalid effect of limiting the content of adult telephone conversations to that which is suitable for children to hear."

Page 1167. After section 1 of the Note, add the following:

1A. *An alternative approach: resurrecting* Ginzburg. In a dissenting opinion in FW/PBS, Inc. v. City of Dallas, 110 S. Ct. 596 (1990), Justice Scalia argued that *Young* and *Renton* did not go far enough in permitting the regulation of "sexually oriented businesses." Building upon Ginzburg v. New York, supra section B, Scalia argued that "a business devoted to the sale of highly explicit sexual material can be found to be engaged in the marketing of obscenity, even though each book or film it sells might, in isolation, [not be] obscene."

Page 1167. At the end of section 2 of the Note, add the following:

Does nude dancing constitute "speech" within the meaning of the first amendment? Consider Wright, A Rationale from J. S. Mill for the Free Speech Clause, 1985 Sup. Ct. Rev. 149, 156, 166:

> [For] something to be speech it must embody or convey a more or less discernible idea, doctrine, conception, or argument of a social nature, where "social" is understood to include broadly political, religious, ethical, and cultural concerns. [The] "message" of commercial nude dancing is [too] attenuated and insubstantial to [constitute "speech" within the meaning of the first amendment].

Page 1168. Before section 4 of the Note, add the following:

3A. *Licensing Sexually Oriented Businesses.* In FW/PBS, Inc. v. City of Dallas, 110 S. Ct. 596 (1990), the Court held that two of the three procedural safeguards recognized in Freedman v. Maryland, supra section C, must be employed in a licensing scheme for sexually oriented business. The Court concluded that such licensing decisions must be made within a reasonable period and that there must be an opportunity for prompt judicial review of adverse decisions, but that the censor need not "go to court to bear the burden [of] justifying the denial."

Page 1169.   Before the Note, add the following:

The Court extended *Pacifica* to the public school setting in Bethel School Dist. No. 403 v. Fraser, 478 U.S. 675 (1986), where it upheld the power of school officials to discipline a student for a speech containing sexual innuendo delivered before an assembly of 600 high school students. In an opinion by Chief Justice Burger, the Court distinguished *Cohen* as follows:

> The First Amendment guarantees wide freedom in matters of adult public discourse. A sharply divided Court upheld the right to express an antidraft viewpoint in a public place, albeit in terms highly offensive to most citizens. See [*Cohen*]. It does not follow, however, that simply because the use of an offensive form of expression may not be prohibited to adults making what the speaker considers a political point, that the same latitude must be permitted to children in a public school.

For a fuller discussion of *Fraser*, see Supplement to Casebook page 1272 infra.

5. Renton *and content-neutrality.* Do you agree with the Court that the ordinance upheld in *Renton* was "content neutral"? Compare *Renton* with the Court's summary affirmance of American Booksellers Assn. v. Hudnut, Supp. to page 1139 of the main text. In *Hudnut*, the court of appeals invalidated an ordinance restricting the distribution of pornography. Although recognizing that the ordinance was motivated by the desire to avoid subordination of women as well as battery and rape, the court nonetheless determined that it was viewpoint-based and, therefore, could not be defended as a restriction of only "low value" speech. Is there a good reason why a statute designed to protect property values should be treated more favorably than one designed to prevent subordination, battery, and rape? Cf. Stone, Comment: Anti-Pornography Legislation as Viewpoint-Discrimination, 9 Harv. J. L. & Pub. Poly. 461 (1986). The issue of content neutrality is examined in section E infra.

6. *Cable.* To what extent, if any, does *Pacifica* govern cable television? See Wardle, Cable Comes of Age: A Constitutional Analysis of the Regulation of "Indecent" Cable Television Programming, 63 Den. U.L. Rev. 621 (1986); Krattenmaker & Esterow, Censoring Indecent Cable Programs: The New Morality Meets the New Media, 51 Ford. L. Rev. 606 (1983).

Page 1169.   At the end of the first paragraph of the Note, add the following:

Consider Sunstein, Pornography and the First Amendment, 1986 Duke L.J. 589, 603-604 (1986):

[In] determining whether speech qualifies as low-value, the cases suggest that four factors are relevant. First, the speech must be far afield from the central concern of the first amendment, which, broadly speaking, is effective popular control of public affairs. [Second], a distinction is drawn between cognitive and noncognitive aspects of speech. [Third], the purpose of the speaker is relevant: if the speaker is seeking to communicate a message, he will be treated more favorably than if he is not. Fourth, the various classes of low-value speech reflect judgments that in certain areas, government is unlikely to be acting for constitutionally impermissible reasons or producing constitutionally troublesome harms.

Does this four-factor analysis adequately explain the Court's decisions? If so, are they the right factors to consider?

E. CONTENT-NEUTRAL RESTRICTIONS: LIMITATIONS ON THE MEANS OF COMMUNICATION

Page 1175.   At the end of section 1 of the Note, add the following:

For a critique of balancing, see Aleinikoff, Constitutional Law in the Age of Balancing, 96 Yale L.J. 943 (1987).

Page 1176.   At the end of subsection e of the Note, add the following:

For an analysis of these issues, see Stone, Content-Neutral Restrictions, 54 U. Chi. L. Rev. 46, 99-114 (1987).

Page 1176.   Before section 3 of the Note, add the following:

For an effort to articulate a comprehensive approach to first amendment balancing, see Zacharias, Flowcharting the First Amendment, 72 Cornell L. Rev. 936 (1987).

Page 1176.   At the bottom of the page, add the following:

4. *The definition of content neutrality.* What makes a restriction content-neutral? Must the restriction be facially neutral regarding content, or is it sufficient that the legislative purpose was unrelated to content? Recall that in City of Renton v. Playtime Theatres, Supplement to Casebook page 1167 supra, the Court held that a zoning ordinance directed against theaters showing "adult" motion pictures was content-neutral. Although the ordinance treated theaters differently based on the content of the films shown, the Court held that it nevertheless satisfied the requirements of content-neutrality because it was *aimed* at the "secondary effects" of such theaters, rather than at the content of the films. Does this approach make sense? Is a

statute prohibiting seditious libel content-neutral if it is aimed at the disruptive effects of the speech rather than at the speech itself?

One theory supporting more lenient review of content-neutral restrictions is that there is less likelihood that such restrictions are motivated by a desire to curb speech. Does that theory survive *Renton*?

The secondary-effects/content-neutrality puzzle is explored further in the debate between Justices O'Connor and Brennan in Boos v. Barry, 485 U.S. 312 (1988). See also Stone, Content-Neutral Restrictions, 54 U. Chi. L. Rev. 46, 114-117 (1987).

The *Renton* Court also rejected the relevance of the lower court's holding that suppression of speech was a motivating factor in the City Council's decision. In doing so it relied on the "familiar principle" that a court should "not strike down an otherwise constitutional statute on the basis of an alleged illicit legislative motive." (Quoting from United States v. O'Brien, 391 U.S. 367 (1968).) If statutes are not content-based unless their purpose is related to content, and if the Court is precluded from inquiring into purpose, how can the party challenging a restriction on speech ever demonstrate that it is content-based?

Page 1177. At the end of the first paragraph of section 2, add the following:

See generally Stone, Content-Neutral Restrictions, 54 U. Chi. L. Rev. 46, 86-94 (1987).

Page 1181. At the end of the second full paragraph, add the following:

See also Boos v. Barry, 485 U.S. 312 (1988), in which the Court upheld against overbreadth challenge a provision of the District of Columbia Code that made it unlawful to congregate within 500 feet of a foreign embassy or to refuse to obey a police order to disperse when the police reasonably believe that the embassy's security or peace is threatened.

Page 1181. Before subsection 3 of the Note, add the following:

2A. *Frisby*. In Frisby v. Shultz, 487 U.S. 474 (1988), a group varying in size from 11 to 40 people picketed in protest on six occasions within one month on the public street outside the residence of a doctor who performed abortions. The picketing was orderly and peaceful. Thereafter, the town enacted an ordinance that the Court interpreted not as prohibiting all residential picketing but, rather, as more narrowly prohibiting only residential picketing that focuses on and takes place in front of a particular residence. With that interpretation, the Court, in a six-to-three decision, upheld the ordinance.

Although emphasizing that "a public street does not lose its status as a traditional public forum because it runs through a residential neighborhood," the Court nonetheless concluded that the ordinance was constitutional because it left "open ample alternative channels of communication" and was "narrowly tailored to serve a significant government interest." The Court found the first requirement "readily" satisfied because the ordinance left protestors free to march, proselytize door-to-door, leaflet, and even picket in a manner that did not focus exclusively on a particular residence.

As to the second requirement, the Court observed that "privacy of the home is [of] the highest order in a free and civilized society, [that] individuals are not required to welcome unwanted speech into their own homes, [and that] the government may protect this freedom." Moreover, the "type of picketers banned by [this ordinance] generally do not seek to disseminate a message to the general public, but to intrude upon the targeted resident, and to do so in an especially offensive way. [And] even if some such picketers have a broader communicative purpose, their activity nonetheless inherently and offensively intrudes on residential privacy." Indeed, the Court noted that "even a solitary picket can invade residential privacy, [for the] target of the focused picketing banned by [this] ordinance is [a] 'captive,' [figuratively], and perhaps literally, trapped within the home." The Court thus concluded that the ordinance was "narrowly tailored" because "the 'evil' of targeted residential picketing, 'the very presence of an unwelcome visitor at the home,' is 'created by the medium of expression itself.' "

In dissent, Justice Brennan, joined by Justice Marshall, conceded that "the government could constitutionally regulate the number of residential picketers, the hours during which a residential picket may take place, or the noise level of such a picket [to] neutralize the intrusive or unduly coercive aspects of picketing around the home." But he rejected the Court's assertion that "the intrusive elements of a residential picket are 'inherent.' " In his view, "the discomfort [of] knowing there is a person outside who disagrees with someone inside [does] not [in itself] implicate the [town's] interest in residential privacy and therefore does not warrant silencing speech." Justice Stevens also dissented.

Page 1183. Insert the following as Note 3c:

c. Ward v. Rock Against Racism, 109 S. Ct. 2746 (1989), relied on *Clark* to hold that

a regulation of the time, place, or manner of protected speech must be narrowly tailored to serve the government's legitimate content-neutral interests but that it need not be the least-restrictive or least-intrusive means of doing so. [The] requirement [is] satisfied "so long as the . . . regulation promotes a substantial government interest that would be achieved less effectively absent the regulation." [*Albertini.*] [But] Government may not regulate expression in such a manner that a substantial portion of the burden on speech does not serve to advance its goals.

Justice Marshall, dissenting (joined by Justices Brennan and Stevens), said that this

> replaces constitutional scrutiny with mandatory deference. . . . [The] majority [instructs] courts to refrain from examining how much speech may be restricted to serve an asserted interest and how that level of restriction is to be achieved. If a court cannot engage in such inquiries, I am at a loss to understand how a court can ascertain whether the government has adopted a regulation that burdens substantially more speech than is necessary.

Page 1185.   At the end of the page, add the following:

For a comprehensive analysis of the fee issue, see Neisser, Charging for Free Speech: User Fees and Insurance in the Marketplace of Ideas, 74 Geo. L.J. 257 (1985).

Page 1187.   The correct citation for Adderley v. Florida is 385 U.S. 39 (1966).

Page 1197.   Before the Note, add the following:

UNITED STATES v. KOKINDA, 110 S. Ct. — (1990):   Respondents, members of a political advocacy group, set up a table on a sidewalk near the entrance to a United States Post Office to distribute literature and solicit contributions. The sidewalk, which is located entirely on Postal Service property, is the sole means by which customers may travel from the parking lot to the post office building. Respondents were convicted of violating a federal regulation prohibiting any person from soliciting contributions "on postal premises." The Court upheld the regulation as applied.

Justice O'Connor, in a plurality opinion joined by Chief Justice Rehnquist and Justices White and Scalia, maintained that the "postal sidewalk [does] not have the characteristics of public sidewalks traditionally open to expressive activity." Rather, "the postal sidewalk was constructed solely to provide for the passage of individuals engaged in postal business." O'Connor invoked *Greer* for the proposition that not "all sidewalks open to the public" are "public fora," adding that "the location and purpose of a publicly-owned sidewalk is critical to determining whether such a sidewalk constitutes a public forum." Although conceding that individuals had generally "been permitted to leaflet, speak, and picket on postal premises," O'Connor argued this did "not add up to the dedication of postal property to speech activities." To the contrary, " '[t]he government does not create a public forum [merely] by . . . *permitting* limited discourse, but only by intentionally opening a nontraditional forum for public discourse.' " O'Connor therefore concluded that "the regulation [must] be analyzed under the standards set forth for nonpublic fora: it must be reasonable and 'not an effort to suppress expression merely because public officials oppose the speaker's view.' "

Applying that standard, O'Connor observed that the "purpose of the forum in this case is to accomplish the most efficient and effective postal delivery system," that "Congress has made clear that 'it wished the Postal Service to be run more like a business,' " and that it "is a long-settled principle that governmental actions are subject to a lower level of First Amendment scrutiny when the government is acting not " 'as lawmaker,' " but " 'as proprietor.' " O'Connor then noted that, "based on its long experience with solicitation," the Postal Service had concluded that "solicitation is inherently disruptive of the postal service's business" because it "impedes the normal flow of traffic," "requires action by those who would respond," and "is more intrusive and intimidating than an encounter with a person giving out information." In such circumstances, O'Connor concluded that the challenged regulation "passes constitutional muster under [the] usual test for reasonableness."

Justice Kennedy concurred in the result. Kennedy found it unnecessary "to make a precise determination whether this sidewalk and others like it are public or nonpublic forums" because the challenged regulation "meets the traditional standards" for "time, place, or manner restrictions" even in public forums. Noting that the challenged regulation prohibits "solicitations on postal property for the immediate payment of money," but not solicitations that do not call for "payments on the premises," Kennedy concluded that the regulation "is narrowly drawn to serve an important governmental interest," while permitting "a broad range" of expressive activity, "including the solicitation of financial support."

Justice Brennan, joined by Justices Marshall, Blackmun, and Stevens, dissented: "The wooden distinctions drawn [by] the plurality have no basis in our cases. [It] is irrelevant that [this sidewalk] may have been constructed only to provide access to [the post office building]. Public sidewalks, parks, and streets have been reserved for public use as forums for speech even though government has not constructed them for expressive purposes. Hence, *why* the sidewalk was built is not salient. [That] the walkway at issue is a sidewalk open and accessible to the general public is alone sufficient to identify it as a public forum. [Thus, although] I agree that the Government has an interest in preventing the obstruction of post office entrances [and] functions, [the challenged] regulation is invalid as applied in this case because [it] 'sweeps an entire category of expressive activity off a public forum solely in the interest of administrative convenience.' "

Page 1197.   At the end of section 1 of the Note, add the following:

For an excellent analysis of deference in this context, see Post, Between Governance and Management: The History and Theory of the Public Forum, 34 U.C.L.A. L. Rev. 1713, 1809-1824 (1987).

Page 1198.   Before section 3 of the Note, add the following:

2A. It has been suggested that public forum doctrine can best be explained, not in terms of a distinction between different types of public property, but in terms of a distinction between different types of government authority. Consider Post, supra, at 1775-1777, 1782:

> When administering its own institutions, the government is invested with a special form of authority, which I shall call "managerial." Managerial authority is controlled by first amendment rules different from those which control the exercise of authority used by the state when it acts to govern the general public. I shall call the latter kind of authority "governance." In situations of governance the state is bound by the ordinary principles of first amendment jurisprudence, but when exercising managerial authority ordinary first amendment rights are subordinated to the instrumental logic characteristic of organizations, and the state can in large measure control speech on the basis of an organization's need to achieve its institutional ends. . . .
>
> There is a striking similarity between this structure and that revealed in modern public forum doctrine. [T]he government's actions within the public forum [are] subject to the same first amendment restraints as are government actions generally. Government authority over the public forum can thus be characterized as a matter of governance. [In the nonpublic forum cases, on the other hand, the Court has been concerned] with the protection of managerial authority from the potentially deleterious effects of judicial review.
>
> The object of public forum doctrine, then, is the constitutional clarification and regulation of government authority over particular resources. Public forum cases require courts to decide whether a resource is subject to a kind of authority "like" that characterized by the government's relationship to a newspaper editorial, which is to say like that involved in the governance of the general public, or whether it is subject to a kind of authority "like" that characterized by the government's control over the internal management of its own institutions, which is to say to the authority of management. If the latter, the questions in the public forum case will concern the legitimate objectives of the managerial authority, the instrumental relationship between the attainment of those objectives and the regulation of speech, and the institutional impact of judicial review.

Page 1201.   At the end of the Note, add the following:

See also Patterson, Free Speech, Copyright, and Fair Use, 40 Vand. L. Rev. 1 (1987).

Compare San Francisco Arts & Athletics, Inc. v. United States Olympic Committee, 483 U.S. 522 (1987), where the Court, in an opinion by Justice Powell, upheld the constitutionality of a statute granting the United States Olympic Committee the exclusive right to use the word "Olympic" for commercial and promotional purposes. Justice Brennan, joined by Justice Marshall, dissented.

Page 1210.   Before section 7 of the Note, add the following:

Compare *O'Brien* with Arcara v. Cloud Books, 478 U.S. 697 (1986). New York law defines places of prostitution, lewdness, and assignation as public health nuisances and provides for the closure of any building found to be such a nuisance. An investigation of respondent's "adult" bookstore determined that sexual acts and solicitation to perform sexual acts were occurring on the premises. Despite this evidence, the New York Court of Appeals held that the closure of the store violated respondent's free speech rights. Applying the four-part *O'Brien* test, it determined that the closure statute incidentally restricted speech and that it was unnecessarily broad to achieve its purpose, since an injunction against the admittedly illegal activity on the premises could achieve the same effect.

In an opinion by Chief Justice Burger, the Supreme Court reversed. The Court emphasized the "crucial distinction" between this case and *O'Brien*:

> The petitioners in *O'Brien* had [at] least the semblance of expressive activity in their claim that the otherwise unlawful burning of a draft card was to "carry a message" of the actor's opposition to the draft. . . .
>
> [Unlike] the symbolic draft card burning in *O'Brien*, the sexual activity carried on in this case manifests absolutely no element of protected expression. . . .
>
> Nor does the distinction drawn by the New York Public Health Law inevitably single out bookstores or others engaged in First Amendment protected activities for the imposition of its burden. [If] the city imposed closure penalties for demonstrated Fire Code violations or health hazards from inadequate sewage treatment, the First Amendment would not aid the owner of premises who had knowingly allowed such violations to persist.

Justice Blackmun dissented in an opinion joined by Justices Brennan and Marshall.

Page 1210.   Before section 7 of the Note, add the following:

For analysis of these issues, see Stone, Content-Neutral Restrictions, 54 U. Chi. L. Rev. 46, 99-114 (1987). See also Shane, Equal Protection, Free Speech, and the Selective Prosecution of Draft Nonregistrants, 72 Iowa L. Rev. 359 (1987); Werhan, The O'Briening of Free Speech Methodology, 19 Ariz. St. L.J. 635 (1987).

Page 1215.   Insert the following as Notes 4 and 5:

4. *Flag desecration*. The Court finally confronted the basic issue of flag desecration in Texas v. Johnson, 109 S. Ct. 2533 (1989). In an opinion by Justice Brennan, the Court overturned the conviction for flag desecration of a man who had burned the flag as part of a political demonstration protesting the policies of the Reagan administration. The Court first found that flag burning in this context was expressive conduct.

> The Government generally has a freer hand in restricting expressive conduct than it has in restricting the written or spoken word. See [*O'Brien; CCNV*]. It may not [proscribe] particular conduct *because* it has expressive elements. ["A] law *directed at* the communicative nature of conduct must, like a law directed at speech itself, be justified by the substantial showing of need that the First Amendment requires" [quoting opinion of Scalia, Circuit Judge, in lower court consideration of *CCNV*].

The state's interest in preventing breaches of the peace as the result of audience responses to flag desecration was not implicated in this case, the Court said, because there was no evidence that a breach of peace was threatened. Nor could the state rely on a "presumption" that "an audience that takes serious offense at particular expression is necessarily likely to disturb the peace and that the expression may be prohibited on this basis. [*Terminiello*.]"

The state's "interest in preserving the flag as a symbol of nationhood and national unity" was "related to expression." The remaining issue was whether that interest justified the statute. The Court said that Johnson "was prosecuted for his expression of dissatisfaction with the policies of this country, expression situated at the core of our First Amendment values," that is, "because of the content of the message he conveyed." As a consequence, the state's asserted interest was subject to "the most exacting scrutiny." The Court continued

> If there is a bedrock principle underlying the First Amendment, it is that the Government may not prohibit the expression of an idea simply because society finds the idea itself offensive or disagreeable.... We have not recognized an exception to this principle even where our flag has been involved. [*Street.*] ... [Nothing] in our precedents suggest that a State may foster its own view of the flag by prohibiting expressive conduct relating to it.... [The] enduring lesson [of those precedents], that the Government may not prohibit expression simply because it disagrees with its message, is not dependent on the particular mode in which one chooses to express an idea. [Otherwise, we] would be permitting a State to "prescribe what shall be orthodox" [*Barnette*] by saying that one may burn a flag to convey one's attitude toward it and its referents only if one does not endanger the flag's representation of nationhood and national unity.... To conclude that the Government may permit designated symbols to be used to communicate only a limited set of messages would be to enter territory having no discernible or defensible boundaries.... We decline [to] create for the flag an exception to the joust of principles protected by the First Amendment.

We are tempted to say [that] the flag's deservedly cherished place in our community will be strengthened, not weakened, by our holding today. Our decision is a reaffimation of the principles of freedom and inclusiveness that the flag best reflects, and of the conviction that our toleration of criticism such as Johnson's is a sign and source of our strength. . . . The way to preserve the flag's special role is not to punish those who feel differently about these matters. It is to persuade them that they are wrong [quoting Brandeis, J., in *Whitney*.] [We] do not consecrate the flag by punishing its desecration, for in doing so we dilute the freedom that this cherished emblem represents.

Chief Justice Rehnquist, joined by Justices White and O'Connor, dissented.

The flag is not simply another "idea" or "point of view" competing for recognition in the marketplace of ideas. [Flag burning is] no essential part of any expression of ideas [referring to *Chaplinsky*], and at the same time it had a tendency to incite a breach of the peace. . . . [Johnson's] act, like Chaplinsky's provocative words, conveyed nothing that could not have been conveyed and was not conveyed just as forcefully in a dozen different ways. . . . Far from being a case of "one picture being worth a thousand words," flag burning is the equivalent of an inarticulate grunt or roar that [is] most likely to be indulged in not to express any particular idea, but to antagonize others. [The] Texas statute deprived Johnson of only one rather inarticulate symbolic form of protest — a form of protest that was profoundly offensive to many — and left him with a full panoply of other symbols and every conceivable form of verbal expression to express his deep disapproval of national policy. Thus, in no way can it be said that Texas is punishing him because his hearers — or any other group of people — were profoundly opposed to the message that he sought to convey. [It] was Johnson's use of this particular symbol, and not the idea that he sought to convey by it or by his many other expressions, for which he was punished.

The Court concludes its opinion with a regrettably patronizing civics lecture. [The] Court's role [as] a platonic guardian admonishing those responsible to public opinion as if they were truant school children has no similar place in our system of government. [Surely] one of the high purposes of a democratic society is to legislate against conduct that is regarded as evil and profoundly offensive to the majority of people — whether it be murder, embezzlement, pollution, or flag burning.

Justice Stevens also dissented.

5. *Flag desecration revisited.* Shortly after the decision in *Johnson*, Congress enacted the Flag Protection Act of 1989, which made it a crime for any person knowingly to mutilate, deface, physically defile, burn, maintain on the floor or ground, or trample upon any flag of the United States. The government maintained that this Act was constitutional because, unlike the statute addressed in *Johnson*, the Act was designed to protect "the physical integrity of the flag under all circumstances," did "not target expressive conduct on the basis of the content of its message," and proscribed "conduct (other than disposal) that damages or mistreats a flag, without regard to the actor's motive, his intended message, or the likely effects of his conduct on onlookers." In United States v.

Eichman, 110 S. Ct. — (1990), the Court, in a five to four decision, invalidated this Act.

Justice Brennan delivered the opinion:

> Although the [Act] contains no explicit content-based limitation on the scope of prohibited conduct, it is nevertheless clear that the Government's asserted *interest* is "related to the suppression of free expression" and concerned with the content of such expression. The Government's interest in protecting the "physical integrity" of a privately owned flag rests upon a perceived need to preserve the flag's status as a symbol of our Nation and certain national ideals. But the mere destruction or disfigurement of a particular physical manifestation of the symbol, without more, does not diminish or otherwise affect the symbol itself in any way. For example, the secret destruction of a flag in one's own basement would not threaten the flag's recognized meaning. Rather, the Government's desire to preserve the flag as a symbol for certain national ideals is implicated "only when a person's treatment of the flag communicates [a] message" to others that is inconsistent with those ideals.
>
> Moreover, the precise language of the Act's prohibitions confirms Congress' interest in the communicative impact of flag destruction. The Act criminalizes the conduct of anyone who "knowingly mutilates, defaces, physically defiles, burns, maintains on the floor or ground, or tramples upon any flag." Each of the specified terms — with the possible exception of "burns" — unmistakably connotes disrespectful treatment. . . .
>
> Although Congress cast the [Act] in somewhat broader terms than the Texas statute at issue in *Johnson,* the Act still suffers from the same fundamental flaw: it suppresses expression out of concern for its likely communicative impact. Despite the Act's wider scope, its restriction on expression cannot be " 'justified without reference to the content of the regulated speech.' " The Act therefore must be subjected to "the most exacting scrutiny," and for the reasons stated in *Johnson,* the Government's interest cannot justify its infringement on First Amendment rights.

Justice Stevens, joined by Chief Justice Rehnquist and Justices White and O'Connor, dissented.

Suppose Congress enacts the following statute: "No person may knowingly impair the physical integrity of the American flag." Do *Johnson* and *Eichman* require the invalidation of this law? Suppose Congress decides that because the bald eagle is the symbol of the United States no one should be allowed to kill bald eagles. (Suppose also that there is no shortage of bald eagles, so the example is not complicated by any concern about preserving the bald eagle as an endangered species). Against this background, is a law that prohibits any person from knowingly killing a bald eagle violative of the first amendment? See Stone, Flag Burning and the Constitution, 75 Iowa L. Rev. 111 (1989).

After the decision in *Eichman,* Congress declined to approve a proposed constitutional amendment that would have authorized Congress and the states to "prohibit the physical desecration of the flag of the United States."

Page 1219.   At the bottom of the page, add the following:

Riley v. National Federation of the Blind of North Carolina, Inc., 108 S. Ct. 2667 (1988) (invalidating various licensing, disclosure, and presumptive fee limitations placed on professional charitable solicitors); United States v. Kokinda, 110 S. Ct. — (1990) (upholding a Postal Service regulation prohibiting any person from soliciting contributions on post office property, as applied to members of a political advocacy group who set up a table on a sidewalk near the entrance to a post office to distribute literature and solicit contributions).

Page 1229.   Before the last paragraph, add the following:

Consider also Fiss, Free Speech and Social Structure, 71 Iowa L. Rev. 1405, 1408-1410, 1412, 1414, 1416 (1986):

> For the most part, the Free Speech Tradition can be understood as a protection of the street corner speaker. [The] problem, however, is that [the] doctrinal edifice that seems . . . so glorious when we have the street corner speaker in mind is largely unresponsive to the conditions of modern society. [The] Tradition assumes that by leaving individuals alone, free from the menacing arm of the policeman, a full and fair consideration of all the issues will emerge. The premise is that autonomy will lead to rich public debate. [But, in a capitalist society], the protection of autonomy [will] produce a public debate that is dominated by those who are economically powerful. [In such circumstances,] the first amendment can just as easily be threatened by a private person as by an agency of the state. [We] should learn to recognize the state not only as an enemy, but also as a friend of speech. [When] the state acts to enhance the quality of public debate, we should recognize its actions as consistent with the first amendment.

See also Fiss, Why the State?, 100 Harv. L. Rev. 781 (1987).

Page 1232.   After section 3 of the Note, add the following:

3A. *Limiting corporate political speech.* In Austin v. Michigan Chamber of Commerce, 110 S. Ct. 1391 (1990), the Court, in a six to three decision, upheld §54(1) of the Michigan Campaign Finance Act, which prohibited corporations from using corporate treasury funds for independent expenditures in support of or in opposition to any candidate for state office, but allowed corporations to make such expenditures from segregated funds used solely for political purposes.

The Court, in an opinion by Justice Marshall, observed that "the unique legal and economic characteristics of corporations" — such as "limited liability, perpetual life, and favorable treatment of the accumulation and distribution of assets" — enable corporations "to use 'resources amassed in the economic marketplace' to obtain 'an unfair advantage in the political marketplace.'" The Court explained that the political advantage of corporations is unfair because "[t]he resources in the treasury of a business corporation [are] not an indication of popular support for the corporation's political ideas. They reflect instead the economically motivated decisions of investors and customers. The availability of these resources may make a corporation a formidable political presence, even though the power of the corporation may be no reflection of the power of its ideas."

Noting that §54(1) was designed to deal with "the corrosive and distorting effects of immense aggregations of wealth that are accumulated with the help of the corporate form and that have little or no correlation to the public's support for the corporation's political ideas," rather than " 'to equalize the relative influence of speakers on elections,' " the Court held that "the State has articulated a sufficiently compelling rationale to support its restriction on independent expenditures by corporations."

The Court also held that the Act is "sufficiently narrowly tailored to achieve its goal" because it is "precisely targeted to eliminate the distortion caused by corporate political spending while also allowing corporations to express their political views [through] separate segregated funds." The Court explained that because "persons contributing to such funds understand that their money will be used solely for political purposes, the speech generated accurately reflects contributors' support for the corporation's political views."

The Court rejected the Michigan Chamber of Commerce's contention that "even if the [Act] is constitutional with respect to for-profit corporations, it nonetheless cannot be applied to a nonprofit ideological corporation like a chamber of commerce." Specifically, the Chamber argued that this case was governed by FEC v. Massachusetts Citizens for Life, Inc., 479 U.S. 238 (1986), in which the Court had invalidated a provision virtually identical to §54(1) as applied to a nonprofit, political corporation. The Court distinguished *MCFL* on the ground that, unlike the Michigan Chamber of Commerce, the corporation involved in *MCFL* "was formed for the express purpose of promoting political ideas and [could not] engage in business activities," had no "shareholders or other persons affiliated so as to have a claim on its assets or earnings," and was independent "from the influence of business corporations."

Justice Scalia dissented:

[Corporations] are, to be sure, given special advantages, [but] so are other associations and private individuals, [ranging] from tax breaks to contract awards to public employment to outright cash subsidies. It is rudimentary that the State cannot exact as the price of those special advantages the forfeiture of First Amendment rights. [Moreover], the fact that corporations "amas[s] large treasuries" [is] not sufficient justification for the suppression of political speech, unless one thinks it would be lawful to prohibit men and women whose net worth is above a certain figure from endorsing political candidates. [The] Court's opinion ultimately rests upon [the] proposition [that] expenditures must "reflect actual public support for the political ideas espoused." [But why] is it perfectly all right if advocacy by an individual billionaire is out of proportion with "actual public support" for his positions? There is no explanation. [The] object of the law we have approved today is not to prevent wrongdoing but to prevent speech. Since those private associations known as corporations have so much money, they will speak so much more, and their views will be given inordinate prominence in election campaigns. This is not an argument that our democratic traditions allow. . . .

Justice Kennedy, joined by Justices O'Connor and Scalia, also dissented:

[L]imitations on independent political expenditures are subject to exacting First Amendment scrutiny. [In] *Buckley* and *Bellotti* [we] rejected the argument that the expenditure of money to increase the quantity of political speech somehow fosters corruption. The key to the majority's reasoning appears to be that because some corporate speakers are well-supported, [government] may ban all corporate speech to ensure that it will not dominate political debate. The argument is flawed in at least two respects. First, the statute is overinclusive because it covers all groups which use the corporate form, including all nonprofit corporations. Second, it assumes that the government has a legitimate interest in equalizing the relative influence of speakers. [Similar arguments were rightly] rejected in *Bellotti*."

Justice Kennedy maintained further that the ability of a corporation to speak through a separate political action committee could not save the Act:

The argument that the availability of a PAC as an alternative means can save a restriction on independent corporate expenditures [is undermined by the fact that it is] a costly and burdensome disincentive to speech. [Between] 25 and 50 percent of a PAC's funds are required to establish and administer the PAC. While the corporation can direct the PAC to make expenditures on behalf of candidates, the PAC can be funded only by contributions from shareholders, directors, officers, and managerial employees, and cannot receive corporate treasury funds. [This] secondhand endorsement structure [debases] the voice [of] corporate speakers.

Page 1232.   Before section 4 of the Note, add the following:

Consider Schneider, Free Speech and Corporate Freedom: A Comment on *First National Bank of Boston v. Bellotti*, 59 S. Cal. L. Rev. 1227, 1257, 1287 (1986):

[The] corporation has a special relationship with the state which justifies treating corporate speech differently from an individual's speech. This special relationship [inheres] in the fact that the corporate form is [the] creature of the state. [The] state may presumably decline to make the corporate form available, and it is hard to see why the corporate form's ability to produce speech ought to constrain the state's authority to define the corporate form's limits. [The] Court's [analysis in *Bellotti* is] impaired by [its] unwillingness to acknowledge that large institutions controlling large agglomerations of wealth are problematic in a democracy. [To] ignore the reality of the corporation [in *Bellotti*] is as unwise as ignoring the reality of the employer's economic power was in *Lochner*.

Page 1234. After the quotation at the top of the page, add the following:

Consider also Austin v. Michigan Chamber of Commerce, 110 S. Ct. 1391 (1990), in which the Court rejected a claim that a law restricting political expenditures by corporations violated the equal protection clause because it does not similarly restrict unincorporated labor unions or "media" corporations. The Court conceded that labor unions, like individuals, may amass large treasuries, but found it dispositive that they do so "without the significant state-conferred advantages of the corporate structure." The Court explained further that a "valid distinction [exists] between corporations that are part of the media industry and other corporations [because of] the unique role the press play in 'informing and educating the public.' "

Page 1236. Before subsection 4 of the Note, add the following:

3A. *Prohibiting paid petitioners.* In Meyer v. Grant, 486 U.S. 414 (1988), the Court invalidated a Colorado statute prohibiting the use of paid circulators to obtain signatures for petitions to qualify proposed state constitutional amendments for inclusion on the general election ballot:

> The circulation of an initiative petition [involves] both the expression of a desire for political change and a discussion of the merits of the proposed change. [Thus], the circulation of a petition involves the type of interactive communication [that] is appropriately described as "core political speech."
>
> The refusal to permit appellees to pay petition circulators restricts political expression in two ways: First, it limits the number of voices who will convey appellees' message and the hours they can speak and, therefore, limits the size of the audience they can reach. Second, it makes it less likely that appellees will garner the number of signatures necessary to place the matter on the ballot, thus limiting their ability to make the matter the focus of statewide attention. . . .
>
> That appellees remain free to employ other means to disseminate their ideas does not take their speech through petition circulators outside the bounds of First Amendment protection. Colorado's prohibition of paid petition circulators restricts access to the most effective, fundamental, and perhaps economical avenue of political discourse, direct one-on-one communication. That it leaves open "more burdensome" avenues of communication, does not relieve its burden on First Amendment expression. The First Amendment protects appellees' right not only to advocate their cause but also to select what they believe to be the most effective means for so doing.
>
> Relying on Posadas [Supplement to Casebook page 1104 supra], Colorado contends that because the power of initiative is a state-created right, it is free to impose limitations on the exercise of that right. [But Posadas] "is inapplicable to the present case [because] the speech restricted in Posadas was merely 'commercial speech' " [whereas this] statute trenches upon an area in which the importance of First Amend-

ment protections "is at its zenith." For that reason the burden that Colorado must overcome to justify this criminal law is well-nigh insurmountable.

We are not persuaded by the State's arguments that the prohibition is justified by its interest in making sure that an initiative has sufficient grass roots support to be placed on the ballot, or by its interest in protecting the integrity of the initiative process.

Page 1243.   After *Roberts*, add the following:

A unanimous Court followed *Roberts* in Board of Directors of Rotary International v. Rotary Club of Duarte, 481 U.S. 537 (1987). The Court upheld the constitutionality of a California antidiscrimination statute that required the Rotary Club to admit women. See also New York State Club Assn., Inc. v. City of New York, 487 U.S. 1 (1988), in which the Court unanimously upheld a New York City Human Rights law that banned discrimination on the basis of race, creed, or sex in any institution, club or place of accommodation that has more than 400 members, provides regular meal service, and regularly receives payment from nonmembers for the furtherance of trade or business.

Page 1243.   At the end of the page, add the following:

In Tashjian v. Republican Party, 479 U.S. 208 (1987), the Court invalidated on first amendment grounds a state law that precluded independents from voting in party primaries. For a fuller discussion, see infra at Supp. to page 1527.

NOTE: CONTENT-NEUTRAL RESTRICTIONS — FINAL THOUGHTS

Consider the following evaluation: The Court has long recognized that by limiting the availability of particular means of communication, content-neutral restrictions can significantly impair the ability of individuals to communicate their views to others. This is a central first amendment concern. The Court generally tests content-neutral restrictions with an implicit balancing approach: The greater the interference with the opportunities for free expression, the greater the burden on government to justify the restriction. When the challenged restriction has a relatively severe effect, the Court invokes strict scrutiny. See, e.g., *Button*; *Buckley* (expenditure limitations); *Roberts*. When the challenged restriction has a significant but not severe effect, the Court employs intermediate scrutiny. See, e.g., *Schneider*; *Buckley*; (contribution limitations); *Martin*. And when the restriction has a relatively modest effect, the Court applies deferential scrutiny. See, e.g., *O'Brien*; *Heffron*; *Clark*. There are exceptions to the pattern and those exceptions are often quite revealing, for they suggest the impact of additional factors, such as public property and incidental effect, that at times trump the central concern of content-neutral analysis. But the general pattern is clear: As the restrictive effect increases, the standard of review increases as well. See Stone, Content-Neutral Restrictions, 54 U. Chi. L. Rev. 46 (1987).

Is this an accurate description of the Court's analysis? If so, does it reflect a satisfactory approach? Consider Stone, supra, at 78-79:

> In its decisions involving content-neutral restrictions that have significant or severe effects on the opportunities for free expression, the Court has been reasonably protective of speech. Decisions such as *Buckley*, *Button*, [and *Roberts*] demonstrate a thoughtful concern for the system of free expression and a healthy skepticism about the government's need to restrict free speech to achieve its ends.
>
> In its decisions involving content-neutral restrictions that have only modest effects on the opportunities for free expression, however, the Court too often has exhibited insensitivity to the importance of nontraditional means of expression, the uncertainty of its own judgments, and the dangers of undue deference to legislative and administrative officials. [Although] the Court has generally applied low-level scrutiny in the right cases, its low-level scrutiny is simply too low.
>
> Even when a particular content-neutral restriction has only a modest effect on the total quantity of public debate because the speaker can shift to alternative means of expression, some weight should be given to the speaker's choice of means, since the speaker can be presumed to have chosen the most effective means available. [A] modest effect, in other words, is not no effect. [And even a modest interference with free expression should be] sufficient to require the government to offer some meaningful explanation for its refusal to accommodate free speech.

See also Lee, Lonely Pamphleteers, Little People, and the Supreme Court: The Doctrine of Time, Place, and Manner Regulations of Expression, 54 Geo. Wash. L. Rev. 757 (1986).

F. ADDITIONAL PROBLEMS

Page 1249.   At the end of subsection 5 of the Note, add the following:

5A. *The reach of* Mosley: Boos. In Boos v. Barry, 485 U.S. 312 (1988), the Court invalidated as an impermissible "content-based restriction on political speech in a public forum" a provision of the District of Columbia Code that made it unlawful, within 500 feet of a foreign embassy, to display any sign that tends to bring the foreign government into "public odium" or "public disrepute."

Page 1249.   Before section 6 of the Note, add the following:

See also Board of Education of Westside Community School v. Mergens, 110 S. Ct. — (1990), holding that the federal Equal Access Act, which requires "any public secondary school which receives Federal financial assistance and which has a limited open forum to deny equal access [to] any students who wish to conduct a meeting within that limited open forum on the basis of the religious, political, philosophical, or other content of the speech at such meetings," does not violate the establishment clause.

Page 1254.   After the quote from Wells & Hellerstein in subsection b of the Note, add the following:

See also United States v. Kokinda, 110 S. Ct. — (1990), in which a plurality, following *Lehman,* invoked the proprietary-governmental distinction in upholding a postal service regulation prohibiting any person from soliciting contributions on post office property.

Page 1259.   Before section 5 of the Note, add the following:

4A. *"Even-handed" regulation in nonpublic forums.* Does it follow from *Perry* that restrictions on first amendment activity are always permissible in a nonpublic forum so long as they do not constitute "an effort to suppress expression merely because public officials oppose the speaker's view"? Consider Board of Airport Commissioners v. Jews for Jesus, 482 U.S. 569 (1987). The Los Angeles Board of Airport Commissioners adopted a resolution banning all first amendment activity in the Los Angeles International Airport. Respondents, who were prevented from distributing religious literature in the airport, claimed that the resolution violated their free speech rights. A unanimous Court, in an opinion by Justice O'Connor, held that it need not decide whether the airport was a public forum because the resolution was facially overbroad even as applied to nonpublic forums.

> On its face, the resolution [reaches] the universe of expressive activity, and, by prohibiting *all* protected expression, purports to create a virtual "First Amendment Free Zone" at [the airport]. . . .
>
> The petitioners suggest that the resolution is not substantially overbroad because it is intended to reach only expressive activity unrelated to airport-related purposes. Such a limiting construction, however, is of little [assistance]. Much nondisruptive speech — such as the wearing of a T-Shirt or button that contains a political message — may not be "airport related," but is still protected speech even in a nonpublic forum.

Justice White, joined by Chief Justice Rehnquist, filed a concurring opinion emphasizing that the Court's opinion "should not be taken as indicating that a majority of the Court considers the Los Angeles International Airport to be a traditional public forum."

4B. *The reach of Perry:* Kokinda. Respondents, members of a political advocacy group, set up a table on a sidewalk near the entrance to a United States Post Office to distribute literature and solicit contributions. The sidewalk is located entirely on post office property and is the sole means by which customers travel from the parking lot to the post office building. Respondents were convicted of violating a regulation prohibiting any person from soliciting contributions on postal premises. In United States v. Kokinda, 110 S. Ct. — (1990), the Court upheld the regulation as applied.

In a plurality opinion, Justice O'Connor, joined by Chief Justice Rehnquist and Justices White and Scalia, concluded that the sidewalk is not a "traditional" public forum because the "postal sidewalk at issue does not have the characteristics of public sidewalks traditionally open to expressive activity." See section E, supra. O'Connor then rejected the claim that the sidewalk, which was available for all conventional forms of expressive activity other than solicitation, was a "limited-purpose" public forum:

> The Postal Service has not expressly dedicated its sidewalks to any expressive activity. [Although] individuals or groups have been permitted to leaflet, speak, and picket on postal premises, [the] practice of allowing some speech activities on postal property [does] not add up to the dedication of postal property to speech activities. ["The] government does not create a public forum by . . . *permitting* limited discouse, but only by intentionally opening a nontraditional forum for public discourse." [*Cornelius*]. [It] is anomalous [to suggest] that the Service's allowance of some avenues of speech would be relied upon as evidence that it is impermissibly suppressing other speech. If anything, the Service's generous accommodation of some types of speech testifies to its willingness to provide as broad a forum as possible, consistent with its postal mission. [Any other view] would create, in the name of the First Amendment, a disincentive for the Government to dedicate its property to any speech activities at all.

Justice Kennedy concurred in the result on the ground that the regulation would be permissible even in a traditional public forum. Justice Brennan, joined by Justices Marshall, Blackmun and Stevens, dissented:

> Even if I did not believe that the postal sidewalk is a "traditional" public [forum], I would find that it is a "limited-purpose" [forum]. We have recognized that even where a forum would not exist but for the decision of government to create it, the government's power to enforce exclusions from the forum is narrowly circumscribed if the government permits a wide range of expression to occur. [This] sidewalk is a limited-purpose forum [in] light of the wide range of expressive activities that are permitted. [The] plurality has collapsed the distinction between exclusions that help define the contours of the forum and those that are imposed *after* the forum is defined. Because the plurality finds that the prohibition on solicitation is part of the definition of the forum, it does not view the regulation as operating on a public forum and hence subjects the postal regulation to only a "reasonableness" inquiry. If, however, the ban

on solicitation were found to be an independent restriction on speech occurring in a limited public forum, it would be judged according to stricter scrutiny. The plurality's approach highlights the fact that there is only a semantic distinction between the two ways in which exclusions from a limited-purpose forum can be characterized. . . .

Page 1272. Before *Jones*, add the following:

In Bethel School Dist. No. 403 v. Fraser, 478 U.S. 675 (1986), the Court distinguished *Tinker* and rejected a first amendment attack on a public high school's decision to discipline a student for speech containing sexual innuendo. Respondent delivered the speech, nominating a fellow student for student elective office, to a high school assembly of approximately 600 students:

> I know a man who is firm — he's firm in his pants, he's firm in his shirt, his character is firm — but most [of] all, his belief in you, the students of Bethel, is firm.
>
> Jeff Kuhlman is a man who takes his point and pounds it in. If necessary, he'll take an issue and nail it to the wall. He doesn't attack things in spurts — he drives hard, pushing and pushing until finally — he succeeds.
>
> Jeff is a man who will go to the very end — even the climax, for each and every one of you.

There was evidence before the trial court that during the speech some students hooted, yelled, and made gestures simulating the sexual activities alluded to in the speech, while others appeared bewildered and embarrassed. One teacher reported that she found it necessary to forgo a portion of her scheduled class on the following day in order to discuss the speech.

When the school disciplined respondent by suspending him for two days, he brought this action alleging a violation of his free speech rights. The district court found that the disciplinary measures were unconstitutional and the court of appeals, relying upon *Tinker*, affirmed.

In an opinion by Chief Justice Burger, the Court reversed. It criticized the lower court for ignoring the "marked distinction between the political 'message' of the armbands in *Tinker* and the sexual content of respondent's speech in this case," and noted that the *Tinker* Court had limited its holding to speech that did not intrude upon the work of the schools or the rights of other students:

> Unlike the sanctions imposed on the students wearing armbands in *Tinker*, the penalties imposed in this case were unrelated to any political viewpoint. The First Amendment does not prevent the school officials from determining that to permit a vulgar and lewd speech such as respondent's would undermine the school's basic educational mission. A high school assembly or classroom is no place for a sexually explicit monologue directed towards an unsuspecting audience of teenage students. Accordingly, it was perfectly appropriate for the school to disassociate itself to make the point to the pupils that vulgar speech and lewd conduct is wholly inconsistent with the "fundamental values" of public school education.

Justice Blackmun concurred in the result, and Justice Brennan wrote a separate concurring opinion. Justices Marshall and Stevens dissented.

In Hazelwood School District v. Kuhlmeier, 484 U.S. 260 (1988), the Court upheld a high school principal's exclusion of two stories from a school newspaper, written and edited by students in conjunction with a course in journalism. One story dealt with the experiences of some of the school's students with pregnancy, the other discussed the impact of divorce on several students at the school. The Court explained:

> The question whether the First Amendment requires a school to tolerate particular student speech — the question [addressed] in *Tinker* — is different from the question whether the First Amendment requires a school affirmatively to promote particular student speech. The former question addresses educators' ability to silence a student's personal expression that happens to occur on the school premises. The latter question concerns educators' authority over school-sponsored publications, theatrical productions, and other expressive activities that students, parents, and members of the public might reasonably perceive to bear the imprimatur of the school. These activities may fairly be characterized as part of the school curriculum, whether or not they occur in a traditional classroom setting, so long as they are supervised by faculty members and designed to impart particular knowledge or skills to student participants and audiences.
>
> Educators are entitled to exercise greater control over this second form of student expression to assure that participants learn whatever lessons the activity is designed to teach, that readers or listeners are not exposed to material that may be inappropriate for their level of maturity, and that the views of the individual speaker are not erroneously attributed to the school. . . .
>
> Accordingly, we conclude that the standard articulated in *Tinker* for determining when a school may punish student expression need not also be the standard for determining when a school may refuse to lend its name and resources to the dissemination of student expression. Instead, we hold that educators do not offend the First Amendment by exercising editorial control over the style and content of student speech in school-sponsored expressive activities so long as their actions are reasonably related to legitimate pedagogical concerns.

Applying this standard, the Court held that the principal's exclusion of the pregnancy story was "reasonable" because, although the students discussed had consented to the article and fictitious names had been used, it was nonetheless possible that the students discussed could be identified by other facts presented in the story, thus breaching "whatever pledge of anonymity had been given to the pregnant students." Moreover, because the article included some discussion of sexuality and birth control, "it was not unreasonable for the principal to have concluded that such frank talk was inappropriate in a school-sponsored publication distributed to 14-year-old freshmen and presumably taken home to be read by students' even younger brothers and sisters." The Court held that the principal's exclusion of the divorce story was reasonable because one of the students quoted in the article had made "comments sharply critical of her father" and the "principal could reasonably have concluded that an individual publicly identified as an inattentive parent [was] entitled to an opportunity to defend himself as a matter of journalistic fairness."

Justice Brennan, joined by Justices Marshall and Blackmun, dissented. Justice Brennan argued that *Tinker* should govern this case and that, under the *Tinker* standard, there was no legitimate basis to exclude the stories. In his view, no special standard was required to deal with the problems of curriculum or school-sponsored expression. Rather, the "disruption" element of *Tinker* should simply be applied in terms of special characteristics of the curriculum or the other school-sponsored activities.

Consider Hafen, *Hazelwood School District* and the Role of First Amendment Institutions, 1988 Duke L.J. 685, 691-692, 704:

> *Hazelwood* now makes clear [that] *Fraser* [was] an important transitional case that signalled the Court's [recognition] that broad interpretations of *Tinker* [had] reduced schools' institutional authority in ways that undermined their educational effectiveness. [*Hazelwood*] reminds us [that] the idea of *in loco parentis* [can be] a needed means of protecting the right of children to develop their capacity for meaningful expression [and that] first amendment institutions such as schools and churches [can] be a vital means of fostering long-term personal liberty. [Indeed, the] first amendment must [protect] not only individual students and teachers, but [the autonomy of schools as well, for such institutions] form a critical part of the constitutional structure. . . .

Page 1273. Before section 3, add the following:

In Turner v. Safley, 482 U.S. 78 (1987), the Court distinguished *Procunier* and upheld a prison regulation generally prohibiting correspondence between inmates at different institutions. In an opinion by Justice O'Connor, the Court held that prison regulations impinging on the constitutional rights of inmates were valid if they are "reasonably related to legitimate penological interests." Justice Stevens, joined by Justices Brennan, Marshall, and Blackmun, dissented. Thornburg v. Abbott, 109 S. Ct. 1874 (1989), partially overruled *Procunier* by holding that prison officials could regulate publications coming into the prison if their rules were reasonably related to legitimate penological standards, although mail from the prison to the outside could be regulated only under the stricter *Martinez* standard. The Court said that the risks to institutional security posed by incoming mail were more substantial than those posed by outgoing mail.

Consider Post, Between Governance and Management: The History and Theory of the Public Forum, 34 U.C.L.A. L. Rev. 1713, 1816-1819 (1987):

> Total institutions, like the military [and] the prison, [attempt] to regulate "all aspects of life . . . in the same place and under the same single authority." Total institutions not only physically separate their members from the larger society, but

they also attempt to the maximum extent possible to strip away from their members statuses associated with that society, and to impose instead a uniform institutional identity. [Judicial] review of administrative decisions in the context of total institutions poses the possibility of three distinct kinds of adverse consequences to managerial authority: ["contamination" of the separateness and insulation of the institution], destruction of organizational culture, and the loss of needed flexibility. [The] pertinence and weight of these [concerns] will vary depending upon the specific kind of decision, authority, and institution that is at issue.

Page 1274. After the Kreimer quotation, add the following:

d. Westen, The Rueful Rhetoric of "Rights," 33 U.C.L.A. L. Rev. 977, 996-997, 999, 1005 (1986):

> Why [do] courts and commentators [regard] the doctrine of unconstitutional conditions as so forceful? [The] answer, I believe, is that the doctrine [exploits] a rhetorical ambiguity in the concept of "rights." [We] use the word "rights" in "two distinct senses." We sometimes use "rights" in a "conclusory" sense to refer to things to which a person is actually *entitled*. An entitlement is the end product of our having determined that a given person [is] justified in demanding something [under certain circumstances]. Sometimes, however, we use "rights" to refer not to entitlements, but to certain kinds of *interests* [which, depending on the circumstances and the strength and nature of the state's countervailing interests may or may not] support an entitlement. [The latter use of the word "rights" in the context of the unconstitutional condition doctrine tends to] give rights discourse undeserved rhetorical force.

Page 1283. At the end of the Note, add the following:

Compare *Connick* with Rankin v. McPherson, 483 U.S. 378 (1987). Respondent, a clerical employee in the office of a county constable, was fired when, after hearing of an assassination attempt against the President, she remarked to a co-worker, "If they go for him again, I hope they get him." The Court, in an opinion by Justice Marshall, held that the remark constituted speech on a matter of public concern and that the discharge violated the first amendment.

> The statement was made in the course of a conversation addressing the policies of the President's administration. It came on the heels of a news bulletin regarding what is certainly a matter of heightened public attention: an attempt on the life of the President. [The] inappropriate or controversial character of a statement is irrelevant to the question whether it deals with a matter of public concern.

Having found that the statement met the threshold "public concern" requirement, the Court went on to balance appellee's first amendment interests against the state's interest in the "effective functioning of the public employer's enterprise." Because the Court found no evidence that appellee's statement had interfered with the efficient functioning of the office, the Court held that the first amendment interests predominated. Justice Scalia, joined by Chief Justice Rehnquist and Justices White and O'Connor, dissented.

Page 1287. Before section d, add the following:

RUTAN v. REPUBLICAN PARTY OF ILLINOIS, 110 S. Ct. — (1990);
In Rutan, the Court, in an opinion by Justice Brennan, rejected the argument that "only those employment decisions that are the 'substantial equivalent of a dismissal' violate a public employee's rights under the First Amendment," and extended *Elrod* and *Branti* to decisions about hiring, "promotions, transfers and recalls after layoffs based on political affiliation or support."

In dissent, Justice Scalia, joined by Chief Justice Rehnquist and Justices O'Connor and Kennedy, called for *Elrod* and *Branti* to be overruled: "The Court [indicates] that the government may prevail [in this case] only if it proves that the practice is 'narrowly tailored to further vital governmental interests.' That strict-scrutiny standard finds no support in our cases. Although our decisions establish that government employees do not lose all constitutional rights, we have consistently applied a lower level of scrutiny when 'the government [functions not] as lawmaker, [but], rather, as proprietor, to manage [its] internal operatio[ns].' When dealing with its own employees, the government may not act in a manner that is 'patently arbitrary or discriminatory,' but its regulations are valid if they bear a 'rational connection' to the governmental end sought to be served, [citing *Mitchell, Letter Carriers, Broadrick, Pickering,* and *Connick*]. Since the government may dismiss an employee for political *speech* 'reasonably deemed by Congress to interfere with the efficiency of the public service,' [*Mitchell*], it follows *a fortiori* that the government may dismiss an employee for political *affiliation* if 'reasonably necessary to promote effective government.' "

Invoking the arguments Justice Powell offered in his *Elrod* dissent about the importance of patronage and pointing to the problems lower courts have encountered in their efforts to apply *Elrod* and *Branti,* Scalia concluded not only that "our balancing test is amply met," but also that "*Elrod* and *Branti* should be overruled": "Even in the field of constitutional adjudication, where the pull of *stare decisis* is at its weakest, one is reluctant to depart from precedent. But when that precedent is not only wrong, not only recent, not only contradicted by a long prior tradition, but also has proved unworkable in practice, then all reluctance ought to disappear. [That] is the situation here."

In another part of his opinion, joined only by Chief Justice Rehnquist and Justice Kennedy, Scalia added: "The provisions of the Bill of Rights were designed to restrain transient majorities from impairing long-recognized personal liberties. They did not create by implication novel individual rights overturning accepted political norms. Thus, when a practice not expressly prohibited by the text of the Bill of Rights bears the endorsement of a long tradition of open, widespread, and unchallenged use that dates back to the beginning of the Republic, we have no proper basis for striking it down. Such a venerable and accepted tradition is not to be laid on the examining table and scrutinized for its conformity to some abstract principle of First-Amendment adjuducation devised by this Court. To the contrary, such traditions are themselves the stuff out of which the Court's principles are to be formed. They are, in these uncertain areas, the very points of reference by which the legitimacy or illegitimacy of *other* practices are to be figured out. When it appears that the latest 'rule,' or 'three-part test,' or 'balancing test' devised by the Court has placed us on a collision course with such a landmark practice, it is the former that must be recalculated by us, and not the latter that must be abandoned by our citizens. I know of no other way to formulate a constitutional jurisprudence that reflects [the] principles adhered to, over time, by the American people, rather than those favored by the personal (and necessarily shifting) philosophical dispositions of a majority of this Court. [Patronage] was, without any thought that it could be unconstitutional, a basis for government employment from the earliest days of the Republic until *Elrod* — and has continued unabated *since Elrod,* to the extent still permitted by that unfortunate decision. [Given] that unbroken tradition regarding the application of an ambiguous constitutional text, there was in my view no basis for holding that patronage-based dismissal violated the First Amendment."

Page 1298. Before subsection 1b of the Note, add the following:

But consider Sunstein, Government Control of Information, 74 Calif. L. Rev. 889, 916-917 (1986):

> This argument relies on property-based notions of information ownership, notions that treat the government like a private citizen who owns information. [But the relevant] precedents here are the public forum cases, which [turn] on the understanding that government ownership of property does not necessarily dispose of a first amendment claim. Government must justify restrictions by reference to something other than ownership.

Page 1299. Before section 2 of the Note, add the following:

For a critique of this view, see Sunstein, Government Control of Information, 74 Calif. L. Rev. 889 (1986).

Page 1299. Before section 3 of the Note, add the following:

But compare Sunstein, Government Control of Information, 74 Calif. L. Rev. 889, 915 (1986):

[The] first amendment is largely a structural provision. [Its] purpose is not only to protect private autonomy, but also to preserve a certain form of government. Citizens may often find it in their interest to give up rights of free speech in exchange for benefits from government. For many, these rights are not extremely valuable as individual possessions. But if government is permitted to obtain enforceable waivers, the aggregate effect may be considerable, and the deliberative processes of the public will be skewed. [Waivers] of first amendment rights thus affect people other than government employees, and effects on third parties are a classic reason to proscribe waivers. The analogy [is] to government purchases of voting rights, which are impermissible even if voters willingly assent.

Page 1302.   Before *Elrod*, add the following:

PACIFIC GAS & ELECTRIC CO. v. PUBLIC UTILITIES COMMISSION, 475 U.S. 1 (1986):   A privately owned electric company distributed in its monthly billing envelope a newsletter, which included political editorials, feature stories, tips on energy conservation, and information about utility services and bills. The state public utilities commission determined that the "extra space" in billing envelopes (i.e., the difference between the weight purchased by a 22-cent stamp and the weight of the bill) used to distribute the newsletter belonged to the ratepayers. It further held that the company must allow Toward Utility Rate Normalization (TURN), a private advocacy group, to utilize the extra space four times per year to communicate with customers of the company. The company contended that requiring it to include in its billing envelopes the speech of a third party with which it disagreed violated its first amendment rights.

Justice Powell announced the Court's judgment in an opinion joined by Chief Justice Burger, Justice Brennan, and Justice O'Connor: "Corporations and other associations, like individuals, contribute to the 'discussion, debate, and the dissemination of information and ideas' that the First Amendment seeks to foster. [*Bellotti*]. [There] is [thus] no doubt that [the Company's] newsletter [receives] the full protection of the First Amendment. . . .

"Compelled access like that ordered in this case both penalizes the expression of particular points of view and forces speakers to alter their speech to conform with an agenda they do not set. These impermissible effects are not remedied by the Commission's definition of the relevant property rights.

"The Court's decision in [*PruneYard*] is not to the contrary. [Notably] absent from *PruneYard* was any concern that access to this area might affect the shopping center owner's exercise of his own right to speak. [*PruneYard*] does not undercut the proposition that forced associations that burden protected speech are impermissible. . . .

"The order does not simply award access to the public at large; rather, it discriminates on the basis of the viewpoints of the selected speakers. Two of the acknowledged purposes of the access order are to offer the public a greater variety of views in [the Company's] billing envelope, and to assist groups (such as TURN) that challenge [the Company] in the Commission's ratemaking proceedings in raising funds. [Access] to the envelopes thus is not content-neutral. . . .

"[Because] access is awarded only to those who disagree with [the Company's] views and who are hostile to its interests, [the Company] must contend with the fact that whenever it speaks out on a given issue, it may be forced — at TURN's discretion — to help disseminate hostile views. [The Company] 'might well conclude' that, under these circumstances, 'the safe course is to avoid controversy,' thereby reducing the free flow of information and ideas that the First Amendment seeks to promote. . . .

"The Commission's access order also impermissibly requires [the Company] to associate with speech with which [it] may disagree. [For] corporations as for individuals, the choice to speak includes within it the choice of what not to say. [Were] the government freely able to compel corporate speakers to propound political messages with which they disagree, this protection would be empty, for the government could require speakers to affirm in one breath that which they deny in the next. . . .

"The Commission expressly declined to hold that under California law [the Company's] customers own the entire billing envelopes and everything contained therein. It decided only that the ratepayers own the 'extra space' in the envelope, defined as that space left over after including the bill and required notices, up to a weight of one ounce. The envelopes themselves, the bills, and [the Company newsletter] all remain [the Company's] property. The Commission's access order thus clearly requires [the Company] to use *its* property as a vehicle for spreading a message with which it disagrees. . . ."

Chief Justice Burger filed a concurring opinion, and Justice Marshall filed an opinion concurring in the judgment.

Justice Rehnquist filed a dissenting opinion. In a portion of the opinion joined by Justices White and Stevens, he made the following argument: "Of course, the First Amendment [prohibits] governmental action affecting the mix of information available to the public if the effect of the action approximates that of direct content-based suppression of speech. [But] the deterrent effect of any statute is an empirical question of degree. When the potential deterrent effect of a particular state law is remote and speculative, the law simply is not subject to heightened First Amendment scrutiny. [This is not a reply statute, which conditions] access upon discrete instances of certain expression, [and] the right of access here bears no relationship to [the Company's] future conduct. [Indeed, the Company here] cannot prevent the access by remaining silent or avoiding discussion of controversial subjects."

In a portion of his dissent not joined by White and Stevens, Rehnquist made the following additional arguments: "This Court has recognized that natural persons enjoy negative free speech rights because of their interest in self-expression. [We have] extended negative free speech rights to newspapers without much discussion. [See *Tornillo*, section 6-C infra of the main text.] Extension of the individual freedom of conscience decisions to business corporations strains the rationale of those cases beyond the breaking point. To ascribe to such artificial entities an 'intellect' or 'mind' for freedom of conscience purposes is to confuse metaphor with reality. Corporations generally have not played the historic role of newspapers as conveyers of individual ideas and opinion."

Justice Stevens filed a separate dissent: "I assume that the plurality would not object to a utility commission rule dictating the format of the bill, even as to required warnings and the type size of various provisos and disclaimers. [I] assume also the plurality would permit the Commission to require the utility to disseminate legal notices of public hearings and ratemaking proceedings written by it. [Given] that the Commission can require the utility to make certain statements and to carry the Commission's own messages to its customers, it seems but a small step to acknowledge that the Commission can also require the utility to act as the conduit for a public interest group's message that bears a close relationship to the purpose of the billing envelope."

Page 1304.   Before the third full paragraph, add the following:

In Chicago Teachers Union Local No. 1 v. Hudson, 475 U.S. 292 (1986), the Court struck down the procedures adopted by a union for considering objections to "fair share" payments assessed against nonunion members. The Court held that the constitutional requirements a union must satisfy in order to collect such payments include provision of an adequate explanation of the basis for the fee, provision of a reasonably prompt opportunity to challenge the amount of the fee before an impartial decisionmaker, and establishment of an escrow account for the amounts reasonably in dispute while such challenges are pending.

Page 1304.   At the end of paragraph before the beginning of the Note, add the following:

See also Keller v. State Bar of California, 110 S. Ct. — (1990) (an integrated state bar association may not use compulsory dues to finance political and ideological activities with which particular members disagree when such expenditures are not "necessarily or reasonably incurred for the purpose of regulating the legal profession or improving the quality of legal services").

Page 1304.   Before the note, add the following:

Consider Harpaz, Justice Jackson's Flag Salute Legacy: The Supreme Court Struggles to Protect Intellectual Individualism, 64 Tex. L. Rev. 817 (1986), arguing that the cases in this section should be understood as posing two distinct problems: Cases like *Barnette*, in which the "government compulsion creates a serious risk of forced conformity to government-favored ideas," should be tested by strict scrutiny; whereas cases like *Wooley, PruneYard, Abood,* and *Pacific Gas & Electric,* which "involve a less serious challenge to first amendment values" because the government coercion involves "a lesser impact on individual conscience" and is "less likely to discourage the individual from expressing contrary ideas," should be tested by more deferential scrutiny.

Page 1305.   After section 2 of the Note, add the following:

2A. *The right to be free of government denigration of speech.* Should there be a constitutional right to suppress *government* speech that has the purpose or effect of denigrating or chilling first amendment activity? In Meese v. Keene, 481 U.S. 465 (1987), the Court, in an opinion by Justice Stevens, rejected the claim that a government decision to label as "political propaganda" three Canadian movies concerning the environmental effects of nuclear war and "acid rain" violated free speech rights.

Under the Foreign Agents Registration Act, all agents of foreign principles must file detailed registration statements describing the nature of their business and their political activities. When a foreign principal disseminates "political propaganda," she must provide the recipient of the material with a disclosure statement on a form prescribed by the Attorney General and label the material with certain information. The Act defines political propaganda to include political material intended to influence the foreign policies of the United States, or that may reasonably be adapted for such use. The films in question were distributed by the National Film Board of Canada, which had registered as an agent of a foreign principle, and the Justice Department determined that they fit within the definition of "political propaganda."

The Court began its first amendment analysis by noting that the attack on the statute rested "not on what [it] actually says, requires, or prohibits, but rather upon a potential misunderstanding of its effect." As defined in the statute, the term "political propaganda" included "advocacy materials that are completely accurate and merit the closest attention and the highest respect." Although others might misinterpret the term, "[as] judges, it is our duty to construe legislation as it is written, not as it might be read by a layman, or as it might be understood by someone who has not even read it."

Moreover, in the Court's view, the statute did not prohibit a distributor "from advising his audience that the films have not been officially censured in any way. [By] compelling some disclosure of information and permitting more, the Act's approach recognizes that the best remedy for misleading or inaccurate speech [is] fair, truthful, and accurate speech."

Justice Blackmun, joined by Justices Brennan and Marshall, dissented:

> I can conclude only that the Court has asked, and has answered, the wrong question. Appellee does not argue that his speech is deterred by the statutory definition of "propaganda." He argues, instead, that his speech is deterred by the common perception that material so classified is unreliable and not to be trusted, bolstered by the added weight and authority accorded any classification made by the all-pervasive Federal Government. Even if the statutory definition is neutral, it is the common understanding of the Government's action that determines the effect on discourse protected by the First Amendment.

Page 1320.   After the quotation from H. Kalven, add the following:

Consider also R. Nagel, Constitutional Cultures 41-42 (1989):

> In *Gibson*, the Court did not deny that knowledge of whether communists had infiltrated the NAACP would have been of great importance [not] only for possible legislation, but also for evaluating both the membership of the NAACP and the messages coming out of the organization. In short, the Court "protected" free speech by denying the public access to important information. Moreover, the Court's reasons for doing so sharply conflicted with traditional first amendment theory. The Court feared that potential exposure of membership lists would burden association rights because the public might misunderstand or misuse the information. The decision thus rested on the belief that an "open market" of ideas could not be trusted.

Page 1326.   Before section c, add the following:

The Court relied upon *Minneapolis Star & Tribune Co.* in Arkansas Writers' Project, Inc. v. Ragland, 481 U.S. 221 (1987), to invalidate an Arkansas statute that imposed a state sales tax on general interest magazines, but exempted newspapers and religious, professional, trade, and sports journals. In an opinion written by Justice Marshall, the Court held that selective taxation of the press — either by singling out the press as a whole, or by singling out individual members of the press — posed particular dangers of governmental abuse. The Arkansas statute evidenced an even more disturbing use of selective taxation than in *Minneapolis Star* because the discrimination was content based.

In a dissenting opinion joined by Chief Justice Rehnquist, Justice Scalia argued that the tax exemption should not be subject to strict scrutiny because it amounted to a subsidy that infringed no one's rights.

> The reason that denial of participation in a tax exemption or other subsidy scheme does not necessarily "infringe" a fundamental right is that — unlike direct restriction

or prohibition — such a denial does not, as a general rule, have any significant coercive effect. . . .

The Kennedy Center, which is subsidized by the Federal Government, [is] authorized by statute to "present classical and contemporary music, opera, drama, dance, and poetry." Is this subsidy subject to strict scrutiny because other kinds of expressive activity, such as learned lectures and political speeches are excluded? Are government research grant programs or the funding activities of the Corporation for Public Broadcasting subject to strict scrutiny because they provide money for the study or exposition of some subject but not others?

Because there is no principled basis to distinguish the subsidization of speech in these areas — which we would surely uphold — from the subsidization that we strike down here, our decision today places the granting or denial of protection within our own idiosyncratic discretion.

Consider Bezanson, Political Agnosticism, Editorial Freedom, and Government Neutrality Toward the Press, 72 Iowa L. Rev. 1359, 1371 (1987): "The Court's reason for making constitutionally suspect any formal singling out of the press was to protect the political neutrality of the press [and to] prevent the government from undermining the [neutrality of the press] by forcing [it] to engage actively in the political process [to] protect its own self-interest."

Page 1327.   At the end of the opinion in *Tornillo*, add the following:

Consider Powe, *Tornillo*, 1987 Sup. Ct. Rev. 345, 380-381:

The principal argument for a right of reply is that under [certain] circumstances editorial discretion can be improved because a reply will enhance public debate by placing more information in the wider public domain. Yet this assertion is incorrect and misleading. [It] is most realistic to expect that a reply to an editorial will displace material that would otherwise appear on the editorial pages. . . . [Thus,] a reply will add information about a subject already discussed, with the result that some other subject, otherwise fit for the editorial pages, will receive less attention or none at all. [A] legislature has concluded that we are better served by [this state of affairs, but it] is not clear [whether] this is accurate or whether any readers of the newspaper will believe they are better served by this substitution.

Page 1327.   After the quotation from Schmidt, add the following:

On the other hand, consider Powe, *Tornillo*, 1987 Sup. Ct. Rev. 345, 391:

Given the principle of press autonomy, what was essential in *Tornillo* was an immediate halt to the notion that newspapers have enjoyed too many rights and should be placed under some legal duties to the reading public. If this movement were not halted in one shot, then the traditional barrier would be down and the legislative experimentation might begin. Where the process would then stop would be anyone's guess. Whether we would still think of freedom of the press in terms of the fierce independence from government would also be open.

Page 1332.   At the end of section b of the Note, add the following:

See also Metro Broadcasting, Inc. v. FCC, 110 S. Ct. — (1990) (holding that the FCC's minority preference policies, which are designed to increase minority ownership and management of broadcast facilities, do not violate the equal protection clause of the fourteenth amendment).

Page 1332.   At the end of subsection c of the Note, add the following:

See also Krattenmaker & Powe, The Fairness Doctrine Today: A Constitutional Curiosity and An Impossible Dream, 1985 Duke L.J. 151.

Page 1332.   At the end of the page, add the following:

For an economic analysis of the issues raised in this Note, see Spitzer, Controlling the Content of Print and Broadcast, 58 S. Cal. L. Rev. 1349 (1985).

Page 1333.   At the top of the page, add the following new section:

3A. *Exclusive cable franchises.* Does the scarcity theory apply to cable television? Does the first amendment permit a municipality to award an exclusive franchise to a single cable operator? To condition a franchise on the willingness of the operator to provide public access or make particular programming decisions? In City of Los Angeles v. Preferred Communications, Inc., 476 U.S. 488 (1986), the Court declined to answer these questions in the absence of a fully developed factual record. However, Justice Rehnquist's opinion for the Court stated that the activities of cable operators "plainly implicate First Amendment interests. [Through] original programming or by exercising editorial discretion over which stations or programs to include in its repertoire, [operators seek] to communicate messages on a wide variety of topics and in a wide variety of formats." Moreover, the Court implied that exclusive franchising must satisfy something more than minimal scrutiny in order to survive constitutional attack. "Where a law is subjected to a colorable First Amendment challenge, the rule of rationality which will sustain legislation against other constitutional challenges typically does not have the same controlling force."

Page 1357.   Before the Note, add the following:

In Press-Enterprise Co. v. Superior Court, 478 U.S. 1 (1986), the Court held that a newspaper had a first amendment right of access to the transcripts of a preliminary hearing growing out of a criminal prosecution. The state court had refused to release the transcript after holding that the first amendment right of access extended only to actual criminal trials and finding that there was a "reasonable likelihood of substantial prejudice" to the accused if the transcripts were released. Writing for the Court, Chief Justice Burger held that "the First Amendment question cannot be resolved solely on the label we give the event, i.e., 'trial' or otherwise, particularly where the preliminary hearing functions much like a full scale trial." Because there was a tradition of accessibility to preliminary hearings and because public access played a positive role in the functioning of such hearings, there was a presumptive first amendment right of access. Therefore, access could not be denied in the absence of specific findings demonstrating that there was a substantial probability that the defendant's right to a fair trial would be prejudiced by publicity that closure would prevent, and that there were no reasonable alternatives to closure adequate to protect the accused's rights.

Justice Stevens, joined by Justice Rehnquist, dissented.

Page 1360.   After the quotation from Nagel, add the following:

On the other hand, consider S. Shiffrin, The First Amendment, Democracy, and Romance 159 (1990):

> . . . American citizens not only feel a deep emotional attachment to the country, but also [a] sense of pride about the first amendment. The first amendment speaks to the kind of people we are and the kind of people we aspire to be. [It] plays an important role in the construction of an appealing story, a story about a nation that promotes independent people, a nation that affords a place of refuge for peoples all over the globe, a nation that welcomes the iconoclast, a nation that respects, tolerates, and even sponsors dissent. [The] image called up by this national picture [encourages] us to picture Walt Whitman's citizenry — vibrant, diverse, vital, stubborn, and independent. It encourages us to believe with Emerson that "America is the idea of emancipation."

Chapter Eight

The Constitution and Religion

B. THE ESTABLISHMENT CLAUSE

Page 1376. At the end of the first Note, add the following:

Bender v. Williamsport Area School Dist., 475 U.S. 534 (1986), posed the issue of *Widmar*'s applicability to high school students. Although the Court failed to reach the merits, see Supplement to Casebook page 90 supra, four dissenting justices thought that *Widmar* was controlling.

Page 1377. Before section 2, add the following:

3. *A critique of the search for impermissible purposes.* In his dissenting opinion in Edwards v. Aguillard, 482 U.S. 578 (1987), Justice Scalia offered this critique of the "purpose" test:

> [While] it is possible to discern the objective "purpose" of a statute (i.e., the public good at which its provisions appear to be directed), or even the formal motivation for a statute where that is explicitly set forth, [discerning] the subjective motivation of those enacting the statute is, to be honest, almost always an impossible task. The number of possible motivations, to begin with, is not binary, or indeed even finite. In the present case [involving a "balanced treatment for creationism" statute, discussed infra at Supp. to page 1408], for example, a particular legislator need not have voted for the Act either because he wanted to foster religion or to improve education. He may have thought the bill would provide jobs for his district, or may have wanted to make amends with a faction of his party he had alienated on another vote, or he may have been a close friend of the bill's sponsor, or he may have hoped the Governor would appreciate his vote and make a fund-raising appearance for him, or he may have been pressured to vote for a bill he disliked by a wealthy contributor or by a flood of constituent mail, or he may have been seeking favorable publicity, or he may have been reluctant to hurt the feelings of a loyal staff member who worked on the bill, or he may have been settling an old score with a legislator who opposed the bill, or he may have been mad at his wife who opposed the bill, or he may have been intoxicated and utterly *un*motivated when the vote was called, or he may have accidentally voted "yes" instead of "no," or, of course, he may have had (and very likely did have) a combination of some of the above and many other considerations.

To look for *the sole purpose* of even a single legislator is probably to look for something that does not exist.

Putting that problem aside, however, where ought we to look for the individual legislator's purpose? We cannot of course assume that every member present [agreed] with the motivation expressed in a particular legislator's pre-enactment floor or committee statement. [Can] we assume, then, that they all agree with the motivation expressed in the staff-prepared committee reports they might have [read]? Should we consider post-enactment floor statements? Or post-enactment testimony from legislators, obtained expressly for the lawsuit? Should we consider media reports on the realities of the legislative bargaining? All of these sources, of course, are eminently manipulable. Legislative histories can be contrived and santized, favorable media coverage orchestrated, and post-enactment recollections conveniently distorted. Perhaps most valuable of all would be more objective indications — for example, evidence regarding the individual legislators' religious affiliations. And if that, why not evidence regarding the fervor or tepidity of their beliefs?

Having achieved, through these simple means, an assessment of what individual legislators intended, we must still confront the question [how] *many* of them must have the invalidating intent. If a state senate approves a bill by vote of 26 to 25, and only one of the 26 intended solely to advance religion, is the law unconstitutional? What if 13 of the 26 had that intent? What if 3 of the 26 had the impermissible intent, but 3 of the 25 were simply attempting to "balance" the votes of their impermissibly motivated colleagues? Or is it possible that the intent of the bill's sponsor is alone enough to invalidate it — on a theory, perhaps, that even though everyone else's intent was pure, what they produced was the fruit of a forbidden tree?

Does this critique cast doubt on the doctrine of Washington v. Davis (page 543 supra in the main text)? On the result in Hunter v. Underwood (page 553 supra in the main text), where the Court's opinion was written by Justice Rehnquist, who joined Justice Scalia's dissent in *Edwards*? Consider the underlying conception of the legislative process reflected in Justice Scalia's comments, and reconsider the discussion, at pages 5-6 supra of the main text, of the antifederalist case against the Constitution.

Page 1394. Insert the following before Note 4:

3A. *Creches and menorahs:* In County of Allegheny v. American Civil Liberties Union, 109 S. Ct. 3086 (1989), shifting majorities on the Court held unconstitutional a freestanding display of a nativity scene on the main staircase of a county courthouse, but upheld the display of a Jewish menorah placed next to the city's Christmas tree and a statement declaring the city's "salute to liberty." A majority of the Court joined an opinion by Justice Blackmun adopting Justice O'Connor's "no endorsement" analysis as a general guide to establishment clause decisions, and concluded that the "setting" of the nativity scene, which was a "single element" in the display, "celebrate[d] Christmas in a way that has the effect of endorsing a patently Christian message."

Justice Blackmun, writing for himself, concluded that the display of the menorah was permissible. "The menorah's message is not exclusively religious," and it stood next to a Christmas tree and a sign saluting liberty, with the effect of "creat[ing] an 'overall holiday setting' that represents both Christmas and Chanukah — two holidays, not one." The setting of the menorah's display led Justice Blackmun to conclude that it "simply recognizes that both Christmas and Chanukah are part of the same winter-holiday season, which has attained a secular status in our society." He also suggested, without making it a central element in the analysis, that it was relevant that the city had "no reasonable alternatives that are less religious in nature" to represent Chanukah.

Justice O'Connor agreed that the display of the menorah was permissible, but criticized Justice Blackmun for unduly minimizing the religious content of the menorah. But, she said, the overall display "sends a message of pluralism and freedom to choose one's own beliefs."

Justices Brennan, Marshall, and Stevens dissented as to the menorah. Justice Brennan argued that the Christmas tree was a religious symbol, that Chanukah was not a holiday with secular dimensions, and that "the government may [not] promote pluralism by sponsoring or condoning displays having strong religious associations on its property." The government's message in the "salute to liberty" was not religious but "patriotic," and "the government's use of religion to promote its own cause is undoubtedly offensive to those whose religious beliefs are not bound up with their attitude toward the Nation." Further, "the uncritical acceptance of a message of religious pluralism [ignores] the extent to which even that message may offend. [To] lump the religious objects and holidays of religions together without regard to their attitudes toward such inclusiveness, or to decide which religions should be excluded because of the possibility of offense, is not a benign or beneficent celebration of pluralism."

Justice Kennedy, joined by Chief Justice Rehnquist and Justices White and Scalia, dissented as to the nativity scene, and rejected the majority's adoption of the "no endorsement" test, saying that it "reflects an unjustified hostility toward religion." To him, the establishment clause "permits government some latitude in recognizing and accommodating the central role religion plays in our society." To him, the Court's decisions

disclose two limiting principles: government may not coerce anyone to support or participate in any religion or its exercise; and it may not, in the guise of avoiding hostility or callous indifference, give direct benefits to religion in such a degree that it in fact "establishes a [state] religiion or religious faith, or tends to do so." [*Lynch*.] . . . [Coercion] need not be a direct tax in aid of religion or a test oath. Symbolic recognition or accommodation of religious faith may violate the Clause in an extreme case, [such as] the permanent erection of a large Latin cross on the roof of city hall [because] such an obtrusive year-round religious display would place the government's weight behind an obvious effort to proselytize on behalf of a particular religion. . . . Absent coercion, the risk of infringement of religious liberty by passive or symbolic accommodation is minimal.

Both displays satisfied Justice Kennedy's test. "No one was compelled to observe or participate in any religious ceremony or activity. [The] creche and the menorah are purely passive symbols of religious holidays. Passersby who disagree with the message conveyed by these displays are free to ignore them, or even to turn their backs."

Justice Kennedy sharply criticized the majority's adoption of the "no endorsement" approach as "flawed in its fundamentals and unworkable in practice." First, "few of our traditional practices recognizing the part religion plays in our society [such as Thanksgiving Proclamations and legislative prayer] can withstand scrutiny under a faithful application of [the] no endorsement" test. Second, the test "threatens to trivialize constitutional adjudication [by requiring] a jurisprudence of minutiae" regarding the overall setting of governmental displays.

The majority responded to Justice Kennedy by saying, first, that he misapprehended the content of permissible accommodations of religion, which were allowed only to relieve government-imposed burdens on peoples' ability to freely exercise their religion (whether or not those burdens themselves violated the free exercise clause). In addition, the Court argued that relying as Justice Kennedy did on traditional practices to determine what is permissible "would gut the core of the Establishment Clause [because] the history of this Nation, it is perhaps sad to say, contains numerous examples of official acts that endorsed Christianity specifically. [This] heritage of official discrimination against non-Christians has no place in the jurisprudence of the Establishment Clause." The Court said that what Justice Kennedy called a "jurisprudence of minutiae" was simply the ordinary judicial process of drawing lines in areas where many considerations must be taken into account, and that Justice Kennedy's "no coercion" approach also would require that lines be drawn, though he might draw them at different places and place a different burden on those who objected to government endorsement of religion.

Finally, the Court responded to Justice Kennedy's assertion that it was hostile to religion and was "issuing national decrees as to what is orthodox and what is not." It said that

> Justice Kennedy apparently has misperceived a respect for religious pluralism, a respect commanded by the Constitution, as hostility or indifference to religion. . . . The government does not discriminate against any citizen on the basis of the citizen's religious faith if the government is secular in its functions and operations. . . . A secular state [is] not the same as an atheistic or antireligious state. [It] follows from the Constitution's proscription against government affiliation with religious beliefs or institutions that there is no orthodoxy on religious matters in the secular state. . . . To be sure, in a pluralistic society there may be some would-be theocrats, who wish that

their religion were an established creed, and some of them perhaps may be audacious enough to claim that the lack of established religion discriminates against their preferences. But this claim gets no relief. . . . Celebrating Christmas as a religious [holiday] necessarily entails professing, proclaiming, or believing that Jesus of Nazareth [is] the Christ. [In] contrast, confining the government's own celebration of Christmas to the holiday's secular aspects does *not* favor the religious belief of non-Christians over those of Christian. Rather, it simply permits the government to acknowledge the holiday without expressing an allegiance to Christian beliefs, an allegiance that would truly favor Christians over non-Christians.

Page 1398.   At the end of the Note, add the following:

Laycock, A Survey of Religious Liberty in the United States, 47 Ohio St. L.J. 409, 443-446 (1986), describes six theories that "have been endorsed by one or more justices." They are (1) the "no-aid theory: that any state money paid to a religious school or its students expands the school's budget and thereby aids religion"; (2) the "purchase-of-services theory: that state money paid to a religious school is simply a purchase of educational services"; (3) the "equal-treatment theory[, which] holds that government is obligated to pay for the secular aspects of education in religious schools [or] that government is free to make such payments if it wishes"; (4) the "child-benefit theory: that the state can provide educational benefits directly to children or their parents, even if the benefits are used at or in connection with a religious school [but] cannot provide the same aid directly to the school"; (5) the "tracing theory, [which] tries to trace each dollar of government money to see what the school spent it on"; and (6) the "little-bit theory [that] a little bit of aid to religious schools is permissible, but it must be structured in a way that keeps it from becoming too much." Which of these theories explains which of the cases? Which, if any, makes sense of the Constitution?

Page 1406.   Before section 2 of the Note, add the following:

In Witters v. Washington Department of Services for the Blind, 474 U.S. 481 (1986), the Court held that the "effects" branch of the *Lemon* test was not violated by a statute authorizing payment to a visually handicapped person for vocational rehabilitation services, where the recipient planned to use the funds to pay his tuition at a Christian college to prepare himself for a career as a minister. The Court found "central" to its analysis the fact that the payments were made "directly to the student, who transmits it to the educational institution of his or her choice." Thus, "any aid provided under [the] program that ultimately flows to religious institutions does so only as a result of the genuinely independent and private choices of aid recipients." It was a general program, which

creates no financial incentive for students to undertake sectarian education [and] does not tend to provide greater or broader benefits for recipients who apply their aid to religious education. [Further], and importantly, nothing [indicates] that [any] significant portion of the aid expended under the [program] as a whole will end up flowing to religious education.

The Court left open the question of entanglement for exploration on remand, and refused to consider whether the free exercise clause required the state to provide the assistance.

Justice Powell, joined by Chief Justice Burger and Justice Rehnquist, wrote a concurring opinion criticizing the Court for not relying directly on *Mueller*. He wrote that *Mueller* meant that "state programs that are wholly neutral in offering educational assistance to a class defined without reference to religion do not violate the second part of the [*Lemon*] test," and that "this conclusion does not depend on the fact that [Witters] appears to be the only handicapped student who has sought to use his assistance to pursue religious training." Justice White wrote a brief concurring opinion stating that he agreed with "most of Justice Powell's opinion regarding *Mueller*." Justice O'Connor concurred in the judgment.

Is *Witters* different from *Mueller*? Note that every justice in the *Mueller* majority expressed separate views in *Witters*.

Page 1408. Before the Note, add the following:

In Edwards v. Aguillard, 482 U.S. 578 (1987), the Court, in an opinion by Justice Brennan, held unconstitutional a Louisiana statute requiring public schools to teach "creation science" whenever they taught the theory of evolution. Examining the structure of the statute and statements made in the course of its adoption, the Court concluded that the statute had no secular purpose despite the statement in the statute's text that it was designed to promote "academic freedom." The Court stated that the statute would not promote academic freedom in the sense of "enhancing the freedom of teachers to teach what they will" or even "teaching all the evidence," in part because it required that curriculum guides be developed for creation science but not for evolution. The Court also stressed that the case presented "[the] same historic and contemporaneous antagonisms between the teachings of certain religious denominations and the teaching of evolution" that it had found in *Epperson*. "The preeminent purpose of the Louisiana legislature was clearly to advance the religious viewpoint that a supernatural being created humankind." The Court's analysis concluded,

> We do not imply that a legislature could never require that scientific critiques of prevailing scientific theories be taught. [Teaching] a variant of scientific theories about the origins of humankind to school children might be validly done with the clear secular intent of enhancing the effectiveness of science instruction. But because the primary purpose of the [Louisiana] Act is to endorse a particular religious doctrine, the Act furthers religion in violation of the Establishment Clause.

Justice Powell's concurring opinion, in which Justice O'Connor joined, agreed that the statute had no secular purpose. It emphasized that

> as a matter of history, school children can and should properly be informed of all aspects of this Nation's religious heritage. I would see no constitutional problem if school children were taught the nature of the Founding Fathers' religious beliefs and how these beliefs affected the attitudes of the times and the structure of our government. [Since] religion permeates our history, a familiarity with the nature of religious beliefs is necessary to understand many historical as well as contemporary events. In addition, [the] Establishment Clause does not prohibit per se the educational use of religious documents in public school education. [It] is properly understood to prohibit the use of the Bible and other religious documents in public school education only when the purpose of the use is to advance a particular religious belief.

Justice White's brief opinion concurring in the judgment said that "this is not a difficult case" in light of the findings by the lower courts that the statute's primary purpose was to advance religion.

Justice Scalia wrote a long dissent, in which Chief Justice Rehnquist joined. His examination of the legislative history led him to conclude that one purpose of the statute was to advance academic freedom, as it stated, in the sense of enhancing "*students'* freedom from *indoctrination*," which the legislature believed was occurring in biology courses that presented only the theory of evolution.

5. *The Adolescent Family Life Act.* In Bowen v. Kendrick, 108 S. Ct. 2562 (1988), the Court considered the constitutionality of the Adolescent Family Life Act, which authorizes federal grants to public and nonpublic private organizations, including organizations with institutional ties to religious denominations, for counseling services and research in the area of premarital adolescent sexual relations and pregnancy. Applying the *Lemon* standard, the Court held that the Act on its face does not violate the Establishment Clause.

Applying the first prong of *Lemon,* the Court maintained that "it is clear from the face of the statute that the [Act] was motivated primarily, if not entirely, by a legitimate secular purpose — the elimination or reduction of social and economic problems caused by teenage sexuality, pregnancy, and parenthood."

Turning to the second prong — whether the "primary effect" of the Act is impermissible — the Court explained that the "services to be provided under the [Act] are not religious in character, nor has there been any suggestion that religious institutions [are] uniquely qualified to carry out those services." Moreover, although the Act "takes a particular approach toward dealing with adolescent sexuality and pregnancy — for example, two of its stated purposes are to 'promote self-discipline' [and] to 'promote adoption as an alternative' [to abortion], that approach is not inherently religious." And although it is clear that religious organizations will participate as recipients of federal funds, "this Court has never held that religious institutions are disabled by the First Amendment from participating in publicly sponsored social welfare programs." Finally, "nothing on the face of the [Act] indicates that a significant proportion of the federal funds will be disbursed to 'pervasively sectarian' institutions." Thus, this "is not a case like *Grand Rapids,* where the challenged aid flowed almost entirely to parochial schools." Instead, the Court argued, "this case more closely resembles *Tilton* and *Roemer,* where it was foreseeable that some proportion of the recipients of government aid would be religiously affiliated, but that only a small portion of these, if any, could be considered 'pervasively sectarian.' "

The Court also rejected the argument that the Act "necessarily has the effect of advancing religion because the religiously affiliated [grantees] will be providing educational and counseling services to adolescents." Although conceding that "the Establishment Clause '[prohibits] government-financed [indoctrination] into the beliefs of a particular religious faith,' " the Court reasoned that when the aid flows to religiously affiliated institutions that are not pervasively sectarian, "we [will not] presume that it [will] be used in a way that would have the primary effect of advancing religion."

The Court also rejected the argument that the Act is invalid because it authorizes teaching by religious grantees "on 'matters that are fundamental elements of religious doctrine,' such as the harm of premarital sex and the reasons for choosing adoption over abortion." The Court explained that on "an issue as sensitive [as] teenage sexuality, it is not surprising that the government's secular concerns would either coincide or conflict with those of religious institutions," but "the possibility or even the likelihood that some of the religious [grantees] will agree with the message that Congress intended to deliver to adolescents through the [Act] is insufficient to warrant a finding that the statute on its face has the primary effect of advancing religion."

Turning to the "excessive entanglement" prong of *Lemon,* the Court concluded that there is "no reason to fear that [the] monitoring involved here will cause Government to intrude unduly in the day-to-day operations of the religiously affiliated [grantees]."

Although holding that the Act was constitutional "on its face," it remanded for a determination whether the Act was unconstitutional "as applied." The Court indicated that the validity of the Act as applied would turn on such determinations as whether any of the grantees under the Act are "pervasively sectarian" and whether any of the "aid has been used to fund 'specifically religious activit[ies] in an otherwise substantially secular setting.' "

Justice Blackmun, joined by Justices Brennan, Marshall and Stevens, dissented on the ground that the Act was invalid under the effects prong of *Lemon:*

> Whereas there may be secular values promoted by the [Act], including the encouragement of adoption and premarital chastity and the discouragement of abortion, it can hardly be doubted that when promoted in theological terms by religious figures, those values take on a religious nature. [And although] the Court has recognized that

the Constitution does not prohibit the government from supporting secular social-welfare services solely because they are provided by a religiously affiliated organization, [there] is a very real and important difference between running a soup kitchen or a hospital, and counseling pregnant teenagers on how to make the difficult decisions facing them. The risk of advancing religion at public expense, and of creating an appearance that the government is endorsing the medium and the message, is much greater when the religious organization is directly engaged in pedagogy, with the express intent of shaping belief and changing behavior, than when it is neutrally dispensing medication, food, or shelter."

Page 1410.   At the end of the Note, add the following:

Consider the suggestion in Paulsen, Religion, Equality, and the Constitution: An Equal Protection Approach to Establishment Clause Adjudication, 61 Notre Dame L. Rev. 311, 313, 315 (1986), that "the establishment clause protects *religious liberty* [by addressing] *the limits of allowable state classifications affecting this liberty.* [This] approach points to a new model for establishment clause adjudication: *The equal protection of the free exercise of religion.*" If the establishment clause protects religious liberty, how does it do so in ways that the free exercise clause does not? That is, on this view, why is there an establishment clause in the first place? Recall that in San Antonio Indep. School Dist. v. Rodriguez, page 821 supra, the Court stated that classifications affecting rights "explicitly or implicitly guaranteed by the Constitution" require "strict judicial scrutiny." Thus, on this view, what does the establishment clause add to the equal protection clause?

C.   THE FREE EXERCISE CLAUSE

Page 1419.   At the end of section 1 of the Note, add the following:

Consider the suggestion that

one can attempt to distinguish between situations [like *Lee*] in which "strategic behavior" is likely to occur and those [like *Yoder*] in which it is less likely. . . .

[But] while few of us desire to educate our children at home, there are some who wish to do so. [Similarly,] while most of us prefer not to lose our jobs, many do at one time or another want to quit. Under *Sherbert,* only a religious basis for voluntarily quitting will provide unemployment insurance benefits. On the other side of the spectrum, avoiding taxes appeals to almost all of us. Free exercise protection would be much more limited on this latter side of the spectrum. This "likelihood of strategic behavior" criterion would protect a meaningful amount of religious conduct and at the same time avoid large scale determinations of sincerity.

[However,] judging credibility is a staple of the adjudicatory and administrative processes, and there is no reason why the burden of proof on this issue ought not to be on the claimant. [Incorrectly] denying some sincere persons shelter for their religious conduct, an occasionally necessary result if sincerity is to be judged, will simply be a cost of granting a meaningful constitutional privilege in this area.

Pepper, Taking the Free Exercise Clause Seriously, 1986 B.Y.U. L. Rev. 299, 327-328.

Page 1419. At the bottom of the page, add the following:

The Court addressed religious-based objections to the provision and use of social security numbers in Bowen v. Roy, 476 U.S. 693 (1986). A federal statute requires applicants for certain welfare benefits to provide the states with their social security numbers and requires the states to use the numbers in administering the program. Appellees, who had applied for Food Stamp and Aid to Families with Dependent Children benefits, contended that providing a social security number for their two-year-old daughter and use of that number by the government would violate their religious beliefs.

Writing for eight justices, Chief Justice Burger rejected appellee's claim that the free exercise clause was infringed when the government used the number.

> Never to our knowledge has the Court interpreted the First Amendment to require the Government *itself* to behave in ways that the individual believes will further his or her spiritual development. [The] Free Exercise Clause affords an individual protection from certain forms of governmental compulsion; it does not afford an individual a right to dictate the conduct of the Government's internal procedures.

When the Chief Justice turned to appellees' claim that they need not provide the number, however, he was no longer able to command a majority of the Court. Writing only for himself and Justices Powell and Rehnquist, he asserted that the government's interest should be subjected to only minimal review because it was not attempting to "affirmatively compel appellees, by threat of sanctions, to refrain from religiously motivated conduct." He argued that

> government regulation that indirectly and incidentally calls for a choice between securing a governmental benefit and adherence to religious beliefs is wholly different from governmental action or legislation that criminalizes religiously inspired activity or inescapably compels conduct that some find objectionable for religious reasons. . . .
>
> The test applied in cases like [*Yoder*] is not appropriate in this setting. In the enforcement of a facially neutral and uniformly applicable requirement for the administration of welfare programs reaching many millions of people, the Government is entitled to wide latitude. [Absent] proof of an intent to discriminate against particular religious beliefs or against religion in general, the Government meets its burden when it demonstrates that a challenged requirement for governmental benefits, neutral and uniform in its application, is a reasonable means of promoting a legitimate public interest.

In an opinion joined by Justices Brennan and Marshall, Justice O'Connor dissented from this portion of Chief Justice Burger's opinion. She asserted that "[the] fact that the underlying dispute involves an award of benefits rather than an exaction of penalties does not grant the Government license to apply a different version of the Constitution." In her opinion, the standard of review advocated by the Chief Justice had

> no basis in precedent and relegates a serious First Amendment value to the barest level of minimal scrutiny that the Equal Protection Clause already provides. I would apply our long line of precedents to hold that the Government must accommodate a legitimate free exercise claim unless pursuing an especially important interest by narrowly tailored means.

Justice White filed a separate, one sentence dissenting opinion stating that the case was controlled by *Thomas* and *Sherbert*.

Both Justice Blackmun and Justice Stevens filed separate concurring opinions that asserted that the dispute concerning provision of the social security number might no longer be justiciable. However, at the conclusion of his opinion, Justice Blackmun noted that "[if] it proves necessary to reach the issue on remand, I agree with Justice O'Connor that [the] Government may not deny assistance to [appellee's daughter] solely because her parents' religious convictions prevent them from supplying the Government with a social security number for their daughter." When Justice Blackmun's vote is added to that of the four dissenters, it appears that a majority of the Court would uphold a free exercise claim relating to provision of a social security number.

The Court revisited and reaffirmed *Sherbert* in Hobbie v. Unemployment Appeals Commn., 480 U.S. 136 (1987). The case was different from *Sherbert* only in that the claimant's beliefs had changed "during the course of her employment, creating a conflict between job and faith that had not previously existed." The Court held that "the timing of [the] conversion is immaterial." The Court also expressly reaffirmed the "strict scrutiny" standard used in *Sherbert* and "rejected" the "less rigorous standard articulated in [the plurality opinion] in Bowen v. Roy." Although only Chief Justice Rehnquist dissented, Justices Powell and Stevens noted their disagreement with the Court's decision to resolve the question of the appropriate standard.

Frazee v. Illinois Department of Employment Security, 109 S. Ct. 1514 (1989), applied *Sherbert* to a person who refused to work on Sunday because he believed that "as a Christian, he could not work on 'the Lord's Day.' " The Court held that it was irrelevant that Frazee was not a member of an established religious sect or church, one of whose tenets was a prohibition on Sunday work. Such membership "would simplify the problem of identifying sincerely held religious beliefs," but in this case there was no question of Frazee's sincerity.

Compare *Hobbie* to Goldman v. Weinberger, 475 U.S. 503 (1986), where a closely divided Court rejected a free exercise challenge to an Air Force regulation prohibiting the wearing of headgear while indoors as applied to an orthodox Jewish officer who was disciplined for wearing a yarmulke. Writing for the Court, Justice Rehnquist repeatedly emphasized the deference owned to military judgments concerning the need to "foster instinctive obedience, unity, commitment, and esprit de corps." The Court rejected petitioners' argument that the Air Force had failed to prove that an exception for the wearing of unobtrusive religious garments would threaten discipline. "The desirability of dress regulations in the military is decided by the appropriate military officials, and they are under no constitutional mandate to abandon their considered professional judgment."

Justice Stevens, joined by Justices White and Powell, wrote a concurring opinion. Although acknowledging that petitioner presented "an especially attractive case for an exception" from the regulations, Stevens worried about the application of such an exemption to members of other religious groups, wishing to wear turbans, saffron robes, and dreadlocks.

> The very strength of [petitioner's] claim creates the danger that a similar claim on behalf of a Sikh or a Rastafarian might readily be dismissed as "so extreme, so unusual, or so faddish an image that public confidence in his ability to perform his duties will be destroyed." [Quoting from Justice Brennan's dissenting opinion.] If exceptions from dress code regulations are to be granted on the basis of a multifactored test[, inevitably] the decisionmaker's evaluation of the character and the sincerity of the requestor's faith — as well as the probable reaction of the majority to the favored treatment of a member of that faith — will play a critical part in the decision. [The] Air Force has no business drawing distinctions between such persons when it is enforcing commands of universal application.

In a dissenting opinion joined by Justice Marshall, Justice Brennan objected to the Court's "subrational-basis" standard of review. "When a military service burdens the free exercise rights of its members in the name of necessity, it must provide, as an initial matter and at a minimum, a *credible* explanation of how the contested practice is likely to interfere with the proffered military interest. Unabashed *ipse dixit* cannot outweigh a constitutional right." Brennan found "totally implausible" the claim that the group identity of the Air Force would be threatened by the wearing of yarmulkes. "To the contrary, a yarmulke worn with a United States military uniform is an eloquent reminder that the shared and proud identity of United States servicemen embraces and unites religious and ethnic pluralism." Although turbans, saffron robes, and dreadlocks were not before the Court, Brennan noted that "a reviewing court could legitimately give deference to dress and grooming rules that have a *reasoned* basis in, for example, functional utility, health and safety considerations, and the goal of a polished, professional appearance. It is the lack of any reasoned basis for prohibiting yarmulkes that is so striking here."

In a separate dissenting opinion, Justice Blackmun acknowledged that the Air Force could consider not only the costs of allowing petitioner to wear a yarmulke, but also the cumulative costs of accommodating other requests for religious exemptions. He also acknowledged that "to allow noncombat personnel to wear yarmulkes but not turbans or dreadlocks because the latter seem more obtrusive [would] be to discriminate in favor of this country's more established, mainstream religions." Nevertheless, he rejected the Air Force's argument because it "simply has not shown any reason to fear that a significant number of enlisted personnel and officers would request religious exemptions that could not be denied on neutral grounds such as safety, let alone that granting these requests would noticeably impair the overall image of the service."

Justice O'Connor also filed a dissenting opinion, in which Justice Marshall joined.

P.L. 100-180 amended 45 U.S.C. section 774 to read: "[A] member of the armed forces may wear an item of religious apparel while wearing the uniform of the member's armed forces [unless] the wearing of the item would interfere with the performance of the member's military duties [or] the item of apparel is not neat and conservative." Does the statute adequately accommodate Justice Stevens' concerns? Is it constitutional?

O'Lone v. Estate of Shabazz, 482 U.S. 342 (1987), like *Goldman*, involved a free exercise challenge in a special institutional context, and the Court again emphasized the needs of the institution in rejecting the challenge. *O'Lone* concerned a challenge by Muslim prisoners to a prison policy that prevented them from attending Jumu'ah, a weekly Muslim congregational service mandated by the Koran. Prison regulations, adopted for security reasons, prevented prisoners with respondents' classification from being inside the building where the service was held. Writing for the Court, Justice Rehnquist conceded that respondents' religious beliefs were sincerely held and that they compelled their attendance at the service. But the Court held that in a prison context, alleged infringements on free exercise interests "are judged under a 'reasonableness' test less restrictive than that ordinarily applied to [infringements] of fundamental constitutional rights." Applying this reasonableness test to the facts before it, the Court had little difficulty in concluding that the restriction was justified by security concerns.

Justice Brennan, joined by Justices Marshall, Blackmun, and Stevens, dissented.

In Lyng v. Northwest Indian Cemetery Protective Assn., 485 U.S. 439 (1988), the Court was confronted with a free exercise challenge to the Forest Service's plan to permit timber harvesting and road construction in an area of a national forest that was traditionally used by various Indian tribes as sacred areas for religious rituals. The Court held, in an opinion by Justice O'Connor, that the burden was not sufficiently severe as to require the Government to show a compelling need to engage in the relevant projects.

> The building of a road or the harvesting of timber on publicly owned land cannot meaningfully be distinguished from the use of a Social Security number in *Roy*. In both cases, the challenged governmental action would interfere significantly with private persons' ability to pursue spiritual fulfillment according to their own religious beliefs. In neither case, however, could the affected individuals be coerced by the Government's action into violating their religious beliefs; nor would either governmental action penalize religious activity by denying any person an equal share of the rights, benefits, and privileges enjoyed by other citizens.

The Court acknowledged that

> indirect coercion or penalties on the free exercise of religion, not just outright prohibitions, are subject to scrutiny under the First Amendment. . . . [But] this does not and cannot imply that incidental effects of government programs, which may make it more difficult to practice certain religions but which have no tendency to coerce individuals into acting contrary to their religious beliefs, require government to bring forward a compelling justification for its otherwise lawful actions. The crucial word in the constitutional text is "prohibit". . . .

The Court noted that the projects at issue "could have devastating effects on traditional Indian religious practices . . . intimately and inextricably bound up with the unique features" of the area, but it concluded that "government simply could not operate if it were required to satisfy every citizen's religious needs and desires."

In a dissenting opinion joined by Justices Marshall and Blackmun, Justice Brennan emphasized the centrality of the area at issue to religious practices and attacked the Court's conception of "coercion."

> Ultimately, the Court's coercion test turns on a distinction between governmental actions that compel affirmative conduct inconsistent with religious belief, and those governmental actions that prevent conduct consistent with religious belief. In my view, such a distinction is without constitutional significance. The crucial word in the constitutional text, as the Court itself acknowledges, is "prohibit," a comprehensive term that in no way suggests that the intended protection is aimed only at governmental actions that coerce affirmative conduct. Nor does the Court's distinction comport with the principal animating the constitutional guarantee: religious freedom is threatened no less by governmental action that makes the practice of one's chosen faith impossible than by governmental programs that pressure one to engage in conduct inconsistent with religious belief.

Justice Brennan argued that as in Sherbert v. Verner, the Government should be required to show a compelling justification for the activities in which it proposed to engage here.

Consider the following views: (a) Sherbert v. Verner has, after *Lyng*, little vitality beyond its precise facts. The land in *Lyng* is no more "the Government's" than was the money in *Sherbert*. (b) Is there difference in the nature of the interference with religion in *Sherbert* and *Lyng*? Consider the view that in *Lyng*, there was even greater coercion — an across-the-board foreclosure rather than a financial inducement to abandon religious practice. (c) The two *Lyng* cases — the other involving the denial of food stamps to strikers, see supplement to casebook page 688 supra — suggest a large development in modern jurisprudence, presaging a dramatic reorientation of the unconstitutional conditions doctrine. That doctrine was designed to prevent government from using financial incentives and property ownership to pressure constitutional rights; but the underlying theory was always obscure. The central problem for the future lies in the development of a theory of "coercion" or "prohibition" in a period of active governmental regulation of economy. Until such a theory is developed, for particular clauses or in general, decisions like those in the two *Lyng* cases, relying largely on common law or pre-governmental conceptions of what "coercion" is, are inevitable.

Consider Epstein, Unconstitutional Conditions, State Power, and the Limits of Consent, 102 Harv. L. Rev. 4, 83-85 (1988), defends the strict *Sherbert* approach:

> [The] government cannot engage in activities that either penalize or subsidize the practice of religion. Judicial scrutiny is high, for whether the government program is sustained or struck down, there is a substantial risk of constitutional error. This test is more stringent than that found in the free speech area, where only restrictions that burden private speech are suspect, while those that subsidize it are not. In contrast, *every* form of error in the religious context is subject to constitutional scrutiny, for to avoid the perils of free exercise may be to land in the thicket of establishment.

Epstein argues that the question in *Sherbert* is

> whether Mrs. Sherbert is [in] the same risk classification as other people within the state. [Suppose] it could be shown that people with religious beliefs have steadier work habits and therefore quit jobs far less frequently than those whose work habits are inferior in part because they are not anchored in religious beliefs. If Mrs. Sherbert is denied benefits, then she is forced to subsidize nonreligious workers. [Alternatively,] it may well be that the coverage for her refusal to work on the Sabbath gives her a better than expected deal from the fund.

Lupu, Where Rights Begin: The Problem of Burdens on the Free Exercise of Religion, 102 Harv. L. Rev. 933, 935, 966, 973-976 (1988), describes *Lyng* as a case that "avoided applying [the free exercise] standard by holding that the harms inflicted by the challenged government policies were not of the sort that would trigger the protections of the free exercise clause," and proposes a principle derived from the common law for defining free exercise burdens: "Whenever religious activity is met by intentional government action analogous to that which, if committed by a private party, would be actionable under general principles of law, a legally cognizable burden on religion is present." Lupu argues that "the doctrine of easement by prescription [seems] especially well tailored to the problem in *Lyng.*" Noting that there are "divergent" rules regarding some aspects of the common law, Lupu argues that the courts should not search for a majority rule or the best rule. It should "engage in a comprehensive analysis of the policies, both general and specific, advanced by the relevant common law norms." Applying this approach to *Lyng* and the common law requirement that one can acquire an easement by prescription only if the possession is hostile to the owner, Lupu concludes that the Indians' religious attachment to the land meant that they "would not have conceded the authority of the United States to evict them," and that this position satisfies the policy underlying the requirement of hostile possession.

EMPLOYMENT DIVISION, DEPARTMENT OF HUMAN RESOURCES v. SMITH
110 S. Ct. 1595 (1990)

JUSTICE SCALIA delivered the opinion of the Court.

This case requires us to decide whether the Free Exercise Clause of the First Amendment permits the State of Oregon to include religiously inspired peyote use within the reach of its general criminal prohibition on use of that drug, and thus permits the State to deny unemployment benefits to persons dismissed from their jobs because of such religiously inspired use. . . .

[Smith was a member of the Native American Church, which has as part of its religious ritual the supervised consumption of peyote. Peyote is a "controlled substance" under Oregon law, possession of which is a criminal offense. Smith was fired from his job at a private drug rehabilitation clinic because he ingested peyote as part of his Church's ritual. He sought and was denied unemployment benefits because he had been discharged for work-related misconduct. On his appeal from the denial of benefits, the Oregon Supreme Court held that state law did not contain an exemption from its criminal statute for religious consumption of peyote, that the criminal ban was unconstitutional as applied to the consumption of peyote in this setting, and that Smith was therefore entitled to unemployment compensation.]

II

Respondents' claim for relief rests on our decisions in [*Sherbert, Thomas,* and *Hobbie*], in which we held that a State could not condition the availability of unemployment insurance on an individual's willingness to forgo conduct required by his religion. [However,] the conduct at issue in those cases was not prohibited by law. . . .

A

[The] free exercise of religion means, first and foremost, the right to believe and profess whatever religious doctrine one desires. . . .

But the "exercise of religion" often involves not only belief and profession but the performance of (or abstention from) physical acts: assembling with others for a worship service, participating in sacramental use of bread and wine, proselytizing, abstaining from certain foods or certain modes of transportation. It would be true, we think (though no case of ours has involved the point), that a state would be "prohibiting the free exercise [of religion]" if it sought to ban such acts or abstentions only when they are engaged in for religious reasons, or only because of the religious belief that they display. It would doubtless be unconstitutional, for example, to ban the casting of "statues that are to be used for worship purposes," or to prohibit bowing down before a golden calf.

Respondents in the present case, however, seek to carry the meaning of "prohibiting the free exercise [of religion]" one large step further. They contend that their religious motivation for using peyote places them beyond the reach of a criminal law that is not specifically directed at their religious practice, and that is concededly constitutional as applied to those who use the drug for other reasons. They assert, in other words, that "prohibiting the free exercise [of religion]" includes requiring any individual to observe a generally applicable law that requires (or forbids) the performance of an act that his religious belief forbids (or requires). As a textual matter, we do not think the words must be given that meaning. It is no more necessary to regard the collection of a general tax, for example, as "prohibiting the free exercise [of religion]" by those citizens who believe support of organized government to be sinful, than it is to regard the same tax as "abridging the freedom . . . of the press" of those publishing companies that must pay the tax as a condition of staying in business. It is a permissible reading of the text, in the one case as in the other, to say that if prohibiting the exercise of religion (or burdening the activity of printing) is not the object of the tax but merely the incidental effect of a generally applicable and otherwise valid provision, the First Amendment has not been offended.

Our decisions reveal that the latter reading is the correct one. We have never held that an individual's religious beliefs excuse him from compliance with an otherwise valid law prohibiting conduct that the State is free to regulate. On the contrary, the record of more than a century of our free exercise jurisprudence contradicts that proposition. [We] first had occasion to assert that principle in [Reynolds], where we rejected the claim that criminal laws against polygamy could not be constitutionally applied to those whose religion commanded the practice. . . .

Subsequent decisions have consistently held that the right of free exercise does not relieve an individual of the obligation to comply with a "valid and neutral law of general applicability on the ground that the law proscribes (or prescribes) conduct that his religion prescribes (or proscribes)." United States v. Lee (Stevens, J., concurring in judgment). . . .

The only decisions in which we have held that the First Amendment bars application of a neutral, generally applicable law to religiously motivated action have involved not the Free Exercise Clause alone, but the Free Exercise Clause in conjunction with other constitutional protections, such as freedom of speech and of the press, see [*Cantwell*], or the right of parents, acknowledged in Pierce v. Society of Sisters, 268 U.S. 510 (1925), to direct the education of their children, see Wisconsin v. Yoder. . . . [1]

The present case does not present such a hybrid situation, but a free exercise claim unconnected with any communicative activity or parental right. Respondents urge us to hold, quite simply, that when otherwise prohibitable conduct is accompanied by religious convictions, not only the convictions but the conduct itself must be free from governmental regulation. We have never held that, and decline to do so now. There being no contention that Oregon's drug law represents an attempt to regulate religious beliefs, the communication of religious beliefs, or the raising of one's children in those beliefs, the rule to which we have adhered ever since *Reynolds* plainly controls. "Our cases do not at their farthest reach support the proposition that a stance of conscientious opposition relieves an objector from any colliding duty fixed by a democratic government." Gillette v. United States.

B

Respondents argue that even though exemption from generally applicable criminal laws need not automatically be extended to religiously motivated actors, at least the claim for a religious exemption must be evaluated under the balancing test set forth in Sherbert v. Verner. Under the *Sherbert* test, governmental actions that substantially burden a religious practice must be justified by a compelling governmental interest. [We] have never invalidated any governmental action on the basis of the *Sherbert* test except the denial of unemployment compensation. Although we have sometimes purported to apply the *Sherbert* test in contexts other than that, we have always found the test satisfied. In recent years we have abstained from applying the *Sherbert* test (outside the unemployment compensation field) at all [citing *Roy, Lyng, Goldman,* and *O'Lone*].

Even if we were inclined to breathe into *Sherbert* some life beyond the unemployment compensation field, we would not apply it to require exemptions from a generally applicable criminal law. The *Sherbert* test, it must be recalled, was

---

1. Both lines of cases have specifically adverted to the non-free exercise principle involved. . . .

developed in a context that lent itself to individualized governmental assessment of the reasons for the relevant conduct. [Our] decisions in the unemployment cases stand for the proposition that where the State has in place a system of individual exemptions, it may not refuse to extend that system to cases of "religious hardship" without compelling reason.

Whether or not the decisions are that limited, they at least have nothing to do with an across-the-board criminal prohibition on a particular form of conduct. [The] government's ability to enforce generally applicable prohibitions of socially harmful conduct, like its ability to carry out other aspects of public policy, "cannot depend on measuring the effects of a governmental action on a religious objector's spiritual development." [*Lyng*]. To make an individual's obligation to obey such a law contingent upon the law's coincidence with his religious beliefs, except where the State's interest is "compelling" — permitting him, by virtue of his beliefs, "to become a law unto himself," [*Reynolds*] — contradicts both constitutional tradition and common sense.[2]

The "compelling interest" requirement seems benign, because it is familiar from other fields. But using it as the standard that must be met before the government may accord different treatment on the basis of race, see, e.g., Palmore v. Sidoti, 466 U.S. 429, 432 (1984), or before the government may regulate the content of speech, see, e.g., Sable Communications of California v. FCC, 492 U.S. — (1989), is not remotely comparable to using it for the purpose asserted here. What it produces in those other fields — equality of treatment, and an unrestricted flow of contending speech — are constitutional norms; what it would produce here — a private right to ignore generally applicable laws — is a constitutional anomaly.[3]

Nor is it possible to limit the impact of respondents' proposal by requiring a "compelling state interest" only when the conduct prohibited is "central" to the individual's religion. It is no more appropriate for judges to determine the "centrality" of religious beliefs before applying a "compelling interest" test in

---

2. Justice O'Connor seeks to distinguish *Lyng* [and] *Roy*, on the ground that those cases involved the government's conduct of "its own internal affairs," which is different because, as Justice Douglas said in *Sherbert*, " 'the Free Exercise Clause is written in terms of what the government cannot do to the individual, not in terms of what the individual can exact from the government.' " [It] is hard to see any reason in principle or practicality why the government should have to tailor its health and safety laws to conform to the diversity of religious belief, but should not have to tailor its management of public lands, or its administration of welfare programs.

3. [Just] as we subject to the most exacting scrutiny laws that make classifications based on race, or on the content of speech, so too we strictly scrutinize governmental classifactions based on religion, see McDaniel v. Paty, 435 U.S. 618 (1978). But we have held that race-neutral laws that have the effect of disproportionately disadvantaging a particular racial group do not thereby become subject to compelling-interest analysis under the Equal Protection Clause, see Washington v. Davis, and we have held that generally applicable laws unconcerned with regulating speech that have the effect of interfering with speech do not thereby become subject to compelling-interest analysis under the First Amendment. . . .

the free exercise field, than it would be for them to determine the "importance" of ideas before applying the "compelling interest" test in the free speech field. What principle of law or logic can be brought to bear to contradict a believer's assertion that a particular act is "central" to his personal faith? Judging the centrality of different religious practices is akin to the unacceptable "business of evaluating the relative merits of differing religious claims." United States v. Lee, (Stevens, J., concurring). [Repeatedly] and in many different contexts, we have warned that courts must not presume to determine the place of a particular belief in a religion or the plausibility of a religious claim.[4]

If the "compelling interest" test is to be applied at all, then, it must be applied across the board, to all actions thought to be religiously commanded. Moreover, if "compelling interest" really means what is says (and watering it down here would subvert its rigor in the other fields where it is applied), manly laws will not meet the test. Any society adopting such a system would be courting anarchy, but that danger increases in direct proportion to the society's diversity of religious beliefs, and its determination to coerce or suppress none of them. Precisely because "we are a cosmopolitan nation made up of people of almost every conceivable religious preference," Braunfeld v. Brown, and precisely because we value and protect that religious divergence, we cannot afford the luxury of deeming presumptively invalid, as applied to the religious objector, every regulation of conduct that does not protect an interest of the highest order. The rule respondents favor would open the prospect of constitutionally required religious exemptions from civic obligations of almost every conceivable kind — ranging from compulsory military service, to the payment of taxes, to health and safety regulation such as manslaughter and child neglect laws, compulsory vaccination laws, drug laws, and traffic laws, to social welfare legislation such as minimum wage laws, child labor laws, animal cruelty laws, environmental protection laws, and laws providing for equality of opportunity for the races. The First Amendment's protection of religious liberty does not require this.

Values that are protected against government interference through enshrinement in the Bill of Rights are not thereby banished from the political process. Just as a society that believes in the negative protection accorded to the press by the First Amendment is likely to enact laws that affirmatively foster the dissemination of the printed word, so also a society that believes in the negative protection accorded to religious belief can be expected to be solicitous of that value in its legislation as well. It is therefore not surprising that a number of

4. [Dispensing] with a "centrality" inquiry is utterly unworkable. It would require, for example, the same degree of "compelling state interest" to impede the practice of throwing rice at church weddings as to impede the practice of getting married in church. There is no way out of the difficulty that, if general laws are to be subjected to a "religious practice" exception, both the importance of the law at issue and the centrality of the practice at issue must reasonably be considered.

States have made an exception to their drug laws for sacramental peyote use. But to say that a nondiscriminatory religious-practice exemption is permitted, or even that it is desirable, is not to say that it is constitutionally required, and that the appropriate occasions for its creation can be discerned by the courts. It may fairly be said that leaving accommodation to the political process will place at a relative disadvantage those religious practices that are not widely engaged in; but that unavoidable consequence of democratic government must be preferred to a system in which each conscience is a law unto itself or in which judges weight the social importance of all laws against the centrality of all religious beliefs.

[Reversed.]

JUSTICE O'CONNOR, with whom JUSTICE BRENNAN, JUSTICE MARSHALL, and JUSTICE BLACKMUN join as to [Part] II, concurring in the judgment.

[Today's] holding dramatically departs from well-settled First Amendment jurisprudence, appears unnecessary to resolve the question presented, and is incompatible with our Nation's fundamental commitment to individual religious liberty. . . .

II . . .

A. . . .

[Because] the First Amendment does not distinguish between religious belief and religious conduct, conduct motivated by sincere religious belief, like the belief itself, must therefore be at least presumptively protected by the Free Exercise Clause.

The Court today, however, interprets the Clause to permit the government to prohibit, without justification, conduct mandated by an individual's religious beliefs, so long as that prohibition is generally applicable. But a law that prohibits certain conduct — conduct that happens to be an act of worship for someone — manifestly does prohibit that person's free exercise of his religion. A person who is barred from engaging in religiously motivated conduct is barred from freely exercising his religion. Moreover, that person is barred from freely exercising his religion regardless of whether the law prohibits the conduct only when engaged in for religious reasons, only by members of that religion, or by all persons. It is difficult to deny that a law that prohibits religiously motivated conduct, even if the law is generally applicable, does not at least implicate First Amendment concerns.

The Court responds that generally applicable laws are "one large step" removed from laws aimed at specific religious practices. The First Amendment, however, does not distinguish between laws that are generally applicable and laws that target particular religious practices. Indeed, few States would be so naive as to enact a law directly prohibiting or burdening a religious practice as such. Our free exercise cases have all concerned generally applicable laws that had the effect of significantly burdening a religious practice. If the First Amendment is to have any vitality, it ought not be construed to cover only the extreme and hypothetical situation in which a State directly targets a religious practice. . . .

To say that a person's right to free exercise has been burdened, of course, does not mean that he has an absolute right to engage in the conduct. Under our established First Amendment jurisprudence, we have recognized that the freedom to act, unlike the freedom to believe, cannot be absolute. Instead, we have respected both the First Amendment's express textual mandate and the governmental interest in regulation of conduct by requiring the Government to justify any substantial burden on religiously motivated conduct by a compelling state interest and by means narrowly tailored to achieve that interest. The compelling interest test effectuates the First Amendment's command that religious liberty is an independent liberty, that it occupies a preferred position, and that the Court will not permit encroachments upon this liberty, whether direct or indirect, unless required by clear and compelling governmental interests "of the highest order," [*Yoder*]. . . .

[In] each of the [cases] cited by the Court to support its categorical rule, we rejected the particular constitutional claims before us only after carefully weighing the competing interests. That we rejected the free exercise claims in those cases hardly calls into question the applicability of First Amendment doctrine in the first place. Indeed, it is surely unusual to judge the vitality of a constitutional doctrine by looking to the win-loss record of the plaintiffs who happen to come before us.

B

Respondents, of course, do not contend that their conduct is automatically immune from all governmental regulations simply because it is motivated by their sincere religious beliefs. Rather, respondents invoke our traditional compelling interest test to argue that the Free Exercise Clause requires the State to grant them a limited exemption from its general criminal prohibition against the possession of peyote. The Court today, however, denies them even the opportunity to make that argument. . . .

In my view, however, the essence of a free exercise claim is relief from a burden imposed by government on religious practices or beliefs, whether the burden is imposed directly through laws that prohibit or compel specific religious practices, or indirectly through laws that, in effect, make abandonment of one's own religious or conformity to the religious beliefs of others the price of an equal place in the civil community. [A] State that makes criminal an individual's religiously motivated conduct burdens that individual's free exercise of religion in the severest manner possible, for it "results in the choice to the individual of either abandoning his religious principle or facing criminal prosecution." I would have thought it beyond argument that such laws implicate free exercise concerns. . . .

Legislatures, of course, have always been "left free to reach actions which were in violation of social duties or subversive of good order." [*Reynolds*]. Yet because of the close relationship between conduct and religious belief, "[i]n every case the power to regulate must be so exercised as not, in attaining a permissible end, unduly to infringe the protected freedom." [*Cantwell*]. Once it has been shown that a government regulation or criminal prohibition burdens the free exercise of religion, we have consistently asked the Government to demonstrate that unbending application of its regulation to the religious objector "is essential to accomplish an overriding governmental interest," [*Lee*], or represents "the least restrictive means of achieving some compelling state interest," [*Thomas*]. To me, the sounder approach — the approach more consistent with our role as judges to decide each case on its individual merits — is to apply this test in each case to determine whether the burden on the specific plaintiffs before us is constitutionally significant and whether the particular criminal interest asserted by the State before us is compelling. Even if, as an empirical matter, a government's criminal laws might usually serve a compelling interest in health, safety, or public order, the First Amendment at least requires a case-by-case determination of the question, sensitive to the facts of each particular claim. Given the range of conduct that a State might legitimately make criminal, we cannot assume, merely because a law carries criminal sanctions and is generally applicable, that the First Amendment never requires the State to grant a limited exemption for religiously motivated conduct. . . .

[The cases] cited by the Court for the proposition that we have rejected application of the *Sherbert* test outside the unemployment compensation field are distinguishable because they arose in the narrow, specialized contexts in which we have not traditionally required the government to justify a burden on religious conduct by articulating a compelling interest. That we did not apply the compelling interest test in these cases says nothing about whether the test should continue to apply in paradigm free exercise cases such as the one presented here.

The Court today gives no convincing reason to depart from settled First Amendment jurisprudence. There is nothing talismanic about neutral laws of general applicability or general criminal prohibitions, for laws neutral toward religion can coerce a person to violate his religious conscience or intrude upon his religious duties just as effectively as laws aimed at religion. Although the Court suggests that the compelling interest test, as applied to generally applicable laws, would result in a "constitutional anomaly," the First Amendment unequivocally makes freedom of religion, like freedom from race discrimination and freedom of speech, a "constitutional nor[m]," not an "anomaly." [As] the language of the Clause itself makes clear, an individual's free exercise of religion is a preferred constitutional activity. See, e.g., McConnell, Accommodation of

Religion, 1985 Sup. Ct. Rev. 1, 9 ("[T]he text of the First Amendment itself 'singles out' religion for special protections"). A law that makes criminal such an activity therefore triggers constitutional concern — and heightened judicial scrutiny — even if it does not target the particular religious conduct at issue. Our free speech cases similarly recognize that neutral regulations that affect free speech values are subject to a balancing, rather than categorical, approach. The Court's parade of horribles, not only fails as a reason for discarding the compelling interest test, it instead demonstrates just the opposite; that courts have been quite capable of applying our free exercise jurisprudence to strike sensible balances between religious liberty and competing state interest.

Finally, the Court today suggests that the disfavoring of minority religions is an "unavoidable consequence" under our system of government and that accommodation of such religions must be left to the political process. In my view, however, the First Amendment was enacted precisely to protect the rights of those whose religious practices are not shared by the majority and may be viewed with hostility. The history of our free exercise doctrine amply demonstrates the harsh impact majoritarian rule has had on unpopular or emerging religious groups such as the Jehovah's Witnesses and the Amish. [The] compelling interest test reflects the First Amendment's mandate of preserving religious liberty to the fullest extent possible in a pluralistic society. For the Court to deem this command a "luxury," to denigrate "[t]he very purpose of a Bill of Rights."

[In Part III of her opinion, in which Justices Brennan, Marshall, and Blackmun did not join, Justice O'Connor concluded that Oregon's prohibition satisfied the compelling state interest test. She agreed that the prohibition placed a "severe burden" on the free exercise of religion, but said that the state had a "significant interest" in controlling drug use. Finding the question close, she concluded that "uniform application" of the prohibition is "essential to accomplish" the overriding purpose of preventing physical harm caused by drug use. Selective exemptions for religious believers would "seriously impair" the state's interest.]

JUSTICE BLACKMUN, with whom JUSTICE BRENNAN and JUSTICE MARSHALL join, dissenting. . . .

[I] do not believe the Founders thought their dearly bought freedom from religious persecution a "luxury," but an essential element of liberty — and they could not have thought religious intolerance "unavoidable," for they drafted the Religion Clauses precisely in order to avoid that intolerance. . . .

In weighing respondents' clear interest in the free exercise of their religion against Oregon's asserted interest in enforcing its drug laws, it is important to articulate in precise terms the state interest involved. It is not the State's broad interest in fighting the critical "war on drugs" that must be weighed against respondents' claim, but the State's narrow interest in refusing to make an exception for the religious, ceremonial use of peyote. [Failure] to reduce the competing interests to the same plane of generality tends to distort the weighing process in the State's favor.

The State's interest in enforcing its prohibition, in order to be sufficiently compelling to outweigh a free exercise claim, cannot be merely abstract or symbolic. The State cannot plausibly assert that unbending application of a criminal prohibition is essential to fulfill any compelling interest, if it does not, in fact, attempt to enforce that prohibition. In this case, the State actually has not evinced any concrete interest in enforcing its drug laws against religious users of peyote. Oregon has never sought to prosecute respondents, and does not claim that it has made significant enforcement efforts against other religious users of peyote. The State's asserted interest thus amounts only to the symbolic preservation of an unenforced prohibition. But a government interest in "symbolism, even symbolism for so worthy a cause as the abolition of unlawful drugs," Treasury Employees v. Von Raab, — U.S. — (1989) (Scalia, J., dissenting) cannot suffice to abrogate the constitutional rights of individuals. . . .

The State proclaims an interest in protecting the health and safety of its citizens from the dangers of unlawful drugs. It offers, however, no evidence that the religious use of peyote has ever harmed anyone. The factual findings of other courts cast doubt on the State's assumption that religious use of peyote is harmful.

[Moreover,] 23 States, including many that have significant Native American populations, have statutory or judicially crafted exemptions in their drug laws for religious use of peyote. Although this does not prove that Oregon must have such an exception too, it is significant that these States, and the Federal Government, all find their (presumably compelling) interests in controlling the use of dangerous drugs compatible with an exemption for religious use of peyote.

The carefully circumscribed ritual context in which respondents used peyote is far removed from the irresponsible and unrestricted recreational use of unlawful drugs. [6] The Native American Church's internal restrictions on, and supervi-

---

6. In this respect, respondents' use of peyote seems closely analogous to the sacramental use of wine by the Roman Catholic Church. During Prohibition, the Federal Government exempted such use of wine from its general ban on possession and use of alcohol. However compelling the Government's then general interest in prohibiting the use of alcohol may have been, it could not plausibly have asserted an interest sufficiently compelling to outweigh Catholics' right to take communion.

sion of, its members' use of peyote substantially obviate the State's health and safety concerns. . . . [7]

[The] State argues that granting an exception for religious peyote use would erode its interest in the uniform, fair, and certain enforcement of its drug laws. The State fears that, if it grants an exemption for religious peyote use, a flood of other claims to religious exemptions will follow. It would then be placed in a dilemma, it says, between allowing a patchwork of exemptions that would hinder its law enforcement efforts, and risking a violation of the Establishment Clause by arbitrarily limiting its religious exemptions. This argument, however, could be made in almost any free exercise case.

The State's apprehension of a flood of other religious claims is purely speculative. Almost half the States and the Federal Government have maintained an exemption for religious peyote use for many years, and apparently have not found themselves overwhelmed by claims to other religious exemptions. [8] Allowing an exemption for religious peyote use would not necessarily oblige the State to grant a similar exemption to other religious groups. The unusual circumstances that make the religious use of peyote compatible with the State's interests in health and safety and in preventing drug trafficking would not apply to other religious claims. Some religions, for example, might not restrict drug use to a limited ceremonial context, as does the native American Church. Some religious claims involve drugs such as marijuana and heroin, in which there is significant illegal traffic, with its attendant greed and violence, so that it would be difficult to grant a religious exemption without seriously compromising law enforcement efforts. That the State might grant an exemption for religious peyote use, but deny other religious claims arising in different circumstances, would not violate the Establishment Clause. Though the State must treat all religions equally, and not favor one over another, this obligation is fulfilled by the uniform application of the "compelling interest" test to all free exercise claims, not by reaching uniform results as to all claims. A showing that religious peyote use does not unduly interfere with the State's interests is "one that probably few other religious groups or sects could make," *Yoder*; this does not mean that an exemption limited to peyote use is tantamount to an establishment of religion.

III . . .

[Respondents] believe, and their sincerity has never been at issue, that the peyote plant embodies their deity, and eating it is an act of worship and

7. The use of peyote is, to some degree, self-limiting. The peyote plant is extremely bitter, and eating it is an unpleasant experience, which would tend to discourage casual or recreational use.

8. Over the past years, various sects have raised free exercise claims regarding drug use. In no reported case, except those involving claims of religious peyote use, has the claimant prevailed.

communion. Without peyote, they could not enact the essential ritual of their religion.

If Oregon can constitutionally prosecute them for this act of worship, they, like the Amish, may be "forced to migrate to some other and more tolerant region." *Yoder.* This potentially devastating impact must be viewed in light of the federal policy — reached in reaction to many years of religious persecution and intolerance — of protecting the religious freedom of Native Americans. See American Indian Religious Freedom Act, 42 U.S.C. §1996 ("it shall be the policy of the United States to protect and preserve for American Indians their inherent right of freedom to believe, express, and exercise the traditional religions . . . , including but not limited to access to sites, use and possession of sacred objects, and the freedom to worship through ceremonials and traditional rites").

The American Indian Religious Freedom Act, in itself, may not create rights enforceable against government action restricting religious freedom, but this Court must scrupulously apply its free exercise analysis to the religious claims of Native Americans, however unorthodox they may be. Otherwise, both the First Amendment and the stated policy of Congress will offer to Native Americans merely an unfulfilled and hollow promise. . . .

[I] dissent.

NOTE: THE SCOPE OF SMITH

How broadly does *Smith* undermine a doctrine of mandatory accommodation? (a) Are the Court's distinctions of *Sherbert* persuasive? Does the Court mean to suggest that the unemployment commission in *Sherbert* was in a position to balance the impairment of free exercise against the prevention of fraudulent claims? If so, why is the Oregon unemployment commission not similarly situated with respect to peyote? Suppose that a state's disapproval of a practice is great enough to induce it to deny various forms of public assistance to those who engage in the practice, but not so great as to lead it to make the practice illegal. That describes the situation in *Sherbert,* where the disapproved practice is voluntary unemployment. Why should accommodation be required in such cases but not in *Smith?*

(b) Is the Court's explanation of *Cantwell* and *Yoder* persuasive? Consider the proposition that because there is no substantive due process right, independent of a religious claim, to keep children out of school, and there is no religious claim, independent of a due process claim, to do so, the two inadequate arguments taken together cannot add up to a valid claim.

(c) Suppose a state adopts an antidiscrimination statute, imposing civil liability, prohibiting discrimination on the basis of religion, and a potential employee, who is Jewish, applies for a job as a Catholic priest. Must the antidiscrimination statute be interpreted to include an exemption for religion-related job qualifications? Does the Court's discussion of cases in which free exercise claims are joined with other claims, such as freedom of association, adequately deal with this problem? Consider the implications of Justice Scalia's reference to the political process at the conclusion of the Court's opinion. Note, however, that, although the political process protected the sacramental use of wine during Prohibition, it has not fully protected the sacramental use of peyote. What limitations does this suggest on reliance on the political process to protect religious liberty interests?

Page 1420.   At the bottom of the page, add the following:

Consider McConnell, Accommodation of Religion, 1985 Sup. Ct. Rev. 1, 1-3:

> The much-discussed "tension" between the two Religion Clauses largely arises from the Court's substitution of a misleading formula (the three-part *Lemon* [test]) and subsidiary, instrumental, values (especially the separation of church and state) in place of the central value of religious liberty. [Between] the accommodations compelled by the Free Exercise Clause and the benefits to religion prohibited by the Establishment Clause there exists a class of permissible government actions toward religion, which have as their purpose and effects the facilitation of religious liberty. Neither strict neutrality nor separationism can account for the idea of accommodation or define its limits. Only an interpretation of the Religion Clauses based on religious liberty [satisfactorily] distinguishes permissible accommodations from impermissible establishments.

See also Simson, The Establishment Clause in the Supreme Court: Rethinking the Court's Approach, 72 Cornell L. Rev. 905 (1987), for another suggested reformation of *Lemon*.

Page 1421.   At the beginning of section 6 of the Note, add the following:

Statutes that attempt to accommodate the concerns of adherents of religion lie at the borderland of the free exercise and establishment clauses. They promote "free exercise values," in the sense that they allow believers to pursue their religious beliefs without hindrance, but legislatures are rarely compelled by the free exercise clause to adopt statutory accommodations. Such statutes are in tension with some formulations of the requirements of the establishment clause, because they have the purpose of advancing religion in the sense just specified. Are such accommodations constitutional? If so, why?

CORPORATION OF PRESIDING BISHOP v. AMOS, 483 U.S. 327 (1987): Appellee Mayson was employed for 16 years as a "building engineer" (janitor) at a nonprofit gymnasium open to the public run by the Mormon

Church. He was fired in 1981 because he failed to qualify for a "temple recommend," a certificate from the Church that he was a church member who observed the Church's standards. He sued his employer, alleging that his discharge violated the prohibition in section 703 of the 1964 Civil Rights Act against discrimination in employment on the basis of religion. The defendants moved to dismiss the claim on the ground that section 702 of the Act shielded them from liability. That section provides that the employment discrimination provisions of the Act "shall not apply [to] a religious corporation [with] respect to the employment of individuals of a particular religion to perform work connected with the carrying on by such corporation [of] its activities." Mayson responded that "if construed to allow religious employers to discriminate on religious grounds in hiring for nonreligious jobs, section 702 violates the Establishment Clause."

The Court, in an opinion by Justice White, unanimously held that the exemption did not violate the establishment clause:

"[The] exemption involved here is in no way questionable under the *Lemon* analysis, [despite the defendant's contention that] an exemption statute will always have the effect of advancing religion." Applying the *Lemon* test, Justice White stated that the law's secular purpose need not be "unrelated to religion — that would amount to a requirement 'that the government show a callous indifference to religious groups.' [Rather], *Lemon*'s 'purpose' requirement aims at preventing the [governmental] decisionmaker [from] abandoning neutrality and acting with the intent of promoting a particular point of view in religious matters. [It] is a permissible legislative purpose to alleviate significant governmental interference with the ability of religious organizations to define and carry out their religious missions. [We] may assume that [an exemption for religious activities of employees of religious organizations] was adequate in the sense that the Free Exercise Clause required no more. Nonetheless, it is a significant burden on a religious organization to require it, on pain of substantial liability, to predict which of its activities a secular court will consider religious. The line is hardly a bright one, and an organization might understandably be concerned that a judge would not understand its religious tenets and sense of mission. Fear of potential liability might affect the way an organization carried out what it understood to be its religious mission."

Turning to the "effects" element in the *Lemon* test, the Court conceded that "religious organizations are better able now to advance their purposes" than they were before they were exempted from the Civil Rights Act. "But religious groups have been better able to advance their purposes on account of many laws that have passed constitutional muster [citing *Walz* and Board of Education v. Allen]. A law is not unconstitutional simply because it *allows* churches to advance religion, which is their very purpose. For a law to have forbidden 'effects,' [it] must be fair to say that the *government itself* has advanced religion through its own activities and influence."

The Court rejected the argument that section 702 was unconstitutional because it "singles out religious entities for a benefit. [Statutes] that give special consideration to religious groups are [not] per se invalid. That would run contrary to the teaching of our cases that there is ample room for accommodation of religion under the Establishment Clause. Where, as here, government acts with the proper purpose of lifting a regulation that burdens the exercise of religion, we see no reason to require that the exemption come packaged with benefits to secular entities."

Justice Brennan concurred in the judgment, in an opinion joined by Justice Marshall:

"This case presents a confrontation between the rights of religious organizations and those of individuals. Any exemption from Title VII's proscription on religious discrimination necessarily has the effect of burdening the religious liberty of [employees]. An exemption says that a person may be put to the choice of either conforming to certain religious tenets or losing a job opportunity. [The] potential for coercion created by such a provision is in serious tension with our commitment to individual freedom of conscience in matters of religious belief."

Justice Brennan noted that "the fact that a religious organization is permitted, rather than required, to impose this burden is irrelevant; what is significant is that the burden is the effect of the exemption." He continued, "[religious] organizations have an interest in autonomy in ordering their internal affairs. [For] many individuals, religious activity derives meaning in large measure from participation in a larger religious community. Such a community represents an ongoing tradition of shared beliefs, an organic entity not reducible to a mere aggregation of individuals. Determining that certain activities are in furtherance of an organization's religious mission, and that only those committed to that mission should conduct them, is thus a means by which a religious community defines itself. Solicitude for a church's ability to do so reflects the idea that furtherance of the autonomy of religious organizations often furthers individual religious freedom as well. The authority to engage in this process of self-definition inevitably involves what we normally regard as infringement on Free Exercise rights. [We] are willing to countenance the imposition of such a condition because we deem it vital that, if certain activities constitute part of a religious community's practice, then a religious organization should be able to require that only members of its community perform those activities. [Because] determining whether an activity is religious or secular requires a searching case-by-case analysis, [considerable] ongoing government entanglement in religious affairs [may result]. Furthermore, this prospect of government intrusion raises concern that a religious organization may be chilled in its Free Exercise activity. [Nonprofit] activities [are] most likely to present cases in which characterization of the activity as religious or secular will be a close question. [This] substantial potential for chilling religious activity makes inappropriate a case-by-case determination of the character of a nonprofit organization, and justifies a categorical exemption for nonprofit activities. [It] permits infringement on employee Free Exercise rights in those instances in which discrimination is most likely to reflect a religious community's self-definition."

Justice Brennan's opinion concluded, "Sensitivity to individual religious freedom dictates that religious discrimination be permitted only with respect to employment in religious activities. Concern for the autonomy of religious organizations demands that we avoid the entanglement and the chill on religious expression that a case-by-case determination would produce. We cannot escape the fact that these aims are in tension."

Justice O'Connor also concurred in the judgment. She said that the Court's distinction between " 'allowing' religious organizations to advance religion, in contrast to government action directly advancing religion [seems] to obscure far more than to enlighten. Almost any government benefit to religion could be recharacterized as simply 'allowing' a religion to better advance itself. [In] nearly every case of a government benefit to religion, the benefit would not be advanced if the religion did not take advantage of the benefit. [Here] the Church had the power to put Mayson to the choice of qualifying for a temple recommend or losing his job because the *government* had lifted from religious organizations the general regulatory burden imposed by section 702. The necessary first step in evaluating an Establishment Clause challenge to a government action lifting from religious organizations a generally applicable regulatory burden is to recognize that such government action *does* have the effect of advancing religion. The necessary second step is to separate those benefits to religion that constitutionally accommodate the free exercise of religion from those that provide unjustifiable benefits to religious organizations." She relied on her opinion in *Lynch* to explain the distinction between the for-profit and the nonprofit activities of religious organizations: "Because there is a probability that a nonprofit activity of a religious organization will itself be involved in the organization's religious mission, in my view the objective observer should perceive the government action as an accommodation of the exercise of religion rather than as a government endorsement of religion. It is not clear, however, that activities conducted by religious organizations solely as profit-making enterprises will be as likely to be directly involved in the religious mission of the organization."

Justice Blackmun concurred in the judgment "essentially for the reasons set forth in Justice O'Connor's opinion."

In Texas Monthly v. Bullock, 109 S. Ct. 890 (1989), a sharply divided Court held unconstitutional a statute that exempted religious publications from a state sales tax. Justice Brennan's opinion, joined by Justices Marshall and Stevens, said that "government policies with secular objectives [may] incidentally benefit religion. The nonsectarian aims of government and religious groups often overlap, and this Court has never required that public authorities refrain from implementing reasonable measures to advance legitimate secular goals merely because they would thereby relieve religious groups of costs they would otherwise incur [citing Widmar v. Vincent (Casebook, p.1248) and *Walz* (Casebook, p. 1392)]." However, in such cases "the benefits derived by religious organizations flowed to a large number of nonreligious groups as well. Indeed, were those benefits confined to religious organizations, they could not have appeared other than as state sponsorship of religion." The exemption for religious publications "lacks sufficient breadth to pass scrutiny under the Establishment Clause. [Insofar] as [the] subsidy is conferred upon a wide array of nonsectarian groups as well as religious groups in pursuit of some legitimate secular end, the fact that religious groups benefit incidentally does not deprive the subsidy of the secular purpose and primary effect mandated by the Establishment Clause. However, when government directs a subsidy exclusively to religious organizations that is not required by the Free Exercise Clause and that either burdens nonbeneficiaries markedly or cannot reasonably be seen as removing a significant state-imposed deterrent to the free exercise of religion, [it] 'provide[s] unjustifiable awards of assistance to religious organizations' and cannot but 'conve[y] a message of endorsement' to slighted members of the community [*Amos*]. This is particularly true where, as here, the subsidy is targeted at writings that *promulgate* the teachings of religious faiths." Justice Brennan's opinion did not describe in detail "how expansive the class of exempt organizations or activities must be to withstand constitutional assault," but said that it "depends on the State's secular aim in granting a tax exemption." If the state subsidized groups contributing to the community's "cultural, intellectual, and moral betterment," the exemption for religious publications would be permitted, but "if Texas sought to promote reflection and discussion about questions of ultimate value and the contours of a good and meaningful life, then a tax exemption would have to be available to an extended range of associations whose publications were substantially devoted to such matters."

Justice Scalia's dissent, joined by Chief Justice Rehnquist and Justice Kennedy, argued that the tax exemption was a permissible accommodation of religion. For him, breadth of coverage is relevant only where the state justifies its legislation on entirely secular grounds, but "where accommodation of religion is the justification, by definition religion is being singled out." Although "it is not always easy to determine when accommodation slides over into promotion, and neutrality into favoritism," the tax exemption was an easy case, because imposing a general sales tax on the sale of religious publications was at least arguably unconstitutional as a burden on religion. Justice Brennan's opinion rejected this argument on the ground that it was obviously not unconstitutional to impose a general sales tax on religious publications. For him, accommodations must not "impose substantial burdens on nonbeneficiaries [or must be] designed to alleviate government intrusions that might significantly deter adherents of a particular faith from conduct protected by the Free Exercise Clause." The tax exemption did burden nonbeneficiaries by increasing their tax bills, and did not alleviate a "demonstrated and possibly grace imposition on religious activity sheltered by the Free Exercise Clause."

Justice Blackmun, whose opinion concurring in the result was joined by Justice O'Connor, expressed more sympathy with the accommodation argument. He argued that the tax exemption was unconstitutional because it was "limited to the sale of religious literature by a religious organization." How is this different from Justice Brennan's concern about the breadth of the exemption? (Justice White also concurred in the result, relying on Arkansas Writers' Project v. Ragland, Supplement p.220.)

Page 1421. At the end of section 6a of the Note, add the following:

The Court upheld the constitutionality of the Equal Access Act in Board of Education of Westside Community Schools v. Mergens, 58 U.S.L.W. 4720 (June 4, 1990). Justice O'Connor's plurality opinion on the constitutional question concluded that "the logic of *Widmar* applies" to the Equal Access Act. Prohibiting discrimination on the basis of political as well as religious speech was a secular purpose under *Lemon*. Equal access would not have the effect of conveying a message of government endorsement of religion. "We think that secondary school students are mature enough and are likely to understand that a school does not endorse or support student speech that it merely permits on a nondiscriminatory basis." Congress had made a similar determination, and she said that the Court should not "lightly second-guess [legislative] judgments, particularly where the judgments are based in part on empirical determinations," as this one was. She noted that the Act limited the permissible participation by school officials at meetings of religious groups, thereby reducing the risk of state endorsement. She also noted that "the broad spectrum of officially recognized student groups [counteracts] any possible message of official endorsement of or preference for religion or a particular religion. [To] the extent that a religious club is merely one of many different student-initiated voluntary clubs, students should perceive no message of government endorsement of religion."

Justice Marshall, joined by Justice Brennan, concurred in the judgment, stressing that schools must take steps to dissociate themselves from religious clubs, particularly where most of the other clubs appear to be "part of the school's effort to inculcate fundamental values." "[If] the religion club is the sole advocacy-oriented group in the forum, or one of a very limited number, and the school continues to promote its student-club program as instrumental to citizenship, then the school's failure to disassociate itself from the religious activity will reasonably be understood as an endorsement of that activity." *Widmar* was different because universities stress student autonomy, decreasing the likelihood that "student speech will be regarded as school speech." But "where a school [regards] its student clubs as a mechanism for defining and transmitting fundamental values, the inclusion of a religious club in the school's program will almost certainly signal school endorsement of the religious practice."

Justice Kennedy, joined by Justice Scalia, also concurred in the judgment, because the Equal Access Act did not give direct benefits to a religion, nor did it coerce students to participate in religious activities. "[No] constitutional violation occurs if the school's action is based upon a recognition of the fact that membership in a religious club is one of many permissible ways for a student to further his or her own personal enrichment." Justice Stevens dissented, finding that the statute, which applied only to schools that have "noncurriculum related" clubs, did not apply to the Westside schools.

Page 1423.   Before the first full paragraph, add the following:

In *Amos*, the Court distinguished *Thornton* in this way:

> [In *Thornton*], Connecticut had given the force of law to the employee's designation of a Sabbath day and required accommodation by the employer regardless of the burden which that constituted for the employer or other employees. [In this case, Mayson] was not legally obligated to take the steps necessary to qualify for a temple recommend, and his discharge was not required by the statute.

Justice O'Connor found this distinction to be of "little significance" because the government placed the employer in a position to insist on a temple recommend by lifting the otherwise applicable prohibition on religious discrimination in employment.

Page 1423.   Before section 7 of the Note, add the following:

6A. *A summary?* Justice Scalia's dissenting opinion in Edwards v. Aguillard, 482 U.S. 578 (1987), offered this summary of circumstances under which "certain kinds of government actions undertaken with the specific intention of improving the position of religion do not 'advance religion' " under *Lemon*:

> [First], since we have consistently described the Establishment Clause as forbidding not only state action motivated by the desire to *advance* religion, but also that intended to "disapprove," "inhibit," or evince "hostility" toward religion, and since we have said that government "neutrality" toward religion is the preeminent goal of the First Amendment, a State which discovers that its employees are inhibiting religion must take steps to prevent them from doing so, even though its purpose would clearly be to advance religion. [Second], we have held that intentional governmental advancement of religion is sometimes required by the Free Exercise Clause. [*Sherbert*; *Yoder*.] [We] have also held that in some circumstances government may act to accommodate religion, even if that action is not required by the First Amemdment. [Few] would contend that Title VII [violates] the Establishment Clause, even though its

"purpose" is, of course, to advance religion, and even though it is almost certainly not required by the Free Exercise Clause.

Page 1423.   At the conclusion of section 7 of the Note, add the following:

In Ohio Civil Rights Comm. v. Dayton Christian Schools, Inc., 477 U.S. 619 (1986), the Court rejected a free exercise challenge to the mere assertion of state jurisdiction to resolve an employment dispute, allegedly involving gender discrimination, between a teacher and a religious institution. The dispute arose when a religious school informed a pregnant teacher that, because its religious doctrine required that she stay at home with her child, her contract would not be renewed. When the teacher consulted a lawyer, the school suspended her immediately for challenging its decision in violation of its internal dispute resolution doctrine, which it also claimed to be based upon religious belief. The teacher then filed a complaint with the Ohio Civil Rights Commission, alleging that the nonrenewal decision constituted gender discrimination in violation of state law. After the commission determined that there was probable cause to proceed with the complaint, the school filed this action seeking to enjoin the state proceedings on the ground that any investigation of its hiring process or imposition of sanctions for its termination decision would violate the free exercise clause. In an opinion by Justice Rehnquist, the Court held that the federal courts should have abstained from adjudicating the case because of the pendency of the state administrative proceeding. It therefore failed to reach appellee's claim that the free exercise clause immunized it from application of the state gender discrimination statute. The Court did hold, however, that the mere exercise of jurisdiction over it by a state administrative body did not violate its first amendment rights.

> Even religious schools cannot claim to be wholly free from some state regulation. We therefore think that however [the school's] constitutional claim should be decided on the merits, the Commission violates no constitutional rights by merely investigating the circumstances of [the teacher's] discharge in this case, if only to ascertain whether the ascribed religious-based reason was in fact the reason for the discharge.

What differences would result from treating regulation of religious institutions as raising problems of establishment rather than problems of free exercise? See Marshall & Blomgren, Regulating Religious Organizations Under the Establishment Clause, 47 Ohio St. L.J. 293 (1986).

Chapter Nine

Economic Liberties and the Constitution: The Contracts and Takings Clauses

A. THE CONTRACTS CLAUSE

Page 1437. Before *United States Trust Co.*, add the following:

4. *Legislative continuity.* The contracts clause might be understood as an effort to deal with problems of legislative continuity and discontinuity, at least when a legislature attempts to modify a bargain made by its predecessors. See the valuable discussion in Sterk, The Continuity of Legislatures: Of Contracts and the Contracts Clause, 88 Colum. L. Rev. 647 (1988):

> [W]hatever deficiencies legislatures have as agents and as deliberative bodies may be magnified when decisions of future impact are at stake. . . . [I]n its contracts clause decisions, the Supreme Court has rejected a model of strong legislative continuity. . . . Judicial intervention in contracts clause [cases] has long reflected a view of legislatures as discontinuous bodies incapable of adequately accounting for the interests of future constituents.

Consider the possibility that a wide range of constitutional doctrines are implicitly influenced by perceptions of this sort.

Page 1444. Before section 4 of the Note, add the following:

The Court adopted a similarly deferential stance in the face of a contract clause claim advanced in Keystone Bituminous Coal Assn. v. DeBenedictis, 480 U.S. 470 (1987). A Pennsylvania statute had the effect of voiding damage waivers that coal companies had obtained from surface owners for damage to surface property caused by mining. The Court, in an opinion by Justice Stevens, upheld the statute. In the Court's view, the state had a strong public interest in preventing the environmental harm caused by the mining. Moreover, in cases where the state itself is not a contracting party, courts should defer to the legislative judgment as to the necessity and reasonableness of the contractual abrogation.

For a discussion of takings clause problems posed by federal retroactive regulation of private penson plans, see Supplement to Casebook page 1464, infra.

B. THE EMINENT DOMAIN CLAUSE

Page 1459.   Before the Note, add the following:

KEYSTONE BITUMINOUS COAL ASSN. v. DeBENEDICTIS, 480 U.S. 470 (1987):   In this case, the Court upheld a modern day analogue of the Kohler Act, invalidated in *Pennsylvania Coal Co.* A Pennsylvania statute enacted in 1966 prohibited mining that caused subsidence damage to public buildings, dwellings used for human habitation, and cemeteries. The administrative agency charged with enforcing the statute generally required 50 percent of the coal beneath such structures to be kept in place as a means of providing surface support. Moreover, the agency was authorized to revoke mining permits if removal of coal caused damage to such structures and the operator had not repaired or paid for the damage.

Justice Stevens delivered the Court's opinion: "Petitioners assert that disposition of their takings claim calls for no more than a straightforward application of the Court's decision in [*Pennsylvania Coal*]. Although there are some obvious similarities between the cases, we agree with the [court below] that the similarities are far less significant than the [differences]. . . .

"The two factors that the [*Pennsylvania Coal*] Court considered relevant have become integral parts of our takings analysis. We have held that land use regulation can effect a taking if it 'does not substantially advance legitimate state interests, . . . or denies an owner economically viable use of his land.' Agins v. Tiburon, 447 U.S. 255, 260 (1980).

"Application of these tests to petitioners' challenge demonstrates that they have not satisfied their burden of showing that the Subsidence Act constitutes a taking. First, unlike the Kohler Act, the character of the governmental action involved here leans heavily against finding a taking; the [state] has acted to arrest what it perceives to be a significant threat to the common welfare. Second, there is no record in this case to support a finding, similar to the one the Court made in *Pennsylvania Coal,* that the Subsidence Act makes it impossible for petitioners to profitably engage in their business, or that there has been undue interference with their investment-backed expectations. . . .

"Unlike the Kohler Act, [the] Subsidence Act does not merely involve a balancing of the private economic interests of coal companies against the private interests of the surface owners. The Pennsylvania Legislature specifically found that important public interests are served by enforcing a policy that is designed to minimize subsidence in certain areas. . . .

"The second factor that distinguishes this case from *Pennsylvania Coal* is the finding in that case that the Kohler Act made mining of 'certain coal' commercially impracticable. In this case, by contrast, petitioners have not shown any deprivation significant enough to satisfy the heavy burden placed upon one alleging a regulatory taking. . . .

"The parties have stipulated that enforcement of the [50%] rule will require petitioners to leave approximately 27 million tons of coal in place. Because they own that coal but cannot mine it, they contend that Pennsylvania has appropriated it for the public purposes described in the Subsidence Act.

"[But the] 27 million tons of coal do not constitute a separate segment of property for takings law purposes. . . .

"We do not consider Justice Holmes' statement that the Kohler Act made mining of 'certain coal' commercially impracticable as requiring us to focus on the individual pillars of coal that must be left in place. . . .

"When the coal that must remain beneath the ground is viewed in the context of any reasonable unit of petitioners' coal mining operations and financial-backed expectations, it is plain that the petitioners have not come close to satisfying their burden of proving that they have been denied the economically viable use of that property."

Chief Justice Rehnquist, in an opinion joined by Justices Powell, O'Connor, and Scalia, dissented.

Page 1461.   Before section 3 of the Note, add the following:

2A. *Remedies for "regulatory" takings*. When government regulation is sufficiently intrusive to constitute a taking, what remedy does the Constitution require? In First English Evangelical Lutheran Church of Glendale v. County of Los Angeles, 482 U.S. 304 (1987), the Court, in an opinion by Justice Rehnquist, held that the mere invalidation of the ordinance restricting use of the property in question was constitutionally insufficient. Although the state was free to end the taking by not enforcing the ordinance, it was also required to pay damages for the temporary taking effected during the period before the ordinance was invalidated. Justice Stevens, joined by Justices Blackmun and O'Connor, filed a dissenting opinion.

Page 1462.   After section 2a of the Note, add the following:

Compare *Andrus* to Hodel v. Irving, 481 U.S. 704 (1987). In the nineteenth century, Congress enacted a law that divided the communal property on the reservation of the Sioux Nation into individual allotments. The allotted lands were held in trust for the Indians by the United States, and after 1910, the allottees were permitted to dispose of their interests by will in accordance with regulations promulgated by the Secretary of the Interior. As successive generations came to hold the allotted lands, ownership became fractionated into extremely small, undivided interests, with the result that it became impractical to make productive use of the lands. In order to deal with this problem, Congress enacted the Indian Land Consolidation Act in 1983, which provided that undivided, fractional interests in trust land could not be devised, but instead would escheat to the tribe if the interest represented 2 percent or less of the total acreage of the tract and had earned its owner less than $100 in the previous year.

The Court, in an opinion by Justice O'Connor held this escheat provision unconstitutional. Applying an "essentially ad hoc, factual" approach, the Court noted that it might well have found the statute constitutionally permissible but for the extraordinary character of the regulation. "[The] regulation here amounts to virtually the abrogation of the right to pass on a certain type of property [to] one's heirs. In one form or another, the right to pass on property — to one's family in particular — has been part of the Anglo-American legal system since feudal times." The Court noted, however, that it would "surely" be permissible for the government to prevent owners from further subdividing the land among future heirs· on pain of escheat and to abolish descent of such interest by rules of intestacy.

Are *Allard* and *Irving* consistent? Justice Scalia, in a concurring opinion joined by Chief Justice Rehnquist and Justice Powell, noted that "the present statute, insofar as concerns the balance between rights taken and rights left untouched [is] indistinguishable from the statute that was at issue in [*Allard*]," and that "in finding a taking today our decision effectively limits *Allard* to its facts." In another concurring opinion, Justice Brennan, joined by Justices Marshall and Blackmun, found "nothing in today's opinion that would limit [*Allard*]. Indeed, [I] am of the view that the unique negotiations giving rise to the property rights and expectations at issue here make this case the unusual one."

Page 1463.   Before the last full paragraph, add the following:

Compare *Kaiser Aetna* to United States v. Riverside Bayview Homes, 474 U.S. 121 (1985). Pursuant to the Clean Water Act, the Army Corps of Engineers issued regulations requiring landowners to secure permits before discharging fill material into wetlands adjacent to navigable bodies of water and their tributaries. The Corps then brought this action against a landowner to enjoin respondents from placing fill material in adjacent wetlands. The district court granted the injunction, but the court of appeals reversed, holding that a narrow construction of the regulations was necessary in order to avoid a taking of private property without just compensation. The Court, in an opinion by Justice White, reversed the court of appeals. Although acknowledging that governmental land-use regulation may "under extreme circumstances" constitute a taking, the Court held that the mere assertion of regulatory jurisdiction does not amount to a taking.

> The reasons are obvious. A requirement that a person obtain a permit before engaging in a certain use of his or her property does not itself "take" the property in any sense: after all, the very existence of a permit system implies that permission may be granted, leaving the landowner free to use the property as desired. Moreover, even if the permit is denied, there may be other viable uses available to the owner. Only when a permit is denied and the effect of the denial is to prevent "economically viable" use of the land in question can it be said that a taking has occurred.

See also MacDonald, Sommer & Frates v. County of Yolo, 477 U.S. 340 (1986). After appellant's proposed subdivision map for development of rural land was rejected by the county planning commission, it brought this action alleging a "taking" of its property and seeking money damages. The trial court granted the defendant's demurrer, and the Supreme Court affirmed. Writing for the Court, Justice Stevens reasoned that until the property owner had obtained a final decision regarding the application of subdivision regulations to its property, it was impossible to determine whether the land retained a reasonable beneficial use. Because the actions of the commission left open the possibility that some development would be permitted, appellant's assertion that his property had been taken was premature. Justice White, joined by Chief Justice Burger and Justices Powell and Rehnquist dissented.

Page 1464. At the end of section 2d of the Note, add the following:

The Court distinguished *Loretto* in FCC v. Florida Power Corp., 480 U.S. 245 (1987), and upheld a federal statute authorizing the Federal Communications Commission to regulate the rates utility companies charge cable operators for the use of utility poles. The Court below had invalidated the act after finding that it authorized a permanent physical occupation of property which, under *Loretto*, constituted a per se taking for which compensation had to be paid. But the Supreme Court, in a unanimous opinion written by Justice Marshall, held that *Loretto* was inapplicable to these facts.

> [While] the statute we considered in *Loretto* specifically *required* landlords to permit permanent occupation of their property by cable companies, nothing in [this act gives] cable companies any right to occupy space on utility poles, or prohibits utility companies from refusing to enter into attachment agreements with cable operators. The Act authorizes the FCC [to] review the rents charged by public utility landlords who have voluntarily entered into leases with cable company tenants renting space on utility poles.

Having determined that there was not a per se taking under *Loretto*, the Court had little difficulty in finding that the mere regulation of rates was not unconstitutional.

It is of course settled beyond dispute that regulation of rates chargeable from the employment of private property devoted to public uses is constitutionally permissible. [So] long as the rates set are not confiscatory, the Fifth Amendment does not bar their imposition.

Page 1464. Before section 3 of the Note, add the following new subsection:

f. In Connolly v. Pension Benefit Guaranty Corp., 475 U.S. 211 (1986), the Court upheld against a takings clause attack the constitutionality of an amendment to the Employee Retirement Income Security Act (ERISA) that required an employer withdrawing from a multiemployer pension plan to pay its proportionate share of the plan's unfunded vested benefits.

As originally enacted, ERISA created a wholly government owned corporation to insure multiemployer pension plans that were in default with insurance premiums assessable against contributors to the plans. Before the legislative scheme had taken full effect, however, Congress became concerned that the insurance system might be subject to liability beyond its means and that the existence of the insurance might actually encourage employers to terminate their participation in, or withdraw from, multiemployer plans. Consequently, Congress amended the law to require an employer withdrawing from a multiemployer plan to pay the employer's proportionate share of the plan's unfunded vested benefits.

Appellants in this action were trustees administering a multiemployer pension plan protecting certain construction workers. By the express terms of the trust agreement, employers participating in the plan obligated themselves to pay only those contributions required by individual collective-bargaining agreements, whether or not those contributions were sufficient to pay the benefits under the plan. Appellants argued that the imposition of the additional noncontractual withdrawal liability violated the takings clause by requiring an uncompensated transfer of assets to the pension trusts. (Note that appellants could not successfully press a contract clause claim because of the inapplicability of that clause to the federal government. See Pension Benefit Guaranty Corp v. Gray & Co., 467 U.S. 717 (1984). For a discussion of the applicability of the contract clause to *state* retroactive regulation of pension plans, see pages 1439-1442 supra of the main text.)

A unanimous Court, in an opinion by Justice White, rejected the takings clause argument. The Court agreed with appellants "that an employer subject to withdrawal liability is permanently deprived of those assets necessary to satisfy its statutory obligation. [If] liability is assessed under the Act, it constitutes a real debt that the employer must satisfy, and it is not an obligation which can be considered insubstantial." But the Court held that

> appellants' submission — that such a statutory liability to a private party always constitutes an uncompensated taking prohibited by the Fifth Amendment — if accepted, would prove too much. In the course of regulating commercial and other human affairs, Congress routinely creates burdens for some that directly benefit others. For example, Congress may set minimum wages, control prices, or create causes of actions that did not previously exist. Given the propriety of the governmental power to regulate, it cannot be said that the Taking Clause is violated whenever legislation requires one person to use his or her assets for the benefit of another.

The Court further held that the fact that the legislation destroyed existing contractual rights did not transform it into an illegal taking. Instead, the Court employed a three-part test based on the economic impact of the regulation, the extent of interference with investment-backed expectations, and the character of the governmental action.

With respect to the economic impact of the regulation, the Court acknowledged that the amendment completely deprived an employer of whatever amount of money it was obligated to pay to fulfill its statutory liability. But it observed that there was "nothing to show that the withdrawal liability actually imposed on an employer will always be out of proportion to his experience with the plan, and the mere fact that the employer must pay money to comply with the Act is but a necessary consequence of the [regulatory] scheme."

Nor was the Court persuaded that there was an impermissible interference with investment-backed expectations. "Pension plans [were] the objects of legislative concern long before the passage of ERISA. [Prudent] employers [had] more than sufficient notice not only that pension plans were currently regulated, but also that withdrawal itself might trigger additional financial obligations."

Finally, with respect to the character of the governmental action, the Court found it significant that the government did not "physically invade or permanently appropriate any of the employer's assets for its own use." Rather, the interference with property rights arose "from a public program that adjusts the benefits and burdens of economic life to promote the common good."

Is *Connolly* consistent with *Loretto*? After *Connolly*, can it still be said that the "traditional rule" defining a "permanent physical occupation authorized by the government" as a taking "avoids otherwise difficult line-drawing problems"? Is there a justification for different treatment of real property on the one hand and statutorily imposed financial liability on the other?

g. Is the takings clause violated when the government conditions the grant of a discretionary benefit upon the recipient's willingness to give up property rights that could not be taken from him without compensation?

In Bowen v. Gilliard, 483 U.S. 587 (1987), the Court considered a takings clause attack on an amendment to the Aid to Families with Dependent Children program that required recipient families to assign to the government child support payments received from a noncustodial parent for a child living in the covered household. The effect of the assignment was to reduce the level of support payments received by the household. Appellees argued that this reduction constituted a taking from the child because the child support payments could be legally used only for the individual child, while the compensating AFDC payments were available for the entire family. The Court, in an opinion by Justice Stevens, rejected the argument:

> Congress is not, by virtue of having instituted a social welfare program, bound to continue it at all, much less at the same benefit level. Thus, notwithstanding the technical legal arguments that have been advanced, it is imperative to recognize that the amendments at issue merely incorporate a definitional element into an entitlement program. It would be quite strange indeed if, by virtue of an offer to *provide* benefits to needy families through the entirely voluntary AFDC program, Congress or the States were deemed to have *taken* some of those very family members' property.

Compare the analysis in *Gilliard* with the following:

NOLLAN v. CALIFORNIA COASTAL COMMISSION, 483 U.S. 825 (1987): The California Coastal Commission conditioned the grant of a permit to rebuild appellants' house on their transfer to the public of an easement across their beachfront property. The Court, in an opinion by Justice Scalia, held that the attempt to impose this condition was a taking:

"Had California simply required the [appellants] to make an easement across their beachfront available to the public on a permanent [basis] we have no doubt there would have been a taking. [We] think a 'permanent physical occupation' has occurred, for purposes of [*Loretto*], where individuals are given a permanent and continuous right to pass to and fro, so that the real property may continuously be traversed, even though no particular individual is permitted to station himself permanently upon the premises. . . . [2]

2. Justice Brennan [suggests] that the Commission's public announcement of its intention to condition the rebuilding of houses on the transfer of easements of access caused the Nollans to have "no reasonable claim to any expectation of being able to exclude members of the public" from walking across their beach. He cites our opinion in Ruckelshaus v. Monsanto Co., 467 U.S. 986 (1984), as support for the peculiar proposition that a unilateral claim of entitlement by the government can alter property rights. In *Monsanto*, however, we found merely that the takings clause was not violated by giving effect to the Government's announcement that application for "*the right to [the] valuable Government benefit,*" (emphasis added) of obtaining registration of an insecticide would confer upon the Government a license to use and disclose the trade secrets contained in the application. See also [Bowen v. Gilliard]. But the right to build on one's own property — even though its exercise can be subjected to legitimate permitting requirements — cannot remotely be described as a "government benefit." [Nor] are the Nollans' rights altered because they acquired the

"Given, then, that requiring uncompensated conveyance of the easement outright would violate the Fourteenth Amendment, the question becomes whether requiring it to be conveyed as a condition for issuing a land use permit alters the outcome. . . .

"[If] the Commission attached to the permit some condition that would have protected the public's ability to see the beach notwithstanding construction of the new house — for example, a height limitation, a width restriction, or a ban on fences — so long as the Commission could have exercised its police power (as we [assume] it could) to forbid construction of the house altogether, imposition of the condition would also be constitutional. Moreover [the] condition would be constitutional even if it consisted of the requirement that the [appellants] provide a viewing spot on their property for passersby with whose sighting of the ocean their new house would interfere. Although such a requirement [would] have to be considered a taking if it were not attached to a development permit, the Commission's assumed power to forbid construction of the house in order to protect the public's view of the beach must surely include the power to condition construction upon some concession by the owner, even a concession of property rights, that serves the same end. . . .

"The evident constitutional propriety disappears, however, if the condition substituted for the prohibition utterly fails to further the end advanced as the justification for the prohibition. When that essential nexus is eliminated, the situation becomes the same as if California law forbade shouting fire in a crowded theater, but granted dispensations to those willing to contribute $100 to the state treasury. [In] short, unless the permit condition serves the same governmental purpose as the development ban, the building restriction is not a valid regulation of land use but 'an out-and-out plan of extortion.' . . .

"Justice Brennan argues that imposition of the access requirement is not irrational. In his version of the Commission's argument, the reason for the requirement is that in its absence, a person looking toward the beach from the road will see a street of residential structures including the Nollans' new home and conclude that there is no public beach nearby. If, however, that person sees people passing and repassing along the dry sand behind the Nollan's home, he will realize that there is a public beach somewhere in the vicinity. The Commission's action, however, was based on the opposite factual finding that the wall of houses completely blocked the view of the beach and that a person looking from the road would not be able to see it at all.

"Even if the Commission had made the finding that Justice Brennan proposes, however, it is not certain that it would suffice. [We] view the Fifth Amend-

land well after the Commission had begun to implement its policy. So long as the Commission could not have deprived the prior owners of the easement without compensating them, the prior owners must be understood to have transferred their full property rights in conveying the lot. [Relocated footnote.]

ment's property clause to be more than a pleading requirement, and compliance with it to be more than an exercise of cleverness and imagination. [Our] cases describe the condition for abridgement of property rights through the police power as '*substantially* advanc[ing]' a legitimate State interest. We are inclined to be particularly careful about the adjective where the actual conveyance of property is made a condition to the lifting of a land use restriction, since in that context there is heightened risk that the purpose is avoidance of the compensation requirement, rather than the stated police power objective."

Justice Brennan, joined by Justice Marshall, wrote a dissenting opinion:

"[The] Court imposes a standard of precision for the exercise of a State's police power that has been discredited for the better part of this century. . . .

"It is [by] now commonplace that this Court's review of the rationality of a State's exercise of its police power demands only that the State '*could rationally have decided*' that the measure adopted might achieve the State's objective. [Minnesota v. Clover Leaf Creamery Co.]

"The Court finds fault with [the Commission's conduct] because it regards the condition as insufficiently tailored to address the precise type of reduction in access produced by the new development. The Nollans' development blocks visual access, the Court tells us, while the Commission seeks to preserve lateral access along the coastline. Such a narrow conception of rationality, however, has long since been discredited as a judicial arrogation of legislative authority. . . .

"Even if we accept the Court's unusual demand for a precise match between the condition imposed and the specific type of burden on access created by the appellants, the State's action easily satisfies this requirement. First, the lateral access condition serves to dissipate the impression that the beach that lies behind the wall of homes along the shore is for private use only. It requires no exceptional imaginative powers to find plausible the Commission's point that the average person passing along the road in front of a phalanx of imposing permanent residences [is] likely to conclude that this particular portion of the shore is not open to the public. If, however, that person can see that numerous people are passing and repassing along the dry sand, this conveys the message that the beach is in fact open for use by the public. . . .

"The second flaw in the Court's analysis [is] more fundamental. The Court assumes that the only burden with which the Coastal Commission was concerned was blockage of visual access to the beach. This is incorrect. The Commission specifically stated in its report [that] '[t]he Commission finds that the applicants' proposed development would present an increase in view blockage, *an increase in private use of the shorefront*, and that this impact would burden the public's ability to traverse to and along the shorefront.'

"[Moreover,] appellants were clearly on notice when requesting a new development permit that a condition of approval would be a provision ensuring [the easement]. [In] this respect, this case is quite similar to [Ruckelshaus v. Monsanto Co.]. In *Monsanto*, the respondent had submitted trade data to the Environmental Protection Agency for the purpose of obtaining registration of certain pesticides. [The] Court conceded that the data in question constituted property under state law. It also found, however, that certain of the data had been submitted to the agency after Congress had made clear that only limited confidentiality would be given data submitted for registration purposes. [The] Court rejected respondent's argument that the requirement that it relinquish some confidentiality imposed an unconstitutional condition upon receipt of a Government benefit. [10]"

Justices Blackmun and Stevens also filed dissenting opinions.

What is the reach of *Nollan*? Professor Michelman speculates that the intensified means-ends scrutiny might signal a "clear and startling" innovation — one that raises a threat to a range of land-use regulations formerly assessed under rational basis review. Michelman, Takings, 1987, 88 Colum. L. Rev. 1600, 1608 (1988). On the other hand, he suggests that the case might more narrowly exemplify "the talismanic force of 'permanent physical occupation' in takings adjudication." Id.

Nollan might well be seen as an unconstitutional conditions case and, on this view, raises the question whether government might condition the receipt of a benefit — here, permission to build — on the grant of an easement. *Nollan* treats this condition as impermissible, partly on the theory that the right to build on one's own property is not a government "benefit," like welfare or social security. But what is the difference between the two kinds of interests? Is the first more "natural" than the others?

The Court also emphasized that the condition imposed by the state (grant of the easement) had no relation to the state's legitimate interest in preserving the view. The Court implied that a concession of property rights that involved a viewing-spot might have been upheld. Here, however, the easement had no connection to the aesthetic goals at stake. As the Court had it, the problem was thus one of "extortion": the beach-access condition was attached to the building permit, to which it was simply not germane. The scrutiny of means-ends con-

---

10. The Court suggests that [*Ruckelshaus*] is distinguishable, because government regulation of property in that case was a condition on receipt of a "government benefit," while here regulation takes the form of a restriction on "the right to build on one's own property." This proffered distinction is not persuasive. Both Monsanto and the Nollans hold property whose use is subject to regulation; Monsanto may not sell its property without obtaining government approval and the Nollans may not build a new development on their property without government approval. Obtaining such approval is as much a "government benefit" for the Nollans as it is for Monsanto. If the Court is somehow suggesting that "the right to build on one's own property" has some privileged natural rights status, the argument is a curious one. By any traditional labor theory of value justification for property rights, for instance, see, e.g., J. Locke, The Second Treatise of Civil Government, Monsanto would have a superior claim, for the chemical formulae which constitute its property only came into being by virtue of Monsanto's efforts. [Relocated footnote.]

nections, through a "relatedness" test, might therefore be seen as an effort to flush out impermissible motivation. See Epstein, Foreword: Unconstitutional Conditions, State Power, and the Limits of Consent, 102 Harv. L. Rev. 1, 62.63 (1988): "The doctrine of unconstitutional conditions limits the abuse of government discretion by severing the denial of the construction permit from the taking of the lateral easement. . . . The 'relatedness' requirements . . . has powerful functional roots, for it . . . reduces the state's ability to extract concessions from individual owners by coordinating separate types of government initiatives."

But see Sullivan, Unconstitutional Conditions, 102 Harv. L. Rev. 1413, 1474: "Germaneness to the purpose of a benefit depends crucially on how broadly or how narrowly that purpose is defined. . . . [T]he condition invalidated in *Nollan* may be interpreted either as nongermane to the provision of visual access to the sea . . . or as germane to a more general state interest in facilitating public use and enjoyment of the beach. . . ." How might a court resolve the problem of characterizing state purpose in resolving the question of germaneness?

For general discussion of this and other issues, see, in addition to the Epstein and Sullivan essays cited above, the articles in The Jurisprudence of Takings, 88 Colum. L. Rev. 1581 (1988).

Page 1464.   Before "3. *Concluding thoughts.*" add the following:

h. In Pennell v. City of San Jose, 485 U.S. 1 (1988), the Supreme Court upheld an unusual rent control ordinance. The ordinance contained a mechanism for automatically increasing annual rents by as much as eight percent. If a tenant objects to an increase greater than eight percent, a hearing is provided, in which a mediation hearing officer decides on whether the proposed increase is "reasonable under the circumstances." The decision about reasonableness is to include consideration of

> the economic and financial hardship imposed on the present tenant or tenants of the unit or units to which such increases apply. If, on balance, the Hearing Officer determinates that the proposed increase constitutes an unreasonably severe financial or economic hardship on a particular tenant, he may order that the excess of the increase . . . be disallowed. Any tenant whose household income and monthly housing expense meets [certain income requirements] shall be deemed to be suffering under financial and economic hardship which must be weighed. . . .

The Court responded:

> We think it would be premature to consider this contention on the present record. As things stand, there simply is no evidence that the "tenant hardship clause" has in fact ever been relied upon by a Hearing Officer to reduce a rent below the figure it

would have been set at on the basis of the other factors set forth in the Ordinance. In addition, there is nothing in the Ordinance requiring that a Hearing Officer in fact reduce a proposed rent increase on grounds of tenant hardship. . . . Given the "essentially ad hoc, factual inquir[y]" involved in the takings analysis, Kaiser Aetna v. United States, we have found it particularly important in takings cases to adhere to our admonition that "the constitutionality of statutes ought not be decided except in an actual factual setting that makes such a decision necessary." . . .

Petitioners argue, however, that it is "arbitrary, discriminatory, or demonstrably irrelevant," for appellees to attempt to accomplish the additional goal of reducing the burden of housing costs on low-income tenants by requiring that "hardship to a tenant" be considered in determining the amount of excess rent increase that is "reasonable under the circumstances." As appellants put it, "The objective of alleviating individual tenant hardship is . . . not a 'policy the legislature is free to adopt' in a rent control ordinance."

[But] the Ordinance establishes a scheme in which a Hearing Officer considers a number of factors in determining the reasonableness of a proposed rent increase which exceeds eight percent *and* which exceeds the amount deemed reasonable. . . . The first six factors of . . . focus on the individual landlord — the Hearing Officer examines the history of the premises, the landlord's costs, and the market for comparable housing. Section 5703.28(c)(5) also allows the landlord to bring forth any other financial evidence — including presumably evidence regarding his own financial status — to be taken into account by the Hearing Officer. It is in only this context that the Ordinance allows tenant hardship to be considered and . . . "balance[d]" with the other factors. . . . Within this scheme, [the Ordinance] represents a rational attempt to accommodate the conflicting interests of protecting tenants from burdensome rent increases while at the same time ensuring that landlords are guaranteed a fair return on their investment. . . .

We accordingly find that the Ordinance, which so carefully considers both the individual circumstances of the landlord and the tenant before determining whether to allow an *additional* increase in rent over and above certain amounts that are deemed reasonable, does not on its face violate the Fourteenth Amendment's Due Process Clause. . . .

We also find that the Ordinance does not violate the Amendment's Equal Protection Clause. . . .

In light of our conclusion above that the Ordinance's tenant hardship provisions are designed to serve the legitimate purpose of protecting tenants, we can hardly conclude that it is irrational for the Ordinance to treat certain landlords differently on the basis of whether or not they have hardship tenants. The Ordinance distinguishes between landlords because doing so furthers the purpose of ensuring that individual tenants do not suffer "unreasonable" hardship; it would be inconsistent to state that hardship is a legitimate factor to be considered but then hold that appellees could not tailor the Ordinance so that only legitimate hardship cases are redressed. . . . We recognize, as appellants point out, that in general it is difficult to say that the landlord "causes" the tenant's hardship. But this is beside the point — if a landlord does have a hardship tenant, regardless of the reason why, it is rational for appellees to take that fact into consideration under . . . of the Ordinance when establishing a rent that is "reasonable under the circumstances."

In a dissenting opinion, Justice Scalia, joined by Justice O'Connor, wrote:

Since the San Jose Ordinance does not require any specification of how much reduction in rent is attributable to each of the various factors that the Hearing Officer is allowed to take into account, it is quite possible that none of the many landlords affected by the ordinance will ever be able to meet the Court's requirement of a "showing in a particular case as to the consequences of [the hardship factor] in the ultimate determination of the rent[.] . . .

The "hardship" provision, is invoked to meet a [distinct] social problem: the existence of some renters who are too poor to afford even reasonably priced housing. But *that* problem is no more caused or exploited by landlords than it is by the grocers who sell needy renters their food, or the department stores that sell them their clothes, or the employers who pay them their wages, or the citizens of San Jose holding the higher-paying jobs from which they are excluded. And even if the neediness of renters could be regarded as a problem distinctively attributable to landlords in general, it is not remotely attributable to the *particular* landlords that the ordinance singles out — namely, those who happen to have a "hardship" tenant at the present time, or who may happen to rent to a "hardship" tenant in the future, or whose current or future affluent tenants may happen to decline into the "hardship" category.

The traditional manner in which American government has met the problem of those who cannot pay reasonable prices for privately sold necessities — a problem caused by the society at large — has been the distribution to such persons of funds raised from the public at large through taxes, either in cash (welfare payments) or in goods (public housing, publicly subsidized housing, and food stamps). Unless we are to abandon the guiding principle of the Takings Clause that "public burdens . . . . should be borne by the public as a whole," this is the only manner that our Constitution permits. . . .

The politically attractive feature of regulation is not that it permits wealth transfers to be achieved that could not be achieved otherwise; but rather that it permits them to be achieved "off budget," with relative invisibility and thus relative immunity from normal democratic processes. San Jose might, for example, have accomplished something like the result here by simply raising the real estate tax upon rental properties and using the additional revenues thus acquired to pay part of the rents of "hardship" tenants. It seems to me doubtful, however, whether the citizens of San Jose would allow funds in the municipal treasury, from wherever derived, to be distributed to a family of four with income as high as $32,400 a year — the generous maximum necessary to qualify automatically as a "hardship" tenant under the rental ordinance. The voters might well see other, more pressing, social priorities. And of course what $32,400-a-year renters can acquire through spurious "regulation," other groups can acquire as well. Once the door is opened it is not unreasonable to expect price regulations requiring private businesses to give special discounts to senior citizens (no matter how affluent), or to students, the handicapped, or war veterans. Subsidies for these groups may well be a good idea, but because of the operation of the Takings Clause our governmental system has required them to be applied, in general, through the process of taxing and spending, where both economic effects and competing priorities are more evident.

That fostering of an intelligent democratic process is one of the happy effects of the constitutional prescription — perhaps accidental, perhaps not. Its essence, however, is simply the unfairness of making one citizen pay, in some fashion other than taxes, to remedy a social problem that is none of his creation. . . . I would hold that the seventh factor in §5703.28(c) of the San Jose Ordinance effects a taking of property without just compensation.

Chapter Ten

The Constitution and the Problem of Private Power

Page 1478. At the end of the second full paragraph, add the following:

Consider I. Shapiro, The Evolution of Rights in Liberal Theory (1986):

At the heart of the negative libertarian ideal is the notion that the state *presence or action* needs to be justified, not state *absence or inaction*. This assumes, fallaciously, some "normal" or "expected course of events," morally benign or at worst morally neutral. It takes as its model of "normal" human interaction a view of simple voluntary transactions among isolated persons, unmediated by external authority structures and power relations, that has never prevailed anywhere in human history, is unimaginable in practice, and even in theory. Thus the negative libertarian conceptions of freedom [are] inevitably loaded ideologically. They clearly presume many of the latent power structures and relationships that in fact prevail in contemporary market [societies].

B. PURE INACTION AND THE THEORY OF GOVERNMENTAL NEUTRALITY

Page 1479.   Before Flagg Bros. v. Brooks, add the following:

DESHANEY v. WINNEBAGO COUNTY DEPARTMENT OF SOCIAL SERVICES, 109 S. Ct. 998 (1989):   When petitioner Joshua Deshaney was one year old, a Wyoming court granted his parents a divorce and awarded custody to his father. Shortly thereafter, the father moved to Winnebago County, Wisconsin. Two years later, respondent social workers working for Winnebago County began receiving reports that the father was physically abusing Joshua. The caseworkers carefully noted each of these reports, as well as Joshua's suspicious injuries, but took no action to remove him from his father's custody. Eventually, when Joshua was four years old, his father beat him so severely that he suffered permanent brain injuries that left him profoundly retarded and confined to an institution for life. This was an action brought by Joshua and his mother claiming that the state's conduct deprived him of his liberty in violation of the Due Process Clause of the fourteenth amendment.

Justice Rehnquist delivered the Court's opinion: "[Nothing] in the language of the Due Process Clause itself requires the State to protect the life, liberty, and property of its citizens against invasion by private actors. The Clause is phrased as a limitation on the State's power to act, not as a guarantee of certain minimal levels of safety and security. [Nor] does history support such an expansive reading of the constitutional text. [Its] purpose was to protect the people from the State, not to ensure that the State protected them from each other. The Framers were content to leave the extent of governmental obligation in the latter area to the democratic political processes. . . .

"Petitioners contend, however, that even if the Due Process Clause imposes no affirmative obligation on the State to provide the general public with adequate protective services, such a duty may arise out of certain 'special relationships' created or assumed by the State with respect to particular individuals. . . .

"We reject this argument. It is true that in certain limited circumstances the Constitution imposes upon the State affirmative duties of care and protection with respect to particular individuals. . . .

"[But these cases] stand only for the proposition that when the State takes a person into its custody and holds him there against his will, the Constitution imposes upon it a corresponding duty to assume some responsibility for his safety and general well-being. [The] affirmative duty to protect arises not from the State's knowledge of the individual's predicament or from its expressions of intent to help him, but from the limitation which it has imposed on his freedom to act on his own behalf.

"Judges and lawyers, like other humans, are moved by natural sympathy in a case like this to find a way for Joshua and his mother to receive adequate compensation for the grievous harm inflicted upon them. But before yielding to that impulse, it is well to remember once again that the harm was inflicted not by the state of Wisconsin, but by Joshua's father. [In] defense of [the state officials] it must also be said that had they moved too soon to take custody of the son away from the father, they would likely have been met with charges of improperly intruding into the parent-child relationship, charges based on the same Due Process Clause that forms the basis for the present charge of failure to provide adequate protection."

Justice Brennan, joined by Justices Marshall and Blackmun, dissented: "It may well be, as the Court decides, that the Due Process Clause as construed by our prior cases creates no general right to basic governmental services. That, however, is not the question presented here. . . .

"I would focus first on the action that Wisconsin *has* taken with respect to Joshua and children like him, rather than on the actions that the State failed to take. . . .

"Wisconsin law invites — indeed, directs — citizens and other governmental entities to depend on local departments of social services such as respondent to protect children from abuse. . . .

"In these circumstances, a private citizen, or even a person working in a government agency other than [the Department of Social Services] would doubtless feel that her job was done as soon as she had reported her suspicions of child abuse to [the Department]. If [the Department] ignores or dismisses these suspicions, no one will step in to fill the gap. [Conceivably], then, children like Joshua are made worse off by the existence of this program when the persons and entities charged with carrying it out fail to do their jobs."

Justice Blackmun also filed a dissenting opinion: "Like the antebellum judges who denied relief to fugitive slaves, the Court today claims that its decision, however harsh, is compelled by existing legal doctrine. On the contrary, the question presented by this case is an open one, and our Fourteenth Amendment precedents may be read more broadly or narrowly depending upon how one chooses to read them. Faced with the choice, I would adopt a 'sympathetic' reading, one which comports with the dictates of fundamental justice and recognizes that compassion need not be exiled from the province of judging.

"Poor Joshua! Victim of repeated attacks by an irresponsible, bullying, cowardly, and intemperate father, and abandoned by respondents who placed him in a dangerous predicament and who knew or learned what was going on, and yet did essentially nothing. [It] is a sad commentary upon American life, and constitutional principles — so full of late of patriotic fervor and proud proclamations about 'liberty and justice for all,' that this child, Joshua Deshaney, now is assigned to live out the remainder of his life profoundly retarded."

NOTE: DeSHANEY, *NATURAL LAW, AND INVISIBLE STATE ACTION*

Is the Court's assertion that the due process clause generally does not require the state to protect citizens against private invasions plausible? Consider Strauss, Due Process, Government Inaction, and Private Wrongs, 1989 S. Ct. Rev. 53, 59:

Suppose a plaintiff seeking, say, to enjoin a trespass by a private party, loses his or her case because the judge is biased. (Suppose the judge has a financial interest aligned with the defendant). That is a clear violation of the Due Process Clause. In what sense, however, is this an instance of government action, as opposed to inaction? The case is just like *DeShaney* [except] that the official who refused to intervene against the private wrongdoing is a judge instead of a social worker. Thus the *DeShaney* approach leads to a wholly implausible conclusion in connection with an issue that goes to the core of the Due Process Clause, the right to trial before an impartial judge.

Notice that none of the *DeShaney* opinions focussed on the most direct way in which state action contributed to Joshua DeShaney's injury: the network of statutes and common law rules that grant custody and control of minor children to their biological parents. (State responsibility for this outcome is particularly obvious on the facts of *DeShaney*, where a state court, albeit in Wyoming, rather than in Wisconsin, had adjudicated a custody dispute regarding the boy in connection with his parents' divorce). Consider whether the state action doctrine has embedded within it unarticulated natural law assumptions about the "rightness" of certain initial allocations — such as the allocation of children to their biological parents — and whether these assumptions blind the court to state action that creates or maintains this "natural" state of affairs.

Compare *DeShaney* to Baltimore City Department of Social Services v. Bouknight, 110 S. Ct. 900 (1990), where the Court rejected the argument that a parent of a child under court supervision could utilize the fifth amendment privilege against compelled incrimination to refuse to produce the child. *Bouknight,* like *DeShaney,* involved a parent who had previously abused her biological child and who was under court supervision. But whereas in *DeShaney,* the Court ignored the governmental conduct relating to child custody decisions, this conduct was crucial to the result in *Bouknight.* The Court analogized child rearing to heavily regulated industries, where the fifth amendment privilege has generally been available in only diluted form.

> When a person assumes control over items that are the legitimate object of the government's non-criminal regulatory powers, the ability to invoke the privilege is reduced. . . . Once Maurce was adjudicated a child in need of assistance, his care and safety became the particular object of the State's regulatory interest. . . . The government demands the production of the very public charge entrusted to a custodian, and makes the demand for compelling reasons unrelated to criminal law enforcement and as part of a broadly applied regulatory regime.

The *Bouknight* Court did not cite *DeShaney* — a case decided a year earlier. Are the two cases consistent? Consider the possibility that the state action doctrine requires courts, but not legislatures, to respect "natural law" allocations.

Page 1488. Before section 2, add the following:

4. Tarkanian. Compare *Flagg Bros.* and *Lugar* with National Collegiate Athletic Association v. Tarkanian, 109 S. Ct. 454 (1988). The case arose out of a National Collegiate Athletic Association investigation of the University of Nevada, Las Vegas (a state university) and its highly successful basketball coach, Tarkanian, for violations of NCAA rules. Under pressure from the NCAA, the University removed Tarkanian, who thereupon sued both the NCAA and the University, claiming that their conduct violated his rights to substantive and procedural due process. The lower courts found that the NCAA's conduct constituted state action subject to constitutional restraint and that both the

NCAA and the University had violated Tarkanian's constitutional rights. In a 5-4 opinion written by Justice Stevens, the Supreme Court reversed the lower court insofar as it had held the NCAA constitutionally liable.

The Court began its analysis by noting that the situation "uniquely mirrors the traditional state action case" and that it required the court "to step through an analytical looking glass to resolve it." In more typical cases, such as *Lugar* and *Flagg Bros.*, a private party has taken steps that cause harm to the plaintiff and the issue is whether the state was sufficiently involved to treat this private conduct as state action. Here, in contrast, the University — concededly a state actor — had suspended Tarkanian. "Thus, the question is not whether [the University] participated to a critical extent in the NCAA's activities, but whether [the University's] actions in compliance with the NCAA rules and recommendations turned the NCAA's conduct into state action."

The Court concluded that University compliance did not transform the NCAA into a state actor. "It would be ironic indeed to conclude that the NCAA's imposition of sanctions against [the University] — sanctions that [the University] and its counsel steadfastly opposed during protracted adversary proceedings — is fairly attributable to the State of Nevada. It would be more appropriate to conclude that [the University] has conducted its athletic program under color of the policies adopted by the NCAA, rather than that those policies were developed and enforced under color of Nevada law."

Justice White filed a dissenting opinion, which was joined by Justices Brennan, Marshall, and O'Connor.

5. *Pope.* Finally, consider the Court's reading of *Lugar* and *Flagg Brothers* in Tulsa Professional Collection Services v. Pope, 485 U.S. — (1988). Oklahoma's probate laws require that claims arising under a contract be presented to the executor of the estate within two months of the publication of a notice advising creditors of the commencement of probate proceedings. A creditor who had not received actual notice and failed to file a claim within two months argued that the constructive notice provision violated due process. In an opinion by Justice O'Connor, the Court held that the creditor had a property interest that was protected by the due process clause. It went on to note, however, that the fourteenth amendment protected this interest only from deprivation by state action. On the state action question, it summarized the holdings of *Lugar* and *Flagg Brothers* as follows:

> Private use of state sanctioned private remedies and procedures does not rise to the level of state action see, e.g., [*Flagg Brothers*]. Nor is the state's involvement in the mere running of a general statute of limitation generally sufficient to implicate due process. [But] when private parties make use of state procedures with the overt, significant assistance of state officials, state action may be found. See, e.g., [*Lugar*].

The Court went on to hold that although the mere state promulgation of the limitation period was insufficient to constitute state action, the probate court's "pervasive and substantial" involvement with the probate proceedings was sufficient.

Is *Pope*'s "pervasive and substantial" involvement test consistent with *Lugar*? Is *Pope* distinguishable because the creditor was invoking the Constitution to secure the affirmative assistance of the state in *Pope*, while the debtor was invoking the Constitution to ward off state interference in *Lugar*?

Page 1493. Before subsection b of the Note, add the following:

Consider San Francisco Arts & Athletics, Inc. v. United States Olympic Committee, 483 U.S. 522 (1987). The Amateur Sports Act of 1978 authorizes the United States Olympic Committee to prohibit certain commercial and promotional uses of the word "Olympic." When petitioner organized and began to promote the "Gay Olympic Games," the Committee brought suit under the statute to enjoin petitioner from using the word "Olympic." Petitioner responded by arguing that such an injunction would violate their free speech rights under the first amendment and that even if the exclusive use of the word granted by Congress did not violate the first amendment, the Committee's discriminatory enforcement of its right of exclusive use violated the equal protection component of the fifth amendment due process clause. With respect to the first argument, the Court, in an opinion by Justice Powell, assumed, without discussion, that there was state action and upheld the statute against first amendment attack. But with respect to the second argument, the Court held that the Committee was not a state actor and that it was therefore not bound by equal protection requirements. Are the two halves of the opinion consistent? Why was there state action under the first amendment, but not under the fifth?

In a footnote at the conclusion of its opinion, the Court noted that the petition for certiorari did not raise the argument, premised on Shelley v. Kramer, that even if the Committee was not a state actor, the entry of an injunction against use of the word "Olympic" constituted governmental action sufficient to require an inquiry into the Committee's discriminatory conduct. If the Court had reached this contention, what result?

C. CONSTITUTIONALLY IMPERMISSIBLE DEPARTURES FROM NEUTRALITY: STATE SUBSIDIZATION, APPROVAL, AND ENCOURAGEMENT

Page 1512. Before section 2 of the Note, add the following:

Consider San Francisco Arts & Athletics, Inc. v. United States Olympic Committee, 483 U.S. 522 (1987). The Amateur Sports Act of 1978 gave to the United States Olympic Committee the exclusive right to use the term

"Olympic." The Committee secured an injunction against petitioners, or-
ganizers of the "Gay Olympics," preventing them from using the word. Petitioners argued, inter alia, that the Committee's selection of groups allowed to
use the word was discriminatory in violation of equal protection principles
embodied in the fifth amendment. The Court, in an opinion by Justice Powell,
held that there was no state action:

> The fact that Congress granted [the Committee] a corporate charter does not render
> [it] a government agent. All corporations act under charters granted by a [govern-
> ment]. [Nor] is the fact that Congress has granted the [Committee] exclusive use of
> the word "Olympic" dispositive. All enforceable rights in trademarks are created by
> some governmental [act]. . . .
>   The [Committee's] choice of how to enforce its exclusive right [simply] is not a
> governmental decision. There is no evidence that the Federal Government coerced or
> encouraged the [Committee] in the exercise of its rights. At most, the Federal Govern-
> ment, by failing to supervise the [Committee's] use of its rights, can be said to exercise
> "[m]ere approval of or acquiescence in the initiatives" of the [Committee]. [*Blum.*]
> This is not enough to make the [Committee's] actions those of the Government.

Justice Brennan, joined by Justice Marshall, dissented:

> The [Committee] and the Federal Government exist in a symbiotic relationship
> sufficient to provide a nexus between the [Committee's] challenged action and the
> Government. First, as in *Burton*, the relationship here confers a variety of mutual
> benefits. [The] Act gave the [Committee] authority and responsibilities that no
> private organization in this country had ever held. . . .
>   Second, in the eye of the public, [the] connection between the decisions of the
> United States Government and those of the United States Olympic Committee is
> profound. . . .
>   Even more importantly, there is a close financial and legislative link between the
> [Committee's] alleged discriminatory exercise of its word-use authority and the finan-
> cial success of both the [Committee] and the Government. It would certainly be
> "irony amounting to grave injustice" if, to finance the team that is to represent the
> virtues of our political system, the [Committee] were free to employ government-
> created economic leverage to prohibit political speech. [*Burton.*]

Justice O'Connor, joined by Justice Blackmun, also dissented from the
Court's state action determination.

Page 1513. Before section 2, add the following:

Compare *Rendell-Baker* to West v. Atkins, 487 U.S. 42 (1988), where the
Court held that a private physician, under contract with the state to provide
medical services for inmates at a state prison, was a state actor for constitutional
purposes. Writing for eight justices, Justice Blackmun rejected the argument
that the doctor's actions were not attributable to the state because he was

exercising independent medical judgment. In a footnote, the Court distinguished *Rendell-Baker* and *Blum* as follows:

> Where the issue is whether a *private* party is engaged in activity that constitutes state action, it may be relevant that the challenged activity turned on judgments controlled by professional standards, where those standards are not established by the State. The Court has held that "a State normally can be held responsible for a private decision only when it has exercised coercive power or has provided such significant encouragement, either overt or covert, that the choice must in law be deemed to be that of the State." [*Blum; Rendell-Baker*]. In both *Blum* and *Rendell-Baker*, the fact that the private entities received state funding and were subject to state regulation did not, without more, convert their conduct into state action. . . .
>
> This determination cannot be transformed into the proposition that no person acts under color of state law where he is exercising independent professional judgment. [*Blum*] and *Rendell-Baker* provide no support for respondent's argument that a physician, employed by the State to fulfill a State's constitutional obligations, does not act under color of state law merely because he renders medical care in accordance with professional obligations.

Why wasn't the New Perspectives School "employed by the State to fulfill the State's constitutional obligations"?

D. CONSTITUTIONALLY REQUIRED DEPARTURES FROM NEUTRALITY: THE PUBLIC FUNCTION DOCTRINE

Page 1527.   After the third paragraph, add the following:

Compare *Terry* to Tashjian v. Republican Party, 479 U.S. 208 (1986). In *Tashjian*, the Court upheld the Republican Party's constitutional challenge to a state law that prohibited nonparty members from participating in party primaries. (The Republicans had adopted a party rule permitting independents to vote in its primaries). The Court held that

> [the] Party's attempt to broaden the base of public participation in and support for its activities is conduct undeniably central to the exercise of the right of association. [The] freedom to join together in furtherance of common political beliefs "necessarily presupposes the freedom to identify the people who constitute the association." Democratic Party of the United States v. Wisconsin, 450 U.S. 107, 122 (1981).

Why wasn't the Jaybirds' "freedom to identify the people who constitute the association" constitutionally protected?

Page 1532.   Before section 2 of the Note, add the following:

e. *Amateur sports.* In San Francisco Arts & Athletics, Inc. v. United States Olympic Committee, 483 U.S. 522 (1987), the Court, in an opinion by Justice

Powell, held that the United States Olympic Committee was not a state actor. The Amateur Sports Act of 1978 created the Committee as a "private [corporation] established under Federal law." The Act imposed certain requirements on the Committee, provided for some funding for it, and granted it exclusive use of the word "Olympic." The Court held that

> [the Act] merely authorized the [Committee] to coordinate activities that always have been performed by private entities. Neither the conduct nor the coordination of amateur sports has been a traditional governmental function.

Compare Justice Brennan's dissenting opinion:

> In the Amateur Sports Act of 1978, Congress placed the power and prestige of the United States Government behind a single, central sports organization. Congress delegated to the [Committee] functions that Government actors traditionally perform — the representation of the Nation abroad and the administration of all private organizations in a particular economic sector. The representation function is of particular significance here [because] an organization that need not adhere to the Constitution cannot meaningfully represent this Nation. The Government is free, of course, to "privatize" some functions it would otherwise perform. But such privatization ought not automatically release those who perform government functions from constitutional obligations.

E. THE CONSTITUTION AND PRIVATE POWER: SOME FINAL THOUGHTS

Page 1536. Before the final paragraph, add the following:

Consider Sunstein, *Lochner*'s Legacy, 87 Colum. L. Rev. 873, 919 (1987):

> [The] central issue in numerous areas of the law [is] whether there is a constitutional requirement of neutrality that commands preservation of the status quo as reflected in market outcomes, or instead whether the Constitution, recognizing the artifactual quality of the market allocation, permits and sometimes demands change. One might understand the *Lochner* era as, above all, a warning about constitutional doctrine that defines neutrality in terms of the perpetuation of current practice, and that treats government conduct tending to sustain it as "inaction" invariably escaping legal sanction, and government conduct proposing change as "action" tending to raise legal doubts.